I0528491

יחזקאל

THE
ISRAEL
BIBLE

EZEKIEL

EDITED BY

Rabbi Tuly Weisz

The Israel Bible: Ezekiel

First Edition, 2021

The Israel Bible was produced by Israel365 in cooperation with Teach for
Israel and is used with permission from Teach for Israel. All rights reserved.
The English translation was adapted by Israel365 from the JPS Tanakh.
Copyright © 1985 by the Jewish Publication Society. All rights reserved.

Cover images used under license from Shutterstock.com

ISBN 978-1-957109-37-4

A CIP catalogue record for this title is available from the British Library

The Israel Bible: Ezekiel is a holy book that contains the
name of God and should be treated with respect.

Table of Contents

Introduction

The Hebrew Bible is commonly known as the *Tanakh* which stands for *Torah* (the Five Books of Moses), *Neviim* (the Prophets) and *Ketuvim* (the Writings). The *Tanakh* consists of 24 books that are considered by Jews to be the word of God. While these books have been referred to as the "Old Testament," many Jews reject this label since it implies the replacement of the Hebrew Bible with something newer and prefer the more authentic Jewish name.

The *Tanakh* is not only the most important book known to man, it is God's word that is perfect and absolute. It is therefore a daunting undertaking to publish an edition of the *Tanakh*, and the responsibilities are awesome. There is no room for error or carelessness in dealing with the eternal word of God. Further, upon embarking on such a serious initiative, we ask ourselves if our efforts are gratuitous. Considering the many editions of the Bible in print, is there truly a need for yet another one?

While there are numerous Bibles in circulation today, its most central aspect – the Land of Israel – has often been overlooked. References to Israel appear on nearly every page, and the city of Jerusalem is specifically referred to hundreds of times throughout the Bible. The essential link between Israel and *Torah* is emphasized repeatedly in verses such as, "For instruction (*Torah*) shall come forth from *Tzion*, the word of *Hashem* from *Yerushalayim*" (Micah 4:2).

The miraculous return of the People of Israel to the Land of Israel in our own generation provides the perfect moment for a new volume to fill this void in biblical literature. *The Israel Bible* includes many special features elucidating God's focus on Israel throughout *Tanakh* and there are many additional, multimedia features available on our website **www.theisraelbible.com**.

Ordering and Presentation – In presenting *The Israel Bible*, our goal is to spread awareness of the biblical significance of the Land of Israel as well as the Jewish people's eternal connection to the land, based on the text of the *Tanakh*, the Hebrew Bible. We aim to honor "the God, the People and the Land of Israel" from an Orthodox Jewish perspective. To that end, *The Israel Bible* follows the traditional Jewish ordering of the books and the customary Hebrew division of chapters. Therefore, for example, we count 24 books of *Tanakh* with *Sefer Divrei Hayamim* (Chronicles) appearing last. It is our hope that our rich content will speak to all Jews and non-Jews who appreciate Israel as the God given land of the Jewish people.

English Translation – Throughout history, Jews have studied the Bible in Hebrew, as any form of translation would miss much of the nuance of the original holy tongue in which *Torah* has been transmitted since the days of Moses. However, as many Jews settled in America in the 19th Century, the need for an English translation became necessary. To be sure, there were already English translations prepared over the centuries by Christians, but in the words of the original editors of the Jewish Publication Society (JPS), "The Jew cannot afford to have his Bible translation prepared for him by others. He cannot have it as a gift, even as he cannot borrow his soul from others."

JPS set out in the late 1800s to publish an authoritative English translation "in the spirit of Jewish tradition." It was compiled over decades by some of the leading Jewish scholars of the time. They formed committees and subcommittees to compare existing English versions, considering medieval and modern Jewish commentators. The monumental JPS translation, originally published in 1917, has been updated in recent years, and *The Israel Bible* is proud to utilize the 1984 New Jewish Publication Society (NJPS) version with its modern, clear language, as well as its wide-ranging acceptance as an accurate and high-quality translation. We applied the NJPS translation verbatim, except for a select list of nouns which we replaced with their traditional Hebrew names. This is true even when we found the NJPS translation to be different than the popular translation of a word or phrase and when the NJPS switched the order of the text for the sake of clarity (see, for example, Ezekiel 24:22–24).

Hebrew Transliteration – To give our readers an authentic *Tanakh* experience, every verse that has commentary is transliterated from Hebrew into English. The Hebrew alphabet chart includes our standards for transliteration and pronunciation of Hebrew verses, enabling readers of *The Israel Bible* to decipher key biblical passages in the holy language. Readers can hear the entire Bible read in Hebrew on our website **www.theisraelbible.com**.

There are various standards when it comes to transliterating Hebrew words into English letters. While we have relied primarily on the classical Hebrew transliteration, we have occasionally deviated for the sake of simplicity, clarity and to reflect common usage.

In addition to whole verses, we have also transliterated many proper nouns in the English translation so that our readers can learn the names of key biblical figures and locations in their Hebrew form. As a rule, we chose to transliterate names of people that were central in the establishment and functioning of the nation of Israel, as well as significant places in the Holy Land. Therefore, regarding Adam's sons, for example, only *Shet* (Seth) is transliterated since it was from him that *Noach* (Noah), and ultimately *Avraham* (Abraham), descended. For this reason, there might be verses or sections of *The Israel Bible* that contains multiple names and only some of them are transliterated.

For the same reason, we have transliterated the names of the books of *Tanakh* when referring to them in our introductions and commentary. When referencing a specific chapter or verse, however, we use the English names of the books in our citations for clarity. We also transliterated ideas and concepts that are central to Judaism such as *Shabbat* (Sabbath), the names of the Jewish holidays and the *Beit Hamikdash* (Temple), as well as biblical measurements. Finally, the name of God is transliterated. Out of respect, Orthodox Jews generally refer to the Lord as *Hashem*, which literally means 'the Name.' Referring to God as *Hashem* reminds us that we feel close to Him but also recognize our distance at the same time. To stress this moniker, we transliterated both the Tetragrammaton as well as the name *Elohim* as *Hashem*.

Study Notes – Our unique commentary was compiled by Orthodox Jewish scholars who live in Israel. It is an anthology in the sense that most of the commentary is not original, but draws from traditional teachings of early Jewish Sages and modern rabbinic commentators. We also include quotations from individuals who have played a significant part in the past century of modern Israeli history including Israeli prime ministers, poets and military leaders.

Our commentary can be broken into four categories, three of which are identified by an icon at the beginning of the study note:

 Israel lessons are indicated with an icon bearing the map of Israel and focus on the Land of Israel and the modern State of Israel.

 Jewish lessons are indicated with a *Torah* scroll and teach a concept in Judaism or a classic idea from rabbinic thought.

 Hebrew lessons are represented by an icon bearing the letter *aleph* and focus on the meaning of a Hebrew word or phrase.

All other comments are considered general comments and are not assigned an icon.

Supplemental Material – In addition to our unique translation and original commentary, *The Israel Bible* offers supplementary material to enrich the learning experience of our readers. Before every book of *Tanakh,* we provide an introduction, as well as information, generally in the form of a map, a chart or a list, which is central to the specific book.

Maps – As the purpose of *The Israel Bible* is to highlight the biblical significance of the Land of Israel, significant time was spent researching and preparing maps to bring the physical contours of the holy land to life with great accuracy. However, since there is a lack of information regarding the precise locations of certain ancient cities, some of the places on our maps are approximate or subject to debate. In these cases, we followed the opinion that we are most comfortable with, but acknowledge that there is room for disagreement. We continue to produce new maps, which are available on our website **www.theisraelbible.com/maps**.

Torah **Readings** – The *Torah* is not just a work that is studied privately, it is also read out loud in synagogue. Every *Shabbat* and holiday a portion of the *Torah* is read, as well as a related section from *Neviim,* the prophets, called the *haftarah.* We included the blessings recited before and after the reading of the *Torah,* a list of the weekly *Torah* portions and their corresponding *haftarot,* and a chart of the *Torah* readings for special days with their corresponding *haftarot.* Readers can always find the current week's *Torah* portion by visiting **www.theisraelbible.com/weekly-torah-portion**. In this volume, we indicate where a new *Torah* portion begins by highlighting the Hebrew verse number with a gray box so readers can follow along with the communal *Torah* readings. Furthermore, we have included prayers for the State of Israel and the soldiers of the Israel Defense Forces (IDF) that are generally recited following the *Torah* reading in synagogue. It is our constant prayer that God watch over the State of Israel and the members of the IDF, who defend Israel every hour of every day.

In 1948, the State of Israel was created providing a modern answer to Isaiah's ancient question, "Is a nation born all at once?" (Isaiah 66:8). *The Israel Bible* was first published in the 70th year of God's miraculous restoration of the People of Israel to the Land of Israel. Jewish wisdom teaches that 70 is a significant number: *Moshe* (Moses) translated the *Torah* into 70 languages for all 70 nations of the world. From our very origins, the Jewish people were meant to be a light unto the 70 nations, spreading God's truth to the masses.

In the seven decades since the modern rebirth of the State of Israel, God's plan has been unfolding with unprecedented speed, dramatic highs and heartbreaking lows. Never has Israel been at the forefront of the world's attention as it is in our generation. Efforts to vilify the Jewish State seem to spread every day across the globe. At the same time, so does the growing movement of millions of non-Jewish biblical Zionists who stand with the nation of Israel as an expression of their commitment to God's word. As we seek to understand the clash of these two conflicting worldviews, the need for *The Israel Bible* has never been so important.

Standing on the great shoulders of those who came before us and emanating from the land that has always served as the birthplace for the Bible, we conclude with a heartfelt prayer: May the Almighty bless our efforts in offering this *Tanakh* to influence the hearts, minds and actions of its readers. In this way, it is our hope to spread God's name so that the publication of *The Israel Bible* brings us one step closer to the final redemption of Israel and the entire world.

Rabbi Tuly Weisz
Editor, *The Israel Bible*

Foreword

The mandate to study God's word daily is interestingly not found in the Five Books of Moses (Pentateuch), but rather in the first book of our prophetic writings: "Let not this Book of the Teaching cease from your lips, but recite it day and night, so that you may observe faithfully all that is written in it. Only then will you prosper in your undertakings and only then will you be successful" (Joshua 1:8). Charged with bringing the Israelites into the land covenantally promised to Abraham, Isaac and Jacob, God ensures Joshua of His protection if the nation observes His ways as dictated in the Divine constitution known as the *Torah*.

In Jewish tradition, Joshua (1:8) is directly linked with Deuteronomy (11:14), "You shall gather in your new grain and wine, and oil."[1] Our Sages deduced from this scriptural combination the importance of merging *Torah* study with a profession. Completely dedicating oneself to the study of *Torah* without having the financial means to sustain this lifestyle can lead one to eventually straying from observance of God's will. Poverty and crime can have an intimate relationship.

We must also be careful that our work does not affect our daily study of Scripture. The addiction of becoming a workaholic and not making *Torah* study a priority can also lead one into temptations that can violate our personal relationship with Him as well as our fellow human beings. The goal is to achieve a healthy balance between our study of God's word and our daily work.

The Deuteronomic verse quoted above is part of the second section of the Shema[2] that discusses the concept of reward and punishment. Sanctifying God by fulfilling His commandments results in the Land of Israel practically benefitting from rains that occur in the right season and reaping the abundance from the fields. However, if the nation follows pagan gods and practices, the consequences are devastating – famine and death. The Land of Israel is intrinsically linked with the keeping of the *Torah*. Covenant Land comes with covenant responsibility.

---

1   Talmud Bavli Berachot 35b
2   Consisting of three sections within the Five Books of Moses (Deut. 6:4–8; 11:13–22 and Numbers 15:37–42), the *Shema* is proclamation of accepting God's Kingdom in our lives, loyalty to His commandments and remembering His redemptive act of liberating us from Egypt. Jews recite the *Shema* twice a day as stated in Deut. 6:7.

Born into slavery, Joshua is now leading His people into the Promised Land. More than 500 years separates him from his ancestral forefather Abraham. The historical narratives that took place between Abraham leaving everything behind to follow God in Genesis 12 and the death of Moses in the last chapter of Deuteronomy are filled with intrigue, suspense, joy, sorrow and hope. What began as a family is now a nation actualizing its mission to be a kingdom of priests to the world. However, for the Israelites to succeed in the Land of Israel, they must see the *Torah* as the only compass to direct their lives.

The biblical episodes after our first entry into the land are well known. Our ancestors' triumphs and sins are all on public record. We learned the harsh reality of Leviticus (18:28) "So let not the land spew you out for defiling it as it spewed out the nation that came before you." Twice, we lost the privilege to be stewards of the Land of Israel and to fulfill our nation state mandate to be a light to the world. However, when the annals of history were ready to archive the Jewish people after the Holocaust, God kept His covenantal promise and gathered us from the four corners of the globe to come home. The year 1948 was a game changer. Biblical prophecies were and are being realized. We are now living in the birth pangs of the messianic era.

In our morning prayers, we recite a series of blessings over the *Torah* that include petitioning God to have a sweet tooth for His word, to study it without any ulterior motive and to have Him to teach it to us. They are some congregations that invoke the following liturgical prayer after the completion of these blessings: *May the Torah be my faith and El Shaddai my help. Blessed be the name of His glorious kingdom forever and all time.*

According to Jewish tradition, the neglect of not blessing the *Torah* before engaging in its study was one of the reasons for the destruction of the Temple.[3] This is deduced from the redundancy of words in Jeremiah (9:12) that talks about Israel not following God: "…Because they forsook the teaching I had set before them. They did not obey Me and they did not follow it [did not make a blessing before studying it]." Our inability to properly cherish God's greatest gift to the world, the *Torah*, led to our eventual exile from our land.

On Israel's Independence Day, Jews around the world recite Psalms 113–118 to express our gratitude to God for His Divine hand in helping establish the State of Israel. We have learned from our past and realize the privilege to see firsthand the land, people and *Torah* operating all together in our generation.

---

3   Babylonian Talmud Nedarim 81a

When Rabbi Tuly Weisz approached me about his intent to publish *The Israel Bible* that would highlight commentary about the special relationship between the land and people, I saw this project as another way to publicly demonstrate our appreciation to God for having the State of Israel. In addition, it is another educational tool to ensure biblical literacy. If we are to truly enjoy the Land of Israel, it is incumbent upon us to continually study the *Torah*. Isaiah once prophesied that the Jewish people would return to Zion with songs, "crowned with everlasting joy" (35:10). *The Israel Bible* provides us the lyrical content to express our joy in living in the land that God calls holy.

Rabbi Shlomo Riskin
Chief Rabbi of Efrat
Founder of the Center for Jewish-Christian
Understanding & Cooperation (CJCUC)

Introduction to Sefer Yechezkel
The Book of Ezekiel

Introduction and commentary by Rabbi Yaakov Beasley

Sefer Yechezkel (Ezekiel) contains the prophecies *Yechezkel* received between the years 593–571 BCE. Since he provides exact dates for a number of his prophecies throughout the book, we can easily pinpoint the moment in history when they are delivered. His messages are intended mainly for the Jews already living in Babylonia, who were exiled from *Yerushalayim* in 597 BCE, and watch from afar as their *Beit Hamikdash* and homeland in *Yehuda* are destroyed. In addition to his prophecies of rebuke, one of *Yechezkel's* central roles involves offering strength to these people who have been torn from the Holy Land. His name thus befits his role as prophet, since *Yechezkel* (יחזקאל) means 'God strengthens'. Hashem chose *Yechezkel* to give strength to His people.

Yechezkel descends from a priestly family in *Yerushalayim*. After being exiled from *Yerushalayim*, he lives in Babylonia, in the city of Tel Abib. His messages of rebuke fall mostly on deaf ears, as the Jews in Babylonia refuse to believe that *Hashem* will destroy His holy city of *Yerushalayim* and His Temple. They also do not accept his words of reproach justifying the upcoming tragedy. After the traumatic destruction, however, the people have become ready to listen to *Yechezkel*, and the focus of his message changes. Instead of emphasizing the catastrophe and its causes, he begins to outline a plan for the Jewish people to survive the temporary loss of their land and to prevail in exile. His messages refer equally to the ritual and the ethical, and he delivers a message of hope that echoes to this day.

Sefer Yechezkel, which is organized chronologically, can be divided into three major sections, paralleling the historical events which unfold around the prophet. Chapters 1–24 speak of the judgment that will befall *Yerushalayim* and provide an explanation for why God has chosen to chastise His people so harshly: The punishments are meant to cleanse His people from their accumulated sins so they can return in purity to their land. In that vein, the actual destruction of *Yerushalayim* is compared to an offering on the altar.

The second section, chapters 25–32, outlines a series of judgments that will befall the nations of the world, either for actively helping Babylonia destroy *Yerushalayim*, or for reveling in the downfall of Israel. Included among these nations are Ammon, Moab, Edom, Philistia, Tyre, Sidon, and Egypt.

The third and final section, chapters 33–48, provides hope for restoration of the exiled remnant of Israel. *Yechezkel* promises that they can, and will, return as a sovereign nation to the Holy Land. This message of deliverance and restoration can be further subdivided into two parts: chapters 33–40 describe the return to the soil of the land, and the final eight chapters envision the rebuilt *Beit Hamikdash* in all its glory, and the Messianic Age. *Yechezkel's* most famous revelation can be found in this section: The vision of the valley of the dry bones (chapter 37).

Sefer Yechezkel is full of unusual symbolic acts and allegories which are intended to help the prophet convey his messages. For example, *Yechezkel* is told to lie on his side for over a year, to shave his hair, and to refrain from mourning for his deceased wife. *Yechezkel's* extravagant, other-worldly descriptions of the "heavenly chariot" and court became the focal point for study of many esoteric mystical traditions. These pursuits have been considered spiritually dangerous for untrained or unprepared students, and studying these chapters was traditionally discouraged, except under the guidance of a master. In fact, there were many who felt that it was not appropriate to include *Sefer Yechezkel* within the biblical canon. The rabbis, however, chose to include *Sefer Yechezkel*, as it was deemed an authentic prophetic work whose eternal messages are meaningful for all generations.

Map of the Ancient Near East

Yechezkel was a contemporary of *Yirmiyahu*. Both lived at the time of the destruction of the first *Beit Hamikdash* and prophesied about its ruin. But while *Yirmiyahu* experienced the destruction in *Eretz Yisrael*, *Yechezkel* prophesied from Babylonia where he had been exiled prior to the final destruction. His presence in the exile, in addition to his prophecies of comfort, brought solace to the rest of the exiles who were eventually brought from *Eretz Yisrael* to Babylonia and reminded them that *Hashem* had not forsaken His people despite the banishment from the land.

The following is a map of the Ancient Near East, including the areas of *Eretz Yisrael,* from where the Jews were taken, and Babylonia, where *Yechezkel* prophesied and the exiled nation was settled.

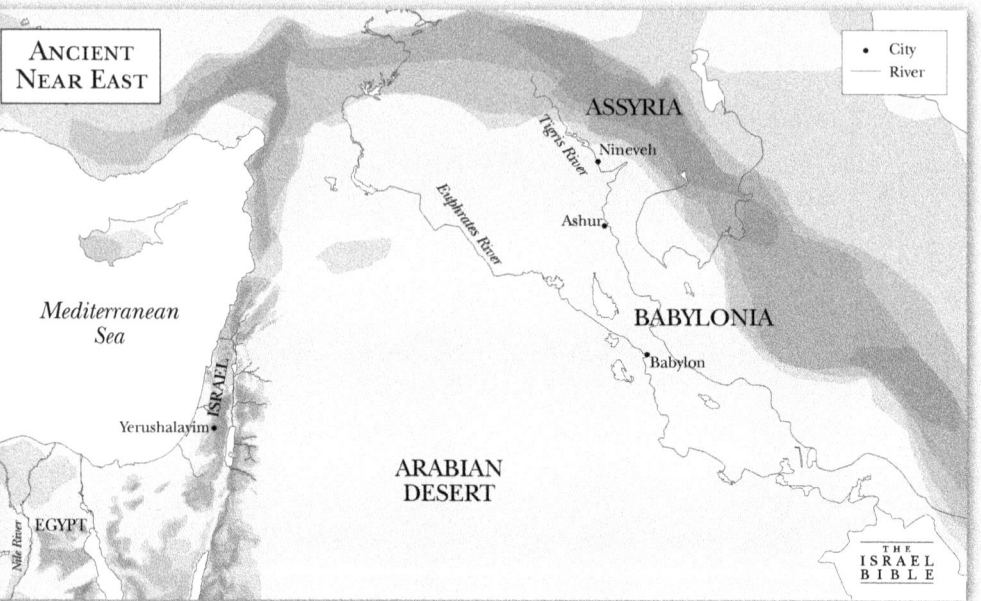

1

1 In the thirtieth year, on the fifth day of the fourth month, when I was in the community of exiles by the Chebar Canal, the heavens opened and I saw visions of *Hashem*.

א וַיְהִי בִּשְׁלֹשִׁים שָׁנָה בָּרְבִיעִי בַּחֲמִשָּׁה לַחֹדֶשׁ וַאֲנִי בְתוֹךְ־הַגּוֹלָה עַל־נְהַר־כְּבָר נִפְתְּחוּ הַשָּׁמַיִם וָאֶרְאֶה מַרְאוֹת אֱלֹהִים:

2 On the fifth day of the month – it was the fifth year of the exile of King *Yehoyachin* –

ב בַּחֲמִשָּׁה לַחֹדֶשׁ הִיא הַשָּׁנָה הַחֲמִישִׁית לְגָלוּת הַמֶּלֶךְ יוֹיָכִין:

3 the word of *Hashem* came to the *Kohen Yechezkel* son of *Buzi*, by the Chebar Canal, in the land of the Chaldeans. And the hand of *Hashem* came upon him there.

ג הָיֹה הָיָה דְבַר־יְהֹוָה אֶל־יְחֶזְקֵאל בֶּן־בּוּזִי הַכֹּהֵן בְּאֶרֶץ כַּשְׂדִּים עַל־נְהַר־כְּבָר וַתְּהִי עָלָיו שָׁם יַד־יְהֹוָה:

ha-YOH ha-YAH d'-var a-do-NAI el y'-khez-KAYL ben bu-ZEE ha-ko-HAYN b'-E-retz kas-DEEM al n'-har k'-VAR va-t'-HEE a-LAV SHAM yad a-do-NAI

4 I looked, and lo, a stormy wind came sweeping out of the north – a huge cloud and flashing fire, surrounded by a radiance; and in the center of it, in the center of the fire, a gleam as of amber.

ד וָאֵרֶא וְהִנֵּה רוּחַ סְעָרָה בָּאָה מִן־הַצָּפוֹן עָנָן גָּדוֹל וְאֵשׁ מִתְלַקַּחַת וְנֹגַהּ לוֹ סָבִיב וּמִתּוֹכָהּ כְּעֵין הַחַשְׁמַל מִתּוֹךְ הָאֵשׁ:

5 In the center of it were also the figures of four creatures. And this was their appearance They had the figures of human beings.

ה וּמִתּוֹכָהּ דְּמוּת אַרְבַּע חַיּוֹת וְזֶה מַרְאֵיהֶן דְּמוּת אָדָם לָהֵנָּה:

6 However, each had four faces, and each of them had four wings;

ו וְאַרְבָּעָה פָנִים לְאֶחָת וְאַרְבַּע כְּנָפַיִם לְאַחַת לָהֶם:

7 the legs of each were [fused into] a single rigid leg, and the feet of each were like a single calf's hoof; and their sparkle was like the luster of burnished bronze.

ז וְרַגְלֵיהֶם רֶגֶל יְשָׁרָה וְכַף רַגְלֵיהֶם כְּכַף רֶגֶל עֵגֶל וְנֹצְצִים כְּעֵין נְחֹשֶׁת קָלָל:

8 They had human hands below their wings. The four of them had their faces and their wings on their four sides.

ח וִידוֹ [וִידֵי] אָדָם מִתַּחַת כַּנְפֵיהֶם עַל אַרְבַּעַת רִבְעֵיהֶם וּפְנֵיהֶם וְכַנְפֵיהֶם לְאַרְבַּעְתָּם:

9 Each one's wings touched those of the other. They did not turn when they moved; each could move in the direction of any of its faces.

ט חֹבְרֹת אִשָּׁה אֶל־אֲחוֹתָהּ כַּנְפֵיהֶם לֹא־יִסַּבּוּ בְלֶכְתָּן אִישׁ אֶל־עֵבֶר פָּנָיו יֵלֵכוּ:

Olive trees on the Mount of Olives overlooking *Yerushalayim*

הָיֹה הָיָה

1:3 The word of *Hashem* came to the *Kohen Yechezkel* *Yechezkel's* prophecy begins with the terrifying and esoteric vision of *Hashem's* holy chariot, symbolic of the Divine Presence leaving the *Beit Hamikdash* and following the Jewish people into exile. The people may be temporarily bereft of their land, but are never abandoned by God. According to Jewish tradition, a prophet cannot receive prophecy outside the Land of Israel, unless he has first received it inside of the land. Therefore, the early commentators such as *Rashi* and *Radak*, note that in Hebrew, the word for the past is doubled in the words *hayo haya* (הָיֹה הָיָה), translated here as "came to," since *Yechezkel's* current prophecy is a continuation of previous prophecies that visited him in *Yerushalayim*. Even when exiled, the people's connection to the holiness and spirituality of *Eretz Yisrael* is never severed or broken.

Ezekiel

10 Each of them had a human face [at the front]; each of the four had the face of a lion on the right; each of the four had the face of an ox on the left; and each of the four had the face of an eagle [at the back].

11 Such were their faces. As for their wings, they were separated: above, each had two touching those of the others, while the other two covered its body.

12 And each could move in the direction of any of its faces; they went wherever the spirit impelled them to go, without turning when they moved.

13 Such then was the appearance of the creatures. With them was something that looked like burning coals of fire. This fire, suggestive of torches, kept moving about among the creatures; the fire had a radiance, and lightning issued from the fire.

14 Dashing to and fro [among] the creatures was something that looked like flares.

15 As I gazed on the creatures, I saw one wheel on the ground next to each of the four-faced creatures.

16 As for the appearance and structure of the wheels, they gleamed like beryl. All four had the same form; the appearance and structure of each was as of two wheels cutting through each other.

17 And when they moved, each could move in the direction of any of its four quarters; they did not veer when they moved.

18 Their rims were tall and frightening, for the rims of all four were covered all over with eyes.

19 And when the creatures moved forward, the wheels moved at their sides; and when the creatures were borne above the earth, the wheels were borne too.

20 Wherever the spirit impelled them to go, they went – wherever the spirit impelled them – and the wheels were borne alongside them; for the spirit of the creatures was in the wheels.

21 When those moved, these moved; and when those stood still, these stood still; and when those were borne above the earth, the wheels were borne alongside them – for the spirit of the creatures was in the wheels.

22 Above the heads of the creatures was a form: an expanse, with an awe-inspiring gleam as of crystal, was spread out above their heads.

י וּדְמוּת פְּנֵיהֶם פְּנֵי אָדָם וּפְנֵי אַרְיֵה אֶל־הַיָּמִין לְאַרְבַּעְתָּם וּפְנֵי־שׁוֹר מֵהַשְּׂמֹאול לְאַרְבַּעְתָּן וּפְנֵי־נֶשֶׁר לְאַרְבַּעְתָּן:

יא וּפְנֵיהֶם וְכַנְפֵיהֶם פְּרֻדוֹת מִלְמָעְלָה לְאִישׁ שְׁתַּיִם חֹבְרוֹת אִישׁ וּשְׁתַּיִם מְכַסּוֹת אֵת גְּוִיֹתֵיהֶנָה:

יב וְאִישׁ אֶל־עֵבֶר פָּנָיו יֵלֵכוּ אֶל אֲשֶׁר יִהְיֶה־שָּׁמָּה הָרוּחַ לָלֶכֶת יֵלֵכוּ לֹא יִסַּבּוּ בְּלֶכְתָּן:

יג וּדְמוּת הַחַיּוֹת מַרְאֵיהֶם כְּגַחֲלֵי־אֵשׁ בֹּעֲרוֹת כְּמַרְאֵה הַלַּפִּדִים הִיא מִתְהַלֶּכֶת בֵּין הַחַיּוֹת וְנֹגַהּ לָאֵשׁ וּמִן־הָאֵשׁ יוֹצֵא בָרָק:

יד וְהַחַיּוֹת רָצוֹא וָשׁוֹב כְּמַרְאֵה הַבָּזָק:

טו וָאֵרֶא הַחַיּוֹת וְהִנֵּה אוֹפַן אֶחָד בָּאָרֶץ אֵצֶל הַחַיּוֹת לְאַרְבַּעַת פָּנָיו:

טז מַרְאֵה הָאוֹפַנִּים וּמַעֲשֵׂיהֶם כְּעֵין תַּרְשִׁישׁ וּדְמוּת אֶחָד לְאַרְבַּעְתָּן וּמַרְאֵיהֶם וּמַעֲשֵׂיהֶם כַּאֲשֶׁר יִהְיֶה הָאוֹפַן בְּתוֹךְ הָאוֹפָן:

יז עַל־אַרְבַּעַת רִבְעֵיהֶן בְּלֶכְתָּם יֵלֵכוּ לֹא יִסַּבּוּ בְּלֶכְתָּן:

יח וְגַבֵּיהֶן וְגֹבַהּ לָהֶם וְיִרְאָה לָהֶם וְגַבֹּתָם מְלֵאֹת עֵינַיִם סָבִיב לְאַרְבַּעְתָּן:

יט וּבְלֶכֶת הַחַיּוֹת יֵלְכוּ הָאוֹפַנִּים אֶצְלָם וּבְהִנָּשֵׂא הַחַיּוֹת מֵעַל הָאָרֶץ יִנָּשְׂאוּ הָאוֹפַנִּים:

כ עַל אֲשֶׁר יִהְיֶה־שָּׁם הָרוּחַ לָלֶכֶת יֵלֵכוּ שָׁמָּה הָרוּחַ לָלֶכֶת וְהָאוֹפַנִּים יִנָּשְׂאוּ לְעֻמָּתָם כִּי רוּחַ הַחַיָּה בָּאוֹפַנִּים:

כא בְּלֶכְתָּם יֵלֵכוּ וּבְעָמְדָם יַעֲמֹדוּ וּבְהִנָּשְׂאָם מֵעַל הָאָרֶץ יִנָּשְׂאוּ הָאוֹפַנִּים לְעֻמָּתָם כִּי רוּחַ הַחַיָּה בָּאוֹפַנִּים:

כב וּדְמוּת עַל־רָאשֵׁי הַחַיָּה רָקִיעַ כְּעֵין הַקֶּרַח הַנּוֹרָא נָטוּי עַל־רָאשֵׁיהֶם מִלְמָעְלָה:

23 Under the expanse, each had one pair of wings extended toward those of the others; and each had another pair covering its body.

כג וְתַחַת הָרָקִיעַ כַּנְפֵיהֶם יְשָׁרוֹת אִשָּׁה אֶל־אֲחוֹתָהּ לְאִישׁ שְׁתַּיִם מְכַסּוֹת לָהֵנָּה וּלְאִישׁ שְׁתַּיִם מְכַסּוֹת לָהֵנָּה אֵת גְּוִיֹּתֵיהֶם:

24 When they moved, I could hear the sound of their wings like the sound of mighty waters, like the sound of *Shaddai*, a tumult like the din of an army. When they stood still, they would let their wings droop.

כד וָאֶשְׁמַע אֶת־קוֹל כַּנְפֵיהֶם כְּקוֹל מַיִם רַבִּים כְּקוֹל־שַׁדַּי בְּלֶכְתָּם קוֹל הֲמֻלָּה כְּקוֹל מַחֲנֶה בְּעָמְדָם תְּרַפֶּינָה כַנְפֵיהֶן:

25 From above the expanse over their heads came a sound. When they stood still, they would let their wings droop.

כה וַיְהִי־קוֹל מֵעַל לָרָקִיעַ אֲשֶׁר עַל־רֹאשָׁם בְּעָמְדָם תְּרַפֶּינָה כַנְפֵיהֶן:

26 Above the expanse over their heads was the semblance of a throne, in appearance like sapphire; and on top, upon this semblance of a throne, there was the semblance of a human form.

כו וּמִמַּעַל לָרָקִיעַ אֲשֶׁר עַל־רֹאשָׁם כְּמַרְאֵה אֶבֶן־סַפִּיר דְּמוּת כִּסֵּא וְעַל דְּמוּת הַכִּסֵּא דְּמוּת כְּמַרְאֵה אָדָם עָלָיו מִלְמָעְלָה:

27 From what appeared as his loins up, I saw a gleam as of amber – what looked like a fire encased in a frame; and from what appeared as his loins down, I saw what looked like fire. There was a radiance all about him.

כז וָאֵרֶא כְּעֵין חַשְׁמַל כְּמַרְאֵה־אֵשׁ בֵּית־לָהּ סָבִיב מִמַּרְאֵה מָתְנָיו וּלְמָעְלָה וּמִמַּרְאֵה מָתְנָיו וּלְמַטָּה רָאִיתִי כְּמַרְאֵה־אֵשׁ וְנֹגַהּ לוֹ סָבִיב:

28 Like the appearance of the bow which shines in the clouds on a day of rain, such was the appearance of the surrounding radiance. That was the appearance of the semblance of the Presence of *Hashem*. When I beheld it, I flung myself down on my face. And I heard the voice of someone speaking.

כח כְּמַרְאֵה הַקֶּשֶׁת אֲשֶׁר יִהְיֶה בֶעָנָן בְּיוֹם הַגֶּשֶׁם כֵּן מַרְאֵה הַנֹּגַהּ סָבִיב הוּא מַרְאֵה דְּמוּת כְּבוֹד־יְהוָה וָאֶרְאֶה וָאֶפֹּל עַל־פָּנַי וָאֶשְׁמַע קוֹל מְדַבֵּר:

2 1 And He said to me, "O mortal, stand up on your feet that I may speak to you."

ב א וַיֹּאמֶר אֵלָי בֶּן־אָדָם עֲמֹד עַל־רַגְלֶיךָ וַאֲדַבֵּר אֹתָךְ:

2 As He spoke to me, a spirit entered into me and set me upon my feet; and I heard what was being spoken to me.

ב וַתָּבֹא בִי רוּחַ כַּאֲשֶׁר דִּבֶּר אֵלַי וַתַּעֲמִדֵנִי עַל־רַגְלָי וָאֶשְׁמַע אֵת מִדַּבֵּר אֵלָי:

3 He said to me, "O mortal, I am sending you to the people of *Yisrael*, that nation of rebels, who have rebelled against Me. – They as well as their fathers have defied Me to this very day;

ג וַיֹּאמֶר אֵלַי בֶּן־אָדָם שׁוֹלֵחַ אֲנִי אוֹתְךָ אֶל־בְּנֵי יִשְׂרָאֵל אֶל־גּוֹיִם הַמּוֹרְדִים אֲשֶׁר מָרְדוּ־בִי הֵמָּה וַאֲבוֹתָם פָּשְׁעוּ בִי עַד־עֶצֶם הַיּוֹם הַזֶּה:

va-YO-mer ay-LAI ben a-DAM sho-LAY-akh a-NEE o-t'-KHA el
b'-NAY yis-ra-AYL el go-YIM ha-mo-r'-DEEM a-SHER ma-r'-du VEE
HAY-mah va-a-vo-TAM PA-sh'-u VEE ad E-tzem ha-YOM ha-ZEH

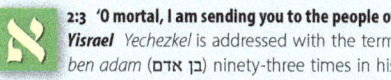

בן אדם

2:3 'O mortal, I am sending you to the people of *Yisrael* *Yechezkel* is addressed with the term *ben adam* (בן אדם) ninety-three times in his book. This expression literally means 'son of man', and is translated here as 'mortal'. This designation alludes to both his humility and mortality, but also to all of man-

4 for the sons are brazen of face and stubborn of heart. I send you to them, and you shall say to them: 'Thus said *Hashem*' –

ד וְהַבָּנִים קְשֵׁי פָנִים וְחִזְקֵי־לֵב אֲנִי שׁוֹלֵחַ אוֹתְךָ אֲלֵיהֶם וְאָמַרְתָּ אֲלֵיהֶם כֹּה אָמַר אֲדֹנָי יֱהֹוִה:

5 whether they listen or not, for they are a rebellious breed – that they may know that there was a *Navi* among them.

ה וְהֵמָּה אִם־יִשְׁמְעוּ וְאִם־יֶחְדָּלוּ כִּי בֵּית מְרִי הֵמָּה וְיָדְעוּ כִּי נָבִיא הָיָה בְתוֹכָם:

6 "And you, mortal, do not fear them and do not fear their words, though thistles and thorns press against you, and you sit upon scorpions. Do not be afraid of their words and do not be dismayed by them, though they are a rebellious breed;

ו וְאַתָּה בֶן־אָדָם אַל־תִּירָא מֵהֶם וּמִדִּבְרֵיהֶם אַל־תִּירָא כִּי סָרָבִים וְסַלּוֹנִים אוֹתָךְ וְאֶל־עַקְרַבִּים אַתָּה יוֹשֵׁב מִדִּבְרֵיהֶם אַל־תִּירָא וּמִפְּנֵיהֶם אַל־תֵּחָת כִּי בֵּית מְרִי הֵמָּה:

7 but speak My words to them, whether they listen or not, for they are rebellious.

ז וְדִבַּרְתָּ אֶת־דְּבָרַי אֲלֵיהֶם אִם־יִשְׁמְעוּ וְאִם־יֶחְדָּלוּ כִּי מְרִי הֵמָּה:

8 "And you, mortal, heed what I say to you: Do not be rebellious like that rebellious breed. Open your mouth and eat what I am giving you."

ח וְאַתָּה בֶן־אָדָם שְׁמַע אֵת אֲשֶׁר־אֲנִי מְדַבֵּר אֵלֶיךָ אַל־תְּהִי־מֶרִי כְּבֵית הַמֶּרִי פְּצֵה פִיךָ וֶאֱכֹל אֵת אֲשֶׁר־אֲנִי נֹתֵן אֵלֶיךָ:

9 As I looked, there was a hand stretched out to me, holding a written scroll.

ט וָאֶרְאֶה וְהִנֵּה־יָד שְׁלוּחָה אֵלָי וְהִנֵּה־בוֹ מְגִלַּת־סֵפֶר:

10 He unrolled it before me, and it was inscribed on both the front and the back; on it were written lamentations, dirges, and woes.

י וַיִּפְרֹשׂ אוֹתָהּ לְפָנַי וְהִיא כְתוּבָה פָּנִים וְאָחוֹר וְכָתוּב אֵלֶיהָ קִנִים וָהֶגֶה וָהִי:

3 1 He said to me, "Mortal, eat what is offered you; eat this scroll, and go speak to the House of *Yisrael*."

ג א וַיֹּאמֶר אֵלַי בֶּן־אָדָם אֵת אֲשֶׁר־תִּמְצָא אֱכוֹל אֱכוֹל אֶת־הַמְּגִלָּה הַזֹּאת וְלֵךְ דַּבֵּר אֶל־בֵּית יִשְׂרָאֵל:

2 So I opened my mouth, and He gave me this scroll to eat,

ב וָאֶפְתַּח אֶת־פִּי וַיַּאֲכִלֵנִי אֵת הַמְּגִלָּה הַזֹּאת:

3 as He said to me, "Mortal, feed your stomach and fill your belly with this scroll that I give you." I ate it, and it tasted as sweet as honey to me.

ג וַיֹּאמֶר אֵלַי בֶּן־אָדָם בִּטְנְךָ תַאֲכֵל וּמֵעֶיךָ תְמַלֵּא אֵת הַמְּגִלָּה הַזֹּאת אֲשֶׁר אֲנִי נֹתֵן אֵלֶיךָ וָאֹכְלָה וַתְּהִי בְּפִי כִּדְבַשׁ לְמָתוֹק:

4 Then He said to me, "Mortal, go to the House of *Yisrael* and repeat My very words to them.

ד וַיֹּאמֶר אֵלַי בֶּן־אָדָם לֶךְ־בֹּא אֶל־בֵּית יִשְׂרָאֵל וְדִבַּרְתָּ בִדְבָרַי אֲלֵיהֶם:

5 For you are sent, not to a people of unintelligible speech and difficult language, but to the House of *Yisrael* –

ה כִּי לֹא אֶל־עַם עִמְקֵי שָׂפָה וְכִבְדֵי לָשׁוֹן אַתָּה שָׁלוּחַ אֶל־בֵּית יִשְׂרָאֵל:

kind's role at God's side in improving the world, as alluded to in *Tehillim* (80:18). As such, *Yechezkel's* messages are intended both for Israel and for the nations. While his message is specific to Israel, the truths it contains are meant for the betterment of all mankind.

Rabbi Tuly Weisz visiting sick children in the hospital

ו לֹא אֶל־עַמִּים רַבִּים עִמְקֵי שָׂפָה וְכִבְדֵי לָשׁוֹן אֲשֶׁר לֹא־תִשְׁמַע דִּבְרֵיהֶם אִם־לֹא אֲלֵיהֶם שְׁלַחְתִּיךָ הֵמָּה יִשְׁמְעוּ אֵלֶיךָ:

ז וּבֵית יִשְׂרָאֵל לֹא יֹאבוּ לִשְׁמֹעַ אֵלֶיךָ כִּי־אֵינָם אֹבִים לִשְׁמֹעַ אֵלָי כִּי כָּל־בֵּית יִשְׂרָאֵל חִזְקֵי־מֵצַח וּקְשֵׁי־לֵב הֵמָּה:

ח הִנֵּה נָתַתִּי אֶת־פָּנֶיךָ חֲזָקִים לְעֻמַּת פְּנֵיהֶם וְאֶת־מִצְחֲךָ חָזָק לְעֻמַּת מִצְחָם:

ט כְּשָׁמִיר חָזָק מִצֹּר נָתַתִּי מִצְחֶךָ לֹא־תִירָא אוֹתָם וְלֹא־תֵחַת מִפְּנֵיהֶם כִּי בֵּית־מְרִי הֵמָּה:

י וַיֹּאמֶר אֵלַי בֶּן־אָדָם אֶת־כָּל־דְּבָרַי אֲשֶׁר אֲדַבֵּר אֵלֶיךָ קַח בִּלְבָבְךָ וּבְאָזְנֶיךָ שְׁמָע:

יא וְלֵךְ בֹּא אֶל־הַגּוֹלָה אֶל־בְּנֵי עַמֶּךָ וְדִבַּרְתָּ אֲלֵיהֶם וְאָמַרְתָּ אֲלֵיהֶם כֹּה אָמַר אֲדֹנָי יְהוִה אִם־יִשְׁמְעוּ וְאִם־יֶחְדָּלוּ:

יב וַתִּשָּׂאֵנִי רוּחַ וָאֶשְׁמַע אַחֲרַי קוֹל רַעַשׁ גָּדוֹל בָּרוּךְ כְּבוֹד־יְהוָה מִמְּקוֹמוֹ:

יג וְקוֹל כַּנְפֵי הַחַיּוֹת מַשִּׁיקוֹת אִשָּׁה אֶל־אֲחוֹתָהּ וְקוֹל הָאוֹפַנִּים לְעֻמָּתָם וְקוֹל רַעַשׁ גָּדוֹל:

יד וְרוּחַ נְשָׂאַתְנִי וַתִּקָּחֵנִי וָאֵלֵךְ מַר בַּחֲמַת רוּחִי וְיַד־יְהוָה עָלַי חָזָקָה:

טו וָאָבוֹא אֶל־הַגּוֹלָה תֵּל אָבִיב הַיֹּשְׁבִים אֶל־נְהַר־כְּבָר וָאֵשֵׁב [וָאֵשֵׁב] הֵמָּה יוֹשְׁבִים שָׁם וָאֵשֵׁב שָׁם שִׁבְעַת יָמִים מַשְׁמִים בְּתוֹכָם:

6 not to the many peoples of unintelligible speech and difficult language, whose talk you cannot understand. If I sent you to them, they would listen to you.

7 But the House of *Yisrael* will refuse to listen to you, for they refuse to listen to Me; for the whole House of *Yisrael* are brazen of forehead and stubborn of heart.

8 But I will make your face as hard as theirs, and your forehead as brazen as theirs.

9 I will make your forehead like adamant, harder than flint. Do not fear them, and do not be dismayed by them, though they are a rebellious breed."

10 Then He said to me: "Mortal, listen with your ears and receive into your mind all the words that I speak to you.

11 Go to your people, the exile community, and speak to them. Say to them: Thus says *Hashem* – whether they listen or not."

12 Then a spirit carried me away, and behind me I heard a great roaring sound: "Blessed is the Presence of *Hashem*, in His place,"

13 with the sound of the wings of the creatures beating against one another, and the sound of the wheels beside them – a great roaring sound.

14 A spirit seized me and carried me away. I went in bitterness, in the fury of my spirit, while the hand of *Hashem* was strong upon me.

15 And I came to the exile community that dwelt in Tel Abib by the Chebar Canal, and I remained where they dwelt. And for seven days I sat there stunned among them.

va-a-VO el ha-go-LAH TAYL a-VEEV ha-yo-sh'-VEEM el n'har k'-VAR
va-ay-SHAYV HAY-mah yo-sh'-VEEM SHAM va-ay-SHAYV SHAM
shiv-AT ya-MEEM mash-MEEM b'-to-KHAM

Tel Aviv

3:15 And I came to the exile community that dwelt in Tel Abib *Yechezkel* goes to the Israelite captives at Tel Abib near the Chebar River. Before he delivers his message of doom, however, he simply sits with them for a week, empathizing with their suffering before sharing the divine message. The name Tel Abib has been linked to the Akkadian "mound of the flood," mentioned in ancient Babylonian sources, so called because it was flooded by the Euphrates River. The great irony is that the name of the city of the exiles has

¹⁶ After those seven days, the word of *Hashem* came to me:

טז וַיְהִי מִקְצֵה שִׁבְעַת יָמִים וַיְהִי דְבַר־יְהֹוָה אֵלַי לֵאמֹר:

¹⁷ "O mortal, I appoint you watchman for the House of *Yisrael*; and when you hear a word from My mouth, you must warn them for Me.

יז בֶּן־אָדָם צֹפֶה נְתַתִּיךָ לְבֵית יִשְׂרָאֵל וְשָׁמַעְתָּ מִפִּי דָּבָר וְהִזְהַרְתָּ אוֹתָם מִמֶּנִּי:

¹⁸ If I say to a wicked man, 'You shall die,' and you do not warn him – you do not speak to warn the wicked man of his wicked course in order to save his life – he, the wicked man, shall die for his iniquity, but I will require a reckoning for his blood from you.

יח בְּאָמְרִי לָרָשָׁע מוֹת תָּמוּת וְלֹא הִזְהַרְתּוֹ וְלֹא דִבַּרְתָּ לְהַזְהִיר רָשָׁע מִדַּרְכּוֹ הָרְשָׁעָה לְחַיֹּתוֹ הוּא רָשָׁע בַּעֲוֹנוֹ יָמוּת וְדָמוֹ מִיָּדְךָ אֲבַקֵּשׁ:

¹⁹ But if you do warn the wicked man, and he does not turn back from his wickedness and his wicked course, he shall die for his iniquity, but you will have saved your own life.

יט וְאַתָּה כִּי־הִזְהַרְתָּ רָשָׁע וְלֹא־שָׁב מֵרִשְׁעוֹ וּמִדַּרְכּוֹ הָרְשָׁעָה הוּא בַּעֲוֹנוֹ יָמוּת וְאַתָּה אֶת־נַפְשְׁךָ הִצַּלְתָּ:

²⁰ Again, if a righteous man abandons his righteousness and does wrong, when I put a stumbling block before him, he shall die. He shall die for his sins; the righteous deeds that he did shall not be remembered; but because you did not warn him, I will require a reckoning for his blood from you.

כ וּבְשׁוּב צַדִּיק מִצִּדְקוֹ וְעָשָׂה עָוֶל וְנָתַתִּי מִכְשׁוֹל לְפָנָיו הוּא יָמוּת כִּי לֹא הִזְהַרְתּוֹ בְּחַטָּאתוֹ יָמוּת וְלֹא תִזָּכַרְןָ צִדְקֹתָו אֲשֶׁר עָשָׂה וְדָמוֹ מִיָּדְךָ אֲבַקֵּשׁ:

²¹ If, however, you warn the righteous man not to sin, and he, the righteous, does not sin, he shall live because he took warning, and you will have saved your own life."

כא וְאַתָּה כִּי הִזְהַרְתּוֹ צַדִּיק לְבִלְתִּי חֲטֹא צַדִּיק וְהוּא לֹא־חָטָא חָיוֹ יִחְיֶה כִּי נִזְהָר וְאַתָּה אֶת־נַפְשְׁךָ הִצַּלְתָּ:

²² Then the hand of *Hashem* came upon me there, and He said to me, "Arise, go out to the valley, and there I will speak with you."

כב וַתְּהִי עָלַי שָׁם יַד־יְהֹוָה וַיֹּאמֶר אֵלַי קוּם צֵא אֶל־הַבִּקְעָה וְשָׁם אֲדַבֵּר אוֹתָךְ:

²³ I arose and went out to the valley, and there stood the Presence of *Hashem*, like the Presence that I had seen at the Chebar Canal; and I flung myself down on my face.

כג וָאָקוּם וָאֵצֵא אֶל־הַבִּקְעָה וְהִנֵּה־שָׁם כְּבוֹד־יְהֹוָה עֹמֵד כַּכָּבוֹד אֲשֶׁר רָאִיתִי עַל־נְהַר־כְּבָר וָאֶפֹּל עַל־פָּנָי:

Ezekiel

become the name of modern Israel's shining metropolis, *Tel Aviv* (תל אביב), which in modern Hebrew means 'the hill of spring.' The name for the city was borrowed from the title of Nahum Sokolow's Hebrew translation of Theodor Herz's *Altneuland*, 'Old New Land.' It was chosen because the word *Tel*, a mound covering ruins of ancient settlements, conjures up images of that which is ancient, while the word *aviv*, spring, implies that which is fresh and new.

24 And a spirit entered into me and set me upon my feet. And He spoke to me, and said to me: "Go, shut yourself up in your house.

כד וַתָּבֹא־בִי רוּחַ וַתַּעֲמִדֵנִי עַל־רַגְלָי וַיְדַבֵּר אֹתִי וַיֹּאמֶר אֵלַי בֹּא הִסָּגֵר בְּתוֹךְ בֵּיתֶךָ:

25 As for you, O mortal, cords have been placed upon you, and you have been bound with them, and you shall not go out among them.

כה וְאַתָּה בֶן־אָדָם הִנֵּה נָתְנוּ עָלֶיךָ עֲבוֹתִים וַאֲסָרוּךָ בָּהֶם וְלֹא תֵצֵא בְּתוֹכָם:

26 And I will make your tongue cleave to your palate, and you shall be dumb; you shall not be a reprover to them, for they are a rebellious breed.

כו וּלְשׁוֹנְךָ אַדְבִּיק אֶל־חִכֶּךָ וְנֶאֱלַמְתָּ וְלֹא־תִהְיֶה לָהֶם לְאִישׁ מוֹכִיחַ כִּי בֵּית מְרִי הֵמָּה:

27 But when I speak with you, I will open your mouth, and you shall say to them, 'Thus says *Hashem*!' He who listens will listen, and he who does not will not – for they are a rebellious breed."

כז וּבְדַבְּרִי אוֹתְךָ אֶפְתַּח אֶת־פִּיךָ וְאָמַרְתָּ אֲלֵיהֶם כֹּה אָמַר אֲדֹנָי יֱהוִֹה הַשֹּׁמֵעַ יִשְׁמָע וְהֶחָדֵל יֶחְדָּל כִּי בֵּית מְרִי הֵמָּה:

4 1 "And you, O mortal, take a brick and put it in front of you, and incise on it a city, *Yerushalayim*.

א וְאַתָּה בֶן־אָדָם קַח־לְךָ לְבֵנָה וְנָתַתָּה אוֹתָהּ לְפָנֶיךָ וְחַקּוֹתָ עָלֶיהָ עִיר אֶת־יְרוּשָׁלָ‍ִם:

2 Set up a siege against it, and build towers against it, and cast a mound against it; pitch camps against it, and bring up battering rams roundabout it.

ב וְנָתַתָּה עָלֶיהָ מָצוֹר וּבָנִיתָ עָלֶיהָ דָּיֵק וְשָׁפַכְתָּ עָלֶיהָ סֹלְלָה וְנָתַתָּה עָלֶיהָ מַחֲנוֹת וְשִׂים־עָלֶיהָ כָּרִים סָבִיב:

3 Then take an iron plate and place it as an iron wall between yourself and the city, and set your face against it. Thus it shall be under siege, you shall besiege it. This shall be an omen for the House of *Yisrael*.

ג וְאַתָּה קַח־לְךָ מַחֲבַת בַּרְזֶל וְנָתַתָּה אוֹתָהּ קִיר בַּרְזֶל בֵּינְךָ וּבֵין הָעִיר וַהֲכִינֹתָה אֶת־פָּנֶיךָ אֵלֶיהָ וְהָיְתָה בַמָּצוֹר וְצַרְתָּ עָלֶיהָ אוֹת הִיא לְבֵית יִשְׂרָאֵל:

4 "Then lie on your left side, and let it bear the punishment of the House of *Yisrael*; for as many days as you lie on it you shall bear their punishment.

ד וְאַתָּה שְׁכַב עַל־צִדְּךָ הַשְּׂמָאלִי וְשַׂמְתָּ אֶת־עֲוֹן בֵּית־יִשְׂרָאֵל עָלָיו מִסְפַּר הַיָּמִים אֲשֶׁר תִּשְׁכַּב עָלָיו תִּשָּׂא אֶת־עֲוֹנָם:

5 For I impose upon you three hundred and ninety days, corresponding to the number of the years of their punishment; and so you shall bear the punishment for the House of *Yisrael*.

ה וַאֲנִי נָתַתִּי לְךָ אֶת־שְׁנֵי עֲוֹנָם לְמִסְפַּר יָמִים שְׁלֹשׁ־מֵאוֹת וְתִשְׁעִים יוֹם וְנָשָׂאתָ עֲוֹן בֵּית־יִשְׂרָאֵל:

6 When you have completed these, you shall lie another forty days on your right side, and bear the punishment of the House of *Yehuda*. I impose on you one day for each year.

ו וְכִלִּיתָ אֶת־אֵלֶּה וְשָׁכַבְתָּ עַל־צִדְּךָ הַיְמוֹנִי [הַיְמָנִי] שֵׁנִית וְנָשָׂאתָ אֶת־עֲוֹן בֵּית־יְהוּדָה אַרְבָּעִים יוֹם יוֹם לַשָּׁנָה יוֹם לַשָּׁנָה נְתַתִּיו לָךְ:

7 "Then, with bared arm, set your face toward besieged *Yerushalayim* and prophesy against it.

ז וְאֶל־מְצוֹר יְרוּשָׁלַ‍ִם תָּכִין פָּנֶיךָ וּזְרֹעֲךָ חֲשׂוּפָה וְנִבֵּאתָ עָלֶיהָ:

8 Now I put cords upon you, so that you cannot turn from side to side until you complete your days of siege.

ח וְהִנֵּה נָתַתִּי עָלֶיךָ עֲבוֹתִים וְלֹא־תֵהָפֵךְ מִצִּדְּךָ אֶל־צִדֶּךָ עַד־כַּלּוֹתְךָ יְמֵי מְצוּרֶךָ:

9 "Further, take wheat, barley, beans, lentils, millet, and emmer. Put them into one vessel and bake them into bread. Eat it as many days as you lie on your side: three hundred and ninety.

ט וְאַתָּה קַח־לְךָ חִטִּין וּשְׂעֹרִים וּפוֹל וַעֲדָשִׁים וְדֹחַן וְכֻסְּמִים וְנָתַתָּה אוֹתָם בִּכְלִי אֶחָד וְעָשִׂיתָ אוֹתָם לְךָ לְלָחֶם מִסְפַּר הַיָּמִים אֲשֶׁר־אַתָּה שׁוֹכֵב עַל־צִדְּךָ שְׁלֹשׁ־מֵאוֹת וְתִשְׁעִים יוֹם תֹּאכֲלֶנּוּ:

v'-a-TAH kakh l'-KHA khi-TEEN us-o-REEM u-FOL va-a-da-SHEEM
v'-DO-khan v'-khu-s'-MEEM v'-na-ta-TAH o-TAM bikh-LEE e-KHAD
v'-a-SEE-ta o-TAM l'-KHA l'-LA-khem mis-PAR ha-ya-MEEM a-sher a-TAH
sho-KHAYV al tzi-d'-KHA sh'-losh may-OT v'-tish-EEM YOM to-kh'-LE-nu

10 The food that you eat shall be by weight, twenty *shekalim* a day; this you shall eat in the space of a day.

י וּמַאֲכָלְךָ אֲשֶׁר תֹּאכְלֶנּוּ בְּמִשְׁקוֹל עֶשְׂרִים שֶׁקֶל לַיּוֹם מֵעֵת עַד־עֵת תֹּאכֲלֶנּוּ:

11 And you shall drink water by measure; drink a sixth of a *hin* in the space of a day.

יא וּמַיִם בִּמְשׂוּרָה תִשְׁתֶּה שִׁשִּׁית הַהִין מֵעֵת עַד־עֵת תִּשְׁתֶּה:

12 "Eat it as a barley cake; you shall bake it on human excrement before their eyes.

יב וְעֻגַת שְׂעֹרִים תֹּאכְלֶנָּה וְהִיא בְּגֶלְלֵי צֵאַת הָאָדָם תְּעֻגֶנָה לְעֵינֵיהֶם:

13 So," said *Hashem*, "shall the people of *Yisrael* eat their bread, unclean, among the nations to which I will banish them."

יג וַיֹּאמֶר יְהֹוָה כָּכָה יֹאכְלוּ בְנֵי־יִשְׂרָאֵל אֶת־לַחְמָם טָמֵא בַּגּוֹיִם אֲשֶׁר אַדִּיחֵם שָׁם:

14 Then I said, "Ah, *Hashem*, my person was never defiled; nor have I eaten anything that died of itself or was torn by beasts from my youth until now, nor has foul flesh entered my mouth."

יד וָאֹמַר אֲהָהּ אֲדֹנָי יֱהֹוִה הִנֵּה נַפְשִׁי לֹא מְטֻמָּאָה וּנְבֵלָה וּטְרֵפָה לֹא־אָכַלְתִּי מִנְּעוּרַי וְעַד־עַתָּה וְלֹא־בָא בְּפִי בְּשַׂר פִּגּוּל:

15 He answered me, "See, I allow you cow's dung instead of human excrement; prepare your bread on that."

טו וַיֹּאמֶר אֵלַי רְאֵה נָתַתִּי לְךָ אֶת־צְפוּעֵי [צְפִיעֵי] הַבָּקָר תַּחַת גֶּלְלֵי הָאָדָם וְעָשִׂיתָ אֶת־לַחְמְךָ עֲלֵיהֶם:

16 And He said to me, "O mortal, I am going to break the staff of bread in *Yerushalayim*, and they shall eat bread by weight, in anxiety, and drink water by measure, in horror,

טז וַיֹּאמֶר אֵלַי בֶּן־אָדָם הִנְנִי שֹׁבֵר מַטֵּה־לֶחֶם בִּירוּשָׁלַ͏ִם וְאָכְלוּ־לֶחֶם בְּמִשְׁקָל וּבִדְאָגָה וּמַיִם בִּמְשׂוּרָה וּבְשִׁמָּמוֹן יִשְׁתּוּ:

17 so that, lacking bread and water, they shall stare at each other, heartsick over their iniquity.

יז לְמַעַן יַחְסְרוּ לֶחֶם וָמָיִם וְנָשַׁמּוּ אִישׁ וְאָחִיו וְנָמַקּוּ בַּעֲוֹנָם:

4:9 **And bake them into bread** *Yechezkel* demonstrates to his listeners the dire straits the people from *Yerushalayim* are in during the final Babylonian siege against the city. According to the Talmud (*Eruvin* 81a), *Yechezkel* rations to himself inedible flour and inferior grains and limits his water in order to portray the austere conditions under which the people of *Yerushalayim* are suffering. As a final blow, these foods are prepared in an impure manner (verse 13), something repulsive to the sensitive prophet-priest.

Indeed, bread and water were very scarce during the Babylonian siege of *Yerushalayim*, as the Bible indicates elsewhere: "The tongue of the suckling cleaves to its palate for thirst. Little children beg for bread; none gives them a morsel." (Lamentations 4:4).

A variety of breads at the Mahane Yehuda market in *Yerushalayim*

5 ¹ And you, O mortal, take a sharp knife; use it as a barber's razor and pass it over your head and beard. Then take scales and divide the hair.

ה א וְאַתָּה בֶן־אָדָם קַח־לְךָ חֶרֶב חַדָּה תַּעַר הַגַּלָּבִים תִּקָּחֶנָּה לָּךְ וְהַעֲבַרְתָּ עַל־רֹאשְׁךָ וְעַל־זְקָנֶךָ וְלָקַחְתָּ לְךָ מֹאזְנֵי מִשְׁקָל וְחִלַּקְתָּם:

² When the days of siege are completed, destroy a third part in fire in the city, take a third and strike it with the sword all around the city, and scatter a third to the wind and unsheathe a sword after them.

ב שְׁלִשִׁית בָּאוּר תַּבְעִיר בְּתוֹךְ הָעִיר כִּמְלֹאת יְמֵי הַמָּצוֹר וְלָקַחְתָּ אֶת־הַשְּׁלִשִׁית תַּכֶּה בַחֶרֶב סְבִיבוֹתֶיהָ וְהַשְּׁלִשִׁית תִּזְרֶה לָרוּחַ וְחֶרֶב אָרִיק אַחֲרֵיהֶם:

³ "Take also a few [hairs] from there and tie them up in your skirts.

ג וְלָקַחְתָּ מִשָּׁם מְעַט בְּמִסְפָּר וְצַרְתָּ אוֹתָם בִּכְנָפֶיךָ:

⁴ And take some more of them and cast them into the fire, and burn them in the fire. From this a fire shall go out upon the whole House of *Yisrael*."

ד וּמֵהֶם עוֹד תִּקָּח וְהִשְׁלַכְתָּ אוֹתָם אֶל־תּוֹךְ הָאֵשׁ וְשָׂרַפְתָּ אֹתָם בָּאֵשׁ מִמֶּנּוּ תֵצֵא־אֵשׁ אֶל־כָּל־בֵּית יִשְׂרָאֵל:

⁵ Thus said *Hashem*: I set this *Yerushalayim* in the midst of nations, with countries round about her.

ה כֹּה אָמַר אֲדֹנָי יֱהֹוִה זֹאת יְרוּשָׁלַ͏ִם בְּתוֹךְ הַגּוֹיִם שַׂמְתִּיהָ וּסְבִיבוֹתֶיהָ אֲרָצוֹת:

KOH a-MAR a-do-NAI e-lo-HEEM ZOT y'7-ru-sha-LA-im b'-TOKH ha-go-YIM sam-TEE-ha us-vee-vo-TE-ha a-ra-TZOT

⁶ But she rebelled against My rules and My laws, acting more wickedly than the nations and the countries round about her; she rejected My rules and disobeyed My laws.

ו וַתֶּמֶר אֶת־מִשְׁפָּטַי לְרִשְׁעָה מִן־הַגּוֹיִם וְאֶת־חֻקּוֹתַי מִן־הָאֲרָצוֹת אֲשֶׁר סְבִיבוֹתֶיהָ כִּי בְמִשְׁפָּטַי מָאָסוּ וְחֻקּוֹתַי לֹא־הָלְכוּ בָהֶם:

⁷ Assuredly, thus said *Hashem*: Because you have outdone the nations that are round about you – you have not obeyed My laws or followed My rules, nor have you observed the rules of the nations round about you –

ז לָכֵן כֹּה־אָמַר אֲדֹנָי יֱהֹוִה יַעַן הֲמָנְכֶם מִן־הַגּוֹיִם אֲשֶׁר סְבִיבוֹתֵיכֶם בְּחֻקּוֹתַי לֹא הֲלַכְתֶּם וְאֶת־מִשְׁפָּטַי לֹא עֲשִׂיתֶם וּכְמִשְׁפְּטֵי הַגּוֹיִם אֲשֶׁר סְבִיבוֹתֵיכֶם לֹא עֲשִׂיתֶם:

⁸ assuredly, thus said *Hashem*: I, in turn, am going to deal with you, and I will execute judgments in your midst in the sight of the nations.

ח לָכֵן כֹּה אָמַר אֲדֹנָי יֱהֹוִה הִנְנִי עָלַיִךְ גַּם־אָנִי וְעָשִׂיתִי בְתוֹכֵךְ מִשְׁפָּטִים לְעֵינֵי הַגּוֹיִם:

⁹ On account of all your abominations, I will do among you what I have never done, and the like of which I will never do again.

ט וְעָשִׂיתִי בָךְ אֵת אֲשֶׁר לֹא־עָשִׂיתִי וְאֵת אֲשֶׁר־לֹא־אֶעֱשֶׂה כָמֹהוּ עוֹד יַעַן כָּל־תּוֹעֲבֹתָיִךְ:

 5:5 I set this *Yerushalayim* in the midst of nations God tells *Yechezkel* that He has set *Yerushalayim* as the center of the world, the rest of the countries around it. In medieval times, *Yerushalayim* was literally thought of as the center of the world, and maps were drawn to reflect that understanding. *Yerushalayim* remains the religious and spiritual center of the world, as it says (Isaiah 2:3) "For instruction shall come forth from *Tzion*, the word of *Hashem* from *Yerushalayim*" Indeed, all the major monotheistic religions of the Western world consider *Yerushalayim* to be their holy city, and it contains their most sacred places. As Rabbi Yitzchak Abarbanel analogizes, "the heart is to the rest of the body as *Yerushalayim* is to the world."

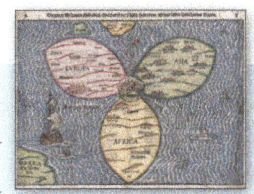

1581 clover leaf world map with *Yerushalayim* at the center

10 Assuredly, parents shall eat their children in your midst, and children shall eat their parents. I will execute judgments against you, and I will scatter all your survivors in every direction.

11 Assuredly, as I live – said *Hashem* – because you defiled My Sanctuary with all your detestable things and all your abominations, I in turn will shear [you] away and show no pity. I in turn will show no compassion:

12 One-third of you shall die of pestilence or perish in your midst by famine, one-third shall fall by the sword around you, and I will scatter one-third in every direction and will unsheathe the sword after them.

13 I will vent all My anger and satisfy My fury upon them; and when I vent all My fury upon them, they shall know that I *Hashem* have spoken in My passion.

14 I will make you a ruin and a mockery among the nations roundabout you, in the sight of every passerby.

15 And when I execute judgment upon you in anger and rage and furious chastisement, you shall be a mockery and a derision, a warning and a horror, to the nations roundabout you: I *Hashem* have spoken.

16 When I loose the deadly arrows of famine against those doomed to destruction, when I loose them against you to destroy you, I will heap more famine upon you and break your staff of bread.

17 I will let loose against you famine and wild beasts and they shall bereave you; pestilence and bloodshed shall sweep through you, and I will bring the sword upon you. I *Hashem* have spoken.

6 1 The word of *Hashem* came to me:

2 O mortal, turn your face toward the mountains of *Yisrael* and prophesy to them

ben a-DAM SEEM pa-NE-kha el ha-RAY yis-ra-AYL v'-hi-na-VAY a-lay-HEM

י לָכֵן אָבוֹת יֹאכְלוּ בָנִים בְּתוֹכֵךְ וּבָנִים יֹאכְלוּ אֲבוֹתָם וְעָשִׂיתִי בָךְ שְׁפָטִים וְזֵרִיתִי אֶת־כָּל־שְׁאֵרִיתֵךְ לְכָל־רוּחַ:

יא לָכֵן חַי־אָנִי נְאֻם אֲדֹנָי יֱהֹוִה אִם־לֹא יַעַן אֶת־מִקְדָּשִׁי טִמֵּאת בְּכָל־שִׁקּוּצַיִךְ וּבְכָל־תּוֹעֲבֹתָיִךְ וְגַם־אֲנִי אֶגְרַע וְלֹא־תָחוֹס עֵינִי וְגַם־אֲנִי לֹא אֶחְמוֹל:

יב שְׁלִשִׁתֵיךְ בַּדֶּבֶר יָמוּתוּ וּבָרָעָב יִכְלוּ בְתוֹכֵךְ וְהַשְּׁלִשִׁית בַּחֶרֶב יִפְּלוּ סְבִיבוֹתָיִךְ וְהַשְּׁלִישִׁית לְכָל־רוּחַ אֱזָרֶה וְחֶרֶב אָרִיק אַחֲרֵיהֶם:

יג וְכָלָה אַפִּי וַהֲנִחוֹתִי חֲמָתִי בָּם וְהִנֶּחָמְתִּי וְיָדְעוּ כִּי־אֲנִי יְהֹוָה דִּבַּרְתִּי בְּקִנְאָתִי בְּכַלּוֹתִי חֲמָתִי בָּם:

יד וְנָתַתִּיךְ לְחָרְבָּה וּלְחֶרְפָּה בַּגּוֹיִם אֲשֶׁר סְבִיבוֹתָיִךְ לְעֵינֵי כָּל־עוֹבֵר:

טו וְהָיְתָה חֶרְפָּה וּגְדוּפָה מוּסָר וּמְשַׁמָּה לַגּוֹיִם אֲשֶׁר סְבִיבוֹתָיִךְ בַּעֲשׂוֹתִי בָךְ שְׁפָטִים בְּאַף וּבְחֵמָה וּבְתֹכְחוֹת חֵמָה אֲנִי יְהֹוָה דִּבַּרְתִּי:

טז בְּשַׁלְּחִי אֶת־חִצֵּי הָרָעָב הָרָעִים בָּהֶם אֲשֶׁר הָיוּ לְמַשְׁחִית אֲשֶׁר־אֲשַׁלַּח אוֹתָם לְשַׁחֶתְכֶם וְרָעָב אֹסֵף עֲלֵיכֶם וְשָׁבַרְתִּי לָכֶם מַטֵּה־לָחֶם:

יז וְשִׁלַּחְתִּי עֲלֵיכֶם רָעָב וְחַיָּה רָעָה וְשִׁכְּלֻךְ וְדֶבֶר וָדָם יַעֲבָר־בָּךְ וְחֶרֶב אָבִיא עָלַיִךְ אֲנִי יְהֹוָה דִּבַּרְתִּי:

א וַיְהִי דְבַר־יְהֹוָה אֵלַי לֵאמֹר:

ב בֶּן־אָדָם שִׂים פָּנֶיךָ אֶל־הָרֵי יִשְׂרָאֵל וְהִנָּבֵא אֲלֵיהֶם:

A baby in a lavender field in the Golan Heights

6:2 O mortal Throughout the book of *Yechezkel*, God consistently refers to *Yechezkel* as ben adam (בן אדם), meaning 'son of man' or 'mortal.' *Adam* (אדם) is the Hebrew word for 'man.' According to Rabbi Matityahu Glazerson, this word is reflective of the three partners who

אדם

Ezekiel

3 and say: O mountains of *Yisrael*, hear the word of *Hashem*. Thus said *Hashem* to the mountains and the hills, to the streams and the valleys: See, I will bring a sword against you and destroy your shrines.

ג וְאָמַרְתָּ הָרֵי יִשְׂרָאֵל שִׁמְעוּ דְּבַר־אֲדֹנָי יֱהֹוִה כֹּה־אָמַר אֲדֹנָי יֱהֹוִה לֶהָרִים וְלַגְּבָעוֹת לָאֲפִיקִים וְלַגֵּאָיוֹת [וְלַגֵּאָיוֹת] הִנְנִי אֲנִי מֵבִיא עֲלֵיכֶם חֶרֶב וְאִבַּדְתִּי בָּמוֹתֵיכֶם:

4 Your altars shall be wrecked and your incense stands smashed, and I will hurl down your slain in front of your fetishes.

ד וְנָשַׁמּוּ מִזְבְּחוֹתֵיכֶם וְנִשְׁבְּרוּ חַמָּנֵיכֶם וְהִפַּלְתִּי חַלְלֵיכֶם לִפְנֵי גִּלּוּלֵיכֶם:

5 I will cast the corpses of the people of *Yisrael* in front of their fetishes, and scatter your bones around your altars

ה וְנָתַתִּי אֶת־פִּגְרֵי בְּנֵי יִשְׂרָאֵל לִפְנֵי גִּלּוּלֵיהֶם וְזֵרִיתִי אֶת־עַצְמוֹתֵיכֶם סְבִיבוֹת מִזְבְּחוֹתֵיכֶם:

6 in all your settlements. The towns shall be laid waste and the shrines shall be devastated. Thus your altars shall be laid waste and bear their punishment; your fetishes shall be smashed and annihilated, your incense stands cut down, and your handiwork wiped out;

ו בְּכֹל מוֹשְׁבוֹתֵיכֶם הֶעָרִים תֶּחֱרַבְנָה וְהַבָּמוֹת תִּישַׁמְנָה לְמַעַן יֶחֶרְבוּ וְיֶאְשְׁמוּ מִזְבְּחוֹתֵיכֶם וְנִשְׁבְּרוּ וְנִשְׁבְּתוּ גִּלּוּלֵיכֶם וְנִגְדְּעוּ חַמָּנֵיכֶם וְנִמְחוּ מַעֲשֵׂיכֶם:

7 and the slain shall fall in your midst. Then you shall know that I am *Hashem*.

ז וְנָפַל חָלָל בְּתוֹכְכֶם וִידַעְתֶּם כִּי־אֲנִי יְהֹוָה:

8 Yet I will leave a remnant, in that some of you shall escape the sword among the nations and be scattered through the lands.

ח וְהוֹתַרְתִּי בִּהְיוֹת לָכֶם פְּלִיטֵי חֶרֶב בַּגּוֹיִם בְּהִזָּרוֹתֵיכֶם בָּאֲרָצוֹת:

9 And those of you that escape will remember Me among the nations where they have been taken captive, how I was brokenhearted through their faithless hearts which turned away from Me, and through their eyes which lusted after their fetishes. And they shall loathe themselves for all the evil they committed and for all their abominable deeds.

ט וְזָכְרוּ פְלִיטֵיכֶם אוֹתִי בַּגּוֹיִם אֲשֶׁר נִשְׁבּוּ־שָׁם אֲשֶׁר נִשְׁבַּרְתִּי אֶת־לִבָּם הַזּוֹנֶה אֲשֶׁר־סָר מֵעָלַי וְאֵת עֵינֵיהֶם הַזֹּנוֹת אַחֲרֵי גִּלּוּלֵיהֶם וְנָקֹטּוּ בִּפְנֵיהֶם אֶל־הָרָעוֹת אֲשֶׁר עָשׂוּ לְכֹל תּוֹעֲבֹתֵיהֶם:

10 Then they shall realize it was not without cause that I *Hashem* resolved to bring this evil upon them.

י וְיָדְעוּ כִּי־אֲנִי יְהֹוָה לֹא אֶל־חִנָּם דִּבַּרְתִּי לַעֲשׂוֹת לָהֶם הָרָעָה הַזֹּאת:

11 Thus said *Hashem*: Strike your hands together and stamp your feet and cry: Aha! over all the vile abominations of the House of *Yisrael* who shall fall by the sword, by famine, and by pestilence.

יא כֹּה־אָמַר אֲדֹנָי יֱהֹוִה הַכֵּה בְכַפְּךָ וּרְקַע בְּרַגְלְךָ וֶאֱמָר־אָח אֶל כָּל־תּוֹעֲבוֹת רָעוֹת בֵּית יִשְׂרָאֵל אֲשֶׁר בַּחֶרֶב בָּרָעָב וּבַדֶּבֶר יִפֹּלוּ:

12 He who is far away shall die of pestilence, and he who is near shall fall by the sword, and he who survives and is protected shall die of famine. Thus I will spend My fury upon them.

יב הָרָחוֹק בַּדֶּבֶר יָמוּת וְהַקָּרוֹב בַּחֶרֶב יִפּוֹל וְהַנִּשְׁאָר וְהַנָּצוּר בָּרָעָב יָמוּת וְכִלֵּיתִי חֲמָתִי בָּם:

---

participate in the creation of a human being: the father, the mother and the Holy One, blessed is He. The letter *alef* (א), whose numerical value is one, represents, the Holy One who provides the spiritual component, the soul. The re- maining two letters, *dalet* (ד) and *mem* (ם), spell *dam* (דם), meaning 'blood,' which symbolizes the physical aspect contributed by the father and mother.

¹³ And you shall know that I am *Hashem*, when your slain lie among the fetishes round about their altars, on every high hill, on all the mountaintops, under every green tree, and under every leafy oak – wherever they presented pleasing odors to all their fetishes.

יג וִידַעְתֶּם כִּי־אֲנִי יְהֹוָה בִּהְיוֹת חַלְלֵיהֶם בְּתוֹךְ גִּלּוּלֵיהֶם סְבִיבוֹת מִזְבְּחוֹתֵיהֶם אֶל כָּל־גִּבְעָה רָמָה בְּכֹל רָאשֵׁי הֶהָרִים וְתַחַת כָּל־עֵץ רַעֲנָן וְתַחַת כָּל־אֵלָה עֲבֻתָּה מְקוֹם אֲשֶׁר נָתְנוּ־שָׁם רֵיחַ נִיחֹחַ לְכֹל גִּלּוּלֵיהֶם:

¹⁴ I will stretch out My hand against them, and lay the land waste and desolate in all their settlements, from the wilderness as far as Diblah; then they shall know that I am *Hashem*.

יד וְנָטִיתִי אֶת־יָדִי עֲלֵיהֶם וְנָתַתִּי אֶת־הָאָרֶץ שְׁמָמָה וּמְשַׁמָּה מִמִּדְבַּר דִּבְלָתָה בְּכֹל מוֹשְׁבוֹתֵיהֶם וְיָדְעוּ כִּי־אֲנִי יְהֹוָה:

7 ¹ The word of *Hashem* came to me:

ז א וַיְהִי דְבַר־יְהֹוָה אֵלַי לֵאמֹר:

² You, O mortal, [say:] Thus said *Hashem* to the land of *Yisrael*: Doom! Doom is coming upon the four corners of the land.

ב וְאַתָּה בֶן־אָדָם כֹּה־אָמַר אֲדֹנָי יְהֹוִה לְאַדְמַת יִשְׂרָאֵל קֵץ בָּא הַקֵּץ עַל־אַרבעת [אַרְבַּע] כַּנְפוֹת הָאָרֶץ:

³ Now doom is upon you! I will let loose My anger against you and judge you according to your ways; I will requite you for all your abominations.

ג עַתָּה הַקֵּץ עָלַיִךְ וְשִׁלַּחְתִּי אַפִּי בָּךְ וּשְׁפַטְתִּיךְ כִּדְרָכָיִךְ וְנָתַתִּי עָלַיִךְ אֵת כָּל־תּוֹעֲבֹתָיִךְ:

⁴ I will show you no pity and no compassion; but I will requite you for your ways and for the abominations in your midst. And you shall know that I am *Hashem*.

ד וְלֹא־תָחוֹס עֵינִי עָלַיִךְ וְלֹא אֶחְמוֹל כִּי דְרָכַיִךְ עָלַיִךְ אֶתֵּן וְתוֹעֲבוֹתַיִךְ בְּתוֹכֵךְ תִּהְיֶיןָ וִידַעְתֶּם כִּי־אֲנִי יְהֹוָה:

⁵ Thus said *Hashem*: A singular disaster; a disaster is coming.

ה כֹּה אָמַר אֲדֹנָי יְהֹוִה רָעָה אַחַת רָעָה הִנֵּה בָאָה:

⁶ Doom is coming! The hour of doom is coming! It stirs against you; there it comes!

ו קֵץ בָּא בָּא הַקֵּץ הֵקִיץ אֵלָיִךְ הִנֵּה בָּאָה:

⁷ The cycle has come around for you, O inhabitants of the land; the time has come; the day is near. There is panic on the mountains, not joy.

ז בָּאָה הַצְּפִירָה אֵלֶיךָ יוֹשֵׁב הָאָרֶץ בָּא הָעֵת קָרוֹב הַיּוֹם מְהוּמָה וְלֹא־הֵד הָרִים:

⁸ Very soon I will pour out My wrath upon you and spend My anger on you; I will judge you according to your ways, and I will requite you for all your abominations.

ח עַתָּה מִקָּרוֹב אֶשְׁפּוֹךְ חֲמָתִי עָלַיִךְ וְכִלֵּיתִי אַפִּי בָּךְ וּשְׁפַטְתִּיךְ כִּדְרָכָיִךְ וְנָתַתִּי עָלַיִךְ אֵת כָּל־תּוֹעֲבוֹתָיִךְ:

⁹ I will show you no pity and no compassion; but I will requite you for your ways, and for the abominations in your midst. And you shall know it was I *Hashem* who punished.

ט וְלֹא־תָחוֹס עֵינִי וְלֹא אֶחְמוֹל כִּדְרָכַיִךְ עָלַיִךְ אֶתֵּן וְתוֹעֲבוֹתַיִךְ בְּתוֹכֵךְ תִּהְיֶיןָ וִידַעְתֶּם כִּי אֲנִי יְהֹוָה מַכֶּה:

¹⁰ Here is the day! See, the cycle has come round; it has appeared. The rod has blossomed; arrogance has budded,

י הִנֵּה הַיּוֹם הִנֵּה בָאָה יָצְאָה הַצְּפִרָה צָץ הַמַּטֶּה פָּרַח הַזָּדוֹן:

¹¹ lawlessness has grown into a rod of wickedness. Nothing comes of them, nor of their abundance, nor of their wealth; nor is there preeminence among them.

יא הֶחָמָס קָם לְמַטֵּה־רֶשַׁע לֹא־מֵהֶם וְלֹא מֵהֲמוֹנָם וְלֹא מֶהֱמֵהֶם וְלֹא־נֹהַּ בָּהֶם:

12 The time has come, the day has arrived. Let not the buyer rejoice nor the seller mourn – for divine wrath shall overtake all her multitude.

יב בָּא הָעֵת הִגִּיעַ הַיּוֹם הַקּוֹנֶה אַל־יִשְׂמָח וְהַמּוֹכֵר אַל־יִתְאַבָּל כִּי חָרוֹן אֶל־כָּל־הֲמוֹנָהּ:

13 For the seller shall not return to what he sold so long as they remain among the living. For the vision concerns all her multitude, it shall not be revoked. And because of his guilt, no man shall hold fast to his life.

יג כִּי הַמּוֹכֵר אֶל־הַמִּמְכָּר לֹא יָשׁוּב וְעוֹד בַּחַיִּים חַיָּתָם כִּי־חָזוֹן אֶל־כָּל־הֲמוֹנָהּ לֹא יָשׁוּב וְאִישׁ בַּעֲוֹנוֹ חַיָּתוֹ לֹא יִתְחַזָּקוּ:

KEE ha-mo-KHAYR el ha-mim-KAR LO ya-SHUV v'-OD ba-kha-YEEM kha-ya-TAM kee kha-ZON el kol ha-mo-NAH LO ya-SHUV v'-EESH ba-a-vo-NO kha-ya-TO lo yit-kha-ZA-ku

14 They have sounded the horn, and all is prepared; but no one goes to battle, for My wrath is directed against all her multitude.

יד תָּקְעוּ בַתָּקוֹעַ וְהָכִין הַכֹּל וְאֵין הֹלֵךְ לַמִּלְחָמָה כִּי חֲרוֹנִי אֶל־כָּל־הֲמוֹנָהּ:

15 The sword is outside and pestilence and famine are inside; he who is in the open shall die by the sword, he who is in the town shall be devoured by famine and pestilence.

טו הַחֶרֶב בַּחוּץ וְהַדֶּבֶר וְהָרָעָב מִבָּיִת אֲשֶׁר בַּשָּׂדֶה בַּחֶרֶב יָמוּת וַאֲשֶׁר בָּעִיר רָעָב וָדֶבֶר יֹאכְלֶנּוּ:

16 And if any survive, they shall take to the mountains; they shall be like doves of the valley, moaning together – every one for his iniquity.

טז וּפָלְטוּ פְּלִיטֵיהֶם וְהָיוּ אֶל־הֶהָרִים כְּיוֹנֵי הַגֵּאָיוֹת כֻּלָּם הֹמוֹת אִישׁ בַּעֲוֹנוֹ:

17 All hands shall grow weak, and all knees shall turn to water.

יז כָּל־הַיָּדַיִם תִּרְפֶּינָה וְכָל־בִּרְכַּיִם תֵּלַכְנָה מָּיִם:

18 They shall gird on sackcloth, and horror shall cover them; every face shall betray shame, and every head shall be made bald.

יח וְחָגְרוּ שַׂקִּים וְכִסְּתָה אוֹתָם פַּלָּצוּת וְאֶל כָּל־פָּנִים בּוּשָׁה וּבְכָל־רָאשֵׁיהֶם קָרְחָה:

19 They shall throw their silver into the streets, and their gold shall be treated as something unclean. Their silver and gold shall not avail to save them in the day of *Hashem*'s wrath – to satisfy their hunger or to fill their stomachs. Because they made them stumble into guilt –

יט כַּסְפָּם בַּחוּצוֹת יַשְׁלִיכוּ וּזְהָבָם לְנִדָּה יִהְיֶה כַּסְפָּם וּזְהָבָם לֹא־יוּכַל לְהַצִּילָם בְּיוֹם עֶבְרַת יְהֹוָה נַפְשָׁם לֹא יְשַׂבֵּעוּ וּמֵעֵיהֶם לֹא יְמַלֵּאוּ כִּי־מִכְשׁוֹל עֲוֹנָם הָיָה:

20 for out of their beautiful adornments, in which they took pride, they made their images and their detestable abominations – therefore I will make them an unclean thing to them.

כ וּצְבִי עֶדְיוֹ לְגָאוֹן שָׂמָהוּ וְצַלְמֵי תוֹעֲבָתָם שִׁקּוּצֵיהֶם עָשׂוּ בוֹ עַל־כֵּן נְתַתִּיו לָהֶם לְנִדָּה:

Fields in Sha'ar Hanegev near Ruhama, Israel.

7:13 For the seller shall not return to what he sold The Land of Israel is a sacred trust from *Hashem*, and in biblical times familial properties could be sold only in times of dire necessity. These sales were always considered temporary, and the family would make extreme efforts to redeem their property, their physical connection to the Holy Land (Leviticus 25). During the *yovel*, the Jubilee year, even lands which had not been redeemed would be returned to the original owners. In this bitter prophecy, *Yechezkel* warns that the upcoming exile will prevent both buyer and seller from enjoying the land, since they will be exiled from *Eretz Yisrael*.

13

21 I will give them as spoil to strangers, and as plunder to the wicked of the earth; and they shall defile them.

כא וּנְתַתִּיו בְּיַד־הַזָּרִים לָבַז וּלְרִשְׁעֵי הָאָרֶץ לְשָׁלָל וְחִלְּלוּהוּ [וְחִלְּלוּהָ]׃

22 I will turn My face from them, and My treasures shall be defiled; ruffians shall invade it and defile it.

כב וַהֲסִבּוֹתִי פָנַי מֵהֶם וְחִלְּלוּ אֶת־צְפוּנִי וּבָאוּ־בָהּ פָּרִיצִים וְחִלְּלוּהָ׃

23 Forge the chain, for the land is full of bloody crimes, and the city is full of lawlessness.

כג עֲשֵׂה הָרַתּוֹק כִּי הָאָרֶץ מָלְאָה מִשְׁפַּט דָּמִים וְהָעִיר מָלְאָה חָמָס׃

24 I will bring in the worst of the nations to take possession of their houses; so shall I turn to naught the pride of the powerful, and their sanctuaries shall be defiled.

כד וְהֵבֵאתִי רָעֵי גוֹיִם וְיָרְשׁוּ אֶת־בָּתֵּיהֶם וְהִשְׁבַּתִּי גְּאוֹן עַזִּים וְנִחֲלוּ מְקַדְשֵׁיהֶם׃

25 Horror comes, and they shall seek safety, but there shall be none.

כה קְפָדָה־בָא וּבִקְשׁוּ שָׁלוֹם וָאָיִן׃

26 Calamity shall follow calamity, and rumor follow rumor. Then they shall seek vision from the *Navi* in vain; instruction shall perish from the *Kohen*, and counsel from the elders.

כו הֹוָה עַל־הֹוָה תָּבוֹא וּשְׁמֻעָה אֶל־שְׁמוּעָה תִּהְיֶה וּבִקְשׁוּ חָזוֹן מִנָּבִיא וְתוֹרָה תֹּאבַד מִכֹּהֵן וְעֵצָה מִזְּקֵנִים׃

27 The king shall mourn, the prince shall clothe himself with desolation, and the hands of the people of the land shall tremble. I will treat them in accordance with their own ways and judge them according to their deserts. And they shall know that I am *Hashem*.

כז הַמֶּלֶךְ יִתְאַבָּל וְנָשִׂיא יִלְבַּשׁ שְׁמָמָה וִידֵי עַם־הָאָרֶץ תִּבָּהַלְנָה מִדַּרְכָּם אֶעֱשֶׂה אוֹתָם וּבְמִשְׁפְּטֵיהֶם אֶשְׁפְּטֵם וְיָדְעוּ כִּי־אֲנִי יְהֹוָה׃

8 1 In the sixth year, on the fifth day of the sixth month, I was sitting at home, and the elders of *Yehuda* were sitting before me, and there the hand of *Hashem* fell upon me.

ח א וַיְהִי בַּשָּׁנָה הַשִּׁשִּׁית בַּשִּׁשִּׁי בַּחֲמִשָּׁה לַחֹדֶשׁ אֲנִי יוֹשֵׁב בְּבֵיתִי וְזִקְנֵי יְהוּדָה יוֹשְׁבִים לְפָנָי וַתִּפֹּל עָלַי שָׁם יַד אֲדֹנָי יְהֹוִה׃

2 As I looked, there was a figure that had the appearance of fire: from what appeared as his loins down, [he was] fire; and from his loins up, his appearance was resplendent and had the color of amber.

ב וָאֶרְאֶה וְהִנֵּה דְמוּת כְּמַרְאֵה־אֵשׁ מִמַּרְאֵה מָתְנָיו וּלְמַטָּה אֵשׁ וּמִמָּתְנָיו וּלְמַעְלָה כְּמַרְאֵה־זֹהַר כְּעֵין הַחַשְׁמַלָה׃

3 He stretched out the form of a hand, and took me by the hair of my head. A spirit lifted me up between heaven and earth and brought me in visions of *Hashem* to *Yerushalayim*, to the entrance of the Penimith Gate that faces north; that was the site of the infuriating image that provokes fury.

ג וַיִּשְׁלַח תַּבְנִית יָד וַיִּקָּחֵנִי בְּצִיצִת רֹאשִׁי וַתִּשָּׂא אֹתִי רוּחַ בֵּין־הָאָרֶץ וּבֵין הַשָּׁמַיִם וַתָּבֵא אֹתִי יְרוּשָׁלַ֫מָה בְּמַרְאוֹת אֱלֹהִים אֶל־פֶּתַח שַׁעַר הַפְּנִימִית הַפּוֹנֶה צָפוֹנָה אֲשֶׁר־שָׁם מוֹשַׁב סֵמֶל הַקִּנְאָה הַמַּקְנֶה׃

4 And the Presence of the God of *Yisrael* appeared there, like the vision that I had seen in the valley.

ד וְהִנֵּה־שָׁם כְּבוֹד אֱלֹהֵי יִשְׂרָאֵל כַּמַּרְאֶה אֲשֶׁר רָאִיתִי בַּבִּקְעָה׃

5 And He said to me, "O mortal, turn your eyes northward." I turned my eyes northward, and there, north of the gate of the *Mizbayach*, was that infuriating image on the approach.

ה וַיֹּאמֶר אֵלַי בֶּן־אָדָם שָׂא־נָא עֵינֶיךָ דֶּרֶךְ צָפוֹנָה וָאֶשָּׂא עֵינַי דֶּרֶךְ צָפוֹנָה וְהִנֵּה מִצָּפוֹן לְשַׁעַר הַמִּזְבֵּחַ סֵמֶל הַקִּנְאָה הַזֶּה בַּבִּאָה׃

6 And He said to me, "Mortal, do you see what they are doing, the terrible abominations that the House of *Yisrael* is practicing here, to drive Me far from My Sanctuary? You shall yet see even greater abominations!"

ו וַיֹּאמֶר אֵלַי בֶּן־אָדָם הֲרֹאֶה אַתָּה מֵהֶם [מֶה] [הֵם] עֹשִׂים תּוֹעֵבוֹת גְּדֹלוֹת אֲשֶׁר בֵּית־יִשְׂרָאֵל עֹשִׂים פֹּה לְרׇחֳקָה מֵעַל מִקְדָּשִׁי וְעוֹד תָּשׁוּב תִּרְאֶה תּוֹעֵבוֹת גְּדֹלוֹת:

7 Then He brought me to the entrance of the court; and I looked, and there was a hole in the wall.

ז וַיָּבֵא אֹתִי אֶל־פֶּתַח הֶחָצֵר וָאֶרְאֶה וְהִנֵּה חֹר־אֶחָד בַּקִּיר:

8 He said to me, "Mortal, break through the wall"; so I broke through the wall and found an entrance.

ח וַיֹּאמֶר אֵלַי בֶּן־אָדָם חֲתׇר־נָא בַקִּיר וָאֶחְתֹּר בַּקִּיר וְהִנֵּה פֶּתַח אֶחָד:

9 And He said to me, "Enter and see the vile abominations that they are practicing here."

ט וַיֹּאמֶר אֵלָי בֹּא וּרְאֵה אֶת־הַתּוֹעֵבוֹת הָרָעוֹת אֲשֶׁר הֵם עֹשִׂים פֹּה:

10 I entered and looked, and there all detestable forms of creeping things and beasts and all the fetishes of the House of *Yisrael* were depicted over the entire wall.

י וָאָבוֹא וָאֶרְאֶה וְהִנֵּה כׇל־תַּבְנִית רֶמֶשׂ וּבְהֵמָה שֶׁקֶץ וְכׇל־גִּלּוּלֵי בֵּית יִשְׂרָאֵל מְחֻקֶּה עַל־הַקִּיר סָבִיב סָבִיב:

11 Before them stood seventy men, elders of the House of *Yisrael*, with Jaazaniah son of *Shafan* standing in their midst. Everyone had a censer in his hand, and a thick cloud of incense smoke ascended.

יא וְשִׁבְעִים אִישׁ מִזִּקְנֵי בֵית־יִשְׂרָאֵל וְיַאֲזַנְיָהוּ בֶן־שָׁפָן עֹמֵד בְּתוֹכָם עֹמְדִים לִפְנֵיהֶם וְאִישׁ מִקְטַרְתּוֹ בְּיָדוֹ וַעֲתַר עֲנַן־הַקְּטֹרֶת עֹלֶה:

12 Again He spoke to me, "O mortal, have you seen what the elders of the House of *Yisrael* are doing in the darkness, everyone in his image-covered chamber? For they say, '*Hashem* does not see us; *Hashem* has abandoned the country.'"

יב וַיֹּאמֶר אֵלַי הֲרָאִיתָ בֶן־אָדָם אֲשֶׁר זִקְנֵי בֵית־יִשְׂרָאֵל עֹשִׂים בַּחֹשֶׁךְ אִישׁ בְּחַדְרֵי מַשְׂכִּיתוֹ כִּי אֹמְרִים אֵין יְהֹוָה רֹאֶה אֹתָנוּ עָזַב יְהֹוָה אֶת־הָאָרֶץ:

*va-YO-mer ay-LAI ha-ra-EE-ta ven a-DAM a-SHER zik-NAY vayt
yis-ra-AYL o-SEEM ba-KHO-shekh EESH b'-khad-RAY mas-kee-TO KEE
o-m'-REEM AYN a-do-NAI ro-EH o-TA-nu a-ZAV a-do-NAI et ha-A-retz*

13 And He said to me, "You shall see even more terrible abominations which they practice."

יג וַיֹּאמֶר אֵלָי עוֹד תָּשׁוּב תִּרְאֶה תּוֹעֵבוֹת גְּדֹלוֹת אֲשֶׁר־הֵמָּה עֹשִׂים:

14 Next He brought me to the entrance of the north gate of the House of *Hashem*; and there sat the women bewailing Tammuz.

יד וַיָּבֵא אֹתִי אֶל־פֶּתַח שַׁעַר בֵּית־יְהֹוָה אֲשֶׁר אֶל־הַצָּפוֹנָה וְהִנֵּה־שָׁם הַנָּשִׁים יֹשְׁבוֹת מְבַכּוֹת אֶת־הַתַּמּוּז:

15 He said to me, "Have you seen, O mortal? You shall see even more terrible abominations than these."

טו וַיֹּאמֶר אֵלַי הֲרָאִיתָ בֶן־אָדָם עוֹד תָּשׁוּב תִּרְאֶה תּוֹעֵבוֹת גְּדֹלוֹת מֵאֵלֶּה:

An elderly man touches the sacred stones of the Western Wall

8:12 Have you seen what the elders of the House of *Yisrael* are doing To explain the upcoming destruction of *Yerushalayim*, *Yechezkel* is shown a scene of the city's elders secretly practicing idolatry within the confines of the Temple. Though they hide their abominations from the public, they do not hesitate to engage in this repugnant behavior. They see the upcoming downfall of *Yehuda* and *Yerushalayim*, but instead of concluding that repentance is needed, the corrupt elders choose to believe that God has rejected His people and "abandoned the country," which leads them to forsake *Hashem* and engage in idolatry.

16 Then He brought me into the inner court of the House of *Hashem*, and there, at the entrance to the Temple of *Hashem*, between the portico and the *Mizbayach*, were about twenty-five men, their backs to the Temple of *Hashem* and their faces to the east; they were bowing low to the sun in the east.

טז וַיָּבֵא אֹתִי אֶל־חֲצַר בֵּית־יְהֹוָה הַפְּנִימִית וְהִנֵּה־פֶתַח הֵיכַל יְהֹוָה בֵּין הָאוּלָם וּבֵין הַמִּזְבֵּחַ כְּעֶשְׂרִים וַחֲמִשָּׁה אִישׁ אֲחֹרֵיהֶם אֶל־הֵיכַל יְהֹוָה וּפְנֵיהֶם קֵדְמָה וְהֵמָּה מִשְׁתַּחֲוִיתֶם קֵדְמָה לַשָּׁמֶשׁ:

17 And He said to me, "Do you see, O mortal? Is it not enough for the House of *Yehuda* to practice the abominations that they have committed here, that they must fill the country with lawlessness and provoke Me still further and thrust the branch to their nostrils?

יז וַיֹּאמֶר אֵלַי הֲרָאִיתָ בֶן־אָדָם הֲנָקֵל לְבֵית יְהוּדָה מֵעֲשׂוֹת אֶת־הַתּוֹעֵבוֹת אֲשֶׁר עָשׂוּ־פֹה כִּי־מָלְאוּ אֶת־הָאָרֶץ חָמָס וַיָּשֻׁבוּ לְהַכְעִיסֵנִי וְהִנָּם שֹׁלְחִים אֶת־הַזְּמוֹרָה אֶל־אַפָּם:

18 I in turn will act with fury, I will show no pity or compassion; though they cry aloud to Me, I will not listen to them."

יח וְגַם־אֲנִי אֶעֱשֶׂה בְחֵמָה לֹא־תָחוֹס עֵינִי וְלֹא אֶחְמֹל וְקָרְאוּ בְאָזְנַי קוֹל גָּדוֹל וְלֹא אֶשְׁמַע אוֹתָם:

9 1 Then He called loudly in my hearing, saying, "Approach, you men in charge of the city, each bearing his weapons of destruction!"

ט א וַיִּקְרָא בְאָזְנַי קוֹל גָּדוֹל לֵאמֹר קָרְבוּ פְּקֻדּוֹת הָעִיר וְאִישׁ כְּלִי מַשְׁחֵתוֹ בְּיָדוֹ:

2 And six men entered by way of the upper gate that faces north, each with his club in his hand; and among them was another, clothed in linen, with a writing case at his waist. They came forward and stopped at the bronze *Mizbayach*.

ב וְהִנֵּה שִׁשָּׁה אֲנָשִׁים בָּאִים מִדֶּרֶךְ־שַׁעַר הָעֶלְיוֹן אֲשֶׁר מָפְנֶה צָפוֹנָה וְאִישׁ כְּלִי מַפָּצוֹ בְּיָדוֹ וְאִישׁ־אֶחָד בְּתוֹכָם לָבֻשׁ בַּדִּים וְקֶסֶת הַסֹּפֵר בְּמָתְנָיו וַיָּבֹאוּ וַיַּעַמְדוּ אֵצֶל מִזְבַּח הַנְּחֹשֶׁת:

3 Now the Presence of the God of *Yisrael* had moved from the cherub on which it had rested to the platform of the House. He called to the man clothed in linen with the writing case at his waist;

ג וּכְבוֹד אֱלֹהֵי יִשְׂרָאֵל נַעֲלָה מֵעַל הַכְּרוּב אֲשֶׁר הָיָה עָלָיו אֶל מִפְתַּן הַבָּיִת וַיִּקְרָא אֶל־הָאִישׁ הַלָּבֻשׁ הַבַּדִּים אֲשֶׁר קֶסֶת הַסֹּפֵר בְּמָתְנָיו:

4 and *Hashem* said to him, "Pass through the city, through *Yerushalayim*, and put a mark on the foreheads of the men who moan and groan because of all the abominations that are committed in it."

ד וַיֹּאמֶר יְהֹוָה אֵלוֹ [אֵלָיו] עֲבֹר בְּתוֹךְ הָעִיר בְּתוֹךְ יְרוּשָׁלָ͏ִם וְהִתְוִיתָ תָּו עַל־מִצְחוֹת הָאֲנָשִׁים הַנֶּאֱנָחִים וְהַנֶּאֱנָקִים עַל כָּל־הַתּוֹעֵבוֹת הַנַּעֲשׂוֹת בְּתוֹכָהּ:

va-YO-mer a-do-NAI ay-LAV a-VOR b'-TOKH ha-EER b'-TOKH y'-ru-sha-LA-im
v'-hit-VEE-ta TAV al mitz-KHOT ha-a-na-SHEEM ha-ne-e-na-KHEEM
v'-ha-ne-e-na-KEEM AL kol ha-TO-ay-VOT ha-na-a-SOT b'-to-KHAH

תו

Iron Dome intercepts Hamas rockets over Ashdod

9:4 And put a mark on the foreheads of the men who moan and groan *Yechezkel* is shown a vision of the death of the guilty in *Yerushalayim*. Before the executions commence, he sees a messenger in white linen mark the foreheads of those who grieve and lament over the destruction, ensuring that a righteous remnant re-

mains. 'To set a mark' in Hebrew is *vi-hitveeta tav* (והתוית תו), based on which the sages explain that the mark that was made was the Hebrew letter *tav* (ת). Like the mark of Cain, which, according to *Rashi* was also a Hebrew letter, this mark is intended to save its bearers from harm.

Ezekiel

5 To the others He said in my hearing, "Follow him through the city and strike; show no pity or compassion.

ה וּלְאֵ֙לֶּה֙ אָמַ֣ר בְּאָזְנַ֔י עִבְר֥וּ בָעִ֛יר אַחֲרָ֖יו וְהַכּ֑וּ עַל־[אַל־] תָּחֹ֤ס עֵינֵיכֶם֙ [עֵינְכֶ֔ם] וְאַל־תַּחְמֹֽלוּ׃

6 Kill off graybeard, youth and maiden, women and children; but do not touch any person who bears the mark. Begin here at My Sanctuary." So they began with the elders who were in front of the House.

ו זָקֵ֡ן בָּח֣וּר וּבְתוּלָה֩ וְטַ֨ף וְנָשִׁ֜ים תַּהַרְג֣וּ לְמַשְׁחִ֗ית וְעַל־כׇּל־אִ֞ישׁ אֲשֶׁר־עָלָ֤יו הַתָּו֙ אַל־תִּגַּ֔שׁוּ וּמִמִּקְדָּשִׁ֖י תָּחֵ֑לּוּ וַיָּחֵ֙לּוּ֙ בָּאֲנָשִׁ֣ים הַזְּקֵנִ֔ים אֲשֶׁ֖ר לִפְנֵ֥י הַבָּֽיִת׃

7 And He said to them, "Defile the House and fill the courts with the slain. Then go forth." So they went forth and began to kill in the city.

ז וַיֹּ֨אמֶר אֲלֵיהֶ֜ם טַמְּא֣וּ אֶת־הַבַּ֗יִת וּמַלְא֧וּ אֶת־הַחֲצֵר֛וֹת חֲלָלִ֖ים צֵ֑אוּ וְיָצְא֖וּ וְהִכּ֥וּ בָעִֽיר׃

8 When they were out killing, and I remained alone, I flung myself on my face and cried out, "Ah, *Hashem*! Are you going to annihilate all that is left of *Yisrael*, pouring out Your fury upon *Yerushalayim*?"

ח וַֽיְהִי֙ כְּהַכּוֹתָ֔ם וְנֵֽאשֲׁאַ֖ר אָ֑נִי וָאֶפְּלָ֨ה עַל־פָּנַ֜י וָאֶזְעַ֗ק וָאֹמַר֙ אֲהָהּ֙ אֲדֹנָ֣י יֱהֹוִ֔ה הֲמַשְׁחִ֣ית אַתָּ֗ה אֵ֚ת כׇּל־שְׁאֵרִ֣ית יִשְׂרָאֵ֔ל בְּשׇׁפְכְּךָ֖ אֶת־חֲמָתְךָ֥ עַל־יְרוּשָׁלָֽͅם׃

9 He answered me, "The iniquity of the Houses of *Yehuda* and *Yisrael* is very very great, the land is full of crime and the city is full of corruption. For they say, '*Hashem* has forsaken the land, and *Hashem* does not see.'

ט וַיֹּ֣אמֶר אֵלַ֗י עֲוֺ֣ן בֵּֽית־יִשְׂרָאֵ֤ל וִֽיהוּדָה֙ גָּדוֹל֙ בִּמְאֹ֣ד מְאֹ֔ד וַתִּמָּלֵ֤א הָאָ֙רֶץ֙ דָּמִ֔ים וְהָעִ֖יר מָלְאָ֣ה מֻטֶּ֑ה כִּ֣י אָמְר֗וּ עָזַ֤ב יְהֹוָה֙ אֶת־הָאָ֔רֶץ וְאֵ֥ין יְהֹוָ֖ה רֹאֶֽה׃

10 I, in turn, will show no pity or compassion; I will give them their deserts."

י וְגַ֙ם־אֲנִ֔י לֹא־תָח֥וֹס עֵינִ֖י וְלֹ֣א אֶחְמֹ֑ל דַּרְכָּ֖ם בְּרֹאשָׁ֥ם נָתָֽתִּי׃

11 And then the man clothed in linen with the writing case at his waist brought back word, saying, "I have done as You commanded me."

יא וְהִנֵּ֞ה הָאִ֣ישׁ ׀ לְבֻ֣שׁ הַבַּדִּ֗ים אֲשֶׁ֤ר הַקֶּ֙סֶת֙ בְּמׇתְנָ֔יו מֵשִׁ֥יב דָּבָ֖ר לֵאמֹ֑ר עָשִׂ֙יתִי֙ כַּאֲשֶׁ֣ר [כְּכֹ֣ל] צִוִּיתָֽנִי [אֲשֶׁ֣ר]׃

10

1 I looked, and on the expanse over the heads of the cherubs, there was something like a sapphire stone; an appearance resembling a throne could be seen over them.

י א וָאֶרְאֶ֗ה וְהִנֵּ֤ה אֶל־הָרָקִ֙יעַ֙ אֲשֶׁר֙ עַל־רֹ֣אשׁ הַכְּרֻבִ֔ים כְּאֶ֣בֶן סַפִּ֔יר כְּמַרְאֵ֖ה דְּמ֣וּת כִּסֵּ֑א נִרְאָ֖ה עֲלֵיהֶֽם׃

va-er-EH v'-hi-NAY el ha-ra-KEE-a a-SHER al ROSH ha-k'-ru-VEEM
k'-E-ven sa-PEER k'-mar-AY d'-MUT ki-SAY nir-AH a-lay-HEM

10:1 On the expanse over the heads of the cherubs Chapter 10 contains the second description of God's throne departing from *Yerushalayim*. The man in white linen, mentioned in chapter 9, takes coals from between the cherubim to set the city ablaze, and the glory of *Hashem* then moves away while fire purges the city. In the Bible, cherubim appear as dividers between *Hashem* and humanity. The first time they appear, they block the entrance to the Garden of Eden (Genesis 3:24). They are also found on the veil that separates the holy places in the *Mishkan* and the *Beit Hamikdash* from the Holy of Holies (Exodus 36:35, I Kings 6:23). Here, the cherubim appear again, as *Hashem* separates Himself from the sinful city.

A replica of the Ark of the Covenant with cherubim on top

² He spoke to the man clothed in linen and said, "Step inside the wheelwork, under the cherubs, and fill your hands with glowing coals from among the cherubs, and scatter them over the city." And he went in as I looked on.

³ Now the cherubs were standing on the south side of the House when the man entered, and the cloud filled the inner court.

⁴ But when the Presence of *Hashem* moved from the cherubs to the platform of the House, the House was filled with the cloud, and the court was filled with the radiance of the Presence of *Hashem*.

⁵ The sound of the cherubs' wings could be heard as far as the outer court, like the voice of *ElShaddai* when He speaks.

⁶ When He commanded the man dressed in linen: "Take fire from among the cherubs within the wheelwork," he went in and stood beside a wheel.

⁷ And a cherub stretched out his hand among the cherubs to the fire that was among the cherubs; he took some and put it into the hands of him who was clothed in linen, who took it and went out.

⁸ The cherubs appeared to have the form of a man's hand under their wings.

⁹ I could see that there were four wheels beside the cherubs, one wheel beside each of the cherubs; as for the appearance of the wheels, they gleamed like the beryl stone.

¹⁰ In appearance, the four had the same form, as if there were two wheels cutting through each other.

¹¹ And when they moved, each could move in the direction of any of its four quarters; they did not veer as they moved. The [cherubs] moved in the direction in which one of the heads faced, without turning as they moved.

¹² Their entire bodies – backs, hands, and wings – and the wheels, the wheels of the four of them, were covered all over with eyes.

¹³ It was these wheels that I had heard called "the wheelwork."

¹⁴ Each one had four faces: One was a cherub's face, the second a human face, the third a lion's face, and the fourth an eagle's face.

ב וַיֹּאמֶר אֶל־הָאִישׁ לְבֻשׁ הַבַּדִּים וַיֹּאמֶר בֹּא אֶל־בֵּינוֹת לַגַּלְגַּל אֶל־תַּחַת לַכְּרוּב וּמַלֵּא חָפְנֶיךָ גַחֲלֵי־אֵשׁ מִבֵּינוֹת לַכְּרֻבִים וּזְרֹק עַל־הָעִיר וַיָּבֹא לְעֵינָי:

ג וְהַכְּרֻבִים עֹמְדִים מִימִין לַבַּיִת בְּבֹאוֹ הָאִישׁ וְהֶעָנָן מָלֵא אֶת־הֶחָצֵר הַפְּנִימִית:

ד וַיָּרָם כְּבוֹד־יְהֹוָה מֵעַל הַכְּרוּב עַל מִפְתַּן הַבָּיִת וַיִּמָּלֵא הַבַּיִת אֶת־הֶעָנָן וְהֶחָצֵר מָלְאָה אֶת־נֹגַהּ כְּבוֹד יְהֹוָה:

ה וְקוֹל כַּנְפֵי הַכְּרוּבִים נִשְׁמַע עַד־הֶחָצֵר הַחִיצֹנָה כְּקוֹל אֵל־שַׁדַּי בְּדַבְּרוֹ:

ו וַיְהִי בְּצַוֺּתוֹ אֶת־הָאִישׁ לְבֻשׁ־הַבַּדִּים לֵאמֹר קַח אֵשׁ מִבֵּינוֹת לַגַּלְגַּל מִבֵּינוֹת לַכְּרוּבִים וַיָּבֹא וַיַּעֲמֹד אֵצֶל הָאוֹפָן:

ז וַיִּשְׁלַח הַכְּרוּב אֶת־יָדוֹ מִבֵּינוֹת לַכְּרוּבִים אֶל־הָאֵשׁ אֲשֶׁר בֵּינוֹת הַכְּרֻבִים וַיִּשָּׂא וַיִּתֵּן אֶל־חָפְנֵי לְבֻשׁ הַבַּדִּים וַיִּקַּח וַיֵּצֵא:

ח וַיֵּרָא לַכְּרֻבִים תַּבְנִית יַד־אָדָם תַּחַת כַּנְפֵיהֶם:

ט וָאֶרְאֶה וְהִנֵּה אַרְבָּעָה אוֹפַנִּים אֵצֶל הַכְּרוּבִים אוֹפַן אֶחָד אֵצֶל הַכְּרוּב אֶחָד וְאוֹפַן אֶחָד אֵצֶל הַכְּרוּב אֶחָד וּמַרְאֵה הָאוֹפַנִּים כְּעֵין אֶבֶן תַּרְשִׁישׁ:

י וּמַרְאֵיהֶם דְּמוּת אֶחָד לְאַרְבַּעְתָּם כַּאֲשֶׁר יִהְיֶה הָאוֹפַן בְּתוֹךְ הָאוֹפָן:

יא בְּלֶכְתָּם אֶל־אַרְבַּעַת רִבְעֵיהֶם יֵלֵכוּ לֹא יִסַּבּוּ בְּלֶכְתָּם כִּי הַמָּקוֹם אֲשֶׁר־יִפְנֶה הָרֹאשׁ אַחֲרָיו יֵלֵכוּ לֹא יִסַּבּוּ בְּלֶכְתָּם:

יב וְכָל־בְּשָׂרָם וְגַבֵּהֶם וִידֵיהֶם וְכַנְפֵיהֶם וְהָאוֹפַנִּים מְלֵאִים עֵינַיִם סָבִיב לְאַרְבַּעְתָּם אוֹפַנֵּיהֶם:

יג לָאוֹפַנִּים לָהֶם קוֹרָא הַגַּלְגַּל בְּאָזְנָי:

יד וְאַרְבָּעָה פָנִים לְאֶחָד פְּנֵי הָאֶחָד פְּנֵי הַכְּרוּב וּפְנֵי הַשֵּׁנִי פְּנֵי אָדָם וְהַשְּׁלִישִׁי פְּנֵי אַרְיֵה וְהָרְבִיעִי פְּנֵי־נָשֶׁר:

15 The cherubs ascended; those were the creatures that I had seen by the Chebar Canal.

טו וַיֵּרֹ֙מּוּ הַכְּרוּבִ֔ים הִ֚יא הַֽחַיָּ֔ה אֲשֶׁ֥ר רָאִ֖יתִי בִּֽנְהַר־כְּבָֽר׃

16 Whenever the cherubs went, the wheels went beside them; and when the cherubs lifted their wings to ascend from the earth, the wheels did not roll away from their side.

טז וּבְלֶ֙כֶת֙ הַכְּרוּבִ֔ים יֵלְכ֥וּ הָאוֹפַנִּ֖ים אֶצְלָ֑ם וּבִשְׂאֵ֣ת הַכְּרוּבִ֗ים אֶת־כַּנְפֵיהֶם֙ לָר֣וּם מֵעַ֣ל הָאָ֔רֶץ לֹא־יִסַּ֧בּוּ הָאוֹפַנִּ֛ים גַּם־הֵ֖ם מֵאֶצְלָֽם׃

17 When those stood still, these stood still; and when those ascended, these ascended with them, for the spirit of the creature was in them.

יז בְּעׇמְדָ֣ם יַֽעֲמֹ֔דוּ וּבְרוֹמָ֖ם יֵרֹ֣מּוּ אוֹתָ֑ם כִּ֛י ר֥וּחַ הַֽחַיָּ֖ה בָּהֶֽם׃

18 Then the Presence of *Hashem* left the platform of the House and stopped above the cherubs.

יח וַיֵּצֵא֙ כְּב֣וֹד יְהֹוָ֔ה מֵעַ֖ל מִפְתַּ֣ן הַבָּ֑יִת וַֽיַּעֲמֹ֖ד עַל־הַכְּרוּבִֽים׃

19 And I saw the cherubs lift their wings and rise from the earth, with the wheels beside them as they departed; and they stopped at the entrance of the eastern gate of the House of *Hashem*, with the Presence of the God of *Yisrael* above them.

יט וַיִּשְׂא֣וּ הַכְּרוּבִ֣ים אֶת־כַּנְפֵיהֶ֗ם וַיֵּר֙וֹמּוּ מִן־הָאָ֤רֶץ לְעֵינַי֙ בְּצֵאתָ֔ם וְהָא֣וֹפַנִּ֔ים לְעֻמָּתָ֑ם וַֽיַּעֲמֹ֗ד פֶּ֣תַח שַׁ֤עַר בֵּית־יְהֹוָה֙ הַקַּדְמוֹנִ֔י וּכְב֧וֹד אֱלֹהֵֽי־יִשְׂרָאֵ֛ל עֲלֵיהֶ֖ם מִלְמָֽעְלָה׃

20 They were the same creatures that I had seen below the God of *Yisrael* at the Chebar Canal; so now I knew that they were cherubs.

כ הִ֣יא הַֽחַיָּ֗ה אֲשֶׁ֥ר רָאִ֛יתִי תַּ֥חַת אֱלֹהֵֽי־יִשְׂרָאֵ֖ל בִּֽנְהַר־כְּבָ֑ר וָאֵדַ֕ע כִּ֥י כְרוּבִ֖ים הֵֽמָּה׃

21 Each one had four faces and each had four wings, with the form of human hands under the wings.

כא אַרְבָּעָ֨ה אַרְבָּעָ֤ה פָנִים֙ לְאֶחָ֔ד וְאַרְבַּ֥ע כְּנָפַ֖יִם לְאֶחָ֑ד וּדְמוּת֙ יְדֵ֣י אָדָ֔ם תַּ֖חַת כַּנְפֵיהֶֽם׃

22 As for the form of their faces, they were the very faces that I had seen by the Chebar Canal – their appearance and their features – and each could move in the direction of any of its faces.1

כב וּדְמ֣וּת פְּנֵיהֶ֗ם הֵ֤מָּה הַפָּנִים֙ אֲשֶׁ֣ר רָאִ֔יתִי עַל־נְהַר־כְּבָ֖ר מַרְאֵיהֶ֣ם וְאוֹתָ֑ם אִ֛ישׁ אֶל־עֵ֥בֶר פָּנָ֖יו יֵלֵֽכוּ׃

11 1 Then a spirit lifted me up and brought me to the east gate of the House of *Hashem*, which faces eastward; and there, at the entrance of the gate, were twenty-five men, among whom I saw Jaazaniah son of Azzur and Pelatiah son of Benaiah, leaders of the people.

א וַתִּשָּׂ֨א אֹתִ֜י ר֗וּחַ וַתָּבֵ֣א אֹתִ֣י אֶל־שַׁ֩עַר֩ בֵּית־יְהֹוָ֨ה הַקַּדְמוֹנִ֜י הַפּוֹנֶ֣ה קָדִ֗ימָה וְהִנֵּה֙ בְּפֶ֣תַח הַשַּׁ֔עַר עֶשְׂרִ֥ים וַֽחֲמִשָּׁ֖ה אִ֑ישׁ וָֽאֶרְאֶ֨ה בְתוֹכָ֜ם אֶת־יַֽאֲזַנְיָ֣ה בֶן־עַזֻּ֗ר וְאֶת־פְּלַטְיָ֙הוּ֙ בֶן־בְּנָיָ֔הוּ שָׂרֵ֖י הָעָֽם׃

2 [*Hashem*] said to me, "O mortal, these are the men who plan iniquity and plot wickedness in this city,

ב וַיֹּ֖אמֶר אֵלָ֑י בֶּן־אָדָ֕ם אֵ֣לֶּה הָֽאֲנָשִׁ֗ים הַחֹֽשְׁבִ֥ים אָ֛וֶן וְהַיֹּֽעֲצִ֥ים עֲצַת־רָ֖ע בָּעִ֥יר הַזֹּֽאת׃

3 who say: 'There is no need now to build houses; this [city] is the pot, and we are the meat.'

ג הָאֹ֣מְרִ֔ים לֹ֥א בְקָר֖וֹב בְּנ֣וֹת בָּתִּ֑ים הִ֣יא הַסִּ֔יר וַֽאֲנַ֖חְנוּ הַבָּשָֽׂר׃

4 I adjure you, prophesy against them; prophesy, O mortal!"

ד לָכֵ֖ן הִנָּבֵ֣א עֲלֵיהֶ֑ם הִנָּבֵ֖א בֶּן־אָדָֽם׃

5 Thereupon the spirit of *Hashem* fell upon me, and He said to me, "Speak: Thus said *Hashem*: Such are your thoughts, O House of *Yisrael*; I know what comes into your mind.

ה וַתִּפֹּ֤ל עָלַי֙ ר֣וּחַ יְהֹוָ֔ה וַיֹּ֣אמֶר אֵלַ֗י אֱמֹר֙ כֹּֽה־אָמַ֣ר יְהֹוָ֔ה כֵּ֥ן אֲמַרְתֶּ֖ם בֵּ֣ית יִשְׂרָאֵ֑ל וּמַעֲל֥וֹת רֽוּחֲכֶ֖ם אֲנִ֥י יְדַעְתִּֽיהָ׃

6 Many have you slain in this city; you have filled its streets with corpses.

ו הִרְבֵּיתֶם חַלְלֵיכֶם בָּעִיר הַזֹּאת וּמִלֵּאתֶם חוּצֹתֶיהָ חָלָל:

7 Assuredly, thus says *Hashem*: The corpses that you have piled up in it are the meat for which it is the pot; but you shall be taken out of it.

ז לָכֵן כֹּה־אָמַר אֲדֹנָי יְהוִה חַלְלֵיכֶם אֲשֶׁר שַׂמְתֶּם בְּתוֹכָהּ הֵמָּה הַבָּשָׂר וְהִיא הַסִּיר וְאֶתְכֶם הוֹצִיא מִתּוֹכָהּ:

8 You feared the sword, and the sword I will bring upon you – declares *Hashem*.

ח חֶרֶב יְרֵאתֶם וְחֶרֶב אָבִיא עֲלֵיכֶם נְאֻם אֲדֹנָי יְהוִה:

9 I will take you out of it and deliver you into the hands of strangers, and I will execute judgments upon you.

ט וְהוֹצֵאתִי אֶתְכֶם מִתּוֹכָהּ וְנָתַתִּי אֶתְכֶם בְּיַד־זָרִים וְעָשִׂיתִי בָכֶם שְׁפָטִים:

10 You shall fall by the sword; I will punish you at the border of *Yisrael*. And you shall know that I am *Hashem*.

י בַּחֶרֶב תִּפֹּלוּ עַל־גְּבוּל יִשְׂרָאֵל אֶשְׁפּוֹט אֶתְכֶם וִידַעְתֶּם כִּי־אֲנִי יְהוָה:

11 This [city] shall not be a pot for you, nor you the meat in it; I will punish you at the border of *Yisrael*.

יא הִיא לֹא־תִהְיֶה לָכֶם לְסִיר וְאַתֶּם תִּהְיוּ בְתוֹכָהּ לְבָשָׂר אֶל־גְּבוּל יִשְׂרָאֵל אֶשְׁפֹּט אֶתְכֶם:

12 Then you shall know that I am *Hashem*, whose laws you did not follow and whose rules you did not obey, acting instead according to the rules of the nations around you."

יב וִידַעְתֶּם כִּי־אֲנִי יְהוָה אֲשֶׁר בְּחֻקַּי לֹא הֲלַכְתֶּם וּמִשְׁפָּטַי לֹא עֲשִׂיתֶם וּכְמִשְׁפְּטֵי הַגּוֹיִם אֲשֶׁר סְבִיבוֹתֵיכֶם עֲשִׂיתֶם:

13 Now, as I prophesied, Pelatiah son of Benaiah dropped dead. I threw myself upon my face and cried out aloud, "Ah, *Hashem*! You are wiping out the remnant of *Yisrael*!"

יג וַיְהִי כְּהִנָּבְאִי וּפְלַטְיָהוּ בֶן־בְּנָיָה מֵת וָאֶפֹּל עַל־פָּנַי וָאֶזְעַק קוֹל־גָּדוֹל וָאֹמַר אֲהָהּ אֲדֹנָי יְהוִה כָּלָה אַתָּה עֹשֶׂה אֵת שְׁאֵרִית יִשְׂרָאֵל:

14 Then the word of *Hashem* came to me:

יד וַיְהִי דְבַר־יְהוָה אֵלַי לֵאמֹר:

15 "O mortal, [I will save] your brothers, your brothers, the men of your kindred, all of that very House of *Yisrael* to whom the inhabitants of *Yerushalayim* say, 'Keep far from *Hashem*; the land has been given as a heritage to us.'

טו בֶּן־אָדָם אַחֶיךָ אַחֶיךָ אַנְשֵׁי גְאֻלָּתֶךָ וְכָל־בֵּית יִשְׂרָאֵל כֻּלֹּה אֲשֶׁר אָמְרוּ לָהֶם יֹשְׁבֵי יְרוּשָׁלַ͏ִם רַחֲקוּ מֵעַל יְהוָה לָנוּ הִיא נִתְּנָה הָאָרֶץ לְמוֹרָשָׁה:

16 Say then: Thus said *Hashem*: I have indeed removed them far among the nations and have scattered them among the countries, and I have become to them a diminished sanctity in the countries whither they have gone.

טז לָכֵן אֱמֹר כֹּה־אָמַר אֲדֹנָי יְהוִה כִּי הִרְחַקְתִּים בַּגּוֹיִם וְכִי הֲפִיצוֹתִים בָּאֲרָצוֹת וָאֱהִי לָהֶם לְמִקְדָּשׁ מְעַט בָּאֲרָצוֹת אֲשֶׁר־בָּאוּ שָׁם:

17 Yet say: Thus said *Hashem*: I will gather you from the peoples and assemble you out of the countries where you have been scattered, and I will give you the Land of *Yisrael*.

יז לָכֵן אֱמֹר כֹּה־אָמַר אֲדֹנָי יְהוִה וְקִבַּצְתִּי אֶתְכֶם מִן־הָעַמִּים וְאָסַפְתִּי אֶתְכֶם מִן־הָאֲרָצוֹת אֲשֶׁר נְפֹצוֹתֶם בָּהֶם וְנָתַתִּי לָכֶם אֶת־אַדְמַת יִשְׂרָאֵל:

18 And they shall return there, and do away with all its detestable things and all its abominations.

יח וּבָאוּ־שָׁמָּה וְהֵסִירוּ אֶת־כָּל־שִׁקּוּצֶיהָ וְאֶת־כָּל־תּוֹעֲבוֹתֶיהָ מִמֶּנָּה:

Ezekiel

19 I will give them one heart and put a new spirit in them; I will remove the heart of stone from their bodies and give them a heart of flesh,

יט וְנָתַתִּי לָהֶם לֵב אֶחָד וְרוּחַ חֲדָשָׁה אֶתֵּן בְּקִרְבְּכֶם וַהֲסִרֹתִי לֵב הָאֶבֶן מִבְּשָׂרָם וְנָתַתִּי לָהֶם לֵב בָּשָׂר:

20 that they may follow My laws and faithfully observe My rules. Then they shall be My people and I will be their God.

כ לְמַעַן בְּחֻקֹּתַי יֵלֵכוּ וְאֶת־מִשְׁפָּטַי יִשְׁמְרוּ וְעָשׂוּ אֹתָם וְהָיוּ־לִי לְעָם וַאֲנִי אֶהְיֶה לָהֶם לֵאלֹהִים:

21 But as for them whose heart is set upon their detestable things and their abominations, I will repay them for their conduct – declares *Hashem*."

כא וְאֶל־לֵב שִׁקּוּצֵיהֶם וְתוֹעֲבוֹתֵיהֶם לִבָּם הֹלֵךְ דַּרְכָּם בְּרֹאשָׁם נָתַתִּי נְאֻם אֲדֹנָי יֱהֹוִה:

22 Then the cherubs, with the wheels beside them, lifted their wings, while the Presence of the God of *Yisrael* rested above them.

כב וַיִּשְׂאוּ הַכְּרוּבִים אֶת־כַּנְפֵיהֶם וְהָאוֹפַנִּים לְעֻמָּתָם וּכְבוֹד אֱלֹהֵי־יִשְׂרָאֵל עֲלֵיהֶם מִלְמָעְלָה:

23 The Presence of *Hashem* ascended from the midst of the city and stood on the hill east of the city.

כג וַיַּעַל כְּבוֹד יֱהֹוָה מֵעַל תּוֹךְ הָעִיר וַיַּעֲמֹד עַל־הָהָר אֲשֶׁר מִקֶּדֶם לָעִיר:

24 A spirit carried me away and brought me in a vision by the spirit of *Hashem* to the exile community in Chaldea. Then the vision that I had seen left me,

כד וְרוּחַ נְשָׂאַתְנִי וַתְּבִיאֵנִי כַשְׂדִּימָה אֶל־הַגּוֹלָה בַּמַּרְאֶה בְּרוּחַ אֱלֹהִים וַיַּעַל מֵעָלַי הַמַּרְאֶה אֲשֶׁר רָאִיתִי:

25 and I told the exiles all the things that *Hashem* had shown me.

כה וָאֲדַבֵּר אֶל־הַגּוֹלָה אֵת כָּל־דִּבְרֵי יֱהֹוָה אֲשֶׁר הֶרְאָנִי:

va-a-da-BAYR el ha-go-LAH AYT kol div-RAY a-do-NAI a-SHER her-A-nee

12 **1** The word of *Hashem* came to me:

א וַיְהִי דְבַר־יֱהֹוָה אֵלַי לֵאמֹר:

2 O mortal, you dwell among the rebellious breed. They have eyes to see but see not, ears to hear but hear not; for they are a rebellious breed.

ב בֶּן־אָדָם בְּתוֹךְ בֵּית־הַמֶּרִי אַתָּה יֹשֵׁב אֲשֶׁר עֵינַיִם לָהֶם לִרְאוֹת וְלֹא רָאוּ אָזְנַיִם לָהֶם לִשְׁמֹעַ וְלֹא שָׁמֵעוּ כִּי בֵּית מְרִי הֵם:

3 Therefore, mortal, get yourself gear for exile, and go into exile by day before their eyes. Go into exile from your home to another place before their very eyes; perhaps they will take note, even though they are a rebellious breed.

ג וְאַתָּה בֶן־אָדָם עֲשֵׂה לְךָ כְּלֵי גוֹלָה וּגְלֵה יוֹמָם לְעֵינֵיהֶם וְגָלִיתָ מִמְּקוֹמְךָ אֶל־מָקוֹם אַחֵר לְעֵינֵיהֶם אוּלַי יִרְאוּ כִּי בֵּית מְרִי הֵמָּה:

11:25 And I told the exiles In verses 16–17, *Hashem* promises that though He has exiled the Children of Israel and scattered them among the nations, in the future He will gather and redeem them: "I will gather you from the peoples and assemble you out of the countries where you have been scattered, and I will give you the Land of Israel." In this verse, *Yechezkel* shares *Hashem's* promise with the Children of Israel already in captivity, giving them hope for

A group of students welcome new immigrants to Israel

the future. The Hebrew word for 'captivity' or 'exile,' found in this verse, is *gola* (גולה), while the term for 'redemption' is *geula* (גאולה). Rabbi Benjamin Blech notes that the two words are spelled almost identically, with the only difference between them being the single letter *aleph* (א). The numerical value of the *aleph* is one, representing the one true God who must be incorporated into the mentality of the *gola* (exile) in order to bring about the *geula* (redemption).

אולה

Ezekiel

4 Carry out your gear as gear for exile by day before their very eyes; and go out again in the evening before their eyes, as one who goes out into exile.

ד וְהוֹצֵאתָ כֵלֶיךָ כִּכְלֵי גוֹלָה יוֹמָם לְעֵינֵיהֶם וְאַתָּה תֵּצֵא בָעֶרֶב לְעֵינֵיהֶם כְּמוֹצָאֵי גוֹלָה:

5 Before their eyes, break through the wall and carry [the gear] out through it;

ה לְעֵינֵיהֶם חֲתָר־לְךָ בַקִּיר וְהוֹצֵאתָ בּוֹ:

6 before their eyes, carry it on your shoulder. Take it out in the dark, and cover your face that you may not see the land; for I make you a portent to the House of *Yisrael*.

ו לְעֵינֵיהֶם עַל־כָּתֵף תִּשָּׂא בָּעֲלָטָה תוֹצִיא פָּנֶיךָ תְכַסֶּה וְלֹא תִרְאֶה אֶת־הָאָרֶץ כִּי־מוֹפֵת נְתַתִּיךָ לְבֵית יִשְׂרָאֵל:

7 I did just as I was ordered: I took out my gear by day as gear for exile, and in the evening I broke through the wall with my own hands. In the darkness I carried [the gear] out on my shoulder, carrying it before their eyes.

ז וָאַעַשׂ כֵּן כַּאֲשֶׁר צֻוֵּיתִי כֵּלַי הוֹצֵאתִי כִּכְלֵי גוֹלָה יוֹמָם וּבָעֶרֶב חָתַרְתִּי־לִי בַקִּיר בְּיָד בָּעֲלָטָה הוֹצֵאתִי עַל־כָּתֵף נָשָׂאתִי לְעֵינֵיהֶם:

8 In the morning, the word of *Hashem* came to me:

ח וַיְהִי דְבַר־יְהֹוָה אֵלַי בַּבֹּקֶר לֵאמֹר:

9 O mortal, did not the House of *Yisrael*, that rebellious breed, ask you, "What are you doing?"

ט בֶּן־אָדָם הֲלֹא אָמְרוּ אֵלֶיךָ בֵּית יִשְׂרָאֵל בֵּית הַמֶּרִי מָה אַתָּה עֹשֶׂה:

10 Say to them: "Thus said *Hashem*: This pronouncement concerns the prince in *Yerushalayim* and all the House of *Yisrael* who are in it."

י אֱמֹר אֲלֵיהֶם כֹּה אָמַר אֲדֹנָי יֱהֹוִה הַנָּשִׂיא הַמַּשָּׂא הַזֶּה בִּירוּשָׁלַם וְכָל־בֵּית יִשְׂרָאֵל אֲשֶׁר־הֵמָּה בְתוֹכָם:

e-MOR a-lay-HEM KOH a-MAR a-do-NAI e-lo-HEEM ha-na-SEE ha-ma-SA ha-ZEH bee-ru-sha-LA-im v'-khol BAYT yis-ra-AYL a-sher HAY-mah v'-to-KHAM

11 Say: "I am a portent for you: As I have done, so shall it be done to them; they shall go into exile, into captivity.

יא אֱמֹר אֲנִי מוֹפֶתְכֶם כַּאֲשֶׁר עָשִׂיתִי כֵּן יֵעָשֶׂה לָהֶם בַּגּוֹלָה בַשְּׁבִי יֵלֵכוּ:

12 And the prince among them shall carry his gear on his shoulder as he goes out in the dark. He shall break through the wall in order to carry [his gear] out through it; he shall cover his face, because he himself shall not see the land with his eyes."

יב וְהַנָּשִׂיא אֲשֶׁר־בְּתוֹכָם אֶל־כָּתֵף יִשָּׂא בָּעֲלָטָה וְיֵצֵא בַּקִּיר יַחְתְּרוּ לְהוֹצִיא בוֹ פָּנָיו יְכַסֶּה יַעַן אֲשֶׁר לֹא־יִרְאֶה לַעַיִן הוּא אֶת־הָאָרֶץ:

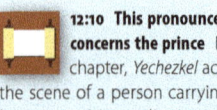

12:10 This pronouncement concerns the prince In this chapter, *Yechezkel* acts out the scene of a person carrying the barest provisions, digging a hole under a stone wall. According to the *Malbim*, these actions reflect the behavior of King *Tzidkiyahu*. Instead of listening to the prophet *Yirmiyahu* and submitting to Babylonia, the Babylonian-appointed king of *Yehuda* at-

The sealed Golden Gate (Gate of Mercy) in the walls of Jerusalem's Old City

tempts to abandon his people by disguising himself and fleeing the siege. However, he is apprehended by the enemy and brought to Babylonia in chains. As hard as it was to surrender, it was the will of God. By refusing to listen and running away, *Tzidkiyahu* seals his fate. We must follow *Hashem's* will even when is not easy, because that path is ultimately best for us.

13 I will spread My net over him, and he shall be caught in My snare. I will bring him to Babylon, the land of the Chaldeans, but he shall not see it; and there he shall die.

יג וּפָרַשְׂתִּי אֶת־רִשְׁתִּי עָלָיו וְנִתְפַּשׂ בִּמְצוּדָתִי וְהֵבֵאתִי אֹתוֹ בָבֶלָה אֶרֶץ כַּשְׂדִּים וְאוֹתָהּ לֹא־יִרְאֶה וְשָׁם יָמוּת:

14 And all those around him, his helpers and all his troops, I will scatter in every direction; and I will unsheathe the sword after them.

יד וְכֹל אֲשֶׁר סְבִיבֹתָיו עֶזְרֹה [עֶזְרוֹ] וְכָל־אֲגַפָּיו אֱזָרֶה לְכָל־רוּחַ וְחֶרֶב אָרִיק אַחֲרֵיהֶם:

15 Then, when I have scattered them among the nations and dispersed them through the countries, they shall know that I am *Hashem*.

טו וְיָדְעוּ כִּי־אֲנִי יְהוָה בַּהֲפִיצִי אוֹתָם בַּגּוֹיִם וְזֵרִיתִי אוֹתָם בָּאֲרָצוֹת:

16 But I will spare a few of them from the sword, from famine, and from pestilence, that they may recount all their abominable deeds among the nations to which they come; and they shall know that I am *Hashem*!

טז וְהוֹתַרְתִּי מֵהֶם אַנְשֵׁי מִסְפָּר מֵחֶרֶב מֵרָעָב וּמִדָּבֶר לְמַעַן יְסַפְּרוּ אֶת־כָּל־תּוֹעֲבוֹתֵיהֶם בַּגּוֹיִם אֲשֶׁר־בָּאוּ שָׁם וְיָדְעוּ כִּי־אֲנִי יְהוָה:

17 The word of *Hashem* came to me:

יז וַיְהִי דְבַר־יְהוָה אֵלַי לֵאמֹר:

18 O mortal, eat your bread in trembling and drink your water in fear and anxiety.

יח בֶּן־אָדָם לַחְמְךָ בְּרַעַשׁ תֹּאכֵל וּמֵימֶיךָ בְּרָגְזָה וּבִדְאָגָה תִּשְׁתֶּה:

19 And say to the people of the land: Thus said *Hashem* concerning the inhabitants of *Yerushalayim* in the land of *Yisrael*: They shall eat their bread in anxiety and drink their water in desolation, because their land will be desolate of its multitudes on account of the lawlessness of all its inhabitants.

יט וְאָמַרְתָּ אֶל־עַם הָאָרֶץ כֹּה־אָמַר אֲדֹנָי יְהוִה לְיוֹשְׁבֵי יְרוּשָׁלַם אֶל־אַדְמַת יִשְׂרָאֵל לַחְמָם בִּדְאָגָה יֹאכֵלוּ וּמֵימֵיהֶם בְּשִׁמָּמוֹן יִשְׁתּוּ לְמַעַן תֵּשַׁם אַרְצָהּ מִמְּלֹאָהּ מֵחֲמַס כָּל־הַיֹּשְׁבִים בָּהּ:

20 The inhabited towns shall be laid waste and the land shall become a desolation; then you shall know that I am *Hashem*.

כ וְהֶעָרִים הַנּוֹשָׁבוֹת תֶּחֱרַבְנָה וְהָאָרֶץ שְׁמָמָה תִהְיֶה וִידַעְתֶּם כִּי־אֲנִי יְהוָה:

21 The word of *Hashem* came to me:

כא וַיְהִי דְבַר־יְהוָה אֵלַי לֵאמֹר:

22 O mortal, what is this proverb that you have in the land of *Yisrael*, that you say, "The days grow many and every vision comes to naught?"

כב בֶּן־אָדָם מָה־הַמָּשָׁל הַזֶּה לָכֶם עַל־אַדְמַת יִשְׂרָאֵל לֵאמֹר יַאַרְכוּ הַיָּמִים וְאָבַד כָּל־חָזוֹן:

23 Assuredly, say to them, Thus said *Hashem*: I will put an end to this proverb; it shall not be used in *Yisrael* any more. Speak rather to them: The days draw near, and the fulfillment of every vision.

כג לָכֵן אֱמֹר אֲלֵיהֶם כֹּה־אָמַר אֲדֹנָי יְהוִה הִשְׁבַּתִּי אֶת־הַמָּשָׁל הַזֶּה וְלֹא־יִמְשְׁלוּ אֹתוֹ עוֹד בְּיִשְׂרָאֵל כִּי אִם־דַּבֵּר אֲלֵיהֶם קָרְבוּ הַיָּמִים וּדְבַר כָּל־חָזוֹן:

24 For there shall no longer be any false vision or soothing divination in the House of *Yisrael*.

כד כִּי לֹא יִהְיֶה עוֹד כָּל־חֲזוֹן שָׁוְא וּמִקְסַם חָלָק בְּתוֹךְ בֵּית יִשְׂרָאֵל:

25 But whenever I *Hashem* speak what I speak, that word shall be fulfilled without any delay; in your days, O rebellious breed, I will fulfill every word I speak – declares *Hashem*.

כה כִּי אֲנִי יְהוָה אֲדַבֵּר אֵת אֲשֶׁר אֲדַבֵּר דָּבָר וְיֵעָשֶׂה לֹא תִמָּשֵׁךְ עוֹד כִּי בִימֵיכֶם בֵּית הַמֶּרִי אֲדַבֵּר דָּבָר וַעֲשִׂיתִיו נְאֻם אֲדֹנָי יְהוִה:

26 The word of *Hashem* came to me:

כו וַיְהִי דְבַר־יְהוָה אֵלַי לֵאמֹר:

²⁷ See, O mortal, the House of *Yisrael* says, "The vision that he sees is far ahead, and he prophesies for the distant future."

²⁸ Assuredly, say to them: Thus said *Hashem*: There shall be no more delay; whenever I speak a word, that word shall be fulfilled – declares *Hashem*.

13 ¹ The word of *Hashem* came to me:

² O mortal, prophesy against the *Neviim* of *Yisrael* who prophesy; say to those who prophesy out of their own imagination: Hear the word of *Hashem*!

³ Thus said *Hashem*: Woe to the degenerate *Neviim*, who follow their own fancy, without having had a vision!

⁴ Your *Neviim*, O *Yisrael*, have been like jackals among ruins.

k'-shu-a-LEEM ba-kha-ra-VOT n'-vee-E-kha yis-ra-AYL ha-YU

⁵ You did not enter the breaches and repair the walls for the House of *Yisrael*, that they might stand up in battle in the day of *Hashem*.

⁶ They prophesied falsehood and lying divination; they said, "Declares *Hashem*," when *Hashem* did not send them, and then they waited for their word to be fulfilled.

⁷ It was false visions you prophesied and lying divination you uttered, saying, "Declares *Hashem*," when I had not spoken.

⁸ Assuredly, thus said *Hashem*: Because you speak falsehood and prophesy lies, assuredly, I will deal with you – declares *Hashem*.

⁹ My hand will be against the *Neviim* who prophesy falsehood and utter lying divination. They shall not remain in the assembly of My people, they shall not be inscribed in the lists of the House of *Yisrael*, and they shall not come back to the land of *Yisrael*. Thus shall you know that I am *Hashem*.

כז בֶּן־אָדָם הִנֵּה בֵית־יִשְׂרָאֵל אֹמְרִים הֶחָזוֹן אֲשֶׁר־הוּא חֹזֶה לְיָמִים רַבִּים וּלְעִתִּים רְחוֹקוֹת הוּא נִבָּא:

כח לָכֵן אֱמֹר אֲלֵיהֶם כֹּה אָמַר אֲדֹנָי יֱהֹוִה לֹא־תִמָּשֵׁךְ עוֹד כָּל־דְּבָרַי אֲשֶׁר אֲדַבֵּר דָּבָר וְיֵעָשֶׂה נְאֻם אֲדֹנָי יֱהֹוִה:

יג א וַיְהִי דְבַר־יְהֹוָה אֵלַי לֵאמֹר:

ב בֶּן־אָדָם הִנָּבֵא אֶל־נְבִיאֵי יִשְׂרָאֵל הַנִּבָּאִים וְאָמַרְתָּ לִנְבִיאֵי מִלִּבָּם שִׁמְעוּ דְּבַר־יְהֹוָה:

ג כֹּה אָמַר אֲדֹנָי יֱהֹוִה הוֹי עַל־הַנְּבִיאִים הַנְּבָלִים אֲשֶׁר הֹלְכִים אַחַר רוּחָם וּלְבִלְתִּי רָאוּ:

ד כְּשֻׁעָלִים בָּחֳרָבוֹת נְבִיאֶיךָ יִשְׂרָאֵל הָיוּ:

ה לֹא עֲלִיתֶם בַּפְּרָצוֹת וַתִּגְדְּרוּ גָדֵר עַל־בֵּית יִשְׂרָאֵל לַעֲמֹד בַּמִּלְחָמָה בְּיוֹם יְהֹוָה:

ו חָזוּ שָׁוְא וְקֶסֶם כָּזָב הָאֹמְרִים נְאֻם־יְהֹוָה וַיהֹוָה לֹא שְׁלָחָם וְיִחֲלוּ לְקַיֵּם דָּבָר:

ז הֲלוֹא מַחֲזֵה־שָׁוְא חֲזִיתֶם וּמִקְסַם כָּזָב אֲמַרְתֶּם וְאֹמְרִים נְאֻם־יְהֹוָה וַאֲנִי לֹא דִבַּרְתִּי:

ח לָכֵן כֹּה אָמַר אֲדֹנָי יֱהֹוִה יַעַן דַּבֶּרְכֶם שָׁוְא וַחֲזִיתֶם כָּזָב לָכֵן הִנְנִי אֲלֵיכֶם נְאֻם אֲדֹנָי יֱהֹוִה:

ט וְהָיְתָה יָדִי אֶל־הַנְּבִיאִים הַחֹזִים שָׁוְא וְהַקֹּסְמִים כָּזָב בְּסוֹד עַמִּי לֹא־יִהְיוּ וּבִכְתָב בֵּית־יִשְׂרָאֵל לֹא יִכָּתֵבוּ וְאֶל־אַדְמַת יִשְׂרָאֵל לֹא יָבֹאוּ וִידַעְתֶּם כִּי אֲנִי אֲדֹנָי יֱהֹוִה:

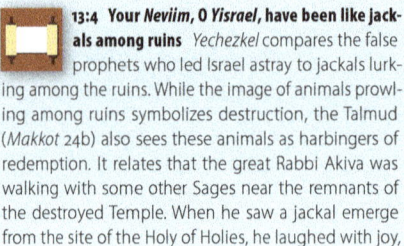

13:4 Your *Neviim*, O *Yisrael*, have been like jackals among ruins *Yechezkel* compares the false prophets who led Israel astray to jackals lurking among the ruins. While the image of animals prowling among ruins symbolizes destruction, the Talmud (*Makkot* 24b) also sees these animals as harbingers of redemption. It relates that the great Rabbi Akiva was walking with some other Sages near the remnants of the destroyed Temple. When he saw a jackal emerge from the site of the Holy of Holies, he laughed with joy, while the others who were with him wept. The Sages were shocked by his laughter, but Rabbi Akiva explained that just as *Hashem* faithfully fulfilled His prophecies of destruction, so too He will be faithful to fulfill the prophecies of redemption, restoration and renewal.

A golden Jackal in Revivim, Israel

¹⁰ Inasmuch as they have misled My people, saying, "It is well," when nothing is well, daubing with plaster the flimsy wall which the people were building,

¹¹ say to those daubers of plaster: It shall collapse; a driving rain shall descend – and you, O great hailstones, shall fall – and a hurricane wind shall rend it.

¹² Then, when the wall collapses, you will be asked, "What became of the plaster you daubed on?"

¹³ Assuredly, thus said *Hashem*: In My fury I will let loose hurricane winds; in My anger a driving rain shall descend, and great hailstones in destructive fury.

¹⁴ I will throw down the wall that you daubed with plaster, and I will raze it to the ground so that its foundation is exposed; and when it falls, you shall perish in its midst; then you shall know that I am *Hashem*.

¹⁵ And when I have spent My fury upon the wall and upon those who daubed it with plaster, I will say to you: Gone is the wall and gone are its daubers,

¹⁶ the *Neviim* of *Yisrael* who prophesy about *Yerushalayim* and see a vision of well-being for her when there is no well-being – declares *Hashem*.

¹⁷ And you, O mortal, set your face against the women of your people, who prophesy out of their own imagination. Prophesy against them

¹⁸ and say: Thus said *Hashem*: Woe to those who sew pads on all arm-joints and make bonnets for the head of every person, in order to entrap! Can you hunt down lives among My people, while you preserve your own lives?

¹⁹ You have profaned My name among My people in return for handfuls of barley and morsels of bread; you have announced the death of persons who will not die and the survival of persons who will not live – lying to My people, who listen to your lies.

²⁰ Assuredly, thus said *Hashem*: I am going to deal with your pads, by which you hunt down lives like birds, and I will tear them from your arms and free the persons whose lives you hunt down like birds.

י יַעַן וּבִיעַן הַטְאוּ אֶת־עַמִּי לֵאמֹר שָׁלוֹם וְאֵין שָׁלוֹם וְהוּא בֹּנֶה חַיִץ וְהִנָּם טָחִים אֹתוֹ תָּפֵל:

יא אֱמֹר אֶל־טָחֵי תָפֵל וְיִפֹּל הָיָה גֶּשֶׁם שׁוֹטֵף וְאַתֵּנָה אַבְנֵי אֶלְגָּבִישׁ תִּפֹּלְנָה וְרוּחַ סְעָרוֹת תְּבַקֵּעַ:

יב וְהִנֵּה נָפַל הַקִּיר הֲלוֹא יֵאָמֵר אֲלֵיכֶם אַיֵּה הַטִּיחַ אֲשֶׁר טַחְתֶּם:

יג לָכֵן כֹּה אָמַר אֲדֹנָי יֱהֹוִה וּבִקַּעְתִּי רוּחַ־ סְעָרוֹת בַּחֲמָתִי וְגֶשֶׁם שֹׁטֵף בְּאַפִּי יִהְיֶה וְאַבְנֵי אֶלְגָּבִישׁ בְּחֵמָה לְכָלָה:

יד וְהָרַסְתִּי אֶת־הַקִּיר אֲשֶׁר־טַחְתֶּם תָּפֵל וְהִגַּעְתִּיהוּ אֶל־הָאָרֶץ וְנִגְלָה יְסֹדוֹ וְנָפְלָה וּכְלִיתֶם בְּתוֹכָהּ וִידַעְתֶּם כִּי־אֲנִי יְהֹוָה:

טו וְכִלֵּיתִי אֶת־חֲמָתִי בַּקִּיר וּבַטָּחִים אֹתוֹ תָּפֵל וְאֹמַר לָכֶם אֵין הַקִּיר וְאֵין הַטָּחִים אֹתוֹ:

טז נְבִיאֵי יִשְׂרָאֵל הַנִּבְּאִים אֶל־יְרוּשָׁלַ͏ִם וְהַחֹזִים לָהּ חֲזוֹן שָׁלֹם וְאֵין שָׁלֹם נְאֻם אֲדֹנָי יֱהֹוִה:

יז וְאַתָּה בֶן־אָדָם שִׂים פָּנֶיךָ אֶל־בְּנוֹת עַמְּךָ הַמִּתְנַבְּאוֹת מִלִּבְּהֶן וְהִנָּבֵא עֲלֵיהֶן:

יח וְאָמַרְתָּ כֹּה־אָמַר אֲדֹנָי יֱהֹוִה הוֹי לִמְתַפְּרוֹת כְּסָתוֹת עַל כָּל־אַצִּילֵי יָדַי וְעֹשׂוֹת הַמִּסְפָּחוֹת עַל־רֹאשׁ כָּל־קוֹמָה לְצוֹדֵד נְפָשׁוֹת הַנְּפָשׁוֹת תְּצוֹדֵדְנָה לְעַמִּי וּנְפָשׁוֹת לָכֶנָה תְחַיֶּינָה:

יט וַתְּחַלֶּלְנָה אֹתִי אֶל־עַמִּי בְּשַׁעֲלֵי שְׂעֹרִים וּבִפְתוֹתֵי לֶחֶם לְהָמִית נְפָשׁוֹת אֲשֶׁר לֹא־תְמוּתֶנָה וּלְחַיּוֹת נְפָשׁוֹת אֲשֶׁר לֹא־תִחְיֶינָה בְּכַזֶּבְכֶם לְעַמִּי שֹׁמְעֵי כָזָב:

כ לָכֵן כֹּה־אָמַר אֲדֹנָי יֱהֹוִה הִנְנִי אֶל־ כִּסְּתוֹתֵיכֶנָה אֲשֶׁר אַתֵּנָה מְצֹדְדוֹת שָׁם אֶת־הַנְּפָשׁוֹת לְפֹרְחוֹת וְקָרַעְתִּי אֹתָם מֵעַל זְרוֹעֹתֵיכֶם וְשִׁלַּחְתִּי אֶת־הַנְּפָשׁוֹת אֲשֶׁר אַתֶּם מְצֹדְדוֹת אֶת־נְפָשִׁים לְפֹרְחֹת:

21 I will tear off your bonnets and rescue My people from your hands, and they shall no longer be prey in your hands; then you shall know that I am *Hashem*.

כא וְקָרַעְתִּי אֶת־מִסְפְּחֹתֵיכֶם וְהִצַּלְתִּי אֶת־עַמִּי מִיֶּדְכֶן וְלֹא־יִהְיוּ עוֹד בְּיֶדְכֶן לִמְצֻדָה וִידַעְתֶּן כִּי־אֲנִי יְהֹוָה:

22 Because you saddened the heart of the innocent with lies, when I would not inflict suffering on him, and encouraged the wicked not to repent of his evil ways and so gain life –

כב יַעַן הַכְאוֹת לֵב־צַדִּיק שֶׁקֶר וַאֲנִי לֹא הִכְאַבְתִּיו וּלְחַזֵּק יְדֵי רָשָׁע לְבִלְתִּי־שׁוּב מִדַּרְכּוֹ הָרָע לְהַחֲיֹתוֹ:

23 assuredly, you shall no longer prophesy lies or practice divination! I will save My people from your hands, and you shall know that I am *Hashem*.

כג לָכֵן שָׁוְא לֹא תֶחֱזֶינָה וְקֶסֶם לֹא־ תִקְסַמְנָה עוֹד וְהִצַּלְתִּי אֶת־עַמִּי מִיֶּדְכֶן וִידַעְתֶּן כִּי־אֲנִי יְהֹוָה:

14 1 Certain elders of *Yisrael* came to me and sat down before me.

יד א וַיָּבוֹא אֵלַי אֲנָשִׁים מִזִּקְנֵי יִשְׂרָאֵל וַיֵּשְׁבוּ לְפָנָי:

2 And the word of *Hashem* came to me:

ב וַיְהִי דְבַר־יְהֹוָה אֵלַי לֵאמֹר:

3 O mortal, these men have turned their thoughts upon their fetishes and set their minds upon the sin through which they stumbled: Shall I respond to their inquiry?

ג בֶּן־אָדָם הָאֲנָשִׁים הָאֵלֶּה הֶעֱלוּ גִלּוּלֵיהֶם עַל־לִבָּם וּמִכְשׁוֹל עֲוֹנָם נָתְנוּ נֹכַח פְּנֵיהֶם הַאִדָּרֹשׁ אִדָּרֵשׁ לָהֶם:

4 Now speak to them and tell them: Thus said *Hashem*: If anyone of the House of *Yisrael* turns his thoughts upon his fetishes and sets his mind upon the sin through which he stumbled, and yet comes to the *Navi*, I *Hashem* will respond to him as he comes with his multitude of fetishes.

ד לָכֵן דַּבֵּר־אוֹתָם וְאָמַרְתָּ אֲלֵיהֶם כֹּה־ אָמַר אֲדֹנָי יֱהֹוִה אִישׁ אִישׁ מִבֵּית יִשְׂרָאֵל אֲשֶׁר יַעֲלֶה אֶת־גִּלּוּלָיו אֶל־לִבּוֹ וּמִכְשׁוֹל עֲוֹנוֹ יָשִׂים נֹכַח פָּנָיו וּבָא אֶל־ הַנָּבִיא אֲנִי יְהֹוָה נַעֲנֵיתִי לוֹ בה [בָא] בְּרֹב גִּלּוּלָיו:

5 Thus I will hold the House of *Yisrael* to account for their thoughts, because they have all been estranged from Me through their fetishes.

ה לְמַעַן תְּפֹשׂ אֶת־בֵּית־יִשְׂרָאֵל בְּלִבָּם אֲשֶׁר נָזֹרוּ מֵעָלַי בְּגִלּוּלֵיהֶם כֻּלָּם:

6 Now say to the House of *Yisrael*: Thus said *Hashem*: Repent, and turn back from your fetishes and turn your minds away from all your abominations.

ו לָכֵן אֱמֹר אֶל־בֵּית יִשְׂרָאֵל כֹּה אָמַר אֲדֹנָי יֱהֹוִה שׁוּבוּ וְהָשִׁיבוּ מֵעַל גִּלּוּלֵיכֶם וּמֵעַל כָּל־תּוֹעֲבֹתֵיכֶם הָשִׁיבוּ פְּנֵיכֶם:

7 For if any man of the House of *Yisrael*, or of the strangers who dwell in *Yisrael*, breaks away from Me and turns his thoughts upon his fetishes and sets his mind upon the sins through which he stumbled, and then goes to the *Navi* to inquire of Me through him, I *Hashem* will respond to him directly.

ז כִּי אִישׁ אִישׁ מִבֵּית יִשְׂרָאֵל וּמֵהַגֵּר אֲשֶׁר־יָגוּר בְּיִשְׂרָאֵל וְיִנָּזֵר מֵאַחֲרַי וְיַעַל גִּלּוּלָיו אֶל־לִבּוֹ וּמִכְשׁוֹל עֲוֹנוֹ יָשִׂים נֹכַח פָּנָיו וּבָא אֶל־הַנָּבִיא לִדְרָשׁ־לוֹ בִי אֲנִי יְהֹוָה נַעֲנֶה־לּוֹ בִּי:

8 I will set My face against that man and make him a sign and a byword, and I will cut him off from the midst of My people. Then you shall know that I am *Hashem*.

ח וְנָתַתִּי פָנַי בָּאִישׁ הַהוּא וַהֲשִׂמֹתִיהוּ לְאוֹת וְלִמְשָׁלִים וְהִכְרַתִּיו מִתּוֹךְ עַמִּי וִידַעְתֶּם כִּי־אֲנִי יְהֹוָה:

9 And if a *Navi* is seduced and does speak a word [to such a man], it was I *Hashem* who seduced that *Navi*; I will stretch out My hand against him and destroy him from among My people *Yisrael*.

ט וְהַנָּבִיא כִי־יְפֻתֶּה וְדִבֶּר דָּבָר אֲנִי יְהֹוָה פִּתֵּיתִי אֵת הַנָּבִיא הַהוּא וְנָטִיתִי אֶת־יָדִי עָלָיו וְהִשְׁמַדְתִּיו מִתּוֹךְ עַמִּי יִשְׂרָאֵל:

10 Thus they shall bear their punishment: The punishment of the inquirer and the punishment of the *Navi* shall be the same,

י וְנָשְׂאוּ עֲוֹנָם כַּעֲוֹן הַדֹּרֵשׁ כַּעֲוֹן הַנָּבִיא יִהְיֶה:

11 so that the House of *Yisrael* may never again stray from Me and defile itself with all its transgressions. Then they shall be My people and I will be their God – declares *Hashem*.

יא לְמַעַן לֹא־יִתְעוּ עוֹד בֵּית־יִשְׂרָאֵל מֵאַחֲרַי וְלֹא־יִטַּמְּאוּ עוֹד בְּכָל־פִּשְׁעֵיהֶם וְהָיוּ לִי לְעָם וַאֲנִי אֶהְיֶה לָהֶם לֵאלֹהִים נְאֻם אֲדֹנָי יֱהֹוִה:

12 The word of *Hashem* came to me:

יב וַיְהִי דְבַר־יְהֹוָה אֵלַי לֵאמֹר:

13 O mortal, if a land were to sin against Me and commit a trespass, and I stretched out My hand against it and broke its staff of bread, and sent famine against it and cut off man and beast from it,

יג בֶּן־אָדָם אֶרֶץ כִּי תֶחֱטָא־לִי לִמְעָל־מַעַל וְנָטִיתִי יָדִי עָלֶיהָ וְשָׁבַרְתִּי לָהּ מַטֵּה־לָחֶם וְהִשְׁלַחְתִּי־בָהּ רָעָב וְהִכְרַתִּי מִמֶּנָּה אָדָם וּבְהֵמָה:

14 even if these three men – *Noach, Daniel,* and *Iyov* – should be in it, they would by their righteousness save only themselves – declares *Hashem*.

יד וְהָיוּ שְׁלֹשֶׁת הָאֲנָשִׁים הָאֵלֶּה בְּתוֹכָהּ נֹחַ דָנִאֵל [דָּנִיֵּאל] וְאִיּוֹב הֵמָּה בְצִדְקָתָם יְנַצְּלוּ נַפְשָׁם נְאֻם אֲדֹנָי יֱהֹוִה:

v'-ha-YU sh'-LO-shet ha-a-na-SHEEM ha-AY-leh b'-to-KHAH
NO-akh da-ni-AYL v'-i-YOV HAY-mah v'-tzid-ka-TAM
y'-na-tz'-LU naf-SHAM n'-UM a-do-NAI e-lo-HEEM

15 Or, if I were to send wild beasts to roam the land and they depopulated it, and it became a desolation with none passing through it because of the beasts,

טו לוּ־חַיָּה רָעָה אַעֲבִיר בָּאָרֶץ וְשִׁכְּלָתָּה וְהָיְתָה שְׁמָמָה מִבְּלִי עוֹבֵר מִפְּנֵי הַחַיָּה:

16 as I live – declares *Hashem* – those three men in it would save neither sons nor daughters; they alone would be saved, but the land would become a desolation.

טז שְׁלֹשֶׁת הָאֲנָשִׁים הָאֵלֶּה בְּתוֹכָהּ חַי־אָנִי נְאֻם אֲדֹנָי יֱהֹוִה אִם־בָּנִים וְאִם־בָּנוֹת יַצִּילוּ הֵמָּה לְבַדָּם יִנָּצֵלוּ וְהָאָרֶץ תִּהְיֶה שְׁמָמָה:

17 Or, if I were to bring the sword upon that land and say, "Let a sword sweep through the land so that I may cut off from it man and beast,"

יז אוֹ חֶרֶב אָבִיא עַל־הָאָרֶץ הַהִיא וְאָמַרְתִּי חֶרֶב תַּעֲבֹר בָּאָרֶץ וְהִכְרַתִּי מִמֶּנָּה אָדָם וּבְהֵמָה:

A pair of religious men walk in a narrow street in *Yerushalayim*

14:14 They would by their righteousness save only themselves Hearing of *Yerushalayim's* imminent demise, one can imagine that *Yechezkel* would have entreated God go save the city, as *Avraham* had before Sodom was destroyed, by means of the following plea: Could the presence of righteous people in the city perhaps prevent its destruction? *Hashem* responds by listing three great people, *Noach, Daniel,* and *Iyov,* whose personal piety was beyond reproach. *Noach* was faced with the destruction of mankind, *Daniel* was faced with the destruction of the nation and *Iyov* was confronted by the destruction of his family. However, each one was able to save only themselves, but not the others around them. The presence of the righteous can only assist others who are willing to learn and be influenced by them.

18 if those three men should be in it, as I live –
declares *Hashem* – they would save neither sons
nor daughters, but they alone would be saved.

וּשְׁלֹשֶׁת הָאֲנָשִׁים הָאֵלֶּה בְּתוֹכָהּ חַי־ יח
אָנִי נְאֻם אֲדֹנָי יֱהוִֹה לֹא יַצִּילוּ בָּנִים
וּבָנוֹת כִּי הֵם לְבַדָּם יִנָּצֵלוּ:

19 Or, if I let loose a pestilence against that land, and
poured out My fury upon it in blood, cutting off
from it man and beast,

אוֹ דֶּבֶר אֲשַׁלַּח אֶל־הָאָרֶץ הַהִיא יט
וְשָׁפַכְתִּי חֲמָתִי עָלֶיהָ בְּדָם לְהַכְרִית
מִמֶּנָּה אָדָם וּבְהֵמָה:

20 should *Noach*, *Daniel*, and *Iyov* be in it, as I live –
declares *Hashem* – they would save neither son
nor daughter; they would save themselves alone by
their righteousness.

וְנֹחַ דָּנִאל [דָּנִיֵּאל] וְאִיּוֹב בְּתוֹכָהּ חַי־ כ
אָנִי נְאֻם אֲדֹנָי יֱהוִֹה אִם־בֵּן אִם־בַּת
יַצִּילוּ הֵמָּה בְצִדְקָתָם יַצִּילוּ נַפְשָׁם:

21 Assuredly, thus said *Hashem*: How much less
[should any escape] now that I have let loose
against *Yerushalayim* all four of My terrible
punishments – the sword, famine, wild beasts, and
pestilence – to cut off man and beast from it!

כִּי כֹה אָמַר אֲדֹנָי יֱהוִֹה אַף כִּי־אַרְבַּעַת כא
שְׁפָטַי הָרָעִים חֶרֶב וְרָעָב וְחַיָּה רָעָה
וְדֶבֶר שִׁלַּחְתִּי אֶל־יְרוּשָׁלָ͏ִם לְהַכְרִית
מִמֶּנָּה אָדָם וּבְהֵמָה:

22 Yet there are survivors left of it, sons and daughters
who are being brought out. They are coming out to
you; and when you see their ways and their deeds,
you will be consoled for the disaster that I brought
on *Yerushalayim*, for all that I brought on it.

וְהִנֵּה נוֹתְרָה־בָּהּ פְּלֵטָה הַמּוּצָאִים בָּנִים כב
וּבָנוֹת הִנָּם יוֹצְאִים אֲלֵיכֶם וּרְאִיתֶם
אֶת־דַּרְכָּם וְאֶת־עֲלִילוֹתָם וְנִחַמְתֶּם עַל־
הָרָעָה אֲשֶׁר הֵבֵאתִי עַל־יְרוּשָׁלַ͏ִם אֵת
כָּל־אֲשֶׁר הֵבֵאתִי עָלֶיהָ:

23 You will be consoled through them, when you
see their ways and their deeds and realize that not
without cause did I do all that I did in it – declares
Hashem.

וְנִחֲמוּ אֶתְכֶם כִּי־תִרְאוּ אֶת־דַּרְכָּם וְאֶת־ כג
עֲלִילוֹתָם וִידַעְתֶּם כִּי לֹא חִנָּם עָשִׂיתִי
אֵת כָּל־אֲשֶׁר־עָשִׂיתִי בָהּ נְאֻם אֲדֹנָי
יֱהוִֹה:

15 1 The word of *Hashem* came to me:

וַיְהִי דְבַר־יְהוָֹה אֵלַי לֵאמֹר: א **טו**

2 O mortal, how is the wood of the grapevine better
than the wood of any branch to be found among
the trees of the forest?

בֶּן־אָדָם מַה־יִּהְיֶה עֵץ־הַגֶּפֶן מִכָּל־עֵץ ב
הַזְּמוֹרָה אֲשֶׁר הָיָה בַּעֲצֵי הַיָּעַר:

3 Can wood be taken from it for use in any work?
Can one take a peg from it to hang any vessel on?

הֲיֻקַּח מִמֶּנּוּ עֵץ לַעֲשׂוֹת לִמְלָאכָה אִם־ ג
יִקְחוּ מִמֶּנּוּ יָתֵד לִתְלוֹת עָלָיו כָּל־כֶּלִי:

4 Now suppose it was thrown into the fire as fuel and
the fire consumed its two ends and its middle was
charred – is it good for any use?

הִנֵּה לָאֵשׁ נִתַּן לְאָכְלָה אֵת שְׁנֵי ד
קְצוֹתָיו אָכְלָה הָאֵשׁ וְתוֹכוֹ נָחָר הֲיִצְלַח
לִמְלָאכָה:

5 Even when it was whole it could not be used for
anything; how much less when fire has consumed it
and it is charred! Can it still be used for anything?

הִנֵּה בִּהְיוֹתוֹ תָמִים לֹא יֵעָשֶׂה לִמְלָאכָה ה
אַף כִּי־אֵשׁ אֲכָלַתְהוּ וַיֵּחָר וְנַעֲשָׂה עוֹד
לִמְלָאכָה:

6 Assuredly, thus said *Hashem*: Like the wood of the
grapevine among the trees of the forest, which I
have designated to be fuel for fire, so will I treat
the inhabitants of *Yerushalayim*.

לָכֵן כֹּה אָמַר אֲדֹנָי יֱהוִֹה כַּאֲשֶׁר עֵץ־ ו
הַגֶּפֶן בְּעֵץ הַיַּעַר אֲשֶׁר־נְתַתִּיו לָאֵשׁ
לְאָכְלָה כֵּן נָתַתִּי אֶת־יֹשְׁבֵי יְרוּשָׁלָ͏ִם:

la-KHAYN KOH a-MAR a-do-NAI e-lo-HEEM ka-a-SHER
aytz ha-GE-fen b'-AYTZ ha-YA-ar a-sher n'-ta-TEEV la-AYSH
l'-okh-LAH KAYN na-TA-tee et yo-sh'-VAY y'-ru-sha-LA-im

7 I will set My face against them; they escaped from fire, but fire shall consume them. When I set my face against them, you shall know that I am *Hashem*.

ז וְנָתַתִּי אֶת־פָּנַי בָּהֶם מֵהָאֵשׁ יָצָאוּ וְהָאֵשׁ תֹּאכְלֵם וִידַעְתֶּם כִּי־אֲנִי יְהוָה בְּשׂוּמִי אֶת־פָּנַי בָּהֶם:

8 I will make the land a desolation, because they committed trespass – declares *Hashem*.

ח וְנָתַתִּי אֶת־הָאָרֶץ שְׁמָמָה יַעַן מָעֲלוּ מַעַל נְאֻם אֲדֹנָי יְהוִה:

16 1 The word of *Hashem* came to me:

טז א וַיְהִי דְבַר־יְהוָה אֵלַי לֵאמֹר:

2 O mortal, proclaim *Yerushalayim*'s abominations to her,

ב בֶּן־אָדָם הוֹדַע אֶת־יְרוּשָׁלַם אֶת־תּוֹעֲבֹתֶיהָ:

3 and say: Thus said *Hashem* to *Yerushalayim*: By origin and birth you are from the land of the Canaanites – your father was an Amorite and your mother a Hittite.

ג וְאָמַרְתָּ כֹּה־אָמַר אֲדֹנָי יְהוִה לִירוּשָׁלַם מְכֹרֹתַיִךְ וּמֹלְדֹתַיִךְ מֵאֶרֶץ הַכְּנַעֲנִי אָבִיךְ הָאֱמֹרִי וְאִמֵּךְ חִתִּית:

4 As for your birth, when you were born your navel cord was not cut, and you were not bathed in water to smooth you; you were not rubbed with salt, nor were you swaddled.

ד וּמוֹלְדוֹתַיִךְ בְּיוֹם הוּלֶּדֶת אֹתָךְ לֹא־כָרַת שָׁרֵּךְ וּבְמַיִם לֹא־רֻחַצְתְּ לְמִשְׁעִי וְהָמְלֵחַ לֹא הֻמְלַחַתְּ וְהָחְתֵּל לֹא חֻתָּלְתְּ:

5 No one pitied you enough to do any one of these things for you out of compassion for you; on the day you were born, you were left lying, rejected, in the open field.

ה לֹא־חָסָה עָלַיִךְ עַיִן לַעֲשׂוֹת לָךְ אַחַת מֵאֵלֶּה לְחֻמְלָה עָלָיִךְ וַתֻּשְׁלְכִי אֶל־פְּנֵי הַשָּׂדֶה בְּגֹעַל נַפְשֵׁךְ בְּיוֹם הֻלֶּדֶת אֹתָךְ:

6 When I passed by you and saw you wallowing in your blood, I said to you: "Live in spite of your blood." Yea, I said to you: "Live in spite of your blood."

ו וָאֶעֱבֹר עָלַיִךְ וָאֶרְאֵךְ מִתְבּוֹסֶסֶת בְּדָמָיִךְ וָאֹמַר לָךְ בְּדָמַיִךְ חֲיִי וָאֹמַר לָךְ בְּדָמַיִךְ חֲיִי:

7 I let you grow like the plants of the field; and you continued to grow up until you attained to womanhood, until your breasts became firm and your hair sprouted. You were still naked and bare

ז רְבָבָה כְּצֶמַח הַשָּׂדֶה נְתַתִּיךְ וַתִּרְבִּי וַתִּגְדְּלִי וַתָּבֹאִי בַּעֲדִי עֲדָיִים שָׁדַיִם נָכֹנוּ וּשְׂעָרֵךְ צִמֵּחַ וְאַתְּ עֵרֹם וְעֶרְיָה:

8 when I passed by you [again] and saw that your time for love had arrived. So I spread My robe over you and covered your nakedness, and I entered into a covenant with you by oath – declares *Hashem*; thus you became Mine.

ח וָאֶעֱבֹר עָלַיִךְ וָאֶרְאֵךְ וְהִנֵּה עִתֵּךְ עֵת דֹּדִים וָאֶפְרֹשׂ כְּנָפִי עָלַיִךְ וָאֲכַסֶּה עֶרְוָתֵךְ וָאֶשָּׁבַע לָךְ וָאָבוֹא בִבְרִית אֹתָךְ נְאֻם אֲדֹנָי יְהוִה וַתִּהְיִי לִי:

Clusters of grapes in a vineyard near *Beit Shemesh*

15:6 Like the wood of the grapevine among the trees of the forest Grapes are one of the seven special agricultural products of *Eretz Yisrael*, and they can teach us a vital life lesson. Contemporary author Rabbi Natan Slifkin explains that grapes must be totally crushed, either underfoot or in a press, to produce valuable wine. He states, "The same is true of the righteous. The difficult question of how bad things can happen to good people is partially resolved through realizing that it is precisely through trials of suffering that latent potential is brought to fruition." In this prophecy, *Yechezkel* promises that the inhabitants of *Yerushalayim* will be destroyed just as a vine that no longer produces grapes is burned for fuel. The message of the grape, however, is that the suffering and hardships are not intended merely as punishments. Rather, *Hashem* hopes that the pain and anguish will eventually bring out the best in them, and inspire their return to Him.

9 I bathed you in water, and washed the blood off you, and anointed you with oil.

ט וָאֶרְחָצֵךְ בַּמַּיִם וָאֶשְׁטֹף דָּמַיִךְ מֵעָלָיִךְ וָאֲסֻכֵךְ בַּשָּׁמֶן:

10 I clothed you with embroidered garments, and gave you sandals of dolphin leather to wear, and wound fine linen about your head, and dressed you in silks.

י וָאַלְבִּישֵׁךְ רִקְמָה וָאֶנְעֲלֵךְ תָּחַשׁ וָאֶחְבְּשֵׁךְ בַּשֵּׁשׁ וָאֲכַסֵּךְ מֶשִׁי:

11 I decked you out in finery and put bracelets on your arms and a chain around your neck.

יא וָאֶעְדֵּךְ עֶדִי וָאֶתְּנָה צְמִידִים עַל־יָדַיִךְ וְרָבִיד עַל־גְּרוֹנֵךְ:

12 I put a ring in your nose, and earrings in your ears, and a splendid crown on your head.

יב וָאֶתֵּן נֶזֶם עַל־אַפֵּךְ וַעֲגִילִים עַל־אָזְנָיִךְ וַעֲטֶרֶת תִּפְאֶרֶת בְּרֹאשֵׁךְ:

13 You adorned yourself with gold and silver, and your apparel was of fine linen, silk, and embroidery. Your food was choice flour, honey, and oil. You grew more and more beautiful, and became fit for royalty.

יג וַתַּעְדִּי זָהָב וָכֶסֶף וּמַלְבּוּשֵׁךְ שֵׁשִׁי [שֵׁשׁ] וָמֶשִׁי וְרִקְמָה סֹלֶת וּדְבַשׁ וָשֶׁמֶן אכלתי [אָכָלְתְּ] וַתִּיפִי בִּמְאֹד מְאֹד וַתִּצְלְחִי לִמְלוּכָה:

14 Your beauty won you fame among the nations, for it was perfected through the splendor which I set upon you – declares *Hashem*.

יד וַיֵּצֵא לָךְ שֵׁם בַּגּוֹיִם בְּיָפְיֵךְ כִּי כָּלִיל הוּא בַּהֲדָרִי אֲשֶׁר־שַׂמְתִּי עָלַיִךְ נְאֻם אֲדֹנָי יְהוִֹה:

15 But confident in your beauty and fame, you played the harlot: you lavished your favors on every passerby; they were his.

טו וַתִּבְטְחִי בְיָפְיֵךְ וַתִּזְנִי עַל־שְׁמֵךְ וַתִּשְׁפְּכִי אֶת־תַּזְנוּתַיִךְ עַל־כָּל־עוֹבֵר לוֹ־יֶהִי:

16 You even took some of your cloths and made yourself tapestried platforms and fornicated on them – not in the future; not in time to come.

טז וַתִּקְחִי מִבְּגָדַיִךְ וַתַּעֲשִׂי־לָךְ בָּמוֹת טְלֻאוֹת וַתִּזְנִי עֲלֵיהֶם לֹא בָאוֹת וְלֹא יִהְיֶה:

17 You took your beautiful things, made of the gold and silver that I had given you, and you made yourself phallic images and fornicated with them.

יז וַתִּקְחִי כְּלֵי תִפְאַרְתֵּךְ מִזְּהָבִי וּמִכַּסְפִּי אֲשֶׁר נָתַתִּי לָךְ וַתַּעֲשִׂי־לָךְ צַלְמֵי זָכָר וַתִּזְנִי־בָם:

18 You took your embroidered cloths to cover them; and you set My oil and My incense before them.

יח וַתִּקְחִי אֶת־בִּגְדֵי רִקְמָתֵךְ וַתְּכַסִּים וְשַׁמְנִי וּקְטָרְתִּי נתתי [נָתַתְּ] לִפְנֵיהֶם:

19 The food that I had given you – the choice flour, the oil, and the honey, which I had provided for you to eat – you set it before them for a pleasing odor. And so it went – declares *Hashem*.

יט וְלַחְמִי אֲשֶׁר־נָתַתִּי לָךְ סֹלֶת וָשֶׁמֶן וּדְבַשׁ הֶאֱכַלְתִּיךְ וּנְתַתִּיהוּ לִפְנֵיהֶם לְרֵיחַ נִיחֹחַ וַיֶּהִי נְאֻם אֲדֹנָי יְהוִֹה:

20 You even took the sons and daughters that you bore to Me and sacrificed them to those [images] as food – as if your harlotries were not enough,

כ וַתִּקְחִי אֶת־בָּנַיִךְ וְאֶת־בְּנוֹתַיִךְ אֲשֶׁר יָלַדְתְּ לִי וַתִּזְבָּחִים לָהֶם לֶאֱכוֹל הַמְעַט מתזנותך [מִתַּזְנוּתָיִךְ]:

21 you slaughtered My children and presented them as offerings to them!

כא וַתִּשְׁחֲטִי אֶת־בָּנָי וַתִּתְּנִים בְּהַעֲבִיר אוֹתָם לָהֶם:

22 In all your abominations and harlotries, you did not remember the days of your youth, when you were naked and bare, and lay wallowing in your blood.

כב וְאֵת כָּל־תּוֹעֲבֹתַיִךְ וְתַזְנֻתַיִךְ לֹא זָכַרְתִּי [זָכַרְתְּ] אֶת־יְמֵי נְעוּרָיִךְ בִּהְיוֹתֵךְ עֵרֹם וְעֶרְיָה מִתְבּוֹסֶסֶת בְּדָמֵךְ הָיִית:

Ezekiel

23 After all your wickedness (woe, woe to
you!) – declares *Hashem* –

כג וַיְהִי אַחֲרֵי כָּל־רָעָתֵךְ אוֹי אוֹי לָךְ נְאֻם
אֲדֹנָי יֱהֹוִה:

24 you built yourself an eminence and made yourself a
mound in every square.

כד וַתִּבְנִי־לָךְ גֶּב וַתַּעֲשִׂי־לָךְ רָמָה בְּכָל־
רְחוֹב:

25 You built your mound at every crossroad; and you
sullied your beauty and spread your legs to every
passerby, and you multiplied your harlotries.

כה אֶל־כָּל־רֹאשׁ דֶּרֶךְ בָּנִית רָמָתֵךְ וַתְּתַעֲבִי
אֶת־יָפְיֵךְ וַתְּפַשְּׂקִי אֶת־רַגְלַיִךְ לְכָל־
עוֹבֵר וַתַּרְבִּי אֶת־תזנתך [תַּזְנוּתָיִךְ]:

26 You played the whore with your neighbors, the
lustful Egyptians – you multiplied your harlotries
to anger Me.

כו וַתִּזְנִי אֶל־בְּנֵי־מִצְרַיִם שְׁכֵנַיִךְ גִּדְלֵי בָשָׂר
וַתַּרְבִּי אֶת־תַּזְנֻתֵךְ לְהַכְעִיסֵנִי:

27 Now, I will stretch out My arm against you and
withhold your maintenance; and I will surrender
you to the will of your enemies, the Philistine
women, who are shocked by your lewd behavior.

כז וְהִנֵּה נָטִיתִי יָדִי עָלַיִךְ וָאֶגְרַע חֻקֵּךְ
וָאֶתְּנֵךְ בְּנֶפֶשׁ שֹׂנְאוֹתַיִךְ בְּנוֹת פְּלִשְׁתִּים
הַנִּכְלָמוֹת מִדַּרְכֵּךְ זִמָּה:

28 In your insatiable lust you also played the whore
with the Assyrians; you played the whore with
them, but were still unsated.

כח וַתִּזְנִי אֶל־בְּנֵי אַשּׁוּר מִבִּלְתִּי שָׂבְעָתֵךְ
וַתִּזְנִים וְגַם לֹא שָׂבָעַתְּ:

29 You multiplied your harlotries with Chaldea, that
land of traders; yet even with this you were not
satisfied.

כט וַתַּרְבִּי אֶת־תַּזְנוּתֵךְ אֶל־אֶרֶץ כְּנַעַן
כַּשְׂדִּימָה וְגַם־בְּזֹאת לֹא שָׂבָעַתְּ:

30 How sick was your heart – declares *Hashem* – when
you did all those things, the acts of a self-willed
whore,

ל מָה אֲמֻלָה לִבָּתֵךְ נְאֻם אֲדֹנָי יֱהֹוִה
בַּעֲשׂוֹתֵךְ אֶת־כָּל־אֵלֶּה מַעֲשֵׂה אִשָּׁה־
זוֹנָה שַׁלָּטֶת:

31 building your eminence at every crossroad and
setting your mound in every square! Yet you were
not like a prostitute, for you spurned fees;

לא בִּבְנוֹתַיִךְ גַּבֵּךְ בְּרֹאשׁ כָּל־דֶּרֶךְ וְרָמָתֵךְ
עשיתי [עָשִׂית] בְּכָל־רְחוֹב וְלֹא־הָיִיתִי
[הָיִית] כַּזּוֹנָה לְקַלֵּס אֶתְנָן:

32 [you were like] the adulterous wife who welcomes
strangers instead of her husband.

לב הָאִשָּׁה הַמְּנָאָפֶת תַּחַת אִישָׁהּ תִּקַּח
אֶת־זָרִים:

33 Gifts are made to all prostitutes, but you made gifts
to all your lovers, and bribed them to come to you
from every quarter for your harlotries.

לג לְכָל־זֹנוֹת יִתְּנוּ־נֵדֶה וְאַתְּ נָתַתְּ אֶת־
נְדָנַיִךְ לְכָל־מְאַהֲבַיִךְ וַתִּשְׁחֳדִי אוֹתָם
לָבוֹא אֵלַיִךְ מִסָּבִיב בְּתַזְנוּתָיִךְ:

34 You were the opposite of other women: you
solicited instead of being solicited; you paid fees
instead of being paid fees. Thus you were just the
opposite!

לד וַיְהִי־בָךְ הֵפֶךְ מִן־הַנָּשִׁים בְּתַזְנוּתַיִךְ
וְאַחֲרַיִךְ לֹא זוּנָּה וּבְתִתֵּךְ אֶתְנָן וְאֶתְנַן
לֹא נִתַּן־לָךְ וַתְּהִי לְהֶפֶךְ:

35 Now, O harlot, hear the word of *Hashem*.

לה לָכֵן זוֹנָה שִׁמְעִי דְּבַר־יְהֹוָה:

36 Thus said *Hashem*: Because of your brazen
effrontery, offering your nakedness to your lovers
for harlotry – just like the blood of your children,
which you gave to all your abominable fetishes: –

לו כֹּה־אָמַר אֲדֹנָי יֱהֹוִה יַעַן הִשָּׁפֵךְ נְחֻשְׁתֵּךְ
וַתִּגָּלֶה עֶרְוָתֵךְ בְּתַזְנוּתַיִךְ עַל־מְאַהֲבָיִךְ
וְעַל כָּל־גִּלּוּלֵי תוֹעֲבוֹתַיִךְ וְכִדְמֵי בָנַיִךְ
אֲשֶׁר נָתַתְּ לָהֶם:

37 I will assuredly assemble all the lovers to whom you gave your favors, along with everybody you accepted and everybody you rejected. I will assemble them against you from every quarter, and I will expose your nakedness to them, and they shall see all your nakedness.

לז לָכֵן הִנְנִי מְקַבֵּץ אֶת־כָּל־מְאַהֲבַיִךְ אֲשֶׁר עָרַבְתְּ עֲלֵיהֶם וְאֵת כָּל־אֲשֶׁר אָהַבְתְּ עַל כָּל־אֲשֶׁר שָׂנֵאת וְקִבַּצְתִּי אֹתָם עָלַיִךְ מִסָּבִיב וְגִלֵּיתִי עֶרְוָתֵךְ אֲלֵהֶם וְרָאוּ אֶת־כָּל־עֶרְוָתֵךְ:

38 I will inflict upon you the punishment of women who commit adultery and murder, and I will direct bloody and impassioned fury against you.

לח וּשְׁפַטְתִּיךְ מִשְׁפְּטֵי נֹאֲפוֹת וְשֹׁפְכֹת דָּם וּנְתַתִּיךְ דַּם חֵמָה וְקִנְאָה:

39 I will deliver you into their hands, and they shall tear down your eminence and level your mounds; and they shall strip you of your clothing and take away your dazzling jewels, leaving you naked and bare.

לט וְנָתַתִּי אוֹתָךְ בְּיָדָם וְהָרְסוּ גַבֵּךְ וְנִתְּצוּ רָמֹתַיִךְ וְהִפְשִׁיטוּ אוֹתָךְ בְּגָדַיִךְ וְלָקְחוּ כְּלֵי תִפְאַרְתֵּךְ וְהִנִּיחוּךְ עֵירֹם וְעֶרְיָה:

40 Then they shall assemble a mob against you to pelt you with stones and pierce you with their swords.

מ וְהֶעֱלוּ עָלַיִךְ קָהָל וְרָגְמוּ אוֹתָךְ בָּאָבֶן וּבִתְּקוּךְ בְּחַרְבוֹתָם:

41 They shall put your houses to the flames and execute punishment upon you in the sight of many women; thus I will put a stop to your harlotry, and you shall pay no more fees.

מא וְשָׂרְפוּ בָתַּיִךְ בָּאֵשׁ וְעָשׂוּ־בָךְ שְׁפָטִים לְעֵינֵי נָשִׁים רַבּוֹת וְהִשְׁבַּתִּיךְ מִזּוֹנָה וְגַם־אֶתְנַן לֹא תִתְּנִי־עוֹד:

42 When I have satisfied My fury upon you and My rage has departed from you, then I will be tranquil; I will be angry no more.

מב וַהֲנִחֹתִי חֲמָתִי בָּךְ וְסָרָה קִנְאָתִי מִמֵּךְ וְשָׁקַטְתִּי וְלֹא אֶכְעַס עוֹד:

43 Because you did not remember the days of your youth, but infuriated Me with all those things, I will pay you back for your conduct – declares *Hashem*. Have you not committed depravity on top of all your other abominations?

מג יַעַן אֲשֶׁר לֹא־זָכַרְתִּי [זָכַרְתְּ] אֶת־יְמֵי נְעוּרַיִךְ וַתִּרְגְּזִי־לִי בְּכָל־אֵלֶּה וְגַם־אֲנִי הֵא דַרְכֵּךְ בְּרֹאשׁ נָתַתִּי נְאֻם אֲדֹנָי יֱהוִֹה וְלֹא עָשִׂיתִי [עָשִׂית] אֶת־הַזִּמָּה עַל כָּל־תּוֹעֲבֹתָיִךְ:

44 Why, everyone who uses proverbs applies to you the proverb "Like mother, like daughter."

מד הִנֵּה כָּל־הַמֹּשֵׁל עָלַיִךְ יִמְשֹׁל לֵאמֹר כְּאִמָּה בִּתָּהּ:

45 You are the daughter of your mother, who rejected her husband and children. And you are the sister of your sisters, who rejected their husbands and children; for you are daughters of a Hittite mother and an Amorite father.

מה בַּת־אִמֵּךְ אַתְּ גֹּעֶלֶת אִישָׁהּ וּבָנֶיהָ וַאֲחוֹת אֲחוֹתֵךְ אַתְּ אֲשֶׁר גָּעֲלוּ אַנְשֵׁיהֶן וּבְנֵיהֶן אִמְּכֶן חִתִּית וַאֲבִיכֶן אֱמֹרִי:

46 Your elder sister was *Shomron*, who lived with her daughters to the north of you; your younger sister was Sodom, who lived with her daughters to the south of you.

מו וַאֲחוֹתֵךְ הַגְּדוֹלָה שֹׁמְרוֹן הִיא וּבְנוֹתֶיהָ הַיּוֹשֶׁבֶת עַל־שְׂמֹאולֵךְ וַאֲחוֹתֵךְ הַקְּטַנָּה מִמֵּךְ הַיּוֹשֶׁבֶת מִימִינֵךְ סְדֹם וּבְנוֹתֶיהָ:

47 Did you not walk in their ways and practice their abominations? Why, you were almost more corrupt than they in all your ways.

מז וְלֹא בְדַרְכֵיהֶן הָלַכְתְּ וּבְתוֹעֲבוֹתֵיהֶן עָשִׂיתִי [עָשִׂית] כִּמְעַט קָט וַתַּשְׁחִתִי מֵהֵן בְּכָל־דְּרָכָיִךְ:

⁴⁸ As I live – declares *Hashem* – your sister Sodom and her daughters did not do what you and your daughters did.

מח חַי־אָנִי נְאֻם אֲדֹנָי יֱהֹוִה אִם־עָשְׂתָה סְדֹם אֲחוֹתֵךְ הִיא וּבְנוֹתֶיהָ כַּאֲשֶׁר עָשִׂית אַתְּ וּבְנוֹתָיִךְ:

⁴⁹ Only this was the sin of your sister Sodom: arrogance! She and her daughters had plenty of bread and untroubled tranquillity; yet she did not support the poor and the needy.

מט הִנֵּה־זֶה הָיָה עֲוֺן סְדֹם אֲחוֹתֵךְ גָּאוֹן שִׂבְעַת־לֶחֶם וְשַׁלְוַת הַשְׁקֵט הָיָה לָהּ וְלִבְנוֹתֶיהָ וְיַד־עָנִי וְאֶבְיוֹן לֹא הֶחֱזִיקָה:

⁵⁰ In their haughtiness, they committed abomination before Me; and so I removed them, as you saw.

נ וַתִּגְבְּהֶינָה וַתַּעֲשֶׂינָה תוֹעֵבָה לְפָנָי וָאָסִיר אֶתְהֶן כַּאֲשֶׁר רָאִיתִי:

⁵¹ Nor did *Shomron* commit even half your sins. You committed more abominations than they, and by all the abominations that you committed you made your sisters look righteous.

נא וְשֹׁמְרוֹן כַּחֲצִי חַטֹּאתַיִךְ לֹא חָטָאָה וַתַּרְבִּי אֶת־תּוֹעֲבוֹתַיִךְ מֵהֵנָּה וַתְּצַדְּקִי אֶת־אֲחוֹתֵךְ [אֲחוֹתַיִךְ] בְּכָל־תּוֹעֲבוֹתַיִךְ אֲשֶׁר עָשִׂיתי [עָשִׂית:]

⁵² Truly, you must bear the disgrace of serving as your sisters' advocate: Since you have sinned more abominably than they, they appear righteous in comparison. So be ashamed and bear your disgrace, because you have made your sisters look righteous.

נב גַּם־אַתְּ שְׂאִי כְלִמָּתֵךְ אֲשֶׁר פִּלַּלְתְּ לַאֲחוֹתֵךְ בְּחַטֹּאתַיִךְ אֲשֶׁר־הִתְעַבְתְּ מֵהֵן תִּצְדַּקְנָה מִמֵּךְ וְגַם־אַתְּ בּוֹשִׁי וּשְׂאִי כְלִמָּתֵךְ בְּצַדֶּקְתֵּךְ אַחְיוֹתֵךְ:

⁵³ I will restore their fortunes – the fortunes of Sodom and her daughters and the fortunes of *Shomron* and her daughters – and your fortunes along with theirs.

נג וְשַׁבְתִּי אֶת־שְׁבִיתְהֶן אֶת־שְׁבִית [שְׁבוּת] סְדֹם וּבְנוֹתֶיהָ וְאֶת־שְׁבִית [שְׁבוּת] שֹׁמְרוֹן וּבְנוֹתֶיהָ וּשְׁבִית [וּשְׁבוּת] שְׁבִיתַיִךְ בְּתוֹכָהְנָה:

⁵⁴ Thus you shall bear your disgrace and feel your disgrace for behaving in such a way that they could take comfort.

נד לְמַעַן תִּשְׂאִי כְלִמָּתֵךְ וְנִכְלַמְתְּ מִכֹּל אֲשֶׁר עָשִׂית בְּנַחֲמֵךְ אֹתָן:

⁵⁵ Then your sister Sodom and her daughters shall return to their former state, and *Shomron* and her daughters shall return to their former state, and you and your daughters shall return to your former state.

נה וַאֲחוֹתַיִךְ סְדֹם וּבְנוֹתֶיהָ תָּשֹׁבְןָ לְקַדְמָתָן וְשֹׁמְרוֹן וּבְנוֹתֶיהָ תָּשֹׁבְןָ לְקַדְמָתָן וְאַתְּ וּבְנוֹתַיִךְ תְּשֻׁבֶינָה לְקַדְמַתְכֶן:

⁵⁶ Was not your sister Sodom a byword in your mouth in the days of your pride,

נו וְלוֹא הָיְתָה סְדֹם אֲחוֹתֵךְ לִשְׁמוּעָה בְּפִיךְ בְּיוֹם גְּאוֹנָיִךְ:

⁵⁷ before your own wickedness was exposed? So must you now bear the mockery of the daughters of Aram and all her neighbors, the daughters of Philistia who jeer at you on every side.

נז בְּטֶרֶם תִּגָּלֶה רָעָתֵךְ כְּמוֹ עֵת חֶרְפַּת בְּנוֹת־אֲרָם וְכָל־סְבִיבוֹתֶיהָ בְּנוֹת פְּלִשְׁתִּים הַשָּׁאטוֹת אוֹתָךְ מִסָּבִיב:

⁵⁸ You yourself must bear your depravity and your abominations – declares *Hashem*.

נח אֶת־זִמָּתֵךְ וְאֶת־תּוֹעֲבוֹתַיִךְ אַתְּ נְשָׂאתִים נְאֻם יְהֹוָה:

⁵⁹ Truly, thus said *Hashem*: I will deal with you as you have dealt, for you have spurned the pact and violated the covenant.

נט כִּי כֹה אָמַר אֲדֹנָי יֱהֹוִה וְעָשִׂית [וְעָשִׂיתי] אוֹתָךְ כַּאֲשֶׁר עָשִׂית אֲשֶׁר־בָּזִית אָלָה לְהָפֵר בְּרִית:

Ezekiel

60 Nevertheless, I will remember the covenant I made with you in the days of your youth, and I will establish it with you as an everlasting covenant.

ס וְזָכַרְתִּי אֲנִי אֶת־בְּרִיתִי אוֹתָךְ בִּימֵי נְעוּרָיִךְ וַהֲקִמוֹתִי לָךְ בְּרִית עוֹלָם:

v'-za-khar-TEE a-NEE et b'-ree-TEE o-TAKH bee-MAY
n'-u-RA-yikh va-ha-kee-mo-TEE LAKH b'-REET o-LAM

61 You shall remember your ways and feel ashamed, when you receive your older sisters and your younger sisters, and I give them to you as daughters, though they are not of your covenant.

סא וְזָכַרְתְּ אֶת־דְּרָכַיִךְ וְנִכְלַמְתְּ בְּקַחְתֵּךְ אֶת־אֲחוֹתַיִךְ הַגְּדֹלוֹת מִמֵּךְ אֶל־הַקְּטַנּוֹת מִמֵּךְ וְנָתַתִּי אֶתְהֶן לָךְ לְבָנוֹת וְלֹא מִבְּרִיתֵךְ:

62 I will establish My covenant with you, and you shall know that I am *Hashem*.

סב וַהֲקִימוֹתִי אֲנִי אֶת־בְּרִיתִי אִתָּךְ וְיָדַעַתְּ כִּי־אֲנִי יהוה:

63 Thus you shall remember and feel shame, and you shall be too abashed to open your mouth again, when I have forgiven you for all that you did – declares *Hashem*.

סג לְמַעַן תִּזְכְּרִי וָבֹשְׁתְּ וְלֹא יִהְיֶה־לָּךְ עוֹד פִּתְחוֹן פֶּה מִפְּנֵי כְּלִמָּתֵךְ בְּכַפְּרִי־לָךְ לְכָל־אֲשֶׁר עָשִׂית נְאֻם אֲדֹנָי יהוה:

17 1 The word of *Hashem* came to me:

יז א וַיְהִי דְבַר־יהוה אֵלַי לֵאמֹר:

2 O mortal, propound a riddle and relate an allegory to the House of *Yisrael*.

ב בֶּן־אָדָם חוּד חִידָה וּמְשֹׁל מָשָׁל אֶל־בֵּית יִשְׂרָאֵל:

3 Say: Thus said *Hashem*: The great eagle with the great wings and the long pinions, with the full plumage and the brilliant colors, came to the Lebanon range and seized the top of the cedar.

ג וְאָמַרְתָּ כֹּה־אָמַר אֲדֹנָי יהוה הַנֶּשֶׁר הַגָּדוֹל גְּדוֹל הַכְּנָפַיִם אֶרֶךְ הָאֵבֶר מָלֵא הַנּוֹצָה אֲשֶׁר־לוֹ הָרִקְמָה בָּא אֶל־הַלְּבָנוֹן וַיִּקַּח אֶת־צַמֶּרֶת הָאָרֶז:

4 He plucked off its topmost bough and carried it off to the land of traders and set it in a city of merchants.

ד אֵת רֹאשׁ יְנִיקוֹתָיו קָטָף וַיְבִיאֵהוּ אֶל־אֶרֶץ כְּנַעַן בְּעִיר רֹכְלִים שָׂמוֹ:

5 He then took some of the seed of the land and planted it in a fertile field; he planted and set it like a willow beside abundant waters.

ה וַיִּקַּח מִזֶּרַע הָאָרֶץ וַיִּתְּנֵהוּ בִּשְׂדֵה־זָרַע קָח עַל־מַיִם רַבִּים צַפְצָפָה שָׂמוֹ:

6 It grew and became a spreading vine of low stature; it became a vine, produced branches, and sent out boughs. [He had intended] that its twigs should turn to him, and that its roots should stay under him.

ו וַיִּצְמַח וַיְהִי לְגֶפֶן סֹרַחַת שִׁפְלַת קוֹמָה לִפְנוֹת דָּלִיּוֹתָיו אֵלָיו וְשָׁרָשָׁיו תַּחְתָּיו יִהְיוּ וַתְּהִי לְגֶפֶן וַתַּעַשׂ בַּדִּים וַתְּשַׁלַּח פֹּארוֹת:

16:60 I will establish it with you as an everlasting covenant This chapter is *Yechezkel's* longest. To explain the unfolding tragedy of destruction and exile, *Yechezkel* employs another metaphor, portraying Israel as a baby abandoned in the wilderness. Ignored by most, a kind passerby picks her up, protects her and cares for her. Upon her reaching the age of maturity, he marries her. Nevertheless, despite his dedication and affection, the young woman becomes unfaithful. Such has been the relationship between the People of Israel and *Hashem*. He saved them from slavery, cared for them and protected them in the desert, entered into a covenant with them at Mount Sinai and brought them to their own land. In return, though, they betrayed Him and abandoned Him, favoring other gods over their own. Unlike mortal man, however, God does not change His mind. He promises that He will renew His relationship with them in an "everlasting covenant" and return them to their land.

A wedding canopy in *Yerushalayim*

7 But there was another great eagle with great wings and full plumage; and this vine now bent its roots in his direction and sent out its twigs toward him, that he might water it more than the bed where it was planted –

ז וַיְהִי נֶשֶׁר־אֶחָד גָּדוֹל גְּדוֹל כְּנָפַיִם וְרַב־נוֹצָה וְהִנֵּה הַגֶּפֶן הַזֹּאת כָּפְנָה שָׁרָשֶׁיהָ עָלָיו וְדָלִיּוֹתָיו שִׁלְחָה־לּוֹ לְהַשְׁקוֹת אוֹתָהּ מֵעֲרֻגוֹת מַטָּעָהּ:

8 though it was planted in rich soil beside abundant water – so that it might grow branches and produce boughs and be a noble vine.

ח אֶל־שָׂדֶה טּוֹב אֶל־מַיִם רַבִּים הִיא שְׁתוּלָה לַעֲשׂוֹת עָנָף וְלָשֵׂאת פֶּרִי לִהְיוֹת לְגֶפֶן אַדָּרֶת:

9 Say: Thus said *Hashem*: Will it thrive? Will he not tear out its roots and rip off its crown, so that its entire foliage withers? It shall wither, despite any strong arm or mighty army [that may come] to remove it from its roots.

ט אֱמֹר כֹּה אָמַר אֲדֹנָי יֱהֹוִה תִּצְלָח הֲלוֹא אֶת־שָׁרָשֶׁיהָ יְנַתֵּק וְאֶת־פִּרְיָהּ יְקוֹסֵס וְיָבֵשׁ כָּל־טַרְפֵּי צִמְחָהּ תִּיבָשׁ וְלֹא־בִזְרֹעַ גְּדוֹלָה וּבְעַם־רָב לְמַשְׂאוֹת אוֹתָהּ מִשָּׁרָשֶׁיהָ:

10 And suppose it is transplanted, will it thrive? When the east wind strikes it, it shall wither – wither upon the bed where it is growing.

י וְהִנֵּה שְׁתוּלָה הֲתִצְלָח הֲלוֹא כְגַעַת בָּהּ רוּחַ הַקָּדִים תִּיבַשׁ יָבֹשׁ עַל־עֲרֻגֹת צִמְחָהּ תִּיבָשׁ:

11 Then the word of *Hashem* came to me:

יא וַיְהִי דְבַר־יְהֹוָה אֵלַי לֵאמֹר:

12 Say to the rebellious breed: Do you not know what these things mean? Say: The king of Babylon came to *Yerushalayim*, and carried away its king and its officers and brought them back with him to Babylon.

יב אֱמָר־נָא לְבֵית הַמֶּרִי הֲלֹא יְדַעְתֶּם מָה־אֵלֶּה אֱמֹר הִנֵּה־בָא מֶלֶךְ־בָּבֶל יְרוּשָׁלִַם וַיִּקַּח אֶת־מַלְכָּהּ וְאֶת־שָׂרֶיהָ וַיָּבֵא אוֹתָם אֵלָיו בָּבֶלָה:

13 He took one of the seed royal and made a covenant with him and imposed an oath on him, and he carried away the nobles of the land –

יג וַיִּקַּח מִזֶּרַע הַמְּלוּכָה וַיִּכְרֹת אִתּוֹ בְּרִית וַיָּבֵא אֹתוֹ בְּאָלָה וְאֶת־אֵילֵי הָאָרֶץ לָקָח:

14 so that it might be a humble kingdom and not exalt itself, but keep his covenant and so endure.

יד לִהְיוֹת מַמְלָכָה שְׁפָלָה לְבִלְתִּי הִתְנַשֵּׂא לִשְׁמֹר אֶת־בְּרִיתוֹ לְעָמְדָהּ:

15 But [that prince] rebelled against him and sent his envoys to Egypt to get horses and a large army. Will he succeed? Will he who does such things escape? Shall he break a covenant and escape?

טו וַיִּמְרָד־בּוֹ לִשְׁלֹחַ מַלְאָכָיו מִצְרַיִם לָתֶת־לוֹ סוּסִים וְעַם־רָב הֲיִצְלָח הֲיִמָּלֵט הָעֹשֵׂה אֵלֶּה וְהֵפֵר בְּרִית וְנִמְלָט:

16 As I live – declares *Hashem* – in the very homeland of the king who made him king, whose oath he flouted and whose covenant he broke – right there, in Babylon, he shall die.

טז חַי־אָנִי נְאֻם אֲדֹנָי יֱהֹוִה אִם־לֹא בִּמְקוֹם הַמֶּלֶךְ הַמַּמְלִיךְ אֹתוֹ אֲשֶׁר בָּזָה אֶת־אָלָתוֹ וַאֲשֶׁר הֵפֵר אֶת־בְּרִיתוֹ אִתּוֹ בְתוֹךְ־בָּבֶל יָמוּת:

17 Pharaoh will not fight at his side with a great army and with numerous troops in the war, when mounds are thrown up and siege towers erected to destroy many lives.

יז וְלֹא בְחַיִל גָּדוֹל וּבְקָהָל רָב יַעֲשֶׂה אוֹתוֹ פַרְעֹה בַּמִּלְחָמָה בִּשְׁפֹּךְ סֹלְלָה וּבִבְנוֹת דָּיֵק לְהַכְרִית נְפָשׁוֹת רַבּוֹת:

18 He flouted a pact and broke a covenant; he gave his promise and did all these things – he shall not escape.

יח וּבָזָה אָלָה לְהָפֵר בְּרִית וְהִנֵּה נָתַן יָדוֹ וְכָל־אֵלֶּה עָשָׂה לֹא יִמָּלֵט:

19 Assuredly, thus said *Hashem*: As I live, I will pay him back for flouting My pact and breaking My covenant.

לָכֵן כֹּה־אָמַר אֲדֹנָי יֱהֹוִה חַי־אָנִי אִם־לֹא אָלָתִי אֲשֶׁר בָּזָה וּבְרִיתִי אֲשֶׁר הֵפִיר וּנְתַתִּיו בְּרֹאשׁוֹ: ט

20 I will spread My net over him and he shall be caught in My snare; I will carry him to Babylon and enter with him into judgment there for the trespass which he committed against Me.

וּפָרַשְׂתִּי עָלָיו רִשְׁתִּי וְנִתְפַּשׂ בִּמְצוּדָתִי וַהֲבִיאוֹתִיהוּ בָבֶלָה וְנִשְׁפַּטְתִּי אִתּוֹ שָׁם מַעֲלוֹ אֲשֶׁר מָעַל־בִּי: כ

21 And all the fugitives of all his battalions shall fall by the sword, and those who remain shall scatter in every direction; then you will know that I *Hashem* have spoken.

וְאֵת כָּל־מִבְרָחוֹ [מִבְרָחָיו] בְּכָל־אֲגַפָּיו בַּחֶרֶב יִפֹּלוּ וְהַנִּשְׁאָרִים לְכָל־רוּחַ יִפָּרֵשׂוּ וִידַעְתֶּם כִּי אֲנִי יְהֹוָה דִּבַּרְתִּי: כא

22 Thus said *Hashem*: Then I in turn will take and set [in the ground a slip] from the lofty top of the cedar; I will pluck a tender twig from the tip of its crown, and I will plant it on a tall, towering mountain.

כֹּה אָמַר אֲדֹנָי יֱהֹוִה וְלָקַחְתִּי אָנִי מִצַּמֶּרֶת הָאֶרֶז הָרָמָה וְנָתָתִּי מֵרֹאשׁ יֹנְקוֹתָיו רַךְ אֶקְטֹף וְשָׁתַלְתִּי אָנִי עַל הַר־גָּבֹהַ וְתָלוּל: כב

23 I will plant it in *Yisrael*'s lofty highlands, and it shall bring forth boughs and produce branches and grow into a noble cedar. Every bird of every feather shall take shelter under it, shelter in the shade of its boughs.

בְּהַר מְרוֹם יִשְׂרָאֵל אֶשְׁתֳּלֶנּוּ וְנָשָׂא עָנָף וְעָשָׂה פֶרִי וְהָיָה לְאֶרֶז אַדִּיר וְשָׁכְנוּ תַחְתָּיו כֹּל צִפּוֹר כָּל־כָּנָף בְּצֵל דָּלִיּוֹתָיו תִּשְׁכֹּנָה: כג

*b'-HAR m'-ROM yis-ra-AYL esh-to-LE-nu v'-na-SA a-NAF v'-A-sah
FE-ree v'-ha-YAH l'-E-rez a-DEER v'-sha-kh'-NU takh-TAV KOL
tzi-POR kol ka-NAF b'-TZAYL da-li-yo-TAV tish-KO-nah*

24 Then shall all the trees of the field know that it is I *Hashem* who have abased the lofty tree and exalted the lowly tree, who have dried up the green tree and made the withered tree bud. I *Hashem* have spoken, and I will act.

וְיָדְעוּ כָּל־עֲצֵי הַשָּׂדֶה כִּי אֲנִי יְהֹוָה הִשְׁפַּלְתִּי עֵץ גָּבֹהַ הִגְבַּהְתִּי עֵץ שָׁפָל הוֹבַשְׁתִּי עֵץ לָח וְהִפְרַחְתִּי עֵץ יָבֵשׁ אֲנִי יְהֹוָה דִּבַּרְתִּי וְעָשִׂיתִי: כד

18 1 The word of *Hashem* came to me:

וַיְהִי דְבַר־יְהֹוָה אֵלַי לֵאמֹר: א **יח**

2 What do you mean by quoting this proverb upon the soil of *Yisrael*, "Parents eat sour grapes and their children's teeth are blunted"?

מַה־לָּכֶם אַתֶּם מֹשְׁלִים אֶת־הַמָּשָׁל הַזֶּה עַל־אַדְמַת יִשְׂרָאֵל לֵאמֹר אָבוֹת יֹאכְלוּ בֹסֶר וְשִׁנֵּי הַבָּנִים תִּקְהֶינָה: ב

*ma la-KHEM a-TEM mo-sh'-LEEM et ha-ma-SHAL ha-ZEH
al ad-MAT yis-ra-AYL lay-MOR a-VOT YO-kh'-lu VO-ser
v'-shi-NAY ha-ba-NEEM tik-HE-nah*

The Hoopoe, Israel's national bird

17:23 Every bird of every feather shall take shelter under it *Yechezkel* reverses the negative prophecies and includes a vision of hope. Referring to *Mashiach*, he describes a small cedar shoot which will be restored to the high mountain of *Yerushalayim*. This tree will grow, bear fruit, and provide protection for all those who seek it. *Yechezkel* is teaching that in the time of redemption, not only will Israel seek out *Hashem*, but all the nations of the world will travel to *Yerushalayim* to seek Israel's friendship and to acknowledge God's sovereignty.

³ As I live – declares *Hashem* – this proverb shall no longer be current among you in *Yisrael*.

ג חַי־אָ֫נִי נְאֻם֙ אֲדֹנָ֣י יְהֹוִ֔ה אִם־יִֽהְיֶ֥ה לָכֶ֛ם ע֥וֹד מְשֹׁ֖ל הַמָּשָׁ֣ל הַזֶּ֑ה בְּיִשְׂרָאֵֽל׃

⁴ Consider, all lives are Mine; the life of the parent and the life of the child are both Mine. The person who sins, only he shall die.

ד הֵ֤ן כׇּל־הַנְּפָשׁוֹת֙ לִ֣י הֵ֔נָּה כְּנֶ֧פֶשׁ הָאָ֛ב וּכְנֶ֥פֶשׁ הַבֵּ֖ן לִי־הֵ֑נָּה הַנֶּ֥פֶשׁ הַחֹטֵ֖את הִ֥יא תָמֽוּת׃

⁵ Thus, if a man is righteous and does what is just and right:

ה וְאִ֖ישׁ כִּי־יִֽהְיֶ֣ה צַדִּ֑יק וְעָשָׂ֥ה מִשְׁפָּ֖ט וּצְדָקָֽה׃

⁶ If he has not eaten on the mountains or raised his eyes to the fetishes of the House of *Yisrael*; if he has not defiled another man's wife or approached a menstruous woman;

ו אֶל־הֶֽהָרִים֙ לֹ֣א אָכָ֔ל וְעֵינָיו֙ לֹ֣א נָשָׂ֔א אֶל־גִּלּוּלֵ֖י בֵּ֣ית יִשְׂרָאֵ֑ל וְאֶת־אֵ֤שֶׁת רֵעֵ֙הוּ֙ לֹ֣א טִמֵּ֔א וְאֶל־אִשָּׁ֥ה נִדָּ֖ה לֹ֥א יִקְרָֽב׃

⁷ if he has not wronged anyone; if he has returned the debtor's pledge to him and has taken nothing by robbery; if he has given bread to the hungry and clothed the naked;

ז וְאִישׁ֙ לֹ֣א יוֹנֶ֔ה חֲבֹלָת֥וֹ חוֹב֙ יָשִׁ֔יב גְּזֵלָ֖ה לֹ֣א יִגְזֹ֑ל לַחְמוֹ֙ לְרָעֵ֣ב יִתֵּ֔ן וְעֵירֹ֖ם יְכַסֶּה־בָּֽגֶד׃

⁸ if he has not lent at advance interest or exacted accrued interest; if he has abstained from wrongdoing and executed true justice between man and man;

ח בַּנֶּ֣שֶׁךְ לֹא־יִתֵּ֗ן וְתַרְבִּית֙ לֹ֣א יִקָּ֔ח מֵעָ֖וֶל יָשִׁ֣יב יָד֑וֹ מִשְׁפַּ֤ט אֱמֶת֙ יַֽעֲשֶׂ֔ה בֵּ֥ין אִ֖ישׁ לְאִֽישׁ׃

⁹ if he has followed My laws and kept My rules and acted honestly – he is righteous. Such a man shall live – declares *Hashem*.

ט בְּחֻקּוֹתַ֥י יְהַלֵּ֛ךְ וּמִשְׁפָּטַ֥י שָׁמַ֖ר לַעֲשׂ֣וֹת אֱמֶ֑ת צַדִּ֥יק הוּא֙ חָיֹ֣ה יִֽחְיֶ֔ה נְאֻ֖ם אֲדֹנָ֥י יְהֹוִֽה׃

¹⁰ Suppose, now, that he has begotten a son who is a ruffian, a shedder of blood, who does any of these things,

י וְהוֹלִ֥יד בֵּן־פָּרִ֖יץ שֹׁפֵ֣ךְ דָּ֑ם וְעָ֣שָׂה אָ֔ח מֵאַחַ֖ד מֵאֵֽלֶּה׃

¹¹ whereas he himself did none of these things. That is, [the son] has eaten on the mountains, has defiled another man's wife,

יא וְה֕וּא אֶת־כׇּל־אֵ֖לֶּה לֹ֣א עָשָׂ֑ה כִּ֣י גַ֤ם אֶל־הֶֽהָרִים֙ אָכָ֔ל וְאֶת־אֵ֥שֶׁת רֵעֵ֖הוּ טִמֵּֽא׃

¹² has wronged the poor and the needy, has taken by robbery, has not returned a pledge, has raised his eyes to the fetishes, has committed abomination,

יב עָנִ֤י וְאֶבְיוֹן֙ הוֹנָ֔ה גְּזֵל֣וֹת גָּזָ֔ל חֲבֹ֖ל לֹ֣א יָשִׁ֑יב וְאֶל־הַגִּלּוּלִים֙ נָשָׂ֣א עֵינָ֔יו תּוֹעֵבָ֖ה עָשָֽׂה׃

¹³ has lent at advance interest, or exacted accrued interest – shall he live? He shall not live! If he has committed any of these abominations, he shall die; he has forfeited his life.

יג בַּנֶּ֧שֶׁךְ נָתַ֛ן וְתַרְבִּ֥ית לָקַ֖ח וָחָ֑י לֹ֣א יִֽחְיֶ֔ה אֵ֣ת כׇּל־הַתּוֹעֵב֤וֹת הָאֵ֙לֶּה֙ עָשָׂ֔ה מ֥וֹת יוּמָ֖ת דָּמָ֥יו בּ֥וֹ יִהְיֶֽה׃

An Israeli toddler holding fresh grapes in honor of *Shavuot*

18:2 What do you mean by quoting this proverb upon the soil of *Yisrael* The sinful nation complains that they are being punished for transgressions committed by their ancestors. *Yechezkel* explains that this is inaccurate; they are being held accountable because they have continued their parents' evil deeds. The prophet specifically reprimands the people for uttering this complaint in the Land of Israel. The fallacy in the children's complaint that they are being punished for their father's sins motivates *Yechezkel* to speak, as the Holy Land cannot tolerate falsehood.

14 Now suppose that he, in turn, has begotten a son who has seen all the sins that his father committed, but has taken heed and has not imitated them:

יד וְהִנֵּה הוֹלִיד בֵּן וַיַּרְא אֶת־כָּל־חַטֹּאת אָבִיו אֲשֶׁר עָשָׂה וַיִּרְאֶה וְלֹא יַעֲשֶׂה כָּהֵן:

15 He has not eaten on the mountains or raised his eyes to the fetishes of the House of *Yisrael*; he has not defiled another man's wife;

טו עַל־הֶהָרִים לֹא אָכָל וְעֵינָיו לֹא נָשָׂא אֶל־גִּלּוּלֵי בֵּית יִשְׂרָאֵל אֶת־אֵשֶׁת רֵעֵהוּ לֹא טִמֵּא:

16 he has not wronged anyone; he has not seized a pledge or taken anything by robbery; he has given his bread to the hungry and clothed the naked;

טז וְאִישׁ לֹא הוֹנָה חֲבֹל לֹא חָבָל וּגְזֵלָה לֹא גָזָל לַחְמוֹ לְרָעֵב נָתָן וְעֵרוֹם כִּסָּה־בָגֶד:

17 he has refrained from oppressing the poor; he has not exacted advance or accrued interest; he has obeyed My rules and followed My laws – he shall not die for the iniquity of his father, but shall live.

יז מֵעָנִי הֵשִׁיב יָדוֹ נֶשֶׁךְ וְתַרְבִּית לֹא לָקָח מִשְׁפָּטַי עָשָׂה בְּחֻקּוֹתַי הָלָךְ הוּא לֹא יָמוּת בַּעֲוֹן אָבִיו חָיֹה יִחְיֶה:

18 To be sure, his father, because he practiced fraud, robbed his brother, and acted wickedly among his kin, did die for his iniquity;

יח אָבִיו כִּי־עָשַׁק עֹשֶׁק גָּזַל גֵּזֶל אָח וַאֲשֶׁר לֹא־טוֹב עָשָׂה בְּתוֹךְ עַמָּיו וְהִנֵּה־מֵת בַּעֲוֹנוֹ:

19 and now you ask, "Why has not the son shared the burden of his father's guilt?" But the son has done what is right and just, and has carefully kept all My laws: he shall live!

יט וַאֲמַרְתֶּם מַדּוּעַ לֹא־נָשָׂא הַבֵּן בַּעֲוֹן הָאָב וְהַבֵּן מִשְׁפָּט וּצְדָקָה עָשָׂה אֵת כָּל־חֻקּוֹתַי שָׁמַר וַיַּעֲשֶׂה אֹתָם חָיֹה יִחְיֶה:

20 The person who sins, he alone shall die. A child shall not share the burden of a parent's guilt, nor shall a parent share the burden of a child's guilt; the righteousness of the righteous shall be accounted to him alone, and the wickedness of the wicked shall be accounted to him alone.

כ הַנֶּפֶשׁ הַחֹטֵאת הִיא תָמוּת בֵּן לֹא־יִשָּׂא בַּעֲוֹן הָאָב וְאָב לֹא יִשָּׂא בַּעֲוֹן הַבֵּן צִדְקַת הַצַּדִּיק עָלָיו תִּהְיֶה וְרִשְׁעַת רשע [הָרָשָׁע] עָלָיו תִּהְיֶה:

21 Moreover, if the wicked one repents of all the sins that he committed and keeps all My laws and does what is just and right, he shall live; he shall not die.

כא וְהָרָשָׁע כִּי יָשׁוּב מִכָּל־חַטֹּאתוֹ [חַטֹּאתָיו] אֲשֶׁר עָשָׂה וְשָׁמַר אֶת־כָּל־חֻקּוֹתַי וְעָשָׂה מִשְׁפָּט וּצְדָקָה חָיֹה יִחְיֶה לֹא יָמוּת:

22 None of the transgressions he committed shall be remembered against him; because of the righteousness he has practiced, he shall live.

כב כָּל־פְּשָׁעָיו אֲשֶׁר עָשָׂה לֹא יִזָּכְרוּ לוֹ בְּצִדְקָתוֹ אֲשֶׁר־עָשָׂה יִחְיֶה:

23 Is it my desire that a wicked person shall die? – says *Hashem*. It is rather that he shall turn back from his ways and live.

כג הֶחָפֹץ אֶחְפֹּץ מוֹת רָשָׁע נְאֻם אֲדֹנָי יֱהֹוִה הֲלוֹא בְּשׁוּבוֹ מִדְּרָכָיו וְחָיָה:

24 So, too, if a righteous person turns away from his righteousness and does wrong, practicing the very abominations that the wicked person practiced, shall he live? None of the righteous deeds that he did shall be remembered; because of the treachery he has practiced and the sins he has committed – because of these, he shall die.

כד וּבְשׁוּב צַדִּיק מִצִּדְקָתוֹ וְעָשָׂה עָוֶל כְּכֹל הַתּוֹעֵבוֹת אֲשֶׁר־עָשָׂה הָרָשָׁע יַעֲשֶׂה וָחָי כָּל־צִדְקֹתוֹ [צִדְקֹתָיו] אֲשֶׁר־עָשָׂה לֹא תִזָּכַרְנָה בְּמַעֲלוֹ אֲשֶׁר־מָעַל וּבְחַטָּאתוֹ אֲשֶׁר־חָטָא בָּם יָמוּת:

²⁵ Yet you say, "The way of *Hashem* is unfair." Listen, O House of *Yisrael*: Is My way unfair? It is your ways that are unfair!

כה וַאֲמַרְתֶּם לֹא יִתָּכֵן דֶּרֶךְ אֲדֹנָי שִׁמְעוּ־נָא בֵּית יִשְׂרָאֵל הֲדַרְכִּי לֹא יִתָּכֵן הֲלֹא דַרְכֵיכֶם לֹא יִתָּכֵנוּ:

²⁶ When a righteous person turns away from his righteousness and does wrong, he shall die for it; he shall die for the wrong he has done.

כו בְּשׁוּב־צַדִּיק מִצִּדְקָתוֹ וְעָשָׂה עָוֶל וּמֵת עֲלֵיהֶם בְּעַוְלוֹ אֲשֶׁר־עָשָׂה יָמוּת:

²⁷ And if a wicked person turns back from the wickedness that he practiced and does what is just and right, such a person shall save his life.

כז וּבְשׁוּב רָשָׁע מֵרִשְׁעָתוֹ אֲשֶׁר עָשָׂה וַיַּעַשׂ מִשְׁפָּט וּצְדָקָה הוּא אֶת־נַפְשׁוֹ יְחַיֶּה:

²⁸ Because he took heed and turned back from all the transgressions that he committed, he shall live; he shall not die.

כח וַיִּרְאֶה וישוב [וַיָּשָׁב] מִכָּל־פְּשָׁעָיו אֲשֶׁר עָשָׂה חָיוֹ יִחְיֶה לֹא יָמוּת:

²⁹ Yet the House of *Yisrael* say, "The way of *Hashem* is unfair." Are My ways unfair, O House of *Yisrael*? It is your ways that are unfair!

כט וְאָמְרוּ בֵּית יִשְׂרָאֵל לֹא יִתָּכֵן דֶּרֶךְ אֲדֹנָי הַדְּרָכַי לֹא יִתָּכֵנוּ בֵּית יִשְׂרָאֵל הֲלֹא דַרְכֵיכֶם לֹא יִתָּכֵן:

³⁰ Be assured, O House of *Yisrael*, I will judge each one of you according to his ways – declares *Hashem*. Repent and turn back from your transgressions; let them not be a stumbling block of guilt for you.

ל לָכֵן אִישׁ כִּדְרָכָיו אֶשְׁפֹּט אֶתְכֶם בֵּית יִשְׂרָאֵל נְאֻם אֲדֹנָי יֱהוִה שׁוּבוּ וְהָשִׁיבוּ מִכָּל־פִּשְׁעֵיכֶם וְלֹא־יִהְיֶה לָכֶם לְמִכְשׁוֹל עָוֹן:

³¹ Cast away all the transgressions by which you have offended, and get yourselves a new heart and a new spirit, that you may not die, O House of *Yisrael*.

לא הַשְׁלִיכוּ מֵעֲלֵיכֶם אֶת־כָּל־פִּשְׁעֵיכֶם אֲשֶׁר פְּשַׁעְתֶּם בָּם וַעֲשׂוּ לָכֶם לֵב חָדָשׁ וְרוּחַ חֲדָשָׁה וְלָמָּה תָמֻתוּ בֵּית יִשְׂרָאֵל:

³² For it is not My desire that anyone shall die – declares *Hashem*. Repent, therefore, and live!

לב כִּי לֹא אֶחְפֹּץ בְּמוֹת הַמֵּת נְאֻם אֲדֹנָי יֱהוִה וְהָשִׁיבוּ וִחְיוּ:

19 ¹ And you are to intone a dirge over the princes of *Yisrael*,

יט א וְאַתָּה שָׂא קִינָה אֶל־נְשִׂיאֵי יִשְׂרָאֵל:

² and say: What a lioness was your mother Among the lions! Crouching among the great beasts, She reared her cubs.

ב וְאָמַרְתָּ מָה אִמְּךָ לְבִיָּא בֵּין אֲרָיוֹת רָבָצָה בְּתוֹךְ כְּפִרִים רִבְּתָה גוּרֶיהָ:

³ She raised up one of her cubs, He became a great beast; He learned to hunt prey – He devoured men.

ג וַתַּעַל אֶחָד מִגֻּרֶיהָ כְּפִיר הָיָה וַיִּלְמַד לִטְרָף־טֶרֶף אָדָם אָכָל:

⁴ Nations heeded [the call] against him; He was caught in their snare. They dragged him off with hooks To the land of Egypt.

ד וַיִּשְׁמְעוּ אֵלָיו גּוֹיִם בְּשַׁחְתָּם נִתְפָּשׂ וַיְבִאֻהוּ בַחַחִים אֶל־אֶרֶץ מִצְרָיִם:

⁵ When she saw herself frustrated, Her hope defeated, She took another of her cubs And set him up as a great beast.

ה וַתֵּרֶא כִּי נוֹחֲלָה אָבְדָה תִּקְוָתָהּ וַתִּקַּח אֶחָד מִגֻּרֶיהָ כְּפִיר שָׂמָתְהוּ:

⁶ He stalked among the lions, He was a great beast; He learned to hunt prey – He devoured men.

ו וַיִּתְהַלֵּךְ בְּתוֹךְ־אֲרָיוֹת כְּפִיר הָיָה וַיִּלְמַד לִטְרָף־טֶרֶף אָדָם אָכָל:

7 He ravished their widows, Laid waste their cities; The land and all in it were appalled At the sound of his roaring.

ז וַיֵּדַע אַלְמְנוֹתָיו וְעָרֵיהֶם הֶחֱרִיב וַתֵּשַׁם אֶרֶץ וּמְלֹאָהּ מִקּוֹל שַׁאֲגָתוֹ׃

va-YAY-da al-m'-no-TAV v'-a-ray-HEM he-khe-REEV
va-tay-SHAM E-retz um-lo-AH mi-KOL sha-a-ga-TO

8 Nations from the countries roundabout Arrayed themselves against him. They spread their net over him, He was caught in their snare.

ח וַיִּתְּנוּ עָלָיו גּוֹיִם סָבִיב מִמְּדִינוֹת וַיִּפְרְשׂוּ עָלָיו רִשְׁתָּם בְּשַׁחְתָּם נִתְפָּשׂ׃

9 With hooks he was put in a cage, They carried him off to the king of Babylon And confined him in a fortress, So that never again should his roar be heard On the hills of *Yisrael*.

ט וַיִּתְּנֻהוּ בַסּוּגַר בַּחַחִים וַיְבִאֻהוּ אֶל־מֶלֶךְ בָּבֶל יְבִאֻהוּ בַּמְּצֹדוֹת לְמַעַן לֹא־יִשָּׁמַע קוֹלוֹ עוֹד אֶל־הָרֵי יִשְׂרָאֵל׃

10 Your mother was like a vine in your blood, Planted beside streams, With luxuriant boughs and branches Thanks to abundant waters.

י אִמְּךָ כַגֶּפֶן בְּדָמְךָ עַל־מַיִם שְׁתוּלָה פֹּרִיָּה וַעֲנֵפָה הָיְתָה מִמַּיִם רַבִּים׃

11 And she had a mighty rod Fit for a ruler's scepter. It towered highest among the leafy trees, It was conspicuous by its height, By the abundance of its boughs.

יא וַיִּהְיוּ־לָהּ מַטּוֹת עֹז אֶל־שִׁבְטֵי מֹשְׁלִים וַתִּגְבַּהּ קוֹמָתוֹ עַל־בֵּין עֲבֹתִים וַיֵּרָא בְגָבְהוֹ בְּרֹב דָּלִיֹּתָיו׃

12 But plucked up in a fury, She was hurled to the ground. The east wind withered her branches, They broke apart and dried up; And her mighty rod was consumed by fire.

יב וַתֻּתַּשׁ בְּחֵמָה לָאָרֶץ הֻשְׁלָכָה וְרוּחַ הַקָּדִים הוֹבִישׁ פִּרְיָהּ הִתְפָּרְקוּ וְיָבֵשׁוּ מַטֵּה עֻזָּהּ אֵשׁ אֲכָלָתְהוּ׃

13 Now she is planted in the desert, In ground that is arid and parched.

יג וְעַתָּה שְׁתוּלָה בַמִּדְבָּר בְּאֶרֶץ צִיָּה וְצָמָא׃

14 Fire has issued from her twig-laden branch And has consumed her boughs, She is left without a mighty rod, A scepter to rule with. This is a dirge, and it has become a [familiar] dirge.

יד וַתֵּצֵא אֵשׁ מִמַּטֵּה בַדֶּיהָ פִּרְיָהּ אָכָלָה וְלֹא־הָיָה בָהּ מַטֵּה־עֹז שֵׁבֶט לִמְשׁוֹל קִינָה הִיא וַתְּהִי לְקִינָה׃

20 1 In the seventh year, on the tenth day of the fifth month, certain elders of *Yisrael* came to inquire of *Hashem*, and sat down before me.

א וַיְהִי בַּשָּׁנָה הַשְּׁבִיעִית בַּחֲמִשִׁי בֶּעָשׂוֹר לַחֹדֶשׁ בָּאוּ אֲנָשִׁים מִזִּקְנֵי יִשְׂרָאֵל לִדְרֹשׁ אֶת־יְהוָה וַיֵּשְׁבוּ לְפָנָי׃

2 And the word of *Hashem* came to me:

ב וַיְהִי דְבַר־יְהוָה אֵלַי לֵאמֹר׃

3 O mortal, speak to the elders of *Yisrael* and say to them: Thus said *Hashem*: Have you come to inquire of Me? As I live, I will not respond to your inquiry – declares *Hashem*.

ג בֶּן־אָדָם דַּבֵּר אֶת־זִקְנֵי יִשְׂרָאֵל וְאָמַרְתָּ אֲלֵהֶם כֹּה אָמַר אֲדֹנָי יְהוִה הֲלִדְרֹשׁ אֹתִי אַתֶּם בָּאִים חַי־אָנִי אִם־אִדָּרֵשׁ לָכֶם נְאֻם אֲדֹנָי יְהוִה׃

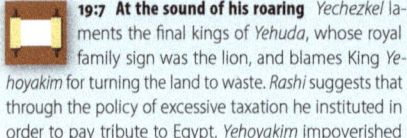

19:7 At the sound of his roaring *Yechezkel* laments the final kings of *Yehuda*, whose royal family sign was the lion, and blames King *Yehoyakim* for turning the land to waste. *Rashi* suggests that through the policy of excessive taxation he instituted in order to pay tribute to Egypt, *Yehoyakim* impoverished the cities, leading to their destruction. A leader has great responsibilities towards his people and the Kings of *Yehuda* are held accountable for impoverishing the nation.

An African lion at the Ramat Gan Safari

⁴ Arraign, arraign them, O mortal! Declare to them the abhorrent deeds of their fathers.

ד הֲתִשְׁפֹּט אֹתָם הֲתִשְׁפּוֹט בֶּן־אָדָם אֶת־תּוֹעֲבֹת אֲבוֹתָם הוֹדִיעֵם:

⁵ Say to them: Thus said *Hashem*: On the day that I chose *Yisrael*, I gave My oath to the stock of the House of *Yaakov*; when I made Myself known to them in the land of Egypt, I gave my oath to them. When I said, "I *Hashem* am your God,"

ה וְאָמַרְתָּ אֲלֵיהֶם כֹּה־אָמַר אֲדֹנָי יֱהֹוִה בְּיוֹם בׇּחֳרִי בְיִשְׂרָאֵל וָאֶשָּׂא יָדִי לְזֶרַע בֵּית יַעֲקֹב וָאִוָּדַע לָהֶם בְּאֶרֶץ מִצְרָיִם וָאֶשָּׂא יָדִי לָהֶם לֵאמֹר אֲנִי יְהֹוָה אֱלֹהֵיכֶם:

⁶ that same day I swore to them to take them out of the land of Egypt into a land flowing with milk and honey, a land which I had sought out for them, the fairest of all lands.

ו בַּיּוֹם הַהוּא נָשָׂאתִי יָדִי לָהֶם לְהוֹצִיאָם מֵאֶרֶץ מִצְרָיִם אֶל־אֶרֶץ אֲשֶׁר־תַּרְתִּי לָהֶם זָבַת חָלָב וּדְבַשׁ צְבִי הִיא לְכׇל־הָאֲרָצוֹת:

ba-YOM ha-HU na-SA-tee ya-DEE la-HEM l'-ho-tzee-AM
may-E-retz mitz-RA-yim el E-retz a-sher TAR-tee la-HEM za-VAT
kha-LAV ud-VASH tz'-VEE HEE l'-khol ha-a-ra-TZOT

⁷ I also said to them: Cast away, every one of you, the detestable things that you are drawn to, and do not defile yourselves with the fetishes of Egypt – I *Hashem* am your God.

ז וָאֹמַר אֲלֵהֶם אִישׁ שִׁקּוּצֵי עֵינָיו הַשְׁלִיכוּ וּבְגִלּוּלֵי מִצְרַיִם אַל־תִּטַּמָּאוּ אֲנִי יְהֹוָה אֱלֹהֵיכֶם:

⁸ But they defied Me and refused to listen to Me. They did not cast away the detestable things they were drawn to, nor did they give up the fetishes of Egypt. Then I resolved to pour out My fury upon them, to vent all My anger upon them there, in the land of Egypt.

ח וַיַּמְרוּ־בִי וְלֹא אָבוּ לִשְׁמֹעַ אֵלַי אִישׁ אֶת־שִׁקּוּצֵי עֵינֵיהֶם לֹא הִשְׁלִיכוּ וְאֶת־גִּלּוּלֵי מִצְרַיִם לֹא עָזָבוּ וָאֹמַר לִשְׁפֹּךְ חֲמָתִי עֲלֵיהֶם לְכַלּוֹת אַפִּי בָּהֶם בְּתוֹךְ אֶרֶץ מִצְרָיִם:

⁹ But I acted for the sake of My name, that it might not be profaned in the sight of the nations among whom they were. For it was before their eyes that I had made Myself known to *Yisrael* to bring them out of the land of Egypt.

ט וָאַעַשׂ לְמַעַן שְׁמִי לְבִלְתִּי הֵחֵל לְעֵינֵי הַגּוֹיִם אֲשֶׁר־הֵמָּה בְתוֹכָם אֲשֶׁר נוֹדַעְתִּי אֲלֵיהֶם לְעֵינֵיהֶם לְהוֹצִיאָם מֵאֶרֶץ מִצְרָיִם:

¹⁰ I brought them out of the land of Egypt and I led them into the wilderness.

י וָאוֹצִיאֵם מֵאֶרֶץ מִצְרָיִם וָאֲבִאֵם אֶל־הַמִּדְבָּר:

¹¹ I gave them My laws and taught them My rules, by the pursuit of which a man shall live.

יא וָאֶתֵּן לָהֶם אֶת־חֻקּוֹתַי וְאֶת־מִשְׁפָּטַי הוֹדַעְתִּי אוֹתָם אֲשֶׁר יַעֲשֶׂה אוֹתָם הָאָדָם וָחַי בָּהֶם:

20:6 The fairest of all lands *Eretz Yisrael* is described here as 'fair' or 'beautiful,' in Hebrew *tzvi* (צבי). The word *tzvi* also means 'gazelle,' which prompts the Talmud (*Ketubot* 112a) to compare the Land of Israel to the skin of a gazelle (see also Daniel 11:16 where the Land of Israel is referred to as *eretz ha-tzvi*, 'the beautiful land'). Just as its skin stretches to fit over the body of the gazelle but shrinks when removed, so do the physical borders of *Eretz Yisrael* stretch to fit its Jewish inhabitants, but shrink when they are exiled from the land. Perhaps a deeper message can be applied for Israel's inhabitants as well. Unlike other places in the world, the inhabitants of Israel must "stretch" themselves morally and spiritually to appreciate the holiness of the Land of the Gazelle, "the fairest of all lands."

A gazelle in the Negev dessert

12 Moreover, I gave them My *Shabbatot* to serve as a sign between Me and them, that they might know that it is I *Hashem* who sanctify them.

יב וְגַם אֶת־שַׁבְּתוֹתַי נָתַתִּי לָהֶם לִהְיוֹת לְאוֹת בֵּינִי וּבֵינֵיהֶם לָדַעַת כִּי אֲנִי יְהֹוָה מְקַדְּשָׁם:

13 But the House of *Yisrael* rebelled against Me in the wilderness; they did not follow My laws and they rejected My rules – by the pursuit of which a man shall live – and they grossly desecrated My *Shabbatot*. Then I thought to pour out My fury upon them in the wilderness and to make an end of them;

יג וַיַּמְרוּ־בִי בֵית־יִשְׂרָאֵל בַּמִּדְבָּר בְּחֻקּוֹתַי לֹא־הָלָכוּ וְאֶת־מִשְׁפָּטַי מָאָסוּ אֲשֶׁר יַעֲשֶׂה אֹתָם הָאָדָם וָחַי בָּהֶם וְאֶת־שַׁבְּתֹתַי חִלְּלוּ מְאֹד וָאֹמַר לִשְׁפֹּךְ חֲמָתִי עֲלֵיהֶם בַּמִּדְבָּר לְכַלּוֹתָם:

14 but I acted for the sake of My name, that it might not be profaned in the sight of the nations before whose eyes I had led them out.

יד וָאֶעֱשֶׂה לְמַעַן שְׁמִי לְבִלְתִּי הֵחֵל לְעֵינֵי הַגּוֹיִם אֲשֶׁר הוֹצֵאתִים לְעֵינֵיהֶם:

15 However, I swore to them in the wilderness that I would not bring them into the land flowing with milk and honey, the fairest of all lands, which I had assigned [to them],

טו וְגַם־אֲנִי נָשָׂאתִי יָדִי לָהֶם בַּמִּדְבָּר לְבִלְתִּי הָבִיא אוֹתָם אֶל־הָאָרֶץ אֲשֶׁר־נָתַתִּי זָבַת חָלָב וּדְבַשׁ צְבִי הִיא לְכָל־הָאֲרָצוֹת:

16 for they had rejected My rules, disobeyed My laws, and desecrated My *Shabbatot*; their hearts followed after their fetishes.

טז יַעַן בְּמִשְׁפָּטַי מָאָסוּ וְאֶת־חֻקּוֹתַי לֹא־הָלְכוּ בָהֶם וְאֶת־שַׁבְּתוֹתַי חִלֵּלוּ כִּי אַחֲרֵי גִלּוּלֵיהֶם לִבָּם הֹלֵךְ:

17 But I had pity on them and did not destroy them; I did not make an end of them in the wilderness.

יז וַתָּחָס עֵינִי עֲלֵיהֶם מִשַּׁחֲתָם וְלֹא־עָשִׂיתִי אוֹתָם כָּלָה בַּמִּדְבָּר:

18 I warned their children in the wilderness: Do not follow the practices of your fathers, do not keep their ways, and do not defile yourselves with their fetishes.

יח וָאֹמַר אֶל־בְּנֵיהֶם בַּמִּדְבָּר בְּחוּקֵּי אֲבוֹתֵיכֶם אַל־תֵּלֵכוּ וְאֶת־מִשְׁפְּטֵיהֶם אַל־תִּשְׁמֹרוּ וּבְגִלּוּלֵיהֶם אַל־תִּטַּמָּאוּ:

19 I *Hashem* am your God: Follow My laws and be careful to observe My rules.

יט אֲנִי יְהֹוָה אֱלֹהֵיכֶם בְּחֻקּוֹתַי לֵכוּ וְאֶת־מִשְׁפָּטַי שִׁמְרוּ וַעֲשׂוּ אוֹתָם:

20 And hallow My *Shabbatot*, that they may be a sign between Me and you, that you may know that I *Hashem* am your God.

כ וְאֶת־שַׁבְּתוֹתַי קַדֵּשׁוּ וְהָיוּ לְאוֹת בֵּינִי וּבֵינֵיכֶם לָדַעַת כִּי אֲנִי יְהֹוָה אֱלֹהֵיכֶם:

21 But the children rebelled against Me: they did not follow My laws and did not faithfully observe My rules, by the pursuit of which man shall live; they profaned My *Shabbatot*. Then I resolved to pour out My fury upon them, to vent all My anger upon them, in the wilderness.

כא וַיַּמְרוּ־בִי הַבָּנִים בְּחֻקּוֹתַי לֹא־הָלָכוּ וְאֶת־מִשְׁפָּטַי לֹא־שָׁמְרוּ לַעֲשׂוֹת אוֹתָם אֲשֶׁר יַעֲשֶׂה אוֹתָם הָאָדָם וָחַי בָּהֶם אֶת־שַׁבְּתוֹתַי חִלֵּלוּ וָאֹמַר לִשְׁפֹּךְ חֲמָתִי עֲלֵיהֶם לְכַלּוֹת אַפִּי בָּם בַּמִּדְבָּר:

22 But I held back My hand and acted for the sake of My name, that it might not be profaned in the sight of the nations before whose eyes I had led them out.

כב וַהֲשִׁבֹתִי אֶת־יָדִי וָאַעַשׂ לְמַעַן שְׁמִי לְבִלְתִּי הֵחֵל לְעֵינֵי הַגּוֹיִם אֲשֶׁר־הוֹצֵאתִי אוֹתָם לְעֵינֵיהֶם:

23 However, I swore to them in the wilderness that I would scatter them among the nations and disperse them through the lands,

כג גַּם־אֲנִי נָשָׂאתִי אֶת־יָדִי לָהֶם בַּמִּדְבָּר לְהָפִיץ אֹתָם בַּגּוֹיִם וּלְזָרוֹת אוֹתָם בָּאֲרָצוֹת:

24 because they did not obey My rules, but rejected My laws, profaned My *Shabbatot*, and looked with longing to the fetishes of their fathers.

כד יַעַן מִשְׁפָּטַי לֹא־עָשׂוּ וְחֻקּוֹתַי מָאָסוּ וְאֶת־שַׁבְּתוֹתַי חִלֵּלוּ וְאַחֲרֵי גִּלּוּלֵי אֲבוֹתָם הָיוּ עֵינֵיהֶם:

25 Moreover, I gave them laws that were not good and rules by which they could not live:

כה וְגַם־אֲנִי נָתַתִּי לָהֶם חֻקִּים לֹא טוֹבִים וּמִשְׁפָּטִים לֹא יִחְיוּ בָּהֶם:

26 When they set aside every first issue of the womb, I defiled them by their very gifts – that I might render them desolate, that they might know that I am *Hashem*.

כו וָאֲטַמֵּא אוֹתָם בְּמַתְּנוֹתָם בְּהַעֲבִיר כָּל־פֶּטֶר רָחַם לְמַעַן אֲשִׁמֵּם לְמַעַן אֲשֶׁר יֵדְעוּ אֲשֶׁר אֲנִי יְהוָה:

27 Now, O mortal, speak to the House of *Yisrael* and say to them: Thus said *Hashem*: By this too your fathers affronted Me and committed trespass against Me:

כז לָכֵן דַּבֵּר אֶל־בֵּית יִשְׂרָאֵל בֶּן־אָדָם וְאָמַרְתָּ אֲלֵיהֶם כֹּה אָמַר אֲדֹנָי יְהוָה עוֹד זֹאת גִּדְּפוּ אוֹתִי אֲבוֹתֵיכֶם בְּמַעֲלָם בִּי מָעַל:

28 When I brought them to the land that I had sworn to give them, and they saw any high hill or any leafy tree, they slaughtered their sacrifices there and presented their offensive offerings there; there they produced their pleasing odors and poured out their libations.

כח וָאֲבִיאֵם אֶל־הָאָרֶץ אֲשֶׁר נָשָׂאתִי אֶת־יָדִי לָתֵת אוֹתָהּ לָהֶם וַיִּרְאוּ כָל־גִּבְעָה רָמָה וְכָל־עֵץ עָבֹת וַיִּזְבְּחוּ־שָׁם אֶת־זִבְחֵיהֶם וַיִּתְּנוּ־שָׁם כַּעַס קָרְבָּנָם וַיָּשִׂימוּ שָׁם רֵיחַ נִיחוֹחֵיהֶם וַיַּסִּיכוּ שָׁם אֶת־נִסְכֵּיהֶם:

29 Then I said to them, "What is this shrine which you visit?" (Therefore such [a shrine] is called bamah to this day.)

כט וָאֹמַר אֲלֵהֶם מָה הַבָּמָה אֲשֶׁר־אַתֶּם הַבָּאִים שָׁם וַיִּקָּרֵא שְׁמָהּ בָּמָה עַד הַיּוֹם הַזֶּה:

30 Now say to the House of *Yisrael*: Thus said *Hashem*: If you defile yourselves as your fathers did and go astray after their detestable things,

ל לָכֵן אֱמֹר אֶל־בֵּית יִשְׂרָאֵל כֹּה אָמַר אֲדֹנָי יְהוָה הַבְּדֶרֶךְ אֲבוֹתֵיכֶם אַתֶּם נִטְמְאִים וְאַחֲרֵי שִׁקּוּצֵיהֶם אַתֶּם זֹנִים:

31 and if to this very day you defile yourselves in the presentation of your gifts by making your children pass through the fire to all your fetishes, shall I respond to your inquiry, O House of *Yisrael*? As I live – declares *Hashem* – I will not respond to you.

לא וּבִשְׂאֵת מַתְּנֹתֵיכֶם בְּהַעֲבִיר בְּנֵיכֶם בָּאֵשׁ אַתֶּם נִטְמְאִים לְכָל־גִּלּוּלֵיכֶם עַד־הַיּוֹם וַאֲנִי אִדָּרֵשׁ לָכֶם בֵּית יִשְׂרָאֵל חַי־אָנִי נְאֻם אֲדֹנָי יְהוָה אִם־אִדָּרֵשׁ לָכֶם:

32 And what you have in mind shall never come to pass – when you say, "We will be like the nations, like the families of the lands, worshiping wood and stone."

לב וְהָעֹלָה עַל־רוּחֲכֶם הָיוֹ לֹא תִהְיֶה אֲשֶׁר אַתֶּם אֹמְרִים נִהְיֶה כַגּוֹיִם כְּמִשְׁפְּחוֹת הָאֲרָצוֹת לְשָׁרֵת עֵץ וָאָבֶן:

33 As I live – declares *Hashem* – I will reign over you with a strong hand, and with an outstretched arm, and with overflowing fury.

לג חַי־אָנִי נְאֻם אֲדֹנָי יְהוָה אִם־לֹא בְּיָד חֲזָקָה וּבִזְרוֹעַ נְטוּיָה וּבְחֵמָה שְׁפוּכָה אֶמְלוֹךְ עֲלֵיכֶם:

34 With a strong hand and an outstretched arm and overflowing fury I will bring you out from the peoples and gather you from the lands where you are scattered,

לד וְהוֹצֵאתִי אֶתְכֶם מִן־הָעַמִּים וְקִבַּצְתִּי אֶתְכֶם מִן־הָאֲרָצוֹת אֲשֶׁר נְפוֹצֹתֶם בָּם בְּיָד חֲזָקָה וּבִזְרוֹעַ נְטוּיָה וּבְחֵמָה שְׁפוּכָה:

35 and I will bring you into the wilderness of the peoples; and there I will enter into judgment with you face to face.

לה וְהֵבֵאתִי אֶתְכֶם אֶל־מִדְבַּר הָעַמִּים וְנִשְׁפַּטְתִּי אִתְּכֶם שָׁם פָּנִים אֶל־פָּנִים:

36 As I entered into judgment with your fathers in the wilderness of the land of Egypt, so will I enter into judgment with you – declares *Hashem*.

לו כַּאֲשֶׁר נִשְׁפַּטְתִּי אֶת־אֲבוֹתֵיכֶם בְּמִדְבַּר אֶרֶץ מִצְרָיִם כֵּן אִשָּׁפֵט אִתְּכֶם נְאֻם אֲדֹנָי יֱהֹוִה:

37 I will make you pass under the shepherd's staff, and I will bring you into the bond of the covenant.

לז וְהַעֲבַרְתִּי אֶתְכֶם תַּחַת הַשָּׁבֶט וְהֵבֵאתִי אֶתְכֶם בְּמָסֹרֶת הַבְּרִית:

38 I will remove from you those who rebel and transgress against Me; I will take them out of the countries where they sojourn, but they shall not enter the land of *Yisrael*. Then you shall know that I am *Hashem*.

לח וּבָרוֹתִי מִכֶּם הַמֹּרְדִים וְהַפּוֹשְׁעִים בִּי מֵאֶרֶץ מְגוּרֵיהֶם אוֹצִיא אוֹתָם וְאֶל־ אַדְמַת יִשְׂרָאֵל לֹא יָבוֹא וִידַעְתֶּם כִּי־ אֲנִי יֱהֹוָה:

39 As for you, O House of *Yisrael*, thus said *Hashem*: Go, every one of you, and worship his fetishes and continue, if you will not obey Me; but do not profane My holy name any more with your idolatrous gifts.

לט וְאַתֶּם בֵּית־יִשְׂרָאֵל כֹּה־אָמַר אֲדֹנָי יֱהֹוִה אִישׁ גִּלּוּלָיו לְכוּ עֲבֹדוּ וְאַחַר אִם־אֵינְכֶם שֹׁמְעִים אֵלָי וְאֶת־שֵׁם קָדְשִׁי לֹא תְחַלְּלוּ־עוֹד בְּמַתְּנוֹתֵיכֶם וּבְגִלּוּלֵיכֶם:

40 For only on My holy mountain, on the lofty mount of *Yisrael* – declares *Hashem* – there, in the land, the entire House of *Yisrael*, all of it, must worship Me. There I will accept them, and there I will take note of your contributions and the choicest offerings of all your sacred things.

מ כִּי בְהַר־קָדְשִׁי בְּהַר מְרוֹם יִשְׂרָאֵל נְאֻם אֲדֹנָי יֱהֹוִה שָׁם יַעַבְדֻנִי כָּל־בֵּית יִשְׂרָאֵל כֻּלֹּה בָּאָרֶץ שָׁם אֶרְצֵם וְשָׁם אֶדְרוֹשׁ אֶת־תְּרוּמֹתֵיכֶם וְאֶת־רֵאשִׁית מַשְׂאוֹתֵיכֶם בְּכָל־קָדְשֵׁיכֶם:

41 When I bring you out from the peoples and gather you from the lands in which you are scattered, I will accept you as a pleasing odor; and I will be sanctified through you in the sight of the nations.

מא בְּרֵיחַ נִיחֹחַ אֶרְצֶה אֶתְכֶם בְּהוֹצִיאִי אֶתְכֶם מִן־הָעַמִּים וְקִבַּצְתִּי אֶתְכֶם מִן־ הָאֲרָצוֹת אֲשֶׁר נְפֹצֹתֶם בָּם וְנִקְדַּשְׁתִּי בָכֶם לְעֵינֵי הַגּוֹיִם:

b'-RAY-akh nee-KHO-akh er-TZEH et-KHEM b'-ho-tzee-EE et-KHEM min ha-a-MEEM v'-ki-batz-TEE et-KHEM min ha-a-ra-TZOT a-SHER n'-fo-tzo-TEM BAM v'-nik-dash-TEE va-KHEM l'-ay-NAY ha-go-YIM

20:41 When I bring you out from the peoples and gather you Having already lived in exile, the prophet *Yechezkel* describes the future miraculous ingathering of the exiles, a miraculous event our generation has been privileged to witness. Yitzchak Ben-Zvi (1884–1963), historian, Zionist leader and the second President of Israel, reflected on the role of the State in this biblical promise: "The ingathering of the exiles is the most central and lofty ideal of this country. The redemptive reestablishment of Israel – this is a complete revolution in the annals of our days, in the chronicles of our entire nation. It serves as a counterweight, opposing our destruction and our extended exile." For 2,000 years, Jews pondered the "When?" of these events, and Yitzchak Ben-Zvi's founding generation of Zionists dealt with the question of "How?" – how could they enable the process to succeed? Now, it is our generation's mission to ask the next question: "Why?" – Why is it that we have merited to witness, and be involved in, such wondrous episodes? The key to appreciating our present day opportunities, and the path to enhancing our future, lies in seeking these answers and working towards their fulfillment.

President Yitzchak Ben-Zvi (1884–1963)

⁴² Then, when I have brought you to the land of *Yisrael*, to the country that I swore to give to your fathers, you shall know that I am *Hashem*.

מב וִידַעְתֶּם כִּי־אֲנִי יְהֹוָה בַּהֲבִיאִי אֶתְכֶם אֶל־אַדְמַת יִשְׂרָאֵל אֶל־הָאָרֶץ אֲשֶׁר נָשָׂאתִי אֶת־יָדִי לָתֵת אוֹתָהּ לַאֲבוֹתֵיכֶם:

⁴³ There you will recall your ways and all the acts by which you defiled yourselves; and you will loathe yourselves for all the evils that you committed.

מג וּזְכַרְתֶּם־שָׁם אֶת־דַּרְכֵיכֶם וְאֵת כָּל־עֲלִילוֹתֵיכֶם אֲשֶׁר נִטְמֵאתֶם בָּם וּנְקֹטֹתֶם בִּפְנֵיכֶם בְּכָל־רָעוֹתֵיכֶם אֲשֶׁר עֲשִׂיתֶם:

⁴⁴ Then, O House of *Yisrael*, you shall know that I am *Hashem*, when I deal with you for My name's sake – not in accordance with your evil ways and corrupt acts – declares *Hashem*.

מד וִידַעְתֶּם כִּי־אֲנִי יְהֹוָה בַּעֲשׂוֹתִי אִתְּכֶם לְמַעַן שְׁמִי לֹא כְדַרְכֵיכֶם הָרָעִים וְכַעֲלִילוֹתֵיכֶם הַנִּשְׁחָתוֹת בֵּית יִשְׂרָאֵל נְאֻם אֲדֹנָי יְהֹוִה:

21 ¹ The word of *Hashem* came to me:

א וַיְהִי דְבַר־יְהֹוָה אֵלַי לֵאמֹר:

² O mortal, set your face toward Teman, and proclaim to Darom, and prophesy against the brushland of the *Negev*.

ב בֶּן־אָדָם שִׂים פָּנֶיךָ דֶּרֶךְ תֵּימָנָה וְהַטֵּף אֶל־דָּרוֹם וְהִנָּבֵא אֶל־יַעַר הַשָּׂדֶה נֶגֶב:

ben a-DAM SEEM pa-NE-kha DE-rekh tay-MA-nah v'-ha-TAYF
el da-ROM v'-hi-na-VAY el YA-ar ha-sa-DEH NE-gev

³ Say to the brushland of the *Negev*: Hear the word of *Hashem*. Thus said *Hashem*: I am going to kindle a fire in you, which shall devour every tree of yours, both green and withered. Its leaping flame shall not go out, and every face from south to north shall be scorched by it.

ג וְאָמַרְתָּ לְיַעַר הַנֶּגֶב שְׁמַע דְּבַר־יְהֹוָה כֹּה־אָמַר אֲדֹנָי יְהֹוִה הִנְנִי מַצִּית־בְּךָ אֵשׁ וְאָכְלָה בְךָ כָל־עֵץ־לַח וְכָל־עֵץ יָבֵשׁ לֹא־תִכְבֶּה לַהֶבֶת שַׁלְהֶבֶת וְנִצְרְבוּ־בָהּ כָּל־פָּנִים מִנֶּגֶב צָפוֹנָה:

⁴ Then all flesh shall recognize that I *Hashem* have kindled it; it shall not go out.

ד וְרָאוּ כָּל־בָּשָׂר כִּי אֲנִי יְהֹוָה בִּעַרְתִּיהָ לֹא תִכְבֶּה:

⁵ And I said, "Ah, *Hashem*! They say of me: He is just a riddlemonger."

ה וָאֹמַר אֲהָהּ אֲדֹנָי יְהֹוִה הֵמָּה אֹמְרִים לִי הֲלֹא מְמַשֵּׁל מְשָׁלִים הוּא:

⁶ Then the word of *Hashem* came to me:

ו וַיְהִי דְבַר־יְהֹוָה אֵלַי לֵאמֹר:

⁷ O mortal, set your face toward *Yerushalayim* and proclaim against her sanctuaries and prophesy against the land of *Yisrael*.

ז בֶּן־אָדָם שִׂים פָּנֶיךָ אֶל־יְרוּשָׁלַ͏ִם וְהַטֵּף אֶל־מִקְדָּשִׁים וְהִנָּבֵא אֶל־אַדְמַת יִשְׂרָאֵל:

Ein Avdat in the Negev

א **21:2 Prophesy against the brushland of the *Negev*** Repeating his warning of *Yerushalayim's* imminent destruction, *Yechezkel* uses the metaphor of a forest fire that will burn without control until all the trees of the forest, dry and healthy alike, are consumed. In Israel's arid climate, forest fires are extremely dangerous, spreading quickly and leaving behind tremendous destruction. Before giving him this prophecy,

נגב *Hashem* tells *Yechezkel* to look southward in the direction of Israel, and uses three Hebrew words for 'south', *tayman* (תימן), *darom* (דרום) and *negev* (נגב). In the following verse, however, only the word *negev* is used. In addition to 'south', *negev* also means 'dry', and refers to the desert region of southern Israel. After the fire, all of Israel will be like the *negev* – a barren, lifeless desert.

8 Say to the land of *Yisrael*: Thus said *Hashem*: I am going to deal with you! I will draw My sword from its sheath, and I will wipe out from you both the righteous and the wicked.

ח וְאָמַרְתָּ לְאַדְמַת יִשְׂרָאֵל כֹּה אָמַר יְהֹוָה הִנְנִי אֵלַיִךְ וְהוֹצֵאתִי חַרְבִּי מִתַּעְרָהּ וְהִכְרַתִּי מִמֵּךְ צַדִּיק וְרָשָׁע:

9 In order to wipe out from you both the righteous and the wicked, My sword shall assuredly be unsheathed against all flesh from south to north;

ט יַעַן אֲשֶׁר־הִכְרַתִּי מִמֵּךְ צַדִּיק וְרָשָׁע לָכֵן תֵּצֵא חַרְבִּי מִתַּעְרָהּ אֶל־כָּל־בָּשָׂר מִנֶּגֶב צָפוֹן:

10 and all flesh shall know that I *Hashem* have drawn My sword from its sheath, not to be sheathed again.

י וְיָדְעוּ כָּל־בָּשָׂר כִּי אֲנִי יְהֹוָה הוֹצֵאתִי חַרְבִּי מִתַּעְרָהּ לֹא תָשׁוּב עוֹד:

11 And you, O mortal, sigh; with tottering limbs and bitter grief, sigh before their eyes.

יא וְאַתָּה בֶן־אָדָם הֵאָנַח בְּשִׁבְרוֹן מָתְנַיִם וּבִמְרִירוּת תֵּאָנַח לְעֵינֵיהֶם:

12 And when they ask you, "Why do you sigh?" answer, "Because of the tidings that have come." Every heart shall sink and all hands hang nerveless; every spirit shall grow faint and all knees turn to water because of the tidings that have come. It is approaching, it shall come to pass – declares *Hashem*.

יב וְהָיָה כִּי־יֹאמְרוּ אֵלֶיךָ עַל־מָה אַתָּה נֶאֱנָח וְאָמַרְתָּ אֶל־שְׁמוּעָה כִי־בָאָה וְנָמֵס כָּל־לֵב וְרָפוּ כָל־יָדַיִם וְכִהֲתָה כָל־רוּחַ וְכָל־בִּרְכַּיִם תֵּלַכְנָה מַּיִם הִנֵּה בָאָה וְנִהְיָתָה נְאֻם אֲדֹנָי יְהֹוִה:

13 The word of *Hashem* came to me:

יג וַיְהִי דְבַר־יְהֹוָה אֵלַי לֵאמֹר:

14 O mortal, prophesy and say: Thus said *Hashem*: A sword! A sword has been whetted and polished.

יד בֶּן־אָדָם הִנָּבֵא וְאָמַרְתָּ כֹּה אָמַר אֲדֹנָי אֱמֹר חֶרֶב חֶרֶב הוּחַדָּה וְגַם־מְרוּטָה:

15 It has been whetted to wreak slaughter; [therefore] it has been ground to a brilliant polish. How can we rejoice? My son, it scorns the rod and every stick.

טו לְמַעַן טְבֹחַ טֶבַח הוּחַדָּה לְמַעַן־הֱיֵה־לָהּ בָּרָק מֹרָטָה אוֹ נָשִׂישׂ שֵׁבֶט בְּנִי מֹאֶסֶת כָּל־עֵץ:

16 It has been given to be polished and then grasped in the hand; for this has the sword been whetted, for this polished – to be put into the hand of a slayer.

טז וַיִּתֵּן אֹתָהּ לְמָרְטָה לִתְפֹּשׂ בַּכָּף הִיא הוּחַדָּה חֶרֶב וְהִיא מֹרָטָה לָתֵת אוֹתָהּ בְּיַד־הוֹרֵג:

17 Cry and wail, O mortal, for this shall befall My people, this shall befall all the chieftains of *Yisrael*: they shall be cast before the sword together with My people; oh, strike the thigh [in grief].

יז זְעַק וְהֵילֵל בֶּן־אָדָם כִּי־הִיא הָיְתָה בְעַמִּי הִיא בְּכָל־נְשִׂיאֵי יִשְׂרָאֵל מְגוּרֵי אֶל־חֶרֶב הָיוּ אֶת־עַמִּי לָכֵן סְפֹק אֶל־יָרֵךְ:

18 Consider: How shall it fail to happen, seeing that it even scorns the rod? – says *Hashem*.

יח כִּי בֹחַן וּמָה אִם־גַּם־שֵׁבֶט מֹאֶסֶת לֹא יִהְיֶה נְאֻם אֲדֹנָי יְהֹוִה:

19 Further, O mortal, prophesy, striking hand against hand. Let the sword strike a second time and yet a third time; it is a sword for massacre, a sword for great carnage, that presses upon them.

יט וְאַתָּה בֶן־אָדָם הִנָּבֵא וְהַךְ כַּף אֶל־כָּף וְתִכָּפֵל חֶרֶב שְׁלִישִׁתָה חֶרֶב חֲלָלִים הִיא חֶרֶב חָלָל הַגָּדוֹל הַחֹדֶרֶת לָהֶם:

20 Thus hearts shall lose courage and many shall fall. At all their gates I have appointed slaughter by the sword. Ah! it is made to flash brilliantly, it is honed for slaughter.

כ לְמַעַן לָמוּג לֵב וְהַרְבֵּה הַמִּכְשֹׁלִים עַל כָּל־שַׁעֲרֵיהֶם נָתַתִּי אִבְחַת־חָרֶב אָח עֲשׂוּיָה לְבָרָק מְעֻטָּה לְטָבַח:

21 Be united, go to the right, turn left; whither are you bound?

כא הִתְאַחֲדִי הֵימִנִי הָשִׂימִי הַשְׂמִילִי אָנָה פָּנַיִךְ מֻעָדוֹת:

22 I, too, will strike hand against hand and will satisfy My fury upon you; I *Hashem* have spoken.

כב וְגַם־אֲנִי אַכֶּה כַפִּי אֶל־כַּפִּי וַהֲנִחֹתִי חֲמָתִי אֲנִי יְהוָֹה דִּבַּרְתִּי:

23 The word of *Hashem* came to me:

כג וַיְהִי דְבַר־יְהוָֹה אֵלַי לֵאמֹר:

24 And you, O mortal, choose two roads on which the sword of the king of Babylon may advance, both issuing from the same country; and select a spot, select it where roads branch off to [two] cities.

כד וְאַתָּה בֶן־אָדָם שִׂים־לְךָ שְׁנַיִם דְּרָכִים לָבוֹא חֶרֶב מֶלֶךְ־בָּבֶל מֵאֶרֶץ אֶחָד יֵצְאוּ שְׁנֵיהֶם וְיָד בָּרֵא בְּרֹאשׁ דֶּרֶךְ־עִיר בָּרֵא:

25 Choose a way for the sword to advance on Rabbah of the Amonites or on fortified *Yerushalayim* in *Yehuda*.

כה דֶּרֶךְ תָּשִׂים לָבוֹא חֶרֶב אֵת רַבַּת בְּנֵי־עַמּוֹן וְאֶת־יְהוּדָה בִירוּשָׁלַ͏ִם בְּצוּרָה:

26 For the king of Babylon has stood at the fork of the road, where two roads branch off, to perform divination: He has shaken arrows, consulted teraphim, and inspected the liver.

כו כִּי־עָמַד מֶלֶךְ־בָּבֶל אֶל־אֵם הַדֶּרֶךְ בְּרֹאשׁ שְׁנֵי הַדְּרָכִים לִקְסָם־קָסֶם קִלְקַל בַּחִצִּים שָׁאַל בַּתְּרָפִים רָאָה בַּכָּבֵד:

27 In his right hand came up the omen against *Yerushalayim* – to set battering rams, to proclaim murder, to raise battle shouts, to set battering rams against the gates, to cast up mounds, to erect towers.

כז בִּימִינוֹ הָיָה הַקֶּסֶם יְרוּשָׁלַ͏ִם לָשׂוּם כָּרִים לִפְתֹּחַ פֶּה בְּרֶצַח לְהָרִים קוֹל בִּתְרוּעָה לָשׂוּם כָּרִים עַל־שְׁעָרִים לִשְׁפֹּךְ סֹלְלָה לִבְנוֹת דָּיֵק:

28 In their eyes, the oaths they had sworn to them were like empty divination; but this shall serve to recall their guilt, for which they shall be taken to task.

כח וְהָיָה לָהֶם כִּקְסָום־[כִּקְסָם־] שָׁוְא בְּעֵינֵיהֶם שְׁבֻעֵי שְׁבֻעוֹת לָהֶם וְהוּא־מַזְכִּיר עָוֹן לְהִתָּפֵשׂ:

29 Assuredly, thus said *Hashem*: For causing your guilt to be recalled, your transgressions to be uncovered, and your sins to be revealed – all your misdeeds – because you have brought yourselves to [My] mind, you shall be taken to task.

כט לָכֵן כֹּה־אָמַר אֲדֹנָי יְהוִֹה יַעַן הַזְכַּרְכֶם עֲוֹנְכֶם בְּהִגָּלוֹת פִּשְׁעֵיכֶם לְהֵרָאוֹת חַטֹּאותֵיכֶם בְּכֹל עֲלִילוֹתֵיכֶם יַעַן הִזָּכֶרְכֶם בַּכַּף תִּתָּפֵשׂוּ:

30 And to you, O dishonored wicked prince of *Yisrael*, whose day has come – the time set for your punishment –

ל וְאַתָּה חָלָל רָשָׁע נְשִׂיא יִשְׂרָאֵל אֲשֶׁר־בָּא יוֹמוֹ בְּעֵת עֲוֹן קֵץ:

31 thus said *Hashem*: Remove the turban and lift off the crown! This shall not remain as it is; exalt the low and abase the high.

לא כֹּה אָמַר אֲדֹנָי יְהוִֹה הָסִיר הַמִּצְנֶפֶת וְהָרִים הָעֲטָרָה זֹאת לֹא־זֹאת הַשָּׁפָלָה הַגְבֵּהַּ וְהַגָּבֹהַּ הַשְׁפִּיל:

32 Ruin, an utter ruin I will make it. It shall be no more until he comes to whom it rightfully belongs; and I will give it to him.

לב עַוָּה עַוָּה עַוָּה אֲשִׂימֶנָּה גַּם־זֹאת לֹא הָיָה עַד־בֹּא אֲשֶׁר־לוֹ הַמִּשְׁפָּט וּנְתַתִּיו:

33 Further, O mortal, prophesy and say: Thus said *Hashem* concerning the Amonites and their blasphemies: Proclaim: O sword! O sword unsheathed for slaughter, polished to the utmost, to a flashing brilliance!

לג וְאַתָּה בֶן־אָדָם הִנָּבֵא וְאָמַרְתָּ כֹּה אָמַר אֲדֹנָי יְהוִֹה אֶל־בְּנֵי עַמּוֹן וְאֶל־חֶרְפָּתָם וְאָמַרְתָּ חֶרֶב חֶרֶב פְּתוּחָה לְטֶבַח מְרוּטָה לְהָכִיל לְמַעַן בָּרָק:

34 Because they have prophesied falsely about you and have divined deceitfully concerning you, you shall be wielded over the necks of the dishonored wicked ones, for their day has come, the time set for their punishment.

לד בַּחֲזוֹת לָךְ שָׁוְא בִּקְסָם־לָךְ כָּזָב לָתֵת אוֹתָךְ אֶל־צַוְּארֵי חַלְלֵי רְשָׁעִים אֲשֶׁר־בָּא יוֹמָם בְּעֵת עֲוֺן קֵץ:

35 Return it to its sheath! In the place where you were created, in the land of your origin, I will judge you.

לה הָשַׁב אֶל־תַּעְרָהּ בִּמְקוֹם אֲשֶׁר־נִבְרֵאת בְּאֶרֶץ מְכֻרוֹתַיִךְ אֶשְׁפֹּט אֹתָךְ:

36 I will pour out My indignation upon you, I will blow upon you with the fire of My wrath; and I will deliver you into the hands of barbarians, craftsmen of destruction.

לו וְשָׁפַכְתִּי עָלַיִךְ זַעְמִי בְּאֵשׁ עֶבְרָתִי אָפִיחַ עָלָיִךְ וּנְתַתִּיךְ בְּיַד אֲנָשִׁים בֹּעֲרִים חָרָשֵׁי מַשְׁחִית:

37 You shall be fuel for the fire, your blood shall sink into the earth, you shall not be remembered, for I *Hashem* have spoken.

לז לָאֵשׁ תִּהְיֶה לְאָכְלָה דָּמֵךְ יִהְיֶה בְּתוֹךְ הָאָרֶץ לֹא תִזָּכֵרִי כִּי אֲנִי יְהֹוָה דִּבַּרְתִּי:

22 1 The word of *Hashem* came to me:

כב א וַיְהִי דְבַר־יְהֹוָה אֵלַי לֵאמֹר:

2 Further, O mortal, arraign, arraign the city of bloodshed; declare to her all her abhorrent deeds!

ב וְאַתָּה בֶן־אָדָם הֲתִשְׁפֹּט הֲתִשְׁפֹּט אֶת־עִיר הַדָּמִים וְהוֹדַעְתָּהּ אֵת כָּל־תּוֹעֲבוֹתֶיהָ:

3 Say: Thus said *Hashem*: O city in whose midst blood is shed, so that your hour is approaching; within which fetishes are made, so that you have become unclean!

ג וְאָמַרְתָּ כֹּה אָמַר אֲדֹנָי יְהֹוִה עִיר שֹׁפֶכֶת דָּם בְּתוֹכָהּ לָבוֹא עִתָּהּ וְעָשְׂתָה גִלּוּלִים עָלֶיהָ לְטָמְאָה:

4 You stand guilty of the blood you have shed, defiled by the fetishes you have made. You have brought on your day; you have reached your year. Therefore I will make you the mockery of the nations and the scorn of all the lands.

ד בְּדָמֵךְ אֲשֶׁר־שָׁפַכְתְּ אָשַׁמְתְּ וּבְגִלּוּלַיִךְ אֲשֶׁר־עָשִׂית טָמֵאת וַתַּקְרִיבִי יָמַיִךְ וַתָּבוֹא עַד־שְׁנוֹתָיִךְ עַל־כֵּן נְתַתִּיךְ חֶרְפָּה לַגּוֹיִם וְקַלָּסָה לְכָל־הָאֲרָצוֹת:

5 Both the near and the far shall scorn you, O besmirched of name, O laden with iniquity!

ה הַקְּרֹבוֹת וְהָרְחֹקוֹת מִמֵּךְ יִתְקַלְּסוּ־בָךְ טְמֵאַת הַשֵּׁם רַבַּת הַמְּהוּמָה:

6 Every one of the princes of *Yisrael* in your midst used his strength for the shedding of blood.

ו הִנֵּה נְשִׂיאֵי יִשְׂרָאֵל אִישׁ לִזְרֹעוֹ הָיוּ בָךְ לְמַעַן שְׁפָךְ־דָּם:

7 Fathers and mothers have been humiliated within you; strangers have been cheated in your midst; orphans and widows have been wronged within you.

ז אָב וָאֵם הֵקַלּוּ בָךְ לַגֵּר עָשׂוּ בַעֹשֶׁק בְּתוֹכֵךְ יָתוֹם וְאַלְמָנָה הוֹנוּ בָךְ:

8 You have despised My holy things and profaned My *Shabbatot*.

ח קָדָשַׁי בָּזִית וְאֶת־שַׁבְּתֹתַי חִלָּלְתְּ:

9 Base men in your midst were intent on shedding blood; in you they have eaten upon the mountains; and they have practiced depravity in your midst.

ט אַנְשֵׁי רָכִיל הָיוּ בָךְ לְמַעַן שְׁפָךְ־דָּם וְאֶל־הֶהָרִים אָכְלוּ בָךְ זִמָּה עָשׂוּ בְתוֹכֵךְ:

10 In you they have uncovered their fathers' nakedness; in you they have ravished women during their impurity.

י עֶרְוַת־אָב גִּלָּה־בָךְ טְמֵאַת הַנִּדָּה עִנּוּ־בָךְ:

11 They have committed abhorrent acts with other men's wives; in their depravity they have defiled their own daughters-in-law; in you they have ravished their own sisters, daughters of their fathers.

וְאִישׁ אֶת־אֵשֶׁת רֵעֵהוּ עָשָׂה תּוֹעֵבָה יא
וְאִישׁ אֶת־כַּלָּתוֹ טִמֵּא בְזִמָּה וְאִישׁ אֶת־
אֲחֹתוֹ בַת־אָבִיו עִנָּה־בָךְ:

12 They have taken bribes within you to shed blood. You have taken advance and accrued interest; you have defrauded your countrymen to your profit. You have forgotten Me – declares *Hashem*.

שֹׁחַד לָקְחוּ־בָךְ לְמַעַן שְׁפָךְ־דָּם נֶשֶׁךְ יב
וְתַרְבִּית לָקַחַתְּ וַתְּבַצְּעִי רֵעַיִךְ בַּעֹשֶׁק
וְאֹתִי שָׁכַחַתְּ נְאֻם אֲדֹנָי יֱהֹוִה:

13 Lo, I will strike My hands over the ill-gotten gains that you have amassed, and over the bloodshed that has been committed in your midst.

וְהִנֵּה הִכֵּיתִי כַפִּי אֶל־בִּצְעֵךְ אֲשֶׁר יג
עָשִׂית וְעַל־דָּמֵךְ אֲשֶׁר הָיוּ בְּתוֹכֵךְ:

14 Will your courage endure, will your hands remain firm in the days when I deal with you? I *Hashem* have spoken and I will act.

הֲיַעֲמֹד לִבֵּךְ אִם־תֶּחֱזַקְנָה יָדַיִךְ לַיָּמִים יד
אֲשֶׁר אֲנִי עֹשֶׂה אוֹתָךְ אֲנִי יְהֹוָה דִּבַּרְתִּי
וְעָשִׂיתִי:

15 I will scatter you among the nations and disperse you through the lands; I will consume the uncleanness out of you.

וַהֲפִיצוֹתִי אוֹתָךְ בַּגּוֹיִם וְזֵרִיתִיךְ טו
בָּאֲרָצוֹת וַהֲתִמֹּתִי טֻמְאָתֵךְ מִמֵּךְ:

16 You shall be dishonored in the sight of nations, and you shall know that I am *Hashem*.

וְנִחַלְתְּ בָּךְ לְעֵינֵי גוֹיִם וְיָדַעַתְּ כִּי־אֲנִי טז
יְהֹוָה:

17 The word of *Hashem* came to me:

וַיְהִי דְבַר־יְהֹוָה אֵלַי לֵאמֹר: יז

18 O mortal, the House of *Yisrael* has become dross to Me; they are all copper, tin, iron, and lead. But in a crucible, the dross shall turn into silver.

בֶּן־אָדָם הָיוּ־לִי בֵית־יִשְׂרָאֵל לְסוּג יח
[לְסִיג] כֻּלָּם נְחֹשֶׁת וּבְדִיל וּבַרְזֶל
וְעוֹפֶרֶת בְּתוֹךְ כּוּר סִגִים כֶּסֶף הָיוּ:

19 Assuredly, thus said *Hashem*: Because you have all become dross, I will gather you into *Yerushalayim*.

לָכֵן כֹּה אָמַר אֲדֹנָי יֱהֹוִה יַעַן הֱיוֹת יט
כֻּלְּכֶם לְסִגִים לָכֵן הִנְנִי קֹבֵץ אֶתְכֶם אֶל־
תּוֹךְ יְרוּשָׁלָ͏ִם:

20 As silver, copper, iron, lead, and tin are gathered into a crucible to blow the fire upon them, so as to melt them, so will I gather you in My fierce anger and cast you [into the fire] and melt you.

קְבֻצַת כֶּסֶף וּנְחֹשֶׁת וּבַרְזֶל וְעוֹפֶרֶת כ
וּבְדִיל אֶל־תּוֹךְ כּוּר לָפַחַת־עָלָיו אֵשׁ
לְהַנְתִּיךְ כֵּן אֶקְבֹּץ בְּאַפִּי וּבַחֲמָתִי
וְהִנַּחְתִּי וְהִתַּכְתִּי אֶתְכֶם:

21 I will gather you and I will blow upon you the fire of My fury, and you shall be melted in it.

וְכִנַּסְתִּי אֶתְכֶם וְנָפַחְתִּי עֲלֵיכֶם בְּאֵשׁ כא
עֶבְרָתִי וְנִתַּכְתֶּם בְּתוֹכָהּ:

22 As silver is melted in a crucible, so shall you be melted in it. And you shall know that I *Hashem* have poured out My fury upon you.

כְּהִתּוּךְ כֶּסֶף בְּתוֹךְ כּוּר כֵּן תֻּתְּכוּ בְתוֹכָהּ כב
וִידַעְתֶּם כִּי־אֲנִי יְהֹוָה שָׁפַכְתִּי חֲמָתִי
עֲלֵיכֶם:

23 The word of *Hashem* came to me:

וַיְהִי דְבַר־יְהֹוָה אֵלַי לֵאמֹר: כג

24 O mortal, say to her: You are an uncleansed land, not to be washed with rain on the day of indignation.

בֶּן־אָדָם אֱמָר־לָהּ אַתְּ אֶרֶץ לֹא מְטֹהָרָה הִיא לֹא גֻשְׁמָהּ בְּיוֹם זָעַם:

ben a-DAM e-mor LAH AT E-retz LO m'-to-ha-RAH
HEE LO gush-MAH b'-YOM ZA-am

25 Her gang of *Neviim* are like roaring lions in her midst, rending prey. They devour human beings; they seize treasure and wealth; they have widowed many women in her midst.

קֶשֶׁר נְבִיאֶיהָ בְּתוֹכָהּ כַּאֲרִי שׁוֹאֵג טֹרֵף טָרֶף נֶפֶשׁ אָכָלוּ חֹסֶן וִיקָר יִקָּחוּ אַלְמְנוֹתֶיהָ הִרְבּוּ בְתוֹכָהּ:

26 Her *Kohanim* have violated My Teaching: they have profaned what is sacred to Me, they have not distinguished between the sacred and the profane, they have not taught the difference between the unclean and the clean, and they have closed their eyes to My *Shabbatot*. I am profaned in their midst.

כֹּהֲנֶיהָ חָמְסוּ תוֹרָתִי וַיְחַלְּלוּ קָדָשַׁי בֵּין־קֹדֶשׁ לְחֹל לֹא הִבְדִּילוּ וּבֵין־הַטָּמֵא לְטָהוֹר לֹא הוֹדִיעוּ וּמִשַּׁבְּתוֹתַי הֶעְלִימוּ עֵינֵיהֶם וָאֵחַל בְּתוֹכָם:

27 Her officials are like wolves rending prey in her midst; they shed blood and destroy lives to win ill-gotten gain.

שָׂרֶיהָ בְקִרְבָּהּ כִּזְאֵבִים טֹרְפֵי טָרֶף לִשְׁפָּךְ־דָּם לְאַבֵּד נְפָשׁוֹת לְמַעַן בְּצֹעַ בָּצַע:

28 Her *Neviim*, too, daub the wall for them with plaster: They prophesy falsely and divine deceitfully for them; they say, "Thus said *Hashem*," when *Hashem* has not spoken.

וּנְבִיאֶיהָ טָחוּ לָהֶם תָּפֵל חֹזִים שָׁוְא וְקֹסְמִים לָהֶם כָּזָב אֹמְרִים כֹּה אָמַר אֲדֹנָי יֱהֹוִה וַיהֹוָה לֹא דִבֵּר:

29 And the people of the land have practiced fraud and committed robbery; they have wronged the poor and needy, have defrauded the stranger without redress.

עַם הָאָרֶץ עָשְׁקוּ עֹשֶׁק וְגָזְלוּ גָּזֵל וְעָנִי וְאֶבְיוֹן הוֹנוּ וְאֶת־הַגֵּר עָשְׁקוּ בְּלֹא מִשְׁפָּט:

30 And I sought a man among them to repair the wall or to stand in the breach before Me in behalf of this land, that I might not destroy it; but I found none.

וָאֲבַקֵּשׁ מֵהֶם אִישׁ גֹּדֵר־גָּדֵר וְעֹמֵד בַּפֶּרֶץ לְפָנַי בְּעַד הָאָרֶץ לְבִלְתִּי שַׁחֲתָהּ וְלֹא מָצָאתִי:

31 I have therefore poured out My indignation upon them; I will consume them with the fire of My fury. I will repay them for their conduct – declares *Hashem*.

וָאֶשְׁפֹּךְ עֲלֵיהֶם זַעְמִי בְּאֵשׁ עֶבְרָתִי כִּלִּיתִים דַּרְכָּם בְּרֹאשָׁם נָתַתִּי נְאֻם אֲדֹנָי יֱהֹוִה:

23 1 The word of *Hashem* came to me:

כג א וַיְהִי דְבַר־יְהֹוָה אֵלַי לֵאמֹר:

2 O mortal, once there were two women, daughters of one mother.

ב בֶּן־אָדָם שְׁתַּיִם נָשִׁים בְּנוֹת אֵם־אַחַת הָיוּ:

22:24 You are an uncleansed land In describing how the entire nation became corrupt, *Hashem* declares "You are an uncleansed land." This is reflective of the extreme spiritual sensitivity of Israel, a special characteristic of the land that appears throughout the Bible. Sinning inside the Holy Land affects not only the sinner, but the land itself becomes defiled as well (see Leviticus 18:24, Numbers 35:34). Thus, because of the sins of the nation, the land has become impure. Conversely, every act of goodness and kindness in Israel strengthens the land in addition to the people.

Israel365 *Tu B'shevat* packages sent to lone soldiers

³ They played the whore in Egypt; they played the whore while still young. There their breasts were squeezed, and there their virgin nipples were handled.

ג וַתִּזְנֶינָה בְמִצְרַיִם בִּנְעוּרֵיהֶן זָנוּ שָׁמָּה מֹעֲכוּ שְׁדֵיהֶן וְשָׁם עִשּׂוּ דַּדֵּי בְּתוּלֵיהֶן:

⁴ Their names were: the elder one, *Ohola*; and her sister, *Oholiva*. They became Mine, and they bore sons and daughters. As for their names, *Ohola* is *Shomron*, and *Oholiva* is *Yerushalayim*.

ד וּשְׁמוֹתָן אָהֳלָה הַגְּדוֹלָה וְאָהֳלִיבָה אֲחוֹתָהּ וַתִּהְיֶינָה לִי וַתֵּלַדְנָה בָּנִים וּבָנוֹת וּשְׁמוֹתָן שֹׁמְרוֹן אָהֳלָה וִירוּשָׁלַ͏ִם אָהֳלִיבָה:

ush-mo-TAN a-ho-LAH ha-g'-do-LAH v'-a-ho-lee-VAH a-kho-TAH va-tih-YE-nah LEE va-tay-LAD-nah ba-NEEM u-va-NOT ush-mo-TAN sho-m'-RON a-ho-LAH vee-ru-sha-LA-im a-ho-lee-VAH

⁵ *Ohola* whored while she was Mine, and she lusted after her lovers, after the Assyrians, warriors

ה וַתִּזֶן אָהֳלָה תַּחְתָּי וַתַּעְגַּב עַל־מְאַהֲבֶיהָ אֶל־אַשּׁוּר קְרוֹבִים:

⁶ clothed in blue, governors and prefects, horsemen mounted on steeds – all of them handsome young fellows.

ו לְבֻשֵׁי תְכֵלֶת פַּחוֹת וּסְגָנִים בַּחוּרֵי חֶמֶד כֻּלָּם פָּרָשִׁים רֹכְבֵי סוּסִים:

⁷ She bestowed her favors upon them – upon all the pick of the Assyrians – and defiled herself with all their fetishes after which she lusted.

ז וַתִּתֵּן תַּזְנוּתֶיהָ עֲלֵיהֶם מִבְחַר בְּנֵי־אַשּׁוּר כֻּלָּם וּבְכֹל אֲשֶׁר־עָגְבָה בְּכָל־גִּלּוּלֵיהֶם נִטְמָאָה:

⁸ She did not give up the whoring she had begun with the Egyptians; for they had lain with her in her youth, and they had handled her virgin nipples and had poured out their lust upon her.

ח וְאֶת־תַּזְנוּתֶיהָ מִמִּצְרַיִם לֹא עָזָבָה כִּי אוֹתָהּ שָׁכְבוּ בִנְעוּרֶיהָ וְהֵמָּה עִשּׂוּ דַּדֵּי בְתוּלֶיהָ וַיִּשְׁפְּכוּ תַזְנוּתָם עָלֶיהָ:

⁹ Therefore I delivered her into the hands of her lovers, into the hands of the Assyrians after whom she lusted.

ט לָכֵן נְתַתִּיהָ בְּיַד־מְאַהֲבֶיהָ בְּיַד בְּנֵי אַשּׁוּר אֲשֶׁר עָגְבָה עֲלֵיהֶם:

¹⁰ They exposed her nakedness; they seized her sons and daughters, and she herself was put to the sword. And because of the punishment inflicted upon her, she became a byword among women.

י הֵמָּה גִּלּוּ עֶרְוָתָהּ בָּנֶיהָ וּבְנוֹתֶיהָ לָקָחוּ וְאוֹתָהּ בַּחֶרֶב הָרָגוּ וַתְּהִי־שֵׁם לַנָּשִׁים וּשְׁפוּטִים עָשׂוּ בָהּ:

¹¹ Her sister *Oholiva* saw this; yet her lusting was more depraved than her sister's, and her whoring more debased.

יא וַתֵּרֶא אֲחוֹתָהּ אָהֳלִיבָה וַתַּשְׁחֵת עַגְבָתָהּ מִמֶּנָּה וְאֶת־תַּזְנוּתֶיהָ מִזְּנוּנֵי אֲחוֹתָהּ:

23:4 *Ohola* is *Shomron*, and *Oholiva* is *Yerushalayim* *Yechezkel* compares the two kingdoms of Israel to two unfaithful sisters named *Ohola* and *Oholiva*. The northern kingdom is represented by the older sister, as it was the first to officially institute idolatrous worship (I Kings 12) and to establish alliances with deceitful foreign powers instead of trusting in God (Hosea 8:9). The southern kingdom of *Yehuda* followed, also worshipping idols and making alliances with foreign nations against God's will. The covenantal relationship between *Hashem* and the Children of Israel is likened to a marriage. By worshipping other gods and relying on foreign powers, the Israelites are being unfaithful to *Hashem* and defiling His land.

A groom breaking a glass at a Jewish wedding; remembering the destruction of *Yerushalayim*

12 She lusted after the Assyrians, governors and prefects, warriors gorgeously clad, horsemen mounted on steeds – all of them handsome young fellows.

אֶל־בְּנֵי אַשּׁוּר עָגְבָה פַּחוֹת וּסְגָנִים קְרֹבִים לְבֻשֵׁי מִכְלוֹל פָּרָשִׁים רֹכְבֵי סוּסִים בַּחוּרֵי חֶמֶד כֻּלָּם: יב

13 And I saw how she had defiled herself. Both of them followed the same course,

וָאֵרֶא כִּי נִטְמָאָה דֶּרֶךְ אֶחָד לִשְׁתֵּיהֶן: יג

14 but she carried her harlotries further. For she saw men sculptured upon the walls, figures of Chaldeans drawn in vermilion,

וַתּוֹסֶף אֶל־תַּזְנוּתֶיהָ וַתֵּרֶא אַנְשֵׁי מְחֻקֶּה עַל־הַקִּיר צַלְמֵי כשדיים [כַשְׂדִּים] חֲקֻקִים בַּשָּׁשַׁר: יד

15 girded with belts round their waists, and with flowing turbans on their heads, all of them looking like officers – a picture of Babylonians whose native land was Chaldea.

חֲגוֹרֵי אֵזוֹר בְּמָתְנֵיהֶם סְרוּחֵי טְבוּלִים בְּרָאשֵׁיהֶם מַרְאֵה שָׁלִשִׁים כֻּלָּם דְּמוּת בְּנֵי־בָבֶל כַּשְׂדִּים אֶרֶץ מוֹלַדְתָּם: טו

16 At the very sight of them she lusted after them, and she sent messengers for them to Chaldea.

ותעגב [וַתַּעְגְּבָה] עֲלֵיהֶם לְמַרְאֵה עֵינֶיהָ וַתִּשְׁלַח מַלְאָכִים אֲלֵיהֶם כַּשְׂדִּימָה: טז

17 So the Babylonians came to her for lovemaking and defiled her with their whoring; and she defiled herself with them until she turned from them in disgust.

וַיָּבֹאוּ אֵלֶיהָ בְנֵי־בָבֶל לְמִשְׁכַּב דֹּדִים וַיְטַמְּאוּ אוֹתָהּ בְּתַזְנוּתָם וַתִּטְמָא־בָם וַתֵּקַע נַפְשָׁהּ מֵהֶם: יז

18 She flaunted her harlotries and exposed her nakedness, and I turned from her in disgust, as I had turned disgusted from her sister.

וַתְּגַל תַּזְנוּתֶיהָ וַתְּגַל אֶת־עֶרְוָתָהּ וַתֵּקַע נַפְשִׁי מֵעָלֶיהָ כַּאֲשֶׁר נָקְעָה נַפְשִׁי מֵעַל אֲחוֹתָהּ: יח

19 But she whored still more, remembering how in her youth she had played the whore in the land of Egypt;

וַתַּרְבֶּה אֶת־תַּזְנוּתֶיהָ לִזְכֹּר אֶת־יְמֵי נְעוּרֶיהָ אֲשֶׁר זָנְתָה בְּאֶרֶץ מִצְרָיִם: יט

20 she lusted for concubinage with them, whose members were like those of asses and whose organs were like those of stallions.

וַתַּעְגְּבָה עַל פִּלַגְשֵׁיהֶם אֲשֶׁר בְּשַׂר־חֲמוֹרִים בְּשָׂרָם וְזִרְמַת סוּסִים זִרְמָתָם: כ

21 Thus you reverted to the wantonness of your youth, remembering your youthful breasts, when the men of Egypt handled your nipples.

וַתִּפְקְדִי אֵת זִמַּת נְעוּרָיִךְ בַּעְשׂוֹת מִמִּצְרַיִם דַּדַּיִךְ לְמַעַן שְׁדֵי נְעוּרָיִךְ: כא

22 Assuredly, *Oholiva*, thus said *Hashem*: I am going to rouse against you the lovers from whom you turned in disgust, and I will bring them upon you from all around –

לָכֵן אָהֳלִיבָה כֹּה־אָמַר אֲדֹנָי יֱהֹוִה הִנְנִי מֵעִיר אֶת־מְאַהֲבַיִךְ עָלַיִךְ אֵת אֲשֶׁר־נָקְעָה נַפְשֵׁךְ מֵהֶם וַהֲבֵאתִים עָלַיִךְ מִסָּבִיב: כב

23 the Babylonians and all the Chaldeans, [the people of] Pekod, Shoa, and Koa, and all the Assyrians with them, all of them handsome young fellows, governors and prefects, officers and warriors, all of them riding on horseback.

בְּנֵי בָבֶל וְכָל־כַּשְׂדִּים פְּקוֹד וְשׁוֹעַ וְקוֹעַ כָּל־בְּנֵי אַשּׁוּר אוֹתָם בַּחוּרֵי חֶמֶד פַּחוֹת וּסְגָנִים כֻּלָּם שָׁלִשִׁים וּקְרוּאִים רֹכְבֵי סוּסִים כֻּלָּם: כג

24 They shall attack you with fleets of wheeled chariots and a host of troops; they shall set themselves against you on all sides with bucklers, shields, and helmets. And I will entrust your punishment to them, and they shall inflict their punishments on you.

כד וּבָאוּ עָלַיִךְ הֹצֶן רֶכֶב וְגַלְגַּל וּבִקְהַל עַמִּים צִנָּה וּמָגֵן וְקוֹבַע יָשִׂימוּ עָלַיִךְ סָבִיב וְנָתַתִּי לִפְנֵיהֶם מִשְׁפָּט וּשְׁפָטוּךְ בְּמִשְׁפְּטֵיהֶם:

25 I will direct My passion against you, and they shall deal with you in fury: they shall cut off your nose and ears. The last of you shall fall by the sword; they shall take away your sons and daughters, and your remnant shall be devoured by fire.

כה וְנָתַתִּי קִנְאָתִי בָּךְ וְעָשׂוּ אוֹתָךְ בְּחֵמָה אַפֵּךְ וְאָזְנַיִךְ יָסִירוּ וְאַחֲרִיתֵךְ בַּחֶרֶב תִּפּוֹל הֵמָּה בָּנַיִךְ וּבְנוֹתַיִךְ יִקָּחוּ וְאַחֲרִיתֵךְ תֵּאָכֵל בָּאֵשׁ:

26 They shall strip you of your clothing and take away your dazzling jewels.

כו וְהִפְשִׁיטוּךְ אֶת־בְּגָדָיִךְ וְלָקְחוּ כְּלֵי תִפְאַרְתֵּךְ:

27 I will put an end to your wantonness and to your whoring in the land of Egypt, and you shall not long for them or remember Egypt any more.

כז וְהִשְׁבַּתִּי זִמָּתֵךְ מִמֵּךְ וְאֶת־זְנוּתֵךְ מֵאֶרֶץ מִצְרָיִם וְלֹא־תִשְׂאִי עֵינַיִךְ אֲלֵיהֶם וּמִצְרַיִם לֹא תִזְכְּרִי־עוֹד:

28 For thus said *Hashem*: I am going to deliver you into the hands of those you hate, into the hands of those from whom you turned in disgust.

כח כִּי כֹה אָמַר אֲדֹנָי יֱהוִֹה הִנְנִי נֹתְנָךְ בְּיַד אֲשֶׁר שָׂנֵאת בְּיַד אֲשֶׁר־נָקְעָה נַפְשֵׁךְ מֵהֶם:

29 They shall treat you with hate, and they shall take away all you have toiled for, and leave you naked and bare; your naked whoredom, wantonness, and harlotry will be exposed.

כט וְעָשׂוּ אוֹתָךְ בְּשִׂנְאָה וְלָקְחוּ כָּל־יְגִיעֵךְ וַעֲזָבוּךְ עֵירֹם וְעֶרְיָה וְנִגְלָה עֶרְוַת זְנוּנַיִךְ וְזִמָּתֵךְ וְתַזְנוּתָיִךְ:

30 These things shall be done to you for your harlotries with the nations, for defiling yourself with their fetishes.

ל עָשֹׂה אֵלֶּה לָךְ בִּזְנוֹתֵךְ אַחֲרֵי גוֹיִם עַל אֲשֶׁר־נִטְמֵאת בְּגִלּוּלֵיהֶם:

31 You walked in your sister's path; therefore I will put her cup into your hand.

לא בְּדֶרֶךְ אֲחוֹתֵךְ הָלָכְתְּ וְנָתַתִּי כוֹסָהּ בְּיָדֵךְ:

32 Thus said *Hashem*: You shall drink of your sister's cup, So deep and wide; It shall cause derision and scorn, It holds so much.

לב כֹּה אָמַר אֲדֹנָי יֱהוִֹה כּוֹס אֲחוֹתֵךְ תִּשְׁתִּי הָעֲמֻקָּה וְהָרְחָבָה תִּהְיֶה לִצְחֹק וּלְלַעַג מִרְבָּה לְהָכִיל:

33 You shall be filled with drunkenness and woe. The cup of desolation and horror, The cup of your sister Shomron –

לג שִׁכָּרוֹן וְיָגוֹן תִּמָּלֵאִי כּוֹס שַׁמָּה וּשְׁמָמָה כּוֹס אֲחוֹתֵךְ שֹׁמְרוֹן:

34 You shall drink it and drain it, And gnaw its shards; And you shall tear your breasts. For I have spoken – declares *Hashem*.

לד וְשָׁתִית אוֹתָהּ וּמָצִית וְאֶת־חֲרָשֶׂיהָ תְּגָרֵמִי וְשָׁדַיִךְ תְּנַתֵּקִי כִּי אֲנִי דִבַּרְתִּי נְאֻם אֲדֹנָי יֱהוִֹה:

35 Assuredly, thus said *Hashem*: Because you have forgotten Me and cast Me behind your back, you in turn must suffer for your wanton whoring.

לה לָכֵן כֹּה אָמַר אֲדֹנָי יֱהוִֹה יַעַן שָׁכַחַתְּ אוֹתִי וַתַּשְׁלִיכִי אוֹתִי אַחֲרֵי גַוֵּךְ וְגַם־אַתְּ שְׂאִי זִמָּתֵךְ וְאֶת־תַּזְנוּתָיִךְ:

36 Then *Hashem* said to me: O mortal, arraign *Ohola* and *Oholiva*, and charge them with their abominations.

לו וַיֹּאמֶר יְהוָֹה אֵלַי בֶּן־אָדָם הֲתִשְׁפּוֹט אֶת־אָהֳלָה וְאֶת־אָהֳלִיבָה וְהַגֵּד לָהֶן אֵת תּוֹעֲבוֹתֵיהֶן:

³⁷ For they have committed adultery, and blood is on their hands; truly they have committed adultery with their fetishes, and have even offered to them as food the children they bore to Me.

כי נִאֵפוּ וְדָם בִּידֵיהֶן וְאֶת־גִּלּוּלֵיהֶן נִאֵפוּ וְגַם אֶת־בְּנֵיהֶן אֲשֶׁר יָלְדוּ־לִי הֶעֱבִירוּ לָהֶם לְאָכְלָה: לז

³⁸ At the same time they also did this to Me: they defiled My Sanctuary and profaned My *Shabbatot*.

עוֹד זֹאת עָשׂוּ לִי טִמְּאוּ אֶת־מִקְדָּשִׁי בַּיּוֹם הַהוּא וְאֶת־שַׁבְּתוֹתַי חִלֵּלוּ: לח

³⁹ On the very day that they slaughtered their children to their fetishes, they entered My Sanctuary to desecrate it. That is what they did in My House.

וּבְשַׁחֲטָם אֶת־בְּנֵיהֶם לְגִלּוּלֵיהֶם וַיָּבֹאוּ אֶל־מִקְדָּשִׁי בַּיּוֹם הַהוּא לְחַלְּלוֹ וְהִנֵּה־כֹה עָשׂוּ בְּתוֹךְ בֵּיתִי: לט

⁴⁰ Moreover, they sent for men to come from afar, [men] to whom a messenger was sent; and they came. For them, [*Oholiva*,] you bathed, painted your eyes, and donned your finery;

וְאַף כִּי תִשְׁלַחְנָה לַאֲנָשִׁים בָּאִים מִמֶּרְחָק אֲשֶׁר מַלְאָךְ שָׁלוּחַ אֲלֵיהֶם וְהִנֵּה־בָאוּ לַאֲשֶׁר רָחַצְתְּ כָּחַלְתְּ עֵינַיִךְ וְעָדִית עֶדִי: מ

⁴¹ and you sat on a grand couch with a set table in front of it – and it was My incense and My oil you laid upon it.

וְיָשַׁבְתְּ עַל־מִטָּה כְבוּדָּה וְשֻׁלְחָן עָרוּךְ לְפָנֶיהָ וּקְטָרְתִּי וְשַׁמְנִי שַׂמְתְּ עָלֶיהָ: מא

⁴² And the noise of a carefree multitude was there, of numerous men brought drunk from the desert; and they put bracelets on their arms and splendid crowns upon their heads.

וְקוֹל הָמוֹן שָׁלֵו בָהּ וְאֶל־אֲנָשִׁים מֵרֹב אָדָם מוּבָאִים סוֹבָאִים [סָבָאִים] מִמִּדְבָּר וַיִּתְּנוּ צְמִידִים אֶל־יְדֵיהֶן וַעֲטֶרֶת תִּפְאֶרֶת עַל־רָאשֵׁיהֶן: מב

⁴³ Then I said, "To destruction with adultery! Look, they are still going on with those same fornications of hers."

וָאֹמַר לַבָּלָה נִאוּפִים עַת [עַתָּה] יִזְנֶה [יִזְנוּ] תַזְנוּתֶהָ וָהִיא: מג

⁴⁴ And they would go to her as one goes to a prostitute; that is how they went to *Ohola* and *Oholiva*, wanton women.

וַיָּבוֹא אֵלֶיהָ כְּבוֹא אֶל־אִשָּׁה זוֹנָה כֵּן בָּאוּ אֶל־אָהֳלָה וְאֶל־אָהֳלִיבָה אִשֹּׁת הַזִּמָּה: מד

⁴⁵ But righteous men shall punish them with the punishments for adultery and for bloodshed, for they are adulteresses and have blood on their hands.

וַאֲנָשִׁים צַדִּיקִם הֵמָּה יִשְׁפְּטוּ אוֹתְהֶם מִשְׁפַּט נֹאֲפוֹת וּמִשְׁפַּט שֹׁפְכוֹת דָּם כִּי נֹאֲפֹת הֵנָּה וְדָם בִּידֵיהֶן: מה

⁴⁶ For thus said *Hashem*: Summon an assembly against them, and make them an object of horror and plunder.

כִּי כֹּה אָמַר אֲדֹנָי יֱהֹוִה הַעֲלֵה עֲלֵיהֶם קָהָל וְנָתֹן אֶתְהֶן לְזַעֲוָה וְלָבַז: מו

⁴⁷ Let the assembly pelt them with stones and cut them down with their swords; let them kill their sons and daughters, and burn down their homes.

וְרָגְמוּ עֲלֵיהֶן אֶבֶן קָהָל וּבָרֵא אוֹתְהֶן בְּחַרְבוֹתָם בְּנֵיהֶם וּבְנוֹתֵיהֶם יַהֲרֹגוּ וּבָתֵּיהֶן בָּאֵשׁ יִשְׂרֹפוּ: מז

⁴⁸ I will put an end to wantonness in the land; and all the women shall take warning not to imitate your wantonness.

וְהִשְׁבַּתִּי זִמָּה מִן־הָאָרֶץ וְנִוַּסְּרוּ כָּל־הַנָּשִׁים וְלֹא תַעֲשֶׂינָה כְּזִמַּתְכֶנָה: מח

⁴⁹ They shall punish you for your wantonness, and you shall suffer the penalty for your sinful idolatry. And you shall know that I am *Hashem*.

וְנָתְנוּ זִמַּתְכֶנָה עֲלֵיכֶן וַחֲטָאֵי גִלּוּלֵיכֶן תִּשֶּׂאינָה וִידַעְתֶּם כִּי אֲנִי אֲדֹנָי יֱהֹוִה: מט

Ezekiel

54

24 **ד** **א** וַיְהִי דְבַר־יְהֹוָה אֵלַי בַּשָּׁנָה הַתְּשִׁיעִית

1 In the ninth year, on the tenth day of the tenth
month, the word of *Hashem* came to me:

בַּחֹדֶשׁ הָעֲשִׂירִי בֶּעָשׂוֹר לַחֹדֶשׁ לֵאמֹר:

*vai-HEE d'-var a-do-NAI ay-LAI ba-sha-NAH ha-t'-shee-EET
ba-KHO-desh ha-a-see-REE be-a-SOR la-KHO-desh lay-MOR*

2 O mortal, record this date, this exact day; for this
very day the king of Babylon has laid siege to
Yerushalayim.

ב בֶּן־אָדָם כתוב־[כְּתָב־] לְךָ אֶת־שֵׁם
הַיּוֹם אֶת־עֶצֶם הַיּוֹם הַזֶּה סָמַךְ מֶלֶךְ־
בָּבֶל אֶל־יְרוּשָׁלַם בְּעֶצֶם הַיּוֹם הַזֶּה:

3 Further, speak in an allegory to the rebellious
breed and say to them: Thus said *Hashem*: Put
the caldron [on the fire], put it on, And then pour
water into it.

ג וּמְשֹׁל אֶל־בֵּית־הַמֶּרִי מָשָׁל וְאָמַרְתָּ
אֲלֵיהֶם כֹּה אָמַר אֲדֹנָי יֱהֹוִה שְׁפֹת הַסִּיר
שְׁפֹת וְגַם־יְצֹק בּוֹ מָיִם:

4 Collect in it the pieces [of meat]. Every choice
piece, thigh and shoulder; Fill it with the best
cuts –

ד אֱסֹף נְתָחֶיהָ אֵלֶיהָ כָּל־נֵתַח טוֹב יָרֵךְ
וְכָתֵף מִבְחַר עֲצָמִים מַלֵּא:

5 Take the best of the flock. Also pile the cuts under
it; Get it boiling briskly, And cook the cuts in it.

ה מִבְחַר הַצֹּאן לָקוֹחַ וְגַם דּוּר הָעֲצָמִים
תַּחְתֶּיהָ רַתַּח רְתָחֶיהָ גַּם־בָּשְׁלוּ עֲצָמֶיהָ
בְּתוֹכָהּ:

6 Assuredly, thus said *Hashem*: Woe to the city of
blood – A caldron whose scum is in it, Whose
scum has not been cleaned out! Empty it piece by
piece; No lot has fallen upon it.

ו לָכֵן כֹּה־אָמַר אֲדֹנָי יֱהֹוִה אוֹי עִיר
הַדָּמִים סִיר אֲשֶׁר חֶלְאָתָה בָהּ וְחֶלְאָתָהּ
לֹא יָצְאָה מִמֶּנָּה לִנְתָחֶיהָ לִנְתָחֶיהָ
הוֹצִיאָהּ לֹא־נָפַל עָלֶיהָ גּוֹרָל:

7 For the blood she shed is still in her; She set it
upon a bare rock; She did not pour it out on the
ground To cover it with earth.

ז כִּי דָמָהּ בְּתוֹכָהּ הָיָה עַל־צְחִיחַ סֶלַע
שָׂמָתְהוּ לֹא שְׁפָכַתְהוּ עַל־הָאָרֶץ
לְכַסּוֹת עָלָיו עָפָר:

8 She set her blood upon the bare rock, So that it was
not covered, So that it may stir up [My] fury To
take vengeance.

ח לְהַעֲלוֹת חֵמָה לִנְקֹם נָקָם נָתַתִּי אֶת־
דָּמָהּ עַל־צְחִיחַ סָלַע לְבִלְתִּי הִכָּסוֹת:

9 Assuredly, thus said *Hashem*: Woe to the city of
blood! I in turn will make a great blaze.

ט לָכֵן כֹּה אָמַר אֲדֹנָי יֱהֹוִה אוֹי עִיר
הַדָּמִים גַּם־אֲנִי אַגְדִּיל הַמְּדוּרָה:

10 Pile on the logs, Kindle the fire, Cook the meat
through And stew it completely, And let the bones
be charred.

י הַרְבֵּה הָעֵצִים הַדְלֵק הָאֵשׁ הָתֵם הַבָּשָׂר
וְהַרְקַח הַמֶּרְקָחָה וְהָעֲצָמוֹת יֵחָרוּ:

11 Let it stand empty on the coals, Until it becomes
so hot That the copper glows. Then its uncleanness
shall melt away in it, And its rust be consumed.

יא וְהַעֲמִידֶהָ עַל־גֶּחָלֶיהָ רֵקָה לְמַעַן תֵּחַם
וְחָרָה נְחֻשְׁתָּהּ וְנִתְּכָה בְתוֹכָהּ טֻמְאָתָהּ
תִּתֻּם חֶלְאָתָהּ:

24:1 On the tenth day of the tenth month In the
final chapter describing *Yerushalayim's* downfall, the prophet mentions the date of the start
of the Babylonian siege of *Yerushalayim*, describing it as
the tenth day of the tenth month. This day, the tenth of
the month of *Tevet*, is one of the four fast days mentioned
in *Zecharya* (8:19) that were instituted after the destruction of the *Beit Hamikdash*, in commemoration of various
stages of its destruc-
tion. Until today,
Jews all over the
world fast on the
tenth of *Tevet*, to re-
member the Babylo-
nian siege of *Yerushalayim*, to mourn over its destruction
and to pray for it to be rebuilt.

Walls of the Old City of *Yerushalayim*

Ezekiel

12 It has frustrated all effort, Its thick scum will not leave it – Into the fire with its scum!

יב תְּאֻנִים הֶלְאָת וְלֹא־תֵצֵא מִמֶּנָּה רַבַּת חֶלְאָתָהּ בָּאֵשׁ חֶלְאָתָהּ:

13 For your vile impurity – because I sought to cleanse you of your impurity, but you would not be cleansed – you shall never be clean again until I have satisfied My fury upon you.

יג בְּטֻמְאָתֵךְ זִמָּה יַעַן טִהַרְתִּיךְ וְלֹא טָהַרְתְּ מִטֻּמְאָתֵךְ לֹא תִטְהֲרִי־עוֹד עַד־הֲנִיחִי אֶת־חֲמָתִי בָּךְ:

14 I *Hashem* have spoken: It shall come to pass and I will do it. I will not refrain or spare or relent. You shall be punished according to your ways and your deeds – declares *Hashem*.

יד אֲנִי יְהֹוָה דִּבַּרְתִּי בָּאָה וְעָשִׂיתִי לֹא־אֶפְרַע וְלֹא־אָחוּס וְלֹא אֶנָּחֵם כִּדְרָכַיִךְ וְכַעֲלִילוֹתַיִךְ שְׁפָטוּךְ נְאֻם אֲדֹנָי יְהֹוִה:

15 The word of *Hashem* came to me:

טו וַיְהִי דְבַר־יְהֹוָה אֵלַי לֵאמֹר:

16 O mortal, I am about to take away the delight of your eyes from you through pestilence; but you shall not lament or weep or let your tears flow.

טז בֶּן־אָדָם הִנְנִי לֹקֵחַ מִמְּךָ אֶת־מַחְמַד עֵינֶיךָ בְּמַגֵּפָה וְלֹא תִסְפֹּד וְלֹא תִבְכֶּה וְלוֹא תָבוֹא דִּמְעָתֶךָ:

17 Moan softly; observe no mourning for the dead: Put on your turban and put your sandals on your feet; do not cover over your upper lip, and do not eat the bread of comforters."

יז הֵאָנֵק דֹּם מֵתִים אֵבֶל לֹא־תַעֲשֶׂה פְּאֵרְךָ חֲבוֹשׁ עָלֶיךָ וּנְעָלֶיךָ תָּשִׂים בְּרַגְלֶיךָ וְלֹא תַעְטֶה עַל־שָׂפָם וְלֶחֶם אֲנָשִׁים לֹא תֹאכֵל:

18 In the evening my wife died, and in the morning I did as I had been commanded. And when I spoke to the people that morning,

יח וָאֲדַבֵּר אֶל־הָעָם בַּבֹּקֶר וַתָּמָת אִשְׁתִּי בָּעָרֶב וָאַעַשׂ בַּבֹּקֶר כַּאֲשֶׁר צֻוֵּיתִי:

19 the people asked me, "Will you not tell us what these things portend for us, that you are acting so?"

יט וַיֹּאמְרוּ אֵלַי הָעָם הֲלֹא־תַגִּיד לָנוּ מָה־אֵלֶּה לָּנוּ כִּי אַתָּה עֹשֶׂה:

20 I answered them, "The word of *Hashem* has come to me:

כ וָאֹמַר אֲלֵיהֶם דְּבַר־יְהֹוָה הָיָה אֵלַי לֵאמֹר:

21 Tell the House of *Yisrael*: Thus said *Hashem*: 'I am going to desecrate My Sanctuary, your pride and glory, the delight of your eyes and the desire of your heart; and the sons and daughters you have left behind shall fall by the sword.

כא אֱמֹר לְבֵית יִשְׂרָאֵל כֹּה־אָמַר אֲדֹנָי יְהֹוִה הִנְנִי מְחַלֵּל אֶת־מִקְדָּשִׁי גְּאוֹן עֻזְּכֶם מַחְמַד עֵינֵיכֶם וּמַחְמַל נַפְשְׁכֶם וּבְנֵיכֶם וּבְנוֹתֵיכֶם אֲשֶׁר עֲזַבְתֶּם בַּחֶרֶב יִפֹּלוּ:

24* *And Yechezkel shall become a portent for you: you shall do just as he has done, when it happens; and you shall know that I am Hashem.'*

22 Accordingly, you shall do as I have done: you shall not cover over your upper lips or eat the bread of comforters;

כב וַעֲשִׂיתֶם כַּאֲשֶׁר עָשִׂיתִי עַל־שָׂפָם לֹא תַעְטוּ וְלֶחֶם אֲנָשִׁים לֹא תֹאכֵלוּ:

23 and your turbans shall remain on your heads, and your sandals upon your feet. You shall not lament or weep, but you shall be heartsick because of your iniquities and shall moan to one another."

כג וּפְאֵרֵכֶם עַל־רָאשֵׁיכֶם וְנַעֲלֵיכֶם בְּרַגְלֵיכֶם לֹא תִסְפְּדוּ וְלֹא תִבְכּוּ וּנְמַקֹּתֶם בַּעֲוֹנֹתֵיכֶם וּנְהַמְתֶּם אִישׁ אֶל־אָחִיו:

24 And *Yechezkel* shall become a portent for you: you shall do just as he has done, when it happens; and you shall know that I am *Hashem*.'

כד וְהָיָה יְחֶזְקֵאל לָכֶם לְמוֹפֵת כְּכֹל אֲשֶׁר־עָשָׂה תַּעֲשׂוּ בְּבֹאָהּ וִידַעְתֶּם כִּי אֲנִי אֲדֹנָי יְהֹוִה:

---

* Verse 24 moved up for clarity

25 You, O mortal, take note: On the day that I take their stronghold from them, their pride and joy, the delight of their eyes and the longing of their hearts – their sons and daughters –

כה וְאַתָּה בֶן־אָדָם הֲלוֹא בְּיוֹם קַחְתִּי מֵהֶם אֶת־מָעוּזָּם מְשׂוֹשׂ תִּפְאַרְתָּם אֶת־מַחְמַד עֵינֵיהֶם וְאֶת־מַשָּׂא נַפְשָׁם בְּנֵיהֶם וּבְנוֹתֵיהֶם:

26 on that day a fugitive will come to you, to let you hear it with your own ears.

כו בַּיּוֹם הַהוּא יָבוֹא הַפָּלִיט אֵלֶיךָ לְהַשְׁמָעוּת אָזְנָיִם:

27 On that day your mouth shall be opened to the fugitive, and you shall speak and no longer be dumb. So you shall be a portent for them, and they shall know that I am *Hashem*.

כז בַּיּוֹם הַהוּא יִפָּתַח פִּיךָ אֶת־הַפָּלִיט וּתְדַבֵּר וְלֹא תֵאָלֵם עוֹד וְהָיִיתָ לָהֶם לְמוֹפֵת וְיָדְעוּ כִּי־אֲנִי יְהֹוָה:

25 1 The word of *Hashem* came to me:

ה א וַיְהִי דְבַר־יְהֹוָה אֵלַי לֵאמֹר:

2 O mortal, set your face toward the Amonites and prophesy against them.

ב בֶּן־אָדָם שִׂים פָּנֶיךָ אֶל־בְּנֵי עַמּוֹן וְהִנָּבֵא עֲלֵיהֶם:

3 Say to the Amonites: Hear the word of *Hashem*! Thus said *Hashem*: Because you cried "Aha!" over My Sanctuary when it was desecrated, and over the land of *Yisrael* when it was laid waste, and over the House of *Yehuda* when it went into exile –

ג וְאָמַרְתָּ לִבְנֵי עַמּוֹן שִׁמְעוּ דְּבַר־אֲדֹנָי יֱהֹוִה כֹּה־אָמַר אֲדֹנָי יֱהֹוִה יַעַן אָמְרֵךְ הֶאָח אֶל־מִקְדָּשִׁי כִי־נִחָל וְאֶל־אַדְמַת יִשְׂרָאֵל כִּי נָשַׁמָּה וְאֶל־בֵּית יְהוּדָה כִּי הָלְכוּ בַּגּוֹלָה:

4 assuredly, I will deliver you to the Kedemites as a possession. They shall set up their encampments among you and pitch their dwellings in your midst; they shall eat your produce and they shall drink your milk.

ד לָכֵן הִנְנִי נֹתְנָךְ לִבְנֵי־קֶדֶם לְמוֹרָשָׁה וְיִשְּׁבוּ טִירוֹתֵיהֶם בָּךְ וְנָתְנוּ בָךְ מִשְׁכְּנֵיהֶם הֵמָּה יֹאכְלוּ פִרְיֵךְ וְהֵמָּה יִשְׁתּוּ חֲלָבֵךְ:

5 I will make Rabbah a pasture for camels and Ammon a place for sheep to lie down. And you shall know that I am *Hashem*.

ה וְנָתַתִּי אֶת־רַבָּה לִנְוֵה גְמַלִּים וְאֶת־בְּנֵי עַמּוֹן לְמִרְבַּץ־צֹאן וִידַעְתֶּם כִּי־אֲנִי יְהֹוָה:

6 For thus said *Hashem*: Because you clapped your hands and stamped your feet and rejoiced over the land of *Yisrael* with such utter scorn –

ו כִּי כֹה אָמַר אֲדֹנָי יֱהֹוִה יַעַן מַחְאֲךָ יָד וְרַקְעֲךָ בְּרָגֶל וַתִּשְׂמַח בְּכָל־שָׁאטְךָ בְּנֶפֶשׁ אֶל־אַדְמַת יִשְׂרָאֵל:

7 assuredly, I will stretch out My hand against you and give you as booty to the nations; I will cut you off from among the peoples and wipe you out from among the countries and destroy you. And you shall know that I am *Hashem*.

ז לָכֵן הִנְנִי נָטִיתִי אֶת־יָדִי עָלֶיךָ וּנְתַתִּיךָ־לְבַג [לְבַז] לַגּוֹיִם וְהִכְרַתִּיךָ מִן־הָעַמִּים וְהַאֲבַדְתִּיךָ מִן־הָאֲרָצוֹת אַשְׁמִידְךָ וְיָדַעְתָּ כִּי־אֲנִי יְהֹוָה:

8 Thus said *Hashem*: Because Moab and Seir said, "See, the House of *Yehuda* is like all other nations" –

ח כֹּה אָמַר אֲדֹנָי יֱהֹוִה יַעַן אֲמֹר מוֹאָב וְשֵׂעִיר הִנֵּה כְּכָל־הַגּוֹיִם בֵּית יְהוּדָה:

9 assuredly, I will lay bare the flank of Moab, all its towns to the last one – Beth-jeshimoth, Baal-meon, and Kiriathaim, the glory of the country.

ט לָכֵן הִנְנִי פֹתֵחַ אֶת־כֶּתֶף מוֹאָב מֵהֶעָרִים מֵעָרָיו מִקָּצֵהוּ צְבִי אֶרֶץ בֵּית הַיְשִׁימֹת בַּעַל מְעוֹן וקריתמה [וְקִרְיָתָיְמָה]:

10 I will deliver it, together with Ammon, to the Kedemites as their possession. Thus Ammon shall not be remembered among the nations,

י לִבְנֵי־קֶדֶם עַל־בְּנֵי עַמּוֹן וּנְתַתִּיהָ לְמוֹרָשָׁה לְמַעַן לֹא־תִזָּכֵר בְּנֵי־עַמּוֹן בַּגּוֹיִם:

11 and I will mete out punishments to Moab. And they shall know that I am *Hashem*.

יא וּבְמוֹאָב אֶעֱשֶׂה שְׁפָטִים וְיָדְעוּ כִּי־אֲנִי יְהֹוָה:

12 Thus said *Hashem*: Because Edom acted vengefully against the House of *Yehuda* and incurred guilt by wreaking revenge upon it –

יב כֹּה אָמַר אֲדֹנָי יְהֹוִה יַעַן עֲשׂוֹת אֱדוֹם בִּנְקֹם נָקָם לְבֵית יְהוּדָה וַיֶּאְשְׁמוּ אָשׁוֹם וְנִקְמוּ בָהֶם:

13 assuredly, thus said *Hashem*: I will stretch out My hand against Edom and cut off from it man and beast, and I will lay it in ruins; from Tema to Dedan they shall fall by the sword.

יג לָכֵן כֹּה אָמַר אֲדֹנָי יְהֹוִה וְנָטִתִי יָדִי עַל־אֱדוֹם וְהִכְרַתִּי מִמֶּנָּה אָדָם וּבְהֵמָה וּנְתַתִּיהָ חָרְבָּה מִתֵּימָן וּדְדָנֶה בַּחֶרֶב יִפֹּלוּ:

14 I will wreak My vengeance on Edom through My people *Yisrael*, and they shall take action against Edom in accordance with My blazing anger; and they shall know My vengeance – declares *Hashem*.

יד וְנָתַתִּי אֶת־נִקְמָתִי בֶּאֱדוֹם בְּיַד עַמִּי יִשְׂרָאֵל וְעָשׂוּ בֶאֱדוֹם כְּאַפִּי וְכַחֲמָתִי וְיָדְעוּ אֶת־נִקְמָתִי נְאֻם אֲדֹנָי יְהֹוִה:

15 Thus said *Hashem*: Because the Philistines, in their ancient hatred, acted vengefully, and with utter scorn sought revenge and destruction –

טו כֹּה אָמַר אֲדֹנָי יְהֹוִה יַעַן עֲשׂוֹת פְּלִשְׁתִּים בִּנְקָמָה וַיִּנָּקְמוּ נָקָם בִּשְׁאָט בְּנֶפֶשׁ לְמַשְׁחִית אֵיבַת עוֹלָם:

16 assuredly, thus said *Hashem*: I will stretch out My hand against the Philistines and cut off the Cherethites and wipe out the last survivors of the seacoast.

טז לָכֵן כֹּה אָמַר אֲדֹנָי יְהֹוִה הִנְנִי נוֹטֶה יָדִי עַל־פְּלִשְׁתִּים וְהִכְרַתִּי אֶת־כְּרֵתִים וְהַאֲבַדְתִּי אֶת־שְׁאֵרִית חוֹף הַיָּם:

17 I will wreak frightful vengeance upon them by furious punishment; and when I inflict My vengeance upon them, they shall know that I am *Hashem*.

יז וְעָשִׂיתִי בָם נְקָמוֹת גְּדֹלוֹת בְּתוֹכְחוֹת חֵמָה וְיָדְעוּ כִּי־אֲנִי יְהֹוָה בְּתִתִּי אֶת־נִקְמָתִי בָּם:

v'-a-SEE-tee VAM n'-ka-MOT g'-do-LOT b'-to-kh'-KHOT khay-MAH
v'-ya-d'-U kee a-NEE a-do-NAI b'-ti-TEE et nik-ma-TEE BAM

כו 1 In the eleventh year, on the first of the month, the word of *Hashem* came to me:

כו א וַיְהִי בְּעַשְׁתֵּי־עֶשְׂרֵה שָׁנָה בְּאֶחָד לַחֹדֶשׁ הָיָה דְבַר־יְהֹוָה אֵלַי לֵאמֹר:

25:17 They shall know that I am *Hashem* Yechezkel begins a series of prophecies against the nations who either assisted the Babylonian destruction of *Yehuda*, or who rejoiced upon *Yehuda's* downfall. *Yechezkel* describes how the Philistines "with utter scorn sought revenge" (verse 15). Therefore, God promises to execute a great vengeance on Philistia. The retribution will be so great that it will be clear that it came from Heaven. *Hashem* loves His people, Israel, even in times of punishment, and He personally involves Himself in their redemption and the downfall of their enemies.

Israeli paratroopers in a training jump

58

2 O mortal, because Tyre gloated over *Yerushalayim*, "Aha! The gateway of the peoples is broken, it has become mine; I shall be filled, now that it is laid in ruins" –

בֶּן־אָדָם יַעַן אֲשֶׁר־אָמְרָה צֹּר עַל־יְרוּשָׁלַם הֶאָח נִשְׁבְּרָה דַּלְתוֹת הָעַמִּים נָסֵבָּה אֵלָי אִמָּלְאָה הָחֳרָבָה:

ben a-DAM YA-an a-sher A-m'-rah TZOR al y'-ru-sha-LA-im he-AKH nish-b'-RAH dal-TOT ha-a-MEEM na-SAY-bah ay-LAI i-ma-l'-AH ha-kho-ra-VAH

3 assuredly, thus said *Hashem*: I am going to deal with you, O Tyre! I will hurl many nations against you, As the sea hurls its waves.

לָכֵן כֹּה אָמַר אֲדֹנָי יְהוִה הִנְנִי עָלַיִךְ צֹר וְהַעֲלֵיתִי עָלַיִךְ גּוֹיִם רַבִּים כְּהַעֲלוֹת הַיָּם לְגַלָּיו:

4 They shall destroy the walls of Tyre And demolish her towers; And I will scrape her soil off her And leave her a naked rock.

וְשִׁחֲתוּ חֹמוֹת צֹר וְהָרְסוּ מִגְדָּלֶיהָ וְסִחֵיתִי עֲפָרָהּ מִמֶּנָּה וְנָתַתִּי אוֹתָהּ לִצְחִיחַ סָלַע:

5 She shall be in the heart of the sea A place for drying nets; For I have spoken it – declares *Hashem*. She shall become spoil for the nations,

מִשְׁטַח חֲרָמִים תִּהְיֶה בְּתוֹךְ הַיָּם כִּי אֲנִי דִבַּרְתִּי נְאֻם אֲדֹנָי יְהוִה וְהָיְתָה לְבַז לַגּוֹיִם:

6 And her daughter-towns in the country Shall be put to the sword. And they shall know that I am *Hashem*.

וּבְנוֹתֶיהָ אֲשֶׁר בַּשָּׂדֶה בַּחֶרֶב תֵּהָרַגְנָה וְיָדְעוּ כִּי־אֲנִי יְהוָה:

7 For thus said *Hashem*: I will bring from the north, against Tyre, King Nebuchadrezzar of Babylon, a king of kings, with horses, chariots, and horsemen – a great mass of troops.

כִּי כֹה אָמַר אֲדֹנָי יְהוִה הִנְנִי מֵבִיא אֶל־צֹר נְבוּכַדְרֶאצַּר מֶלֶךְ־בָּבֶל מִצָּפוֹן מֶלֶךְ מְלָכִים בְּסוּס וּבְרֶכֶב וּבְפָרָשִׁים וְקָהָל וְעַם־רָב:

8 Your daughter-towns in the country He shall put to the sword; He shall erect towers against you, And cast up mounds against you, And raise [a wall of] bucklers against you.

בְּנוֹתַיִךְ בַּשָּׂדֶה בַּחֶרֶב יַהֲרֹג וְנָתַן עָלַיִךְ דָּיֵק וְשָׁפַךְ עָלַיִךְ סֹלְלָה וְהֵקִים עָלַיִךְ צִנָּה:

9 He shall turn the force of his battering rams Against your walls And smash your towers with his axes.

וּמְחִי קָבָלּוֹ יִתֵּן בְּחֹמוֹתָיִךְ וּמִגְדְּלֹתַיִךְ יִתֹּץ בְּחַרְבוֹתָיו:

10 From the cloud raised by his horses Dust shall cover you; From the clatter of horsemen And wheels and chariots, Your walls shall shake – When he enters your gates As men enter a breached city.

מִשִּׁפְעַת סוּסָיו יְכַסֵּךְ אֲבָקָם מִקּוֹל פָּרַשׁ וְגַלְגַּל וָרֶכֶב תִּרְעַשְׁנָה חוֹמוֹתַיִךְ בְּבֹאוֹ בִּשְׁעָרַיִךְ כִּמְבוֹאֵי עִיר מְבֻקָּעָה:

Ruins near the southern wall of the Temple Mount

26:2 Because Tyre gloated over *Yerushalayim* Tyre, the capital city of the Phoenician empire, was besieged by Nebuchadnezzar and ultimately destroyed by Alexander the Great. Tyre was a great commercial center, with a rock fortress located offshore that was nearly impregnable. Its ability to withstand great armies made Tyre's inhabitants arrogant and insensitive. They rejoice at the misfortune of their neighbors, trying to profit from the sufferings of others. Since their attitude towards *Yerushalayim* is described as "I shall be filled, now that it is laid in ruins," Tyre is deserving of the divine punishments that will befall it.

11 With the hoofs of his steeds He shall trample all your streets. He shall put your people to the sword, And your mighty pillars shall crash to the ground.

יא בְּפַרְסוֹת סוּסָיו יִרְמֹס אֶת־כָּל־חוּצוֹתָיִךְ עַמֵּךְ בַּחֶרֶב יַהֲרֹג וּמַצְּבוֹת עֻזֵּךְ לָאָרֶץ תֵּרֵד:

12 They shall plunder your wealth And loot your merchandise. They shall raze your walls And tear down your splendid houses, And they shall cast into the water Your stones and timber and soil.

יב וְשָׁלְלוּ חֵילֵךְ וּבָזְזוּ רְכֻלָּתֵךְ וְהָרְסוּ חוֹמוֹתַיִךְ וּבָתֵּי חֶמְדָּתֵךְ יִתֹּצוּ וַאֲבָנַיִךְ וְעֵצַיִךְ וַעֲפָרֵךְ בְּתוֹךְ מַיִם יָשִׂימוּ:

13 I will put an end to the murmur of your songs, And the sound of your lyres shall be heard no more.

יג וְהִשְׁבַּתִּי הֲמוֹן שִׁירָיִךְ וְקוֹל כִּנּוֹרַיִךְ לֹא יִשָּׁמַע עוֹד:

14 I will make you a naked rock, You shall be a place for drying nets; You shall never be rebuilt. For I have spoken – declares *Hashem*.

יד וּנְתַתִּיךְ לִצְחִיחַ סֶלַע מִשְׁטַח חֲרָמִים תִּהְיֶה לֹא תִבָּנֶה עוֹד כִּי אֲנִי יְהוָה דִּבַּרְתִּי נְאֻם אֲדֹנָי יְהוִה:

15 Thus said *Hashem* to Tyre: The coastlands shall quake at the sound of your downfall, when the wounded groan, when slaughter is rife within you.

טו כֹּה אָמַר אֲדֹנָי יְהוִה לְצוֹר הֲלֹא מִקּוֹל מַפַּלְתֵּךְ בֶּאֱנֹק חָלָל בֵּהָרֵג הֶרֶג בְּתוֹכֵךְ יִרְעֲשׁוּ הָאִיִּים:

16 All the rulers of the sea shall descend from their thrones; they shall remove their robes and strip off their embroidered garments. They shall clothe themselves with trembling, and shall sit on the ground; they shall tremble every moment, and they shall be aghast at you.

טז וְיָרְדוּ מֵעַל כִּסְאוֹתָם כֹּל נְשִׂיאֵי הַיָּם וְהֵסִירוּ אֶת־מְעִילֵיהֶם וְאֶת־בִּגְדֵי רִקְמָתָם יִפְשֹׁטוּ חֲרָדוֹת יִלְבָּשׁוּ עַל־הָאָרֶץ יֵשֵׁבוּ וְחָרְדוּ לִרְגָעִים וְשָׁמְמוּ עָלָיִךְ:

17 And they shall intone a dirge over you, and they shall say to you: How you have perished, you who were peopled from the seas, O renowned city! Mighty on the sea were she and her inhabitants, Who cast their terror on all its inhabitants.

יז וְנָשְׂאוּ עָלַיִךְ קִינָה וְאָמְרוּ לָךְ אֵיךְ אָבַדְתְּ נוֹשֶׁבֶת מִיַּמִּים הָעִיר הַהֻלָּלָה אֲשֶׁר הָיְתָה חֲזָקָה בַיָּם הִיא וְיֹשְׁבֶיהָ אֲשֶׁר־נָתְנוּ חִתִּיתָם לְכָל־יוֹשְׁבֶיהָ:

18 Now shall the coastlands tremble On the day of your downfall, And the coastlands by the sea Be terrified at your end.

יח עַתָּה יֶחְרְדוּ הָאִיִּן יוֹם מַפַּלְתֵּךְ וְנִבְהֲלוּ הָאִיִּים אֲשֶׁר־בַּיָּם מִצֵּאתֵךְ:

19 For thus said *Hashem*: When I make you a ruined city, like cities empty of inhabitants; when I bring the deep over you, and its mighty waters cover you,

יט כִּי כֹה אָמַר אֲדֹנָי יְהוִה בְּתִתִּי אֹתָךְ עִיר נֶחֱרֶבֶת כֶּעָרִים אֲשֶׁר לֹא־נוֹשָׁבוּ בְּהַעֲלוֹת עָלַיִךְ אֶת־תְּהוֹם וְכִסּוּךְ הַמַּיִם הָרַבִּים:

20 then I will bring you down, with those who go down to the Pit, to the people of old. I will install you in the netherworld, with those that go down to the Pit, like the ruins of old, so that you shall not be inhabited and shall not radiate splendor in the land of the living.

כ וְהוֹרַדְתִּיךְ אֶת־יוֹרְדֵי בוֹר אֶל־עַם עוֹלָם וְהוֹשַׁבְתִּיךְ בְּאֶרֶץ תַּחְתִּיּוֹת כָּחֳרָבוֹת מֵעוֹלָם אֶת־יוֹרְדֵי בוֹר לְמַעַן לֹא תֵשֵׁבִי וְנָתַתִּי צְבִי בְּאֶרֶץ חַיִּים:

21 I will make you a horror, and you shall cease to be; you shall be sought, but shall never be found again – declares *Hashem*.

כא בַּלָּהוֹת אֶתְּנֵךְ וְאֵינֵךְ וּתְבֻקְשִׁי וְלֹא־תִמָּצְאִי עוֹד לְעוֹלָם נְאֻם אֲדֹנָי יְהוִה:

27 1 The word of *Hashem* came to me:

וַיְהִי דְבַר־יְהֹוָה אֵלַי לֵאמֹר: א

2 Now you, O mortal, intone a dirge over Tyre.

וְאַתָּה בֶן־אָדָם שָׂא עַל־צֹר קִינָה: ב

3 Say to Tyre: O you who dwell at the gateway of the sea, Who trade with the peoples on many coastlands: Thus said *Hashem*: O Tyre, you boasted, I am perfect in beauty.

וְאָמַרְתָּ לְצוֹר הישבתי [הַיֹּשֶׁבֶת] עַל־ ג
מְבוֹאֹת יָם רֹכֶלֶת הָעַמִּים אֶל־אִיִּים
רַבִּים כֹּה אָמַר אֲדֹנָי יֱהֹוִה צוֹר אַתְּ
אָמַרְתְּ אֲנִי כְּלִילַת יֹפִי:

v'-a-mar-TA l'-TZOR ha-yo-SHE-vet al m'-vo-OT YAM ro-KHE-let
ha-a-MEEM el i-YEEM ra-BEEM KOH a-MAR a-do-NAI
e-lo-HEEM TZOR AT a-MAR-t' a-NEE k'-LEE-lat YO-fee

4 Your frontiers were on the high seas, Your builders perfected your beauty.

בְּלֵב יַמִּים גְּבוּלָיִךְ בֹּנַיִךְ כָּלְלוּ יָפְיֵךְ: ד

5 From cypress trees of Senir They fashioned your planks; They took a cedar from Lebanon To make a mast for you.

בְּרוֹשִׁים מִשְּׂנִיר בָּנוּ לָךְ אֵת כָּל־לֻחֹתָיִם ה
אֶרֶז מִלְּבָנוֹן לָקָחוּ לַעֲשׂוֹת תֹּרֶן עָלָיִךְ:

6 From oak trees of Bashan They made your oars; Of boxwood from the isles of Kittim, Inlaid with ivory, They made your decks.

אַלּוֹנִים מִבָּשָׁן עָשׂוּ מִשּׁוֹטָיִךְ קַרְשֵׁךְ ו
עָשׂוּ־שֵׁן בַּת־אֲשֻׁרִים מֵאִיֵּי כִּתִּים
[כִּתִּיִּים]:

7 Embroidered linen from Egypt Was the cloth That served you for sails; Of blue and purple from the coasts of Elishah Were your awnings.

שֵׁשׁ־בְּרִקְמָה מִמִּצְרַיִם הָיָה מִפְרָשֵׂךְ ז
לִהְיוֹת לָךְ לְנֵס תְּכֵלֶת וְאַרְגָּמָן מֵאִיֵּי
אֱלִישָׁה הָיָה מְכַסֵּךְ:

8 The inhabitants of Sidon and Arvad Were your rowers; Your skilled men, O Tyre, were within you, They were your pilots.

יֹשְׁבֵי צִידוֹן וְאַרְוַד הָיוּ שָׁטִים לָךְ ח
חֲכָמַיִךְ צוֹר הָיוּ בָךְ הֵמָּה חֹבְלָיִךְ:

9 Gebal's elders and craftsmen were within you, Making your repairs. All the ships of the sea, with their crews, Were in your harbor To traffic in your wares.

זִקְנֵי גְבַל וַחֲכָמֶיהָ הָיוּ בָךְ מַחֲזִיקֵי ט
בִּדְקֵךְ כָּל־אֳנִיּוֹת הַיָּם וּמַלָּחֵיהֶם הָיוּ בָךְ
לַעֲרֹב מַעֲרָבֵךְ:

10 Men of Persia, Lud, and Put Were in your army, Your fighting men; They hung shields and helmets in your midst, They lent splendor to you.

פָּרַס וְלוּד וּפוּט הָיוּ בְחֵילֵךְ אַנְשֵׁי י
מִלְחַמְתֵּךְ מָגֵן וְכוֹבַע תִּלּוּ־בָךְ הֵמָּה נָתְנוּ
הֲדָרֵךְ:

11 Men of Arvad and Helech Manned your walls all around, And men of Gammad were stationed in your towers; They hung their quivers all about your walls; They perfected your beauty.

בְּנֵי אַרְוַד וְחֵילֵךְ עַל־חוֹמוֹתַיִךְ סָבִיב יא
וְגַמָּדִים בְּמִגְדְּלוֹתַיִךְ הָיוּ שִׁלְטֵיהֶם תִּלּוּ
עַל־חוֹמוֹתַיִךְ סָבִיב הֵמָּה כָּלְלוּ יָפְיֵךְ:

A ship on the Mediterranean Sea near *Ashkelon*

27:3 I am perfect in beauty *Yechezkel* laments the downfall of Tyre, blaming her ruin on arrogance. He compares Tyre to a beautiful ship, made of the finest materials by expert craftsmen (verses 4–11). He then gives a detailed description of the commercial activity that enriched the port city (verses 12–25). However, the proud ship, reliant on its wealth for its success and safety, was too full and heavy, a dangerous state for a vessel in deep waters. It therefore sank at the first storm (verses 26–36). As an expression of her arrogance, Tyre says about herself "I am perfect in beauty," a biblical phrase that had been used by *Yirmiyahu* to describe *Yerushalayim* (Lamentations 2:15).

12 Tarshish traded with you because of your wealth of all kinds of goods; they bartered silver, iron, tin, and lead for your wares.

יב תַּרְשִׁישׁ סֹחַרְתֵּךְ מֵרֹב כָּל־הוֹן בְּכֶסֶף בַּרְזֶל בְּדִיל וְעוֹפֶרֶת נָתְנוּ עִזְבוֹנָיִךְ:

13 Javan, Tubal, and Meshech – they were your merchants; they trafficked with you in human beings and copper utensils.

יג יָוָן תֻּבַל וָמֶשֶׁךְ הֵמָּה רֹכְלָיִךְ בְּנֶפֶשׁ אָדָם וּכְלֵי נְחֹשֶׁת נָתְנוּ מַעֲרָבֵךְ:

14 From Beth-togarmah they bartered horses, horsemen, and mules for your wares.

יד מִבֵּית תּוֹגַרְמָה סוּסִים וּפָרָשִׁים וּפְרָדִים נָתְנוּ עִזְבוֹנָיִךְ:

15 The people of Dedan were your merchants; many coastlands traded under your rule and rendered you tribute in ivory tusks and ebony.

טו בְּנֵי דְדָן רֹכְלַיִךְ אִיִּים רַבִּים סְחֹרַת יָדֵךְ קַרְנוֹת שֵׁן והובנים [וְהָבְנִים] הֵשִׁיבוּ אֶשְׁכָּרֵךְ:

16 Aram traded with you because of your wealth of merchandise, dealing with you in turquoise, purple stuff, embroidery, fine linen, coral, and agate.

טז אֲרָם סֹחַרְתֵּךְ מֵרֹב מַעֲשָׂיִךְ בְּנֹפֶךְ אַרְגָּמָן וְרִקְמָה וּבוּץ וְרָאמֹת וְכַדְכֹּד נָתְנוּ בְּעִזְבוֹנָיִךְ:

17 *Yehuda* and the land of *Yisrael* were your merchants; they trafficked with you in wheat of Minnith and Pannag, honey, oil, and balm.

יז יְהוּדָה וְאֶרֶץ יִשְׂרָאֵל הֵמָּה רֹכְלָיִךְ בְּחִטֵּי מִנִּית וּפַנַּג וּדְבַשׁ וָשֶׁמֶן וָצֹרִי נָתְנוּ מַעֲרָבֵךְ:

18 Because of your wealth of merchandise, because of your great wealth, Damascus traded with you in Helbon wine and white wool.

יח דַּמֶּשֶׂק סֹחַרְתֵּךְ בְּרֹב מַעֲשַׂיִךְ מֵרֹב כָּל־הוֹן בְּיֵין חֶלְבּוֹן וְצֶמֶר צָחַר:

19 Vedan and Javan from Uzal traded for your wares; they trafficked with you in polished iron, cassia, and calamus.

יט וְדָן וְיָוָן מְאוּזָּל בְּעִזְבוֹנַיִךְ נָתָנּוּ בַּרְזֶל עָשׁוֹת קִדָּה וְקָנֶה בְּמַעֲרָבֵךְ הָיָה:

20 Dedan was your merchant in saddlecloths for riding.

כ דְּדָן רֹכַלְתֵּךְ בְּבִגְדֵי־חֹפֶשׁ לְרִכְבָּה:

21 Arabia and all Kedar's chiefs were traders under your rule; they traded with you in lambs, rams, and goats.

כא עֲרַב וְכָל־נְשִׂיאֵי קֵדָר הֵמָּה סֹחֲרֵי יָדֵךְ בְּכָרִים וְאֵילִים וְעַתּוּדִים בָּם סֹחֲרָיִךְ:

22 The merchants of Sheba and Raamah were your merchants; they bartered for your wares all the finest spices, all kinds of precious stones, and gold.

כב רֹכְלֵי שְׁבָא וְרַעְמָה הֵמָּה רֹכְלָיִךְ בְּרֹאשׁ כָּל־בֹּשֶׂם וּבְכָל־אֶבֶן יְקָרָה וְזָהָב נָתְנוּ עִזְבוֹנָיִךְ:

23 Haran, Canneh, and Eden, the merchants of Sheba, Assyria, and Chilmad traded with you.

כג חָרָן וְכַנֵּה וָעֶדֶן רֹכְלֵי שְׁבָא אַשּׁוּר כִּלְמַד רֹכַלְתֵּךְ:

24 These were your merchants in choice fabrics, embroidered cloaks of blue, and many-colored carpets tied up with cords and preserved with cedar – among your wares.

כד הֵמָּה רֹכְלַיִךְ בְּמַכְלֻלִים בִּגְלוֹמֵי תְּכֵלֶת וְרִקְמָה וּבְגִנְזֵי בְּרֹמִים בַּחֲבָלִים חֲבֻשִׁים וַאֲרֻזִים בְּמַרְכֻלְתֵּךְ:

25 The ships of Tarshish were in the service of your trade. So you were full and richly laden On the high seas.

כה אֳנִיּוֹת תַּרְשִׁישׁ שָׁרוֹתַיִךְ מַעֲרָבֵךְ וַתִּמָּלְאִי וַתִּכְבְּדִי מְאֹד בְּלֵב־יַמִּים:

26 Your oarsmen brought you out Into the mighty waters; The tempest wrecked you On the high seas.

כו בְּמַיִם רַבִּים הֱבִיאוּךְ הַשָּׁטִים אֹתָךְ רוּחַ הַקָּדִים שְׁבָרֵךְ בְּלֵב יַמִּים:

27 Your wealth, your wares, your merchandise, Your sailors and your pilots, The men who made your repairs, Those who carried on your traffic, And all the fighting men within you – All the multitude within you – Shall go down into the depths of the sea On the day of your downfall.

כז הוֹנֵךְ וְעִזְבוֹנַיִךְ מַעֲרָבֵךְ וְחֹבְלָיִךְ מַחֲזִיקֵי בִדְקֵךְ וְעֹרְבֵי מַעֲרָבֵךְ וְכָל־אַנְשֵׁי מִלְחַמְתֵּךְ אֲשֶׁר־בָּךְ וּבְכָל־קְהָלֵךְ אֲשֶׁר בְּתוֹכֵךְ יִפְּלוּ בְּלֵב יַמִּים בְּיוֹם מַפַּלְתֵּךְ:

28 At the outcry of your pilots The billows shall heave;

כח לְקוֹל זַעֲקַת חֹבְלָיִךְ יִרְעֲשׁוּ מִגְרֹשׁוֹת:

29 And all the oarsmen and mariners, All the pilots of the sea, Shall come down from their ships And stand on the ground.

כט וְיָרְדוּ מֵאֳנִיּוֹתֵיהֶם כֹּל תֹּפְשֵׂי מָשׁוֹט מַלָּחִים כֹּל חֹבְלֵי הַיָּם אֶל־הָאָרֶץ יַעֲמֹדוּ:

30 They shall raise their voices over you And cry out bitterly; They shall cast dust on their heads And strew ashes on themselves.

ל וְהִשְׁמִיעוּ עָלַיִךְ בְּקוֹלָם וְיִזְעֲקוּ מָרָה וְיַעֲלוּ עָפָר עַל־רָאשֵׁיהֶם בָּאֵפֶר יִתְפַּלָּשׁוּ:

31 On your account, they shall make Bald patches on their heads, And shall gird themselves with sackcloth. They shall weep over you, broken-hearted, With bitter lamenting;

לא וְהִקְרִיחוּ אֵלַיִךְ קָרְחָה וְחָגְרוּ שַׂקִּים וּבָכוּ אֵלַיִךְ בְּמַר־נֶפֶשׁ מִסְפֵּד מָר:

32 They shall intone a dirge over you as they wail, And lament for you thus: Who was like Tyre when she was silenced In the midst of the sea?

לב וְנָשְׂאוּ אֵלַיִךְ בְּנִיהֶם קִינָה וְקוֹנְנוּ עָלָיִךְ מִי כְצוֹר כְּדֻמָּה בְּתוֹךְ הַיָּם:

33 When your wares were unloaded from the seas, You satisfied many peoples; With your great wealth and merchandise You enriched the kings of the earth.

לג בְּצֵאת עִזְבוֹנַיִךְ מִיַּמִּים הִשְׂבַּעַתְּ עַמִּים רַבִּים בְּרֹב הוֹנַיִךְ וּמַעֲרָבַיִךְ הֶעֱשַׁרְתְּ מַלְכֵי־אָרֶץ:

34 But when you were wrecked on the seas, In the deep waters sank your merchandise And all the crew aboard you.

לד עֵת נִשְׁבֶּרֶת מִיַּמִּים בְּמַעֲמַקֵּי־מָיִם מַעֲרָבֵךְ וְכָל־קְהָלֵךְ בְּתוֹכֵךְ נָפָלוּ:

35 All the inhabitants of the coastlands Are appalled over you; Their kings are aghast, Their faces contorted.

לה כֹּל יֹשְׁבֵי הָאִיִּים שָׁמְמוּ עָלָיִךְ וּמַלְכֵיהֶם שָׂעֲרוּ שַׂעַר רָעֲמוּ פָּנִים:

36 The merchants among the peoples hissed at you; You have become a horror, And have ceased to be forever.

לו סֹחֲרִים בָּעַמִּים שָׁרְקוּ עָלָיִךְ בַּלָּהוֹת הָיִית וְאֵינֵךְ עַד־עוֹלָם:

28 1 The word of *Hashem* came to me:

ח א וַיְהִי דְבַר־יְהוָה אֵלַי לֵאמֹר:

2 O mortal, say to the prince of Tyre: Thus said *Hashem*: Because you have been so haughty and have said, "I am a god; I sit enthroned like a god in the heart of the seas," whereas you are not a god but a man, though you deemed your mind equal to a god's –

ב בֶּן־אָדָם אֱמֹר לִנְגִיד צֹר כֹּה־אָמַר אֲדֹנָי יְהוִה יַעַן גָּבַהּ לִבְּךָ וַתֹּאמֶר אֵל אָנִי מוֹשַׁב אֱלֹהִים יָשַׁבְתִּי בְּלֵב יַמִּים וְאַתָּה אָדָם וְלֹא־אֵל וַתִּתֵּן לִבְּךָ כְּלֵב אֱלֹהִים:

3 Yes, you are wiser than *Daniel*; In no hidden matter can anyone Compare to you.

ג הִנֵּה חָכָם אַתָּה מִדָּנִאֵל [מִדָּנִיֵּאל] כָּל־סָתוּם לֹא עֲמָמוּךָ:

⁴ By your shrewd understanding You have gained riches, And have amassed gold and silver In your treasuries.

ד בְּחָכְמָתְךָ֙ וּבִתְבוּנָ֣תְךָ֔ עָשִׂ֥יתָ לְּךָ֖ חָ֑יִל וַתַּ֛עַשׂ זָהָ֥ב וָכֶ֖סֶף בְּאוֹצְרוֹתֶֽיךָ׃

⁵ By your great shrewdness in trade You have increased your wealth, And you have grown haughty Because of your wealth.

ה בְּרֹ֧ב חׇכְמָתְךָ֛ בִּרְכֻלָּתְךָ֖ הִרְבִּ֣יתָ חֵילֶ֑ךָ וַיִּגְבַּ֥הּ לְבָבְךָ֖ בְּחֵילֶֽךָ׃

⁶ Assuredly, thus said *Hashem*: Because you have deemed your mind equal to a god's,

ו לָכֵ֗ן כֹּ֤ה אָמַר֙ אֲדֹנָ֣י יֱהֹוִ֔ה יַ֛עַן תִּתְּךָ֥ אֶת־לְבָבְךָ֖ כְּלֵ֥ב אֱלֹהִֽים׃

⁷ I swear I will bring against you Strangers, the most ruthless of nations. They shall unsheathe their swords Against your prized shrewdness, And they shall strike down your splendor.

ז לָכֵ֗ן הִנְנִ֨י מֵבִ֤יא עָלֶ֙יךָ֙ זָרִ֔ים עָרִיצֵ֖י גּוֹיִ֑ם וְהֵרִ֤יקוּ חַרְבוֹתָם֙ עַל־יְפִ֣י חׇכְמָתֶ֔ךָ וְחִלְּל֖וּ יִפְעָתֶֽךָ׃

⁸ They shall bring you down to the Pit; In the heart of the sea you shall die The death of the slain.

ח לַשַּׁ֖חַת יֽוֹרִד֑וּךָ וָמַ֛תָּה מְמוֹתֵ֥י חָלָ֖ל בְּלֵ֥ב יַמִּֽים׃

⁹ Will you still say, "I am a god" Before your slayers, When you are proved a man, not a god, At the hands of those who strike you down?

ט הֶאָמֹ֤ר תֹּאמַר֙ אֱלֹהִ֣ים אָ֔נִי לִפְנֵ֖י הֹֽרְגֶ֑ךָ וְאַתָּ֥ה אָדָ֛ם וְלֹא־אֵ֖ל בְּיַ֥ד מְחַלְלֶֽיךָ׃

¹⁰ By the hands of strangers you shall die The death of the uncircumcised; For I have spoken – declares *Hashem*.

י מוֹתֵ֧י עֲרֵלִ֛ים תָּמ֖וּת בְּיַד־זָרִ֑ים כִּ֚י אֲנִ֣י דִבַּ֔רְתִּי נְאֻ֖ם אֲדֹנָ֥י יֱהֹוִֽה׃

¹¹ The word of *Hashem* came to me:

יא וַיְהִ֥י דְבַר־יְהֹוָ֖ה אֵלַ֥י לֵאמֹֽר׃

¹² O mortal, intone a dirge over the king of Tyre and say to him: Thus said *Hashem*: You were the seal of perfection, Full of wisdom and flawless in beauty.

יב בֶּן־אָדָ֕ם שָׂ֥א קִינָ֖ה עַל־מֶ֣לֶךְ צ֑וֹר וְאָמַרְתָּ֣ ל֗וֹ כֹּ֤ה אָמַר֙ אֲדֹנָ֣י יֱהֹוִ֔ה אַתָּה֙ חוֹתֵ֣ם תׇּכְנִ֔ית מָלֵ֥א חׇכְמָ֖ה וּכְלִ֥יל יֹֽפִי׃

¹³ You were in Eden, the garden of *Hashem*; Every precious stone was your adornment: Carnelian, chrysolite, and amethyst; Beryl, lapis lazuli, and jasper; Sapphire, turquoise, and emerald; And gold beautifully wrought for you, Mined for you, prepared the day you were created.

יג בְּעֵ֨דֶן גַּן־אֱלֹהִ֜ים הָיִ֗יתָ כׇּל־אֶ֨בֶן יְקָרָ֤ה מְסֻכָתֶ֙ךָ֙ אֹ֣דֶם פִּטְדָ֞ה וְיָהֲלֹ֗ם תַּרְשִׁ֥ישׁ שֹׁ֙הַם֙ וְיָ֣שְׁפֵ֔ה סַפִּ֣יר נֹ֔פֶךְ וּבָרְקַ֖ת וְזָהָ֑ב מְלֶ֨אכֶת תֻּפֶּ֤יךָ וּנְקָבֶ֙יךָ֙ בָּ֔ךְ בְּי֥וֹם הִבָּרַאֲךָ֖ כּוֹנָֽנוּ׃

¹⁴ I created you as a cherub With outstretched shielding wings; And you resided on *Hashem*'s holy mountain; You walked among stones of fire.

יד אַ֨תְּ־כְּר֔וּב מִמְשַׁ֖ח הַסּוֹכֵ֑ךְ וּנְתַתִּ֗יךָ בְּהַ֨ר קֹ֤דֶשׁ אֱלֹהִים֙ הָיִ֔יתָ בְּת֥וֹךְ אַבְנֵי־אֵ֖שׁ הִתְהַלָּֽכְתָּ׃

¹⁵ You were blameless in your ways, From the day you were created Until wrongdoing was found in you.

טו תָּמִ֤ים אַתָּה֙ בִּדְרָכֶ֔יךָ מִיּ֖וֹם הִבָּרְאָ֑ךְ עַד־נִמְצָ֥א עַוְלָ֖תָה בָּֽךְ׃

¹⁶ By your far-flung commerce You were filled with lawlessness And you sinned. So I have struck you down From the mountain of *Hashem*, And I have destroyed you, O shielding cherub, From among the stones of fire.

טז בְּרֹ֣ב רְכֻלָּתְךָ֗ מָל֧וּ תוֹכְךָ֛ חָמָ֖ס וַֽתֶּחֱטָ֑א וָאֶחַלֶּלְךָ֩ מֵהַ֨ר אֱלֹהִ֜ים וָֽאַבֶּדְךָ֙ כְּר֣וּב הַסֹּכֵ֔ךְ מִתּ֖וֹךְ אַבְנֵי־אֵֽשׁ׃

¹⁷ You grew haughty because of your beauty, You debased your wisdom for the sake of your splendor; I have cast you to the ground, I have made you an object for kings to stare at.

יז גָּבַ֤הּ לִבְּךָ֙ בְּיׇפְיֶ֔ךָ שִׁחַ֥תָּ חׇכְמָתְךָ֖ עַל־יִפְעָתֶ֑ךָ עַל־אֶ֣רֶץ הִשְׁלַכְתִּ֗יךָ לִפְנֵ֧י מְלָכִ֛ים נְתַתִּ֖יךָ לְרַ֥אֲוָה בָֽךְ׃

18 By the greatness of your guilt, Through the dishonesty of your trading, You desecrated your sanctuaries. So I made a fire issue from you, And it has devoured you; I have reduced you to ashes on the ground, In the sight of all who behold you.

יח מֵרֹב עֲוֺנֶיךָ בְּעֶוֶל רְכֻלָּתְךָ חִלַּלְתָּ מִקְדָּשֶׁיךָ וָאוֹצִא־אֵשׁ מִתּוֹכְךָ הִיא אֲכָלָתְךָ וָאֶתֶּנְךָ לְאֵפֶר עַל־הָאָרֶץ לְעֵינֵי כָּל־רֹאֶיךָ:

19 All who knew you among the peoples Are appalled at your doom. You have become a horror And have ceased to be, forever.

יט כָּל־יוֹדְעֶיךָ בָּעַמִּים שָׁמְמוּ עָלֶיךָ בַּלָּהוֹת הָיִיתָ וְאֵינְךָ עַד־עוֹלָם:

20 The word of *Hashem* came to me:

כ וַיְהִי דְבַר־יְהֹוָה אֵלַי לֵאמֹר:

21 O mortal, set your face toward Sidon and prophesy against her.

כא בֶּן־אָדָם שִׂים פָּנֶיךָ אֶל־צִידוֹן וְהִנָּבֵא עָלֶיהָ:

22 Say: Thus said *Hashem*: I am going to deal with you, O Sidon. I will gain glory in your midst; And they shall know that I am *Hashem*, When I wreak punishment upon her And show Myself holy through her.

כב וְאָמַרְתָּ כֹּה אָמַר אֲדֹנָי יְהֹוִה הִנְנִי עָלַיִךְ צִידוֹן וְנִכְבַּדְתִּי בְּתוֹכֵךְ וְיָדְעוּ כִּי־אֲנִי יְהֹוָה בַּעֲשׂוֹתִי בָהּ שְׁפָטִים וְנִקְדַּשְׁתִּי בָהּ:

23 I will let pestilence loose against her And bloodshed into her streets. And the slain shall fall in her midst When the sword comes upon her from all sides. And they shall know that I am *Hashem*.

כג וְשִׁלַּחְתִּי־בָהּ דֶּבֶר וָדָם בְּחוּצוֹתֶיהָ וְנִפְלַל חָלָל בְּתוֹכָהּ בְּחֶרֶב עָלֶיהָ מִסָּבִיב וְיָדְעוּ כִּי־אֲנִי יְהֹוָה:

24 Then shall the House of *Yisrael* no longer be afflicted with prickling briers and lacerating thorns from all the neighbors who despise them; and they shall know that I am *Hashem*.

כד וְלֹא־יִהְיֶה עוֹד לְבֵית יִשְׂרָאֵל סִלּוֹן מַמְאִיר וְקוֹץ מַכְאִב מִכֹּל סְבִיבֹתָם הַשָּׁאטִים אוֹתָם וְיָדְעוּ כִּי אֲנִי אֲדֹנָי יְהֹוִה:

25 Thus said *Hashem*: When I have gathered the House of *Yisrael* from the peoples among which they have been dispersed, and have shown Myself holy through them in the sight of the nations, they shall settle on their own soil, which I gave to My servant *Yaakov*,

כה כֹּה־אָמַר אֲדֹנָי יְהֹוִה בְּקַבְּצִי אֶת־בֵּית יִשְׂרָאֵל מִן־הָעַמִּים אֲשֶׁר נָפֹצוּ בָם וְנִקְדַּשְׁתִּי בָם לְעֵינֵי הַגּוֹיִם וְיָשְׁבוּ עַל־אַדְמָתָם אֲשֶׁר נָתַתִּי לְעַבְדִּי לְיַעֲקֹב:

koh a-MAR a-do-NAI e-lo-HEEM b'-ka-b'-TZEE et BAYT yis-ra-AYL min ha-a-MEEM a-SHER na-FO-tzu VAM v'-nik-DASH-tee VAM l'-ay-NAY ha-go-YIM v'-ya-sh'-VU al ad-ma-TAM a-SHER na-TA-tee l'-av-DEE l'-ya-a-KOV

28:25 When I have gathered the House of *Yisrael* This verse describes the future redemption of the Jewish people from all the nations amongst whom they are scattered. The "ingathering of the exiles" was the stated goal of the first Zionist Congress in 1897, and remains a central mission of the State of Israel. This objective is reflected in the Knesset's 1950 "Law of Return," which grants full automatic citizenship to any Jew who desires to settle in the Jewish State. Modern Israel was founded to serve as the homeland for the Jewish people scattered throughout the earth. Over the past several decades, millions of Jews from over one-hundred countries have returned home in dramatic fulfillment of this prophecy.

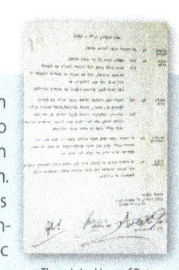
The original Law of Return

²⁶ and they shall dwell on it in security. They shall build houses and plant vineyards, and shall dwell on it in security, when I have meted out punishment to all those about them who despise them. And they shall know that I *Hashem* am their God.

כו וְיָשְׁבוּ עָלֶיהָ לָבֶטַח וּבָנוּ בָתִּים וְנָטְעוּ כְרָמִים וְיָשְׁבוּ לָבֶטַח בַּעֲשׂוֹתִי שְׁפָטִים בְּכֹל הַשָּׁאטִים אֹתָם מִסְּבִיבוֹתָם וְיָדְעוּ כִּי אֲנִי יְהֹוָה אֱלֹהֵיהֶם:

כט ¹ In the tenth year, on the twelfth day of the tenth month, the word of *Hashem* came to me:

כט א בַּשָּׁנָה הָעֲשִׂירִית בָּעֲשִׂרִי בִּשְׁנֵים עָשָׂר לַחֹדֶשׁ הָיָה דְבַר־יְהֹוָה אֵלַי לֵאמֹר:

² O mortal, turn your face against Pharaoh king of Egypt, and prophesy against him and against all Egypt.

ב בֶּן־אָדָם שִׂים פָּנֶיךָ עַל־פַּרְעֹה מֶלֶךְ מִצְרָיִם וְהִנָּבֵא עָלָיו וְעַל־מִצְרַיִם כֻּלָּהּ:

³ Speak these words: Thus said *Hashem*: I am going to deal with you, O Pharaoh king of Egypt, Mighty monster, sprawling in your channels, Who said, My Nile is my own I made it for myself.

ג דַּבֵּר וְאָמַרְתָּ כֹּה־אָמַר אֲדֹנָי יְהֹוִה הִנְנִי עָלֶיךָ פַּרְעֹה מֶלֶךְ־מִצְרַיִם הַתַּנִּים הַגָּדוֹל הָרֹבֵץ בְּתוֹךְ יְאֹרָיו אֲשֶׁר אָמַר לִי יְאֹרִי וַאֲנִי עֲשִׂיתִנִי:

da-BAYR v'-a-mar-TA koh a-MAR a-do-NAI e-lo-HEEM hi-n'-NEE a-LE-kha par-OH me-lekh mitz-RA-yim ha-ta-NEEM ha-ga-DOL ha-ro-VAYTZ b'-TOKH y'-o-RAV a-SHER a-MAR LEE y'-o-REE va-a-NEE a-see-TI-nee

⁴ I will put hooks in your jaws, And make the fish of your channels Cling to your scales; I will haul you up from your channels, With all the fish of your channels Clinging to your scales.

ד וְנָתַתִּי חַחִיים [חַחִים] בִּלְחָיֶיךָ וְהִדְבַּקְתִּי דְגַת־יְאֹרֶיךָ בְּקַשְׂקְשֹׂתֶיךָ וְהַעֲלִיתִיךָ מִתּוֹךְ יְאֹרֶיךָ וְאֵת כָּל־דְּגַת יְאֹרֶיךָ בְּקַשְׂקְשֹׂתֶיךָ תִּדְבָּק:

⁵ And I will fling you into the desert, With all the fish of your channels. You shall be left lying in the open, Ungathered and unburied: I have given you as food To the beasts of the earth And the birds of the sky.

ה וּנְטַשְׁתִּיךָ הַמִּדְבָּרָה אוֹתְךָ וְאֵת כָּל־דְּגַת יְאֹרֶיךָ עַל־פְּנֵי הַשָּׂדֶה תִּפּוֹל לֹא תֵאָסֵף וְלֹא תִקָּבֵץ לְחַיַּת הָאָרֶץ וּלְעוֹף הַשָּׁמַיִם נְתַתִּיךָ לְאָכְלָה:

⁶ Then all the inhabitants of Egypt shall know That I am *Hashem*. Because you were a staff of reed To the House of *Yisrael*:

ו וְיָדְעוּ כָּל־יֹשְׁבֵי מִצְרַיִם כִּי אֲנִי יְהֹוָה יַעַן הֱיוֹתָם מִשְׁעֶנֶת קָנֶה לְבֵית יִשְׂרָאֵל:

⁷ When they grasped you with the hand, you would splinter, And wound all their shoulders, And when they leaned on you, you would break, And make all their loins unsteady.

ז בְּתָפְשָׂם בְּךָ בכפך [בַכַּף] תֵּרוֹץ וּבָקַעְתָּ לָהֶם כָּל־כָּתֵף וּבְהִשָּׁעֲנָם עָלֶיךָ תִּשָּׁבֵר וְהַעֲמַדְתָּ לָהֶם כָּל־מָתְנָיִם:

⁸ Assuredly, thus said *Hashem*: Lo, I will bring a sword against you, and will cut off man and beast from you,

ח לָכֵן כֹּה אָמַר אֲדֹנָי יְהֹוִה הִנְנִי מֵבִיא עָלַיִךְ חָרֶב וְהִכְרַתִּי מִמֵּךְ אָדָם וּבְהֵמָה:

29:3 My Nile is my own The wicked Pharaoh boasts that he has no need for heavenly powers, as his nation does not depend on rainfall for its sustenance. Each year, the mighty Nile river would overflow, ensuring the irrigation and growth of Egyptian crops. In contrast, *Eretz Yisrael* does not have a water source that it can depend on; rather it "soaks up its water from the rains of heaven" (Deuteronomy 11:11). While at first glance it may appear that the Nile is entirely reliable, Pharaoh fails to recognize that he is missing the singular relationship with God which exists in the Land of Israel. As the *Torah* states, since *Eretz Yisrael* is dependent on rainfall, it is the land "which *Hashem* your God looks after, on which *Hashem* your God always keeps His eye" (ibid 12).

Rain at the Western Wall in *Yerushalayim*

9 so that the land of Egypt shall fall into desolation and ruin. And they shall know that I am *Hashem* – because he boasted, "The Nile is mine, and I made it."

ט וְהָיְתָה אֶרֶץ־מִצְרַיִם לִשְׁמָמָה וְחׇרְבָּה וְיָדְעוּ כִּי־אֲנִי יְהֹוָה יַעַן אָמַר יְאֹר לִי וַאֲנִי עָשִׂיתִי:

10 Assuredly, I am going to deal with you and your channels, and I will reduce the land of Egypt to utter ruin and desolation, from Migdol to Syene, all the way to the border of Nubia.

י לָכֵן הִנְנִי אֵלֶיךָ וְאֶל־יְאֹרֶיךָ וְנָתַתִּי אֶת־אֶרֶץ מִצְרַיִם לְחׇרְבוֹת חֹרֶב שְׁמָמָה מִמִּגְדֹּל סְוֵנֵה וְעַד־גְּבוּל כּוּשׁ:

11 No foot of man shall traverse it, and no foot of beast shall traverse it; and it shall remain uninhabited for forty years.

יא לֹא תַעֲבׇר־בָּהּ רֶגֶל אָדָם וְרֶגֶל בְּהֵמָה לֹא תַעֲבׇר־בָּהּ וְלֹא תֵשֵׁב אַרְבָּעִים שָׁנָה:

12 For forty years I will make the land of Egypt the most desolate of desolate lands, and its cities shall be the most desolate of ruined cities. And I will scatter the Egyptians among the nations and disperse them throughout the countries.

יב וְנָתַתִּי אֶת־אֶרֶץ מִצְרַיִם שְׁמָמָה בְּתוֹךְ אֲרָצוֹת נְשַׁמּוֹת וְעָרֶיהָ בְּתוֹךְ עָרִים מׇחֳרָבוֹת תִּהְיֶיןָ שְׁמָמָה אַרְבָּעִים שָׁנָה וַהֲפִצֹתִי אֶת־מִצְרַיִם בַּגּוֹיִם וְזֵרִיתִים בָּאֲרָצוֹת:

13 Further, thus said *Hashem*: After a period of forty years I will gather the Egyptians from the peoples among whom they were dispersed.

יג כִּי כֹּה אָמַר אֲדֹנָי יְהֹוָה מִקֵּץ אַרְבָּעִים שָׁנָה אֲקַבֵּץ אֶת־מִצְרַיִם מִן־הָעַמִּים אֲשֶׁר־נָפֹצוּ שָׁמָּה:

14 I will restore the fortunes of the Egyptians and bring them back to the land of their origin, the land of Pathros, and there they shall be a lowly kingdom.

יד וְשַׁבְתִּי אֶת־שְׁבוּת מִצְרַיִם וַהֲשִׁבֹתִי אֹתָם אֶרֶץ פַּתְרוֹס עַל־אֶרֶץ מְכוּרָתָם וְהָיוּ שָׁם מַמְלָכָה שְׁפָלָה:

15 It shall be the lowliest of all the kingdoms, and shall not lord it over the nations again. I will reduce the Egyptians, so that they shall have no dominion over the nations.

טו מִן־הַמַּמְלָכוֹת תִּהְיֶה שְׁפָלָה וְלֹא־תִתְנַשֵּׂא עוֹד עַל־הַגּוֹיִם וְהִמְעַטְתִּים לְבִלְתִּי רְדוֹת בַּגּוֹיִם:

16 Never again shall they be the trust of the House of *Yisrael*, recalling its guilt in having turned to them. And they shall know that I am *Hashem*.

טז וְלֹא יִהְיֶה־עוֹד לְבֵית יִשְׂרָאֵל לְמִבְטָח מַזְכִּיר עָוֺן בִּפְנוֹתָם אַחֲרֵיהֶם וְיָדְעוּ כִּי אֲנִי אֲדֹנָי יְהֹוָה:

17 In the twenty-seventh year, on the first day of the first month, the word of *Hashem* came to me:

יז וַיְהִי בְּעֶשְׂרִים וָשֶׁבַע שָׁנָה בָּרִאשׁוֹן בְּאֶחָד לַחֹדֶשׁ הָיָה דְבַר־יְהֹוָה אֵלַי לֵאמֹר:

18 O mortal, King Nebuchadrezzar of Babylon has made his army expend vast labor on Tyre; every head is rubbed bald and every shoulder scraped. But he and his army have had no return for the labor he expended on Tyre.

יח בֶּן־אָדָם נְבוּכַדְרֶאצַּר מֶלֶךְ־בָּבֶל הֶעֱבִיד אֶת־חֵילוֹ עֲבֹדָה גְדֹלָה אֶל־צֹר כׇּל־רֹאשׁ מֻקְרָח וְכׇל־כָּתֵף מְרוּטָה וְשָׂכָר לֹא־הָיָה לוֹ וּלְחֵילוֹ מִצֹּר עַל־הָעֲבֹדָה אֲשֶׁר־עָבַד עָלֶיהָ:

19 Assuredly, thus said *Hashem*: I will give the land of Egypt to Nebuchadrezzar, king of Babylon. He shall carry off her wealth and take her spoil and seize her booty; and she shall be the recompense of his army.

יט לָכֵן כֹּה אָמַר אֲדֹנָי יְהֹוָה הִנְנִי נֹתֵן לִנְבוּכַדְרֶאצַּר מֶלֶךְ־בָּבֶל אֶת־אֶרֶץ מִצְרַיִם וְנָשָׂא הֲמֹנָהּ וְשָׁלַל שְׁלָלָהּ וּבָזַז בִּזָּהּ וְהָיְתָה שָׂכָר לְחֵילוֹ:

20 As the wage for which he labored, for what they did for Me, I give him the land of Egypt – declares *Hashem*.

כ פְּעֻלָּתוֹ אֲשֶׁר־עָבַד בָּהּ נָתַתִּי לוֹ אֶת־אֶרֶץ מִצְרָיִם אֲשֶׁר עָשׂוּ לִי נְאֻם אֲדֹנָי יֱהֹוִה:

21 On that day I will endow the House of *Yisrael* with strength, and you shall be vindicated among them. And they shall know that I am *Hashem*.

כא בַּיּוֹם הַהוּא אַצְמִיחַ קֶרֶן לְבֵית יִשְׂרָאֵל וּלְךָ אֶתֵּן פִּתְחוֹן־פֶּה בְּתוֹכָם וְיָדְעוּ כִּי־אֲנִי יֱהֹוִה:

30 1 The word of *Hashem* came to me:

ל א וַיְהִי דְבַר־יְהֹוָה אֵלַי לֵאמֹר:

2 O mortal, prophesy and say: Thus said *Hashem*: Wail, alas for the day!

ב בֶּן־אָדָם הִנָּבֵא וְאָמַרְתָּ כֹּה אָמַר אֲדֹנָי יֱהֹוִה הֵילִילוּ הָהּ לַיּוֹם:

3 For a day is near; A day of *Hashem* is near. It will be a day of cloud, An hour of [invading] nations.

ג כִּי־קָרוֹב יוֹם וְקָרוֹב יוֹם לַיהֹוָה יוֹם עָנָן עֵת גּוֹיִם יִהְיֶה:

4 A sword shall pierce Egypt, And Nubia shall be seized with trembling, When men fall slain in Egypt And her wealth is seized And her foundations are overthrown.

ד וּבָאָה חֶרֶב בְּמִצְרַיִם וְהָיְתָה חַלְחָלָה בְּכוּשׁ בִּנְפֹל חָלָל בְּמִצְרָיִם וְלָקְחוּ הֲמוֹנָהּ וְנֶהֶרְסוּ יְסוֹדֹתֶיהָ:

5 Nubia, Put, and Lud, and all the mixed populations, and Cub, and the inhabitants of the allied countries shall fall by the sword with them.

ה כּוּשׁ וּפוּט וְלוּד וְכָל־הָעֶרֶב וְכוּב וּבְנֵי אֶרֶץ הַבְּרִית אִתָּם בַּחֶרֶב יִפֹּלוּ:

6 Thus said *Hashem*: Those who support Egypt shall fall, And her proud strength shall sink; There they shall fall by the sword, From Migdol to Syene – declares *Hashem*.

ו כֹּה אָמַר יְהֹוָה וְנָפְלוּ סֹמְכֵי מִצְרַיִם וְיָרַד גְּאוֹן עֻזָּהּ מִמִּגְדֹּל סְוֵנֵה בַּחֶרֶב יִפְּלוּ־בָהּ נְאֻם אֲדֹנָי יֱהֹוִה:

7 They shall be the most desolate of desolate lands, and her cities shall be the most ruined of cities,

ז וְנָשַׁמּוּ בְּתוֹךְ אֲרָצוֹת נְשַׁמּוֹת וְעָרָיו בְּתוֹךְ־עָרִים נַחֲרָבוֹת תִּהְיֶינָה:

8 when I set fire to Egypt and all who help her are broken. Thus they shall know that I am *Hashem*.

ח וְיָדְעוּ כִּי־אֲנִי יְהֹוָה בְּתִתִּי־אֵשׁ בְּמִצְרַיִם וְנִשְׁבְּרוּ כָּל־עֹזְרֶיהָ:

9 On that day, messengers shall set out at My bidding to strike terror into confident Nubia. And they shall be seized with trembling on Egypt's day [of doom] – for it is at hand.

ט בַּיּוֹם הַהוּא יֵצְאוּ מַלְאָכִים מִלְּפָנַי בַּצִּים לְהַחֲרִיד אֶת־כּוּשׁ בֶּטַח וְהָיְתָה חַלְחָלָה בָהֶם בְּיוֹם מִצְרַיִם כִּי הִנֵּה בָּאָה:

10 Thus said *Hashem*: I will put an end to the wealth of Egypt through King Nebuchadrezzar of Babylon.

י כֹּה אָמַר אֲדֹנָי יֱהֹוִה וְהִשְׁבַּתִּי אֶת־הֲמוֹן מִצְרַיִם בְּיַד נְבוּכַדְרֶאצַּר מֶלֶךְ־בָּבֶל:

11 He, together with his troops, the most ruthless of the nations, shall be brought to ravage the land. And they shall unsheathe the sword against Egypt and fill the land with the slain.

יא הוּא וְעַמּוֹ אִתּוֹ עָרִיצֵי גוֹיִם מוּבָאִים לְשַׁחֵת הָאָרֶץ וְהֵרִיקוּ חַרְבוֹתָם עַל־מִצְרַיִם וּמָלְאוּ אֶת־הָאָרֶץ חָלָל:

12 I will turn the channels into dry ground, and I will deliver the land into the hands of evil men. I will lay waste the land and everything in it by the hands of strangers. I *Hashem* have spoken.

יב וְנָתַתִּי יְאֹרִים חָרָבָה וּמָכַרְתִּי אֶת־הָאָרֶץ בְּיַד־רָעִים וַהֲשִׁמֹּתִי אֶרֶץ וּמְלֹאָהּ בְּיַד־זָרִים אֲנִי יְהֹוָה דִּבַּרְתִּי:

Ezekiel

13 Thus said *Hashem*: I will destroy the fetishes and make an end of the idols in Noph; and no longer shall there be a prince in the land of Egypt; and I will strike the land of Egypt with fear.

כֹּה־אָמַר אֲדֹנָי יְהֹוִה וְהַאֲבַדְתִּי גִלּוּלִים יג
וְהִשְׁבַּתִּי אֱלִילִים מִנֹּף וְנָשִׂיא מֵאֶרֶץ־
מִצְרַיִם לֹא יִהְיֶה־עוֹד וְנָתַתִּי יִרְאָה
בְּאֶרֶץ מִצְרָיִם:

14 I will lay Pathros waste, I will set fire to Zoan, and I will execute judgment on No.

וַהֲשִׁמֹּתִי אֶת־פַּתְרוֹס וְנָתַתִּי אֵשׁ בְּצֹעַן יד
וְעָשִׂיתִי שְׁפָטִים בְּנֹא:

15 I will pour out my anger upon Sin, the stronghold of Egypt, and I will destroy the wealth of No.

וְשָׁפַכְתִּי חֲמָתִי עַל־סִין מָעוֹז מִצְרָיִם טו
וְהִכְרַתִּי אֶת־הֲמוֹן נֹא:

16 I will set fire to Egypt; Sin shall writhe in anguish and No shall be torn apart; and Noph [shall face] adversaries in broad daylight.

וְנָתַתִּי אֵשׁ בְּמִצְרַיִם חוּל תחיל [תָּחוּל] טז
סִין וְנֹא תִּהְיֶה לְהִבָּקֵעַ וְנֹף צָרֵי יוֹמָם:

17 The young men of Aven and Pi-beseth shall fall by the sword, and those [towns] shall go into captivity.

בַּחוּרֵי אָוֶן וּפִי־בֶסֶת בַּחֶרֶב יִפֹּלוּ וְהֵנָּה יז
בַּשְּׁבִי תֵלַכְנָה:

18 In Tehaphnehes daylight shall be withheld, when I break there the power of Egypt, and there her proud strength comes to an end. [The city] itself shall be covered with cloud, and its daughter towns shall go into captivity.

וּבִתְחַפְנְחֵס חָשַׂךְ הַיּוֹם בְּשִׁבְרִי־שָׁם יח
אֶת־מֹטוֹת מִצְרַיִם וְנִשְׁבַּת־בָּהּ גְּאוֹן
עֻזָּהּ הִיא עָנָן יְכַסֶּנָּה וּבְנוֹתֶיהָ בַּשְּׁבִי
תֵלַכְנָה:

19 Thus I will execute judgment on Egypt; And they shall know that I am *Hashem*.

וְעָשִׂיתִי שְׁפָטִים בְּמִצְרָיִם וְיָדְעוּ כִּי־אֲנִי יט
יְהֹוָה:

20 In the eleventh year, on the seventh day of the first month, the word of *Hashem* came to me:

וַיְהִי בְּאַחַת עֶשְׂרֵה שָׁנָה בָּרִאשׁוֹן כ
בְּשִׁבְעָה לַחֹדֶשׁ הָיָה דְבַר־יְהֹוָה אֵלַי
לֵאמֹר:

21 O mortal, I have broken the arm of Pharaoh king of Egypt; it has not been bound up to be healed nor firmly bandaged to make it strong enough to grasp the sword.

בֶּן־אָדָם אֶת־זְרוֹעַ פַּרְעֹה מֶלֶךְ־מִצְרַיִם כא
שָׁבָרְתִּי וְהִנֵּה לֹא־חֻבְּשָׁה לָתֵת רְפֻאוֹת
לָשׂוּם חִתּוּל לְחָבְשָׁהּ לְחָזְקָהּ לִתְפֹּשׂ
בֶּחָרֶב:

22 Assuredly, thus said *Hashem*: I am going to deal with Pharaoh king of Egypt. I will break his arms, both the sound one and the injured, and make the sword drop from his hand.

לָכֵן כֹּה־אָמַר אֲדֹנָי יְהֹוִה הִנְנִי אֶל־ כב
פַּרְעֹה מֶלֶךְ־מִצְרַיִם וְשָׁבַרְתִּי אֶת־
זְרֹעֹתָיו אֶת־הַחֲזָקָה וְאֶת־הַנִּשְׁבָּרֶת
וְהִפַּלְתִּי אֶת־הַחֶרֶב מִיָּדוֹ:

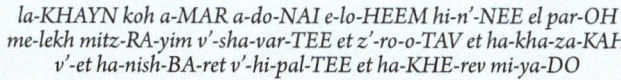

*la-KHAYN koh a-MAR a-do-NAI e-lo-HEEM hi-n'-NEE el par-OH
me-lekh mitz-RA-yim v'-sha-var-TEE et z'-ro-o-TAV et ha-kha-za-KAH
v'-et ha-nish-BA-ret v'-hi-pal-TEE et ha-KHE-rev mi-ya-DO*

An Israeli soldier with his arm raised in a salute to the flag

30:22 And make the sword drop from his hand This prophecy was stated in the spring of 587 BCE, one year before the destruction of the first *Beit Hamikdash*. When Nebuchadnezzar first attacks *Yerushalayim* in 588 BCE, Pharaoh Hophra comes to assist *Tzidkiyahu*. However, Hophra's armies are soundly defeated, and he retreats, leaving *Yerushalayim* alone against the onslaught.

Yechezkel portrays Egypt as having one broken arm, unable to hold a sword to defend itself (verse 21). He then states that Babylonia will finish the conquest, breaking Egypt's good arm as well. Indeed, after its defeat by Nebuchadnezzar, Egypt never regains its status as a superpower in the ancient world. As the prophets had predicted, relying on foreign powers for help instead of turning to God was of no benefit to *Yehuda*.

²³ I will scatter the Egyptians among the nations and disperse them throughout the countries.

כג וַהֲפִצוֹתִ֥י אֶת־מִצְרַ֖יִם בַּגּוֹיִ֑ם וְזֵרִיתִ֖ם בָּאֲרָצֽוֹת׃

²⁴ I will strengthen the arms of the king of Babylon and put My sword in his hand; and I will break the arms of Pharaoh, and he shall groan before him with the groans of one struck down.

כד וְחִזַּקְתִּ֗י אֶת־זְרֹע֣וֹת מֶ֣לֶךְ בָּבֶ֔ל וְנָתַתִּ֥י אֶת־חַרְבִּ֖י בְּיָד֑וֹ וְשָׁבַרְתִּי֙ אֶת־זְרֹע֣וֹת פַּרְעֹ֔ה וְנָאַ֛ק נַאֲק֥וֹת חָלָ֖ל לְפָנָֽיו׃

²⁵ I will make firm the arms of the king of Babylon, but the arms of Pharaoh shall fail. And they shall know that I am *Hashem*, when I put My sword into the hand of the king of Babylon, and he lifts it against the land of Egypt.

כה וְהַחֲזַקְתִּ֗י אֶת־זְרֹעוֹת֙ מֶ֣לֶךְ בָּבֶ֔ל וּזְרֹע֥וֹת פַּרְעֹ֖ה תִּפֹּ֑לְנָה וְיָדְע֞וּ כִּֽי־אֲנִ֣י יְהֹוָ֗ה בְּתִתִּ֤י חַרְבִּי֙ בְּיַד־מֶ֣לֶךְ בָּבֶ֔ל וְנָטָ֥ה אוֹתָ֖הּ אֶל־אֶ֥רֶץ מִצְרָֽיִם׃

²⁶ I will scatter the Egyptians among the nations and disperse them throughout the countries. Thus they shall know that I am *Hashem*.

כו וַהֲפִצוֹתִ֤י אֶת־מִצְרַ֙יִם֙ בַּגּוֹיִ֔ם וְזֵרִיתִ֥י אוֹתָ֖ם בָּאֲרָצ֑וֹת וְיָדְע֖וּ כִּֽי־אֲנִ֥י יְהֹוָֽה׃

³¹ ¹ In the eleventh year, on the first day of the third month, the word of *Hashem* came to me:

לא א וַיְהִ֗י בְּאַחַ֤ת עֶשְׂרֵה֙ שָׁנָ֔ה בַּשְּׁלִישִׁ֖י בְּאֶחָ֣ד לַחֹ֑דֶשׁ הָיָ֥ה דְבַר־יְהֹוָ֖ה אֵלַ֥י לֵאמֹֽר׃

² O mortal, say to Pharaoh king of Egypt and his hordes: Who was comparable to you in greatness?

ב בֶּן־אָדָ֕ם אֱמֹ֛ר אֶל־פַּרְעֹ֥ה מֶֽלֶךְ־מִצְרַ֖יִם וְאֶל־הֲמוֹנ֑וֹ אֶל־מִ֖י דָּמִ֥יתָ בְגׇדְלֶֽךָ׃

³ Assyria was a cedar in Lebanon With beautiful branches and shady thickets, Of lofty stature, With its top among leafy trees.

ג הִנֵּ֨ה אַשּׁ֜וּר אֶ֣רֶז בַּלְּבָנ֗וֹן יְפֵ֥ה עָנָ֛ף וְחֹ֥רֶשׁ מֵצַ֖ל וּגְבַ֣הּ קוֹמָ֑ה וּבֵ֣ין עֲבֹתִ֔ים הָיְתָ֖ה צַמַּרְתּֽוֹ׃

hi-NAY a-SHUR E-rez ba-l'-va-NON y'-FAY a-NAF v'-KHO-resh may-TZAL
ug-VAH ko-MAH u-VAYN a-vo-TEEM ha-y'-TAH tza-mar-TO

⁴ Waters nourished it, The deep made it grow tall, Washing with its streams The place where it was planted, Making its channels well up To all the trees of the field.

ד מַ֣יִם גִּדְּל֔וּהוּ תְּה֖וֹם רֹֽמְמָ֑תְהוּ אֶת־נַהֲרֹתֶ֗יהָ הֹלֵךְ֙ סְבִיב֣וֹת מַטָּעָ֔הּ וְאֶת־תְּעָלֹתֶ֣יהָ שִׁלְּחָ֔ה אֶ֖ל כׇּל־עֲצֵ֥י הַשָּׂדֶֽה׃

⁵ Therefore it exceeded in stature All the trees of the field; Its branches multiplied and its boughs grew long Because of the abundant water That welled up for it.

ה עַל־כֵּן֙ גָּבְהָ֣א קֹֽמָת֔וֹ מִכֹּ֖ל עֲצֵ֣י הַשָּׂדֶ֑ה וַתִּרְבֶּ֤ינָה סַֽרְעַפֹּתָיו֙ וַתֶּאֱרַ֣כְנָה פֹארֹתָ֔ו [פֹּארֹתָ֔יו] מִמַּ֥יִם רַבִּ֖ים בְּשַׁלְּחֽוֹ׃

⁶ In its branches nested All the birds of the sky; All the beasts of the field Bore their young under its boughs, And in its shadow lived All the great nations.

ו בִּסְעַפֹּתָ֤יו קִֽנְנוּ֙ כׇּל־ע֣וֹף הַשָּׁמַ֔יִם וְתַ֤חַת פֹּארֹתָיו֙ יָֽלְד֔וּ כֹּ֖ל חַיַּ֣ת הַשָּׂדֶ֑ה וּבְצִלּ֣וֹ יֵֽשְׁב֔וּ כֹּ֖ל גּוֹיִ֥ם רַבִּֽים׃

31:3 Assyria was a cedar in Lebanon For people who refused to believe that Egypt could be defeated after centuries of hegemony, *Yechezkel* points to Assyria. The mighty Assyrians had ruled for centuries, secure in their dominant position as a world power, like a solid and strong cedar tree. Yet they were ultimately chopped down and quickly fell. The cedar trees from Lebanon are remarkably thick and tall trees, reaching up to ninety feet in height and having a girth of over thirty feet. Because of its quality and resistance to decay and worms, cedar wood was a highly valued construction material. Indeed, King *Shlomo* imported cedars from Lebanon to use in the construction of his own palace, as well the *Beit Hamikdash*.

Israeli landscape behind the branches of a cedar tree

7 It was beautiful in its height, In the length of its branches, Because its stock stood By abundant waters.

ז וַיְּיִף בְּגׇדְלוֹ בְּאֹרֶךְ דָּלִיּוֹתָיו כִּי־הָיָה שׇׁרְשׁוֹ אֶל־מַיִם רַבִּים:

8 Cedars in the garden of *Hashem* Could not compare with it; Cypresses could not match its boughs, And plane trees could not vie with its branches; No tree in the garden of *Hashem* Was its peer in beauty.

ח אֲרָזִים לֹא־עֲמָמֻהוּ בְּגַן־אֱלֹהִים בְּרוֹשִׁים לֹא דָמוּ אֶל־סְעַפֹּתָיו וְעַרְמֹנִים לֹא־הָיוּ כְּפֹארֹתָיו כׇּל־עֵץ בְּגַן־אֱלֹהִים לֹא־דָמָה אֵלָיו בְּיׇפְיוֹ:

9 I made it beautiful In the profusion of its branches; And all the trees of Eden envied it In the garden of *Hashem*.

ט יָפֶה עֲשִׂיתִיו בְּרֹב דָּלִיּוֹתָיו וַיְקַנְאֻהוּ כׇּל־עֲצֵי־עֵדֶן אֲשֶׁר בְּגַן הָאֱלֹהִים:

10 Assuredly, thus said *Hashem*: Because it towered high in stature, and thrust its top up among the leafy trees, and it was arrogant in its height,

י לָכֵן כֹּה אָמַר אֲדֹנָי יְהֹוִה יַעַן אֲשֶׁר גָּבַהְתָּ בְּקוֹמָה וַיִּתֵּן צַמַּרְתּוֹ אֶל־בֵּין עֲבוֹתִים וְרָם לְבָבוֹ בְּגׇבְהוֹ:

11 I delivered it into the hands of the mightiest of nations. They treated it as befitted its wickedness. I banished it.

יא וְאֶתְּנֵהוּ בְּיַד אֵיל גּוֹיִם עָשׂוֹ יַעֲשֶׂה לוֹ כְּרִשְׁעוֹ גֵּרַשְׁתִּהוּ:

12 Strangers, the most ruthless of nations, cut it down and abandoned it; its branches fell on the mountains and in every valley; its boughs were splintered in every watercourse of the earth; and all the peoples of the earth departed from its shade and abandoned it.

יב וַיִּכְרְתֻהוּ זָרִים עָרִיצֵי גוֹיִם וַיִּטְּשֻׁהוּ אֶל־הֶהָרִים וּבְכׇל־גֵּאָיוֹת נָפְלוּ דָלִיּוֹתָיו וַתִּשָּׁבַרְנָה פֹארֹתָיו בְּכֹל אֲפִיקֵי הָאָרֶץ וַיֵּרְדוּ מִצִּלּוֹ כׇּל־עַמֵּי הָאָרֶץ וַיִּטְּשֻׁהוּ:

13 Upon its fallen trunk all the birds of the sky nest, and all the beasts of the field lodge among its boughs –

יג עַל־מַפַּלְתּוֹ יִשְׁכְּנוּ כׇּל־עוֹף הַשָּׁמָיִם וְאֶל־פֹּארֹתָיו הָיוּ כֹּל חַיַּת הַשָּׂדֶה:

14 so that no trees by water should exalt themselves in stature or set their tops among the leafy trees, and that no well-watered tree may reach up to them in height. For they are all consigned to death, to the lowest part of the netherworld, together with human beings who descend into the Pit.

יד לְמַעַן אֲשֶׁר לֹא־יִגְבְּהוּ בְקוֹמָתָם כׇּל־עֲצֵי־מַיִם וְלֹא־יִתְּנוּ אֶת־צַמַּרְתָּם אֶל־בֵּין עֲבֹתִים וְלֹא־יַעַמְדוּ אֵלֵיהֶם בְּגׇבְהָם כׇּל־שֹׁתֵי מָיִם כִּי־כֻלָּם נִתְּנוּ לַמָּוֶת אֶל־אֶרֶץ תַּחְתִּית בְּתוֹךְ בְּנֵי אָדָם אֶל־יוֹרְדֵי בוֹר:

15 Thus said *Hashem*: On the day it went down to Sheol, I closed the deep over it and covered it; I held back its streams, and the great waters were checked. I made Lebanon mourn deeply for it, and all the trees of the field languished on its account.

טו כֹּה־אָמַר אֲדֹנָי יְהֹוִה בְּיוֹם רִדְתּוֹ שְׁאוֹלָה הֶאֱבַּלְתִּי כִּסֵּתִי עָלָיו אֶת־תְּהוֹם וָאֶמְנַע נַהֲרוֹתֶיהָ וַיִּכָּלְאוּ מַיִם רַבִּים וָאַקְדִּר עָלָיו לְבָנוֹן וְכׇל־עֲצֵי הַשָּׂדֶה עָלָיו עֻלְפֶּה:

16 I made nations quake at the crash of its fall, when I cast it down to Sheol with those who descend into the Pit; and all the trees of Eden, the choicest and best of Lebanon, all that were well watered, were consoled in the lowest part of the netherworld.

טז מִקּוֹל מַפַּלְתּוֹ הִרְעַשְׁתִּי גוֹיִם בְּהוֹרִדִי אֹתוֹ שְׁאוֹלָה אֶת־יוֹרְדֵי בוֹר וַיִּנָּחֲמוּ בְּאֶרֶץ תַּחְתִּית כׇּל־עֲצֵי־עֵדֶן מִבְחַר וְטוֹב־לְבָנוֹן כׇּל־שֹׁתֵי מָיִם:

17 They also descended with it into Sheol, to those slain by the sword, together with its supporters, they who had lived under its shadow among the nations.

יז גַּם־הֵם אִתּוֹ יָרְדוּ שְׁאוֹלָה אֶל־חַלְלֵי־חָרֶב וּזְרֹעוֹ יָשְׁבוּ בְצִלּוֹ בְּתוֹךְ גּוֹיִם:

18 [Now you know] who is comparable to you in glory and greatness among the trees of Eden. And you too shall be brought down with the trees of Eden to the lowest part of the netherworld; you shall lie among the uncircumcised and those slain by the sword. Such shall be [the fate of] Pharaoh and all his hordes – declares *Hashem*.

יח אֶל־מִי דָמִיתָ כָּכָה בְּכָבוֹד וּבְגֹדֶל בַּעֲצֵי־עֵדֶן וְהוֹרַדְתָּ אֶת־עֲצֵי־עֵדֶן אֶל־אֶרֶץ תַּחְתִּית בְּתוֹךְ עֲרֵלִים תִּשְׁכַּב אֶת־חַלְלֵי־חֶרֶב הוּא פַרְעֹה וְכָל־הֲמוֹנֹה נְאֻם אֲדֹנָי יְהֹוִה:

לב 1 In the twelfth year, on the first day of the twelfth month, the word of *Hashem* came to me:

א וַיְהִי בִּשְׁתֵּי עֶשְׂרֵה שָׁנָה בִּשְׁנֵי־עָשָׂר חֹדֶשׁ בְּאֶחָד לַחֹדֶשׁ הָיָה דְבַר־יְהֹוָה אֵלַי לֵאמֹר:

2 O mortal, intone a dirge over Pharaoh king of Egypt. Say to him: O great beast among the nations, you are doomed! You are like the dragon in the seas, Thrusting through their streams, Stirring up the water with your feet And muddying their streams!

ב בֶּן־אָדָם שָׂא קִינָה עַל־פַּרְעֹה מֶלֶךְ־מִצְרַיִם וְאָמַרְתָּ אֵלָיו כְּפִיר גּוֹיִם נִדְמֵיתָ וְאַתָּה כַּתַּנִּים בַּיַּמִּים וַתָּגַח בְּנַהֲרוֹתֶיךָ וַתִּדְלַח־מַיִם בְּרַגְלֶיךָ וַתִּרְפֹּס נַהֲרוֹתָם:

*ben a-DAM SA kee-NAH al par-OH me-lekh mitz-RA-yim v'-a-mar-TA ay-LAV
k'-FEER go-YIM nid-MAY-ta v'-a-TAH ka-ta-NEEM ba-ya-MEEM va-TA-gakh
b'-na-ha-ro-TE-kha va-tid-lakh MA-yim b'-rag-LE-kha va-tir-POS na-ha-ro-TAM*

3 Thus said *Hashem*: I will cast My net over you In an assembly of many peoples, And you shall be hauled up in My toils.

ג כֹּה אָמַר אֲדֹנָי יְהֹוִה וּפָרַשְׂתִּי עָלֶיךָ אֶת־רִשְׁתִּי בִּקְהַל עַמִּים רַבִּים וְהֶעֱלוּךָ בְּחֶרְמִי:

4 And I will fling you to the ground, Hurl you upon the open field. I will cause all the birds of the sky To settle upon you. I will cause the beasts of all the earth To batten on you.

ד וּנְטַשְׁתִּיךָ בָאָרֶץ עַל־פְּנֵי הַשָּׂדֶה אֲטִילֶךָ וְהִשְׁכַּנְתִּי עָלֶיךָ כָּל־עוֹף הַשָּׁמַיִם וְהִשְׂבַּעְתִּי מִמְּךָ חַיַּת כָּל־הָאָרֶץ:

5 I will cast your carcass upon the hill And fill the valleys with your rotting flesh.

ה וְנָתַתִּי אֶת־בְּשָׂרְךָ עַל־הֶהָרִים וּמִלֵּאתִי הַגֵּאָיוֹת רָמוּתֶךָ:

6 I will drench the earth With your oozing blood upon the hills, And the watercourses shall be filled with your [gore].

ו וְהִשְׁקֵיתִי אֶרֶץ צָפָתְךָ מִדָּמְךָ אֶל־הֶהָרִים וַאֲפִקִים יִמָּלְאוּן מִמֶּךָּ:

32:2 You are like the dragon in the seas With the exile and destruction of Israel and *Yehuda* complete, *Yechezkel* turns his attention to the other nations. Though Egypt views itself as a fierce lion among the nations, able to roam freely and terrorize its neighbors, *Yechezkel* taunts them, saying that they are nothing more than a wretched beast in a swamp who will be thrashed like a crocodile away from the water. Though Israel has suffered at the hands of many enemies, they have no reason to fear. Ultimately, all the enemy nations will fall and Israel will return triumphantly to the Promised Land.

Crocodiles at Hamat Gader

Ezekiel

7 When you are snuffed out, I will cover the sky And darken its stars; I will cover the sun with clouds And the moon shall not give its light.

8 All the lights that shine in the sky I will darken above you; And I will bring darkness upon your land – declares *Hashem*.

9 I will vex the hearts of many peoples When I bring your shattered remnants among the nations, To countries which you never knew.

10 I will strike many peoples with horror over your fate; And their kings shall be aghast over you, When I brandish My sword before them. They shall tremble continually, Each man for his own life, On the day of your downfall.

11 For thus said *Hashem*: The sword of the king of Babylon shall come upon you.

12 I will cause your multitude to fall By the swords of warriors, All the most ruthless among the nations. They shall ravage the splendor of Egypt, And all her masses shall be wiped out.

13 I will make all her cattle vanish from beside abundant waters; The feet of man shall not muddy them any more, Nor shall the hoofs of cattle muddy them.

14 Then I will let their waters settle, And make their rivers flow like oil – declares *Hashem*:

15 When I lay the land of Egypt waste, When the land is emptied of [the life] that filled it, When I strike down all its inhabitants. And they shall know that I am *Hashem*.

16 This is a dirge, and it shall be intoned; The women of the nations shall intone it, They shall intone it over Egypt and all her multitude – declares *Hashem*.

17 In the twelfth year, on the fifteenth day of the month, the word of *Hashem* came to me:

18 O mortal, wail [the dirge] – along with the women of the mighty nations – over the masses of Egypt, accompanying their descent to the lowest part of the netherworld, among those who have gone down into the Pit.

19 Whom do you surpass in beauty? Down with you, and be laid to rest with the uncircumcised!

ז וְכִסֵּיתִי בְכַבּֽוֹתְךָ֙ שָׁמַ֔יִם וְהִקְדַּרְתִּ֖י אֶת־כֹּֽכְבֵיהֶ֑ם שֶׁ֚מֶשׁ בֶּֽעָנָ֣ן אֲכַסֶּ֔נּוּ וְיָרֵ֖חַ לֹא־יָאִ֥יר אוֹרֽוֹ׃

ח כָּל־מְא֤וֹרֵי אוֹר֙ בַּשָּׁמַ֔יִם אַקְדִּירֵ֖ם עָלֶ֑יךָ וְנָתַ֤תִּי חֹ֨שֶׁךְ֙ עַל־אַרְצְךָ֔ נְאֻ֖ם אֲדֹנָ֥י יֱהֹוִֽה׃

ט וְהִכְעַסְתִּ֔י לֵ֖ב עַמִּ֣ים רַבִּ֑ים בַּהֲבִיאִ֤י שִׁבְרְךָ֙ בַּגּוֹיִ֔ם עַל־אֲרָצ֖וֹת אֲשֶׁ֥ר לֹֽא־יְדַעְתָּֽם׃

י וַהֲשִׁמּוֹתִ֨י עָלֶ֜יךָ עַמִּ֣ים רַבִּ֗ים וּמַלְכֵיהֶ֞ם יִשְׂעֲר֤וּ עָלֶ֨יךָ֙ שַׂ֔עַר בְּעוֹפְפִ֥י חַרְבִּ֖י עַל־פְּנֵיהֶ֑ם וְחָרְד֤וּ לִרְגָעִים֙ אִ֣ישׁ לְנַפְשׁ֔וֹ בְּי֖וֹם מַפַּלְתֶּֽךָ׃

יא כִּ֛י כֹּ֥ה אָמַ֖ר אֲדֹנָ֣י יֱהֹוִ֑ה חֶ֚רֶב מֶֽלֶךְ־בָּבֶ֖ל תְּבוֹאֶֽךָ׃

יב בְּחַרְב֣וֹת גִּבּוֹרִ֔ים אַפִּ֖יל הֲמוֹנֶ֑ךָ עָרִיצֵ֤י גוֹיִם֙ כֻּלָּ֔ם וְשָֽׁדְדוּ֙ אֶת־גְּא֣וֹן מִצְרַ֔יִם וְנִשְׁמַ֖ד כָּל־הֲמוֹנָֽהּ׃

יג וְהַֽאֲבַדְתִּ֣י אֶת־כָּל־בְּהֶמְתָּ֔הּ מֵעַ֖ל מַ֣יִם רַבִּ֑ים וְלֹ֨א תִדְלָחֵ֤ם רֶֽגֶל־אָדָם֙ ע֔וֹד וּפַרְס֥וֹת בְּהֵמָ֖ה לֹ֥א תִדְלָחֵֽם׃

יד אָ֚ז אַשְׁקִ֣יעַ מֵֽימֵיהֶ֔ם וְנַהֲרוֹתָ֖ם כַּשֶּׁ֣מֶן אוֹלִ֑יךְ נְאֻ֖ם אֲדֹנָ֥י יֱהֹוִֽה׃

טו בְּתִתִּי֩ אֶת־אֶ֨רֶץ מִצְרַ֜יִם שְׁמָמָ֣ה וּנְשַׁמָּ֗ה אֶ֚רֶץ מִמְּלֹאָ֔הּ בְּהַכּוֹתִ֖י אֶת־כָּל־י֣וֹשְׁבֵי בָ֑הּ וְיָדְע֖וּ כִּֽי־אֲנִ֥י יֱהֹוִֽה׃

טז קִינָ֥ה הִיא֙ וְקֽוֹנְנ֔וּהָ בְּנ֥וֹת הַגּוֹיִ֖ם תְּקוֹנֵ֣נָּה אוֹתָ֑הּ עַל־מִצְרַ֤יִם וְעַל־כָּל־הֲמוֹנָהּ֙ תְּקוֹנֵ֣נָּה אוֹתָ֔הּ נְאֻ֖ם אֲדֹנָ֥י יֱהֹוִֽה׃

יז וַֽיְהִי֙ בִּשְׁתֵּ֣י עֶשְׂרֵ֣ה שָׁנָ֔ה בַּֽחֲמִשָּׁ֥ה עָשָׂ֖ר לַחֹ֑דֶשׁ הָיָ֥ה דְבַר־יְהֹוָ֖ה אֵלַ֥י לֵאמֹֽר׃

יח בֶּן־אָדָ֡ם נְהֵ֣ה עַל־הֲמ֪וֹן מִצְרַ֟יִם וְהֽוֹרִדֵ֡הוּ אוֹתָ֣הּ וּבְנ֣וֹת גּוֹיִ֣ם אַדִּרִ֡ם אֶל־אֶ֣רֶץ תַּחְתִּיּ֖וֹת אֶת־י֥וֹרְדֵי בֽוֹר׃

יט מִמִּ֖י נָעָ֑מְתָּ רְדָ֥ה וְהׇשְׁכְּבָ֖ה אֶת־עֲרֵלִֽים׃

²⁰ They shall lie amid those slain by the sword, [amid those slain by] the sword [Egypt] has been dragged and left with all her masses.

כ בְּתוֹךְ חַלְלֵי־חֶרֶב יִפֹּלוּ חֶרֶב נִתָּנָה מָשְׁכוּ אוֹתָהּ וְכָל־הֲמוֹנֶיהָ:

²¹ From the depths of Sheol the mightiest of warriors speak to him and his allies; the uncircumcised, the slain by the sword, have gone down and lie [there].

כא יְדַבְּרוּ־לוֹ אֵלֵי גִבּוֹרִים מִתּוֹךְ שְׁאוֹל אֶת־עֹזְרָיו יָרְדוּ שָׁכְבוּ הָעֲרֵלִים חַלְלֵי־חָרֶב:

²² Assyria is there with all her company, their graves round about, all of them slain, fallen by the sword.

כב שָׁם אַשּׁוּר וְכָל־קְהָלָהּ סְבִיבוֹתָיו קִבְרֹתָיו כֻּלָּם חֲלָלִים הַנֹּפְלִים בֶּחָרֶב:

²³ Their graves set in the farthest recesses of the Pit, all her company are round about her tomb, all of them slain, fallen by the sword – they who struck terror in the land of the living.

כג אֲשֶׁר נִתְּנוּ קִבְרֹתֶיהָ בְּיַרְכְּתֵי־בוֹר וַיְהִי קְהָלָהּ סְבִיבוֹת קְבֻרָתָהּ כֻּלָּם חֲלָלִים נֹפְלִים בַּחֶרֶב אֲשֶׁר־נָתְנוּ חִתִּית בְּאֶרֶץ חַיִּים:

²⁴ There too is Elam and all her masses round about her tomb, all of them slain, fallen by the sword – they who descended uncircumcised to the lowest part of the netherworld, who struck terror in the land of the living – now they bear their shame with those who have gone down to the Pit.

כד שָׁם עֵילָם וְכָל־הֲמוֹנָהּ סְבִיבוֹת קְבֻרָתָהּ כֻּלָּם חֲלָלִים הַנֹּפְלִים בַּחֶרֶב אֲשֶׁר־יָרְדוּ עֲרֵלִים אֶל־אֶרֶץ תַּחְתִּיּוֹת אֲשֶׁר נָתְנוּ חִתִּיתָם בְּאֶרֶץ חַיִּים וַיִּשְׂאוּ כְלִמָּתָם אֶת־יוֹרְדֵי בוֹר:

²⁵ They made a bed for her among the slain, with all her masses; their graves are round about her. They are all uncircumcised, slain by the sword. Though their terror was once spread over the land of the living, they bear their shame with those who have gone into the Pit; they are placed among the slain.

כה בְּתוֹךְ חֲלָלִים נָתְנוּ מִשְׁכָּב לָהּ בְּכָל־הֲמוֹנָהּ סְבִיבוֹתָיו קִבְרֹתֶהָ כֻּלָּם עֲרֵלִים חַלְלֵי־חֶרֶב כִּי־נִתַּן חִתִּיתָם בְּאֶרֶץ חַיִּים וַיִּשְׂאוּ כְלִמָּתָם אֶת־יוֹרְדֵי בוֹר בְּתוֹךְ חֲלָלִים נִתָּן:

²⁶ Meshech and Tubal and all their masses are there; their graves are round about. They are all uncircumcised, pierced through by the sword – they who once struck terror in the land of the living.

כו שָׁם מֶשֶׁךְ תֻּבַל וְכָל־הֲמוֹנָהּ סְבִיבוֹתָיו קִבְרוֹתֶיהָ כֻּלָּם עֲרֵלִים מְחֻלְלֵי חֶרֶב כִּי־נָתְנוּ חִתִּיתָם בְּאֶרֶץ חַיִּים:

²⁷ And they do not lie with the fallen uncircumcised warriors, who went down to Sheol with their battle gear, who put their swords beneath their heads and their iniquities upon thei bones – for the terror of the warriors was upon the land of the living.

כז וְלֹא יִשְׁכְּבוּ אֶת־גִּבּוֹרִים נֹפְלִים מֵעֲרֵלִים אֲשֶׁר יָרְדוּ־שְׁאוֹל בִּכְלֵי־מִלְחַמְתָּם וַיִּתְּנוּ אֶת־חַרְבוֹתָם תַּחַת רָאשֵׁיהֶם וַתְּהִי עֲוֺנֹתָם עַל־עַצְמוֹתָם כִּי־חִתִּית גִּבּוֹרִים בְּאֶרֶץ חַיִּים:

²⁸ And you too shall be shattered amid the uncircumcised, and lie among those slain by the sword.

כח וְאַתָּה בְּתוֹךְ עֲרֵלִים תִּשָּׁבֵר וְתִשְׁכַּב אֶת־חַלְלֵי־חָרֶב:

²⁹ Edom is there, her kings and all her chieftains, who, for all their might, are laid among those who are slain by the sword; they too lie with the uncircumcised and with those who have gone down to the Pit.

כט שָׁמָּה אֱדוֹם מְלָכֶיהָ וְכָל־נְשִׂיאֶיהָ אֲשֶׁר־נִתְּנוּ בִגְבוּרָתָם אֶת־חַלְלֵי־חָרֶב הֵמָּה אֶת־עֲרֵלִים יִשְׁכָּבוּ וְאֶת־יֹרְדֵי בוֹר:

Ezekiel

Ezekiel

30 All the princes of the north and all the Sidonians are there, who went down in disgrace with the slain, in spite of the terror that their might inspired; and they lie, uncircumcised, with those who are slain by the sword, and bear their shame with those who have gone down to the Pit.

ל שָׁמָּה נְסִיכֵי צָפוֹן כֻּלָּם וְכָל־צִדֹנִי אֲשֶׁר־יָרְדוּ אֶת־חֲלָלִים בְּחִתִּיתָם מִגְּבוּרָתָם בּוֹשִׁים וַיִּשְׁכְּבוּ עֲרֵלִים אֶת־חַלְלֵי־חֶרֶב וַיִּשְׂאוּ כְלִמָּתָם אֶת־יוֹרְדֵי בוֹר:

31 These Pharaoh shall see, and he shall be consoled for all his masses, those of Pharaoh's men slain by the sword and all his army – declares *Hashem*.

לא אוֹתָם יִרְאֶה פַרְעֹה וְנִחַם עַל־כָּל־הֲמוֹנֹה [הֲמוֹנוֹ] חַלְלֵי־חֶרֶב פַּרְעֹה וְכָל־חֵילוֹ נְאֻם אֲדֹנָי יְהוִֹה:

32 I strike terror into the land of the living; Pharaoh and all his masses are laid among the uncircumcised, along with those who were slain by the sword – said *Hashem*.

לב כִּי־נָתַתִּי אֶת־חִתִּיתוֹ [חִתִּיתִי] בְּאֶרֶץ חַיִּים וְהֻשְׁכַּב בְּתוֹךְ עֲרֵלִים אֶת־חַלְלֵי־חֶרֶב פַּרְעֹה וְכָל־הֲמוֹנֹה נְאֻם אֲדֹנָי יְהוִֹה:

33 1 The word of *Hashem* came to me:

ג א וַיְהִי דְבַר־יְהוָֹה אֵלַי לֵאמֹר:

2 O mortal, speak to your fellow countrymen and say to them: When I bring the sword against a country, the citizens of that country take one of their number and appoint him their watchman.

ב בֶּן־אָדָם דַּבֵּר אֶל־בְּנֵי־עַמְּךָ וְאָמַרְתָּ אֲלֵיהֶם אֶרֶץ כִּי־אָבִיא עָלֶיהָ חָרֶב וְלָקְחוּ עַם־הָאָרֶץ אִישׁ אֶחָד מִקְצֵיהֶם וְנָתְנוּ אֹתוֹ לָהֶם לְצֹפֶה:

3 Suppose he sees the sword advancing against the country, and he blows the *shofar* and warns the people.

ג וְרָאָה אֶת־הַחֶרֶב בָּאָה עַל־הָאָרֶץ וְתָקַע בַּשּׁוֹפָר וְהִזְהִיר אֶת־הָעָם:

v'-ra-AH et ha-KHE-rev ba-AH al ha-A-retz v'-ta-KA
ba-sho-FAR v'-hiz-HEER et ha-AM

4 If anybody hears the sound of the *shofar* but ignores the warning, and the sword comes and dispatches him, his blood shall be on his own head.

ד וְשָׁמַע הַשֹּׁמֵעַ אֶת־קוֹל הַשּׁוֹפָר וְלֹא נִזְהָר וַתָּבוֹא חֶרֶב וַתִּקָּחֵהוּ דָּמוֹ בְרֹאשׁוֹ יִהְיֶה:

5 Since he heard the sound of the *shofar* but ignored the warning, his bloodguilt shall be upon himself; had he taken the warning, he would have saved his life.

ה אֵת קוֹל הַשּׁוֹפָר שָׁמַע וְלֹא נִזְהָר דָּמוֹ בּוֹ יִהְיֶה וְהוּא נִזְהָר נַפְשׁוֹ מִלֵּט:

6 But if the watchman sees the sword advancing and does not blow the *shofar*, so that the people are not warned, and the sword comes and destroys one of them, that person was destroyed for his own sins; however, I will demand a reckoning for his blood from the watchman.

ו וְהַצֹּפֶה כִּי־יִרְאֶה אֶת־הַחֶרֶב בָּאָה וְלֹא־תָקַע בַּשּׁוֹפָר וְהָעָם לֹא־נִזְהָר וַתָּבוֹא חֶרֶב וַתִּקַּח מֵהֶם נָפֶשׁ הוּא בַּעֲוֺנוֹ נִלְקָח וְדָמוֹ מִיַּד־הַצֹּפֶה אֶדְרֹשׁ:

33:3 He blows the horn At the beginning of this chapter, *Yechezkel* compares the job of a prophet to a city's watchman. Just as the guard alerts the townsfolk of impending danger, so is the prophet responsible for warning the people about the consequences of their actions. Ancient Israelite cities were built with towers connected to their walls where the watchmen would sit. In order to warn inhabitants of approaching enemies, the watchman would blow a 'horn', in Hebrew *shofar* (שופר). In Judaism, the shofar has both military significance (see also Joshua 6), and religious significance, as it is sounded on *Rosh Hashana*, the Jewish New Year. By using the image of a *shofar*, *Yechezkel* deftly combines the two themes of military and spiritual preparedness.

Man blowing the shofar at the Western Wall

7 Now, O mortal, I have appointed you a watchman for the House of *Yisrael*; and whenever you hear a message from My mouth, you must transmit My warning to them.

8 When I say to the wicked, "Wicked man, you shall die," but you have not spoken to warn the wicked man against his way, he, that wicked man, shall die for his sins, but I will demand a reckoning for his blood from you.

9 But if you have warned the wicked man to turn back from his way, and he has not turned from his way, he shall die for his own sins, but you will have saved your life.

10 Now, O mortal, say to the House of *Yisrael*: This is what you have been saying: "Our transgressions and our sins weigh heavily upon us; we are sick at heart about them. How can we survive?"

11 Say to them: As I live – declares *Hashem* – it is not My desire that the wicked shall die, but that the wicked turn from his [evil] ways and live. Turn back, turn back from your evil ways, that you may not die, O House of *Yisrael*!

12 Now, O mortal, say to your fellow countrymen: The righteousness of the righteous shall not save him when he transgresses, nor shall the wickedness of the wicked cause him to stumble when he turns back from his wickedness. The righteous shall not survive through his righteousness when he sins.

13 When I say of the righteous "He shall surely live," and, relying on his righteousness, he commits iniquity, none of his righteous deeds shall be remembered; but for the iniquity that he has committed he shall die.

14 So, too, when I say to the wicked, "You shall die," and he turns back from his sinfulness and does what is just and right –

15 if the wicked man restores a pledge, makes good what he has taken by robbery, follows the laws of life, and does not commit iniquity – he shall live, he shall not die.

16 None of the sins that he committed shall be remembered against him; since he does what is just and right, he shall live.

ז וְאַתָּה בֶן־אָדָם צֹפֶה נְתַתִּיךָ לְבֵית יִשְׂרָאֵל וְשָׁמַעְתָּ מִפִּי דָּבָר וְהִזְהַרְתָּ אֹתָם מִמֶּנִּי:

ח בְּאָמְרִי לָרָשָׁע רָשָׁע מוֹת תָּמוּת וְלֹא דִבַּרְתָּ לְהַזְהִיר רָשָׁע מִדַּרְכּוֹ הוּא רָשָׁע בַּעֲוֹנוֹ יָמוּת וְדָמוֹ מִיָּדְךָ אֲבַקֵּשׁ:

ט וְאַתָּה כִּי־הִזְהַרְתָּ רָשָׁע מִדַּרְכּוֹ לָשׁוּב מִמֶּנָּה וְלֹא־שָׁב מִדַּרְכּוֹ הוּא בַּעֲוֹנוֹ יָמוּת וְאַתָּה נַפְשְׁךָ הִצַּלְתָּ:

י וְאַתָּה בֶן־אָדָם אֱמֹר אֶל־בֵּית יִשְׂרָאֵל כֵּן אֲמַרְתֶּם לֵאמֹר כִּי־פְשָׁעֵינוּ וְחַטֹּאתֵינוּ עָלֵינוּ וּבָם אֲנַחְנוּ נְמַקִּים וְאֵיךְ נִחְיֶה:

יא אֱמֹר אֲלֵיהֶם חַי־אָנִי נְאֻם אֲדֹנָי יֱהֹוִה אִם־אֶחְפֹּץ בְּמוֹת הָרָשָׁע כִּי אִם־בְּשׁוּב רָשָׁע מִדַּרְכּוֹ וְחָיָה שׁוּבוּ שׁוּבוּ מִדַּרְכֵיכֶם הָרָעִים וְלָמָּה תָמוּתוּ בֵּית יִשְׂרָאֵל:

יב וְאַתָּה בֶן־אָדָם אֱמֹר אֶל־בְּנֵי־עַמְּךָ צִדְקַת הַצַּדִּיק לֹא תַצִּילֶנּוּ בְּיוֹם פִּשְׁעוֹ וְרִשְׁעַת הָרָשָׁע לֹא־יִכָּשֶׁל בָּהּ בְּיוֹם שׁוּבוֹ מֵרִשְׁעוֹ וְצַדִּיק לֹא יוּכַל לִחְיוֹת בָּהּ בְּיוֹם חֲטֹאתוֹ:

יג בְּאָמְרִי לַצַּדִּיק חָיֹה יִחְיֶה וְהוּא־בָטַח עַל־צִדְקָתוֹ וְעָשָׂה עָוֶל כָּל־צִדְקָתוֹ [צִדְקֹתָיו] לֹא תִזָּכַרְנָה וּבְעַוְלוֹ אֲשֶׁר־עָשָׂה בּוֹ יָמוּת:

יד וּבְאָמְרִי לָרָשָׁע מוֹת תָּמוּת וְשָׁב מֵחַטָּאתוֹ וְעָשָׂה מִשְׁפָּט וּצְדָקָה:

טו חֲבֹל יָשִׁיב רָשָׁע גְּזֵלָה יְשַׁלֵּם בְּחֻקּוֹת הַחַיִּים הָלַךְ לְבִלְתִּי עֲשׂוֹת עָוֶל חָיוֹ יִחְיֶה לֹא יָמוּת:

טז כָּל־חטאתו [חַטֹּאתָיו] אֲשֶׁר חָטָא לֹא תִזָּכַרְנָה לוֹ מִשְׁפָּט וּצְדָקָה עָשָׂה חָיוֹ יִחְיֶה:

17 Your fellow countrymen say, "The way of *Hashem* is unfair." But it is their way that is unfair!

יז וְאָמְרוּ בְּנֵי עַמְּךָ לֹא יִתָּכֵן דֶּרֶךְ אֲדֹנָי וְהֵמָּה דַּרְכָּם לֹא־יִתָּכֵן:

18 When a righteous man turns away from his righteous deeds and commits iniquity, he shall die for it.

יח בְּשׁוּב־צַדִּיק מִצִּדְקָתוֹ וְעָשָׂה עָוֶל וּמֵת בָּהֶם:

19 And when a wicked man turns back from his wickedness and does what is just and right, it is he who shall live by virtue of these things.

יט וּבְשׁוּב רָשָׁע מֵרִשְׁעָתוֹ וְעָשָׂה מִשְׁפָּט וּצְדָקָה עֲלֵיהֶם הוּא יִחְיֶה:

20 And will you say, "The way of *Hashem* is unfair"? I will judge each one of you according to his ways, O House of *Yisrael*!

כ וַאֲמַרְתֶּם לֹא יִתָּכֵן דֶּרֶךְ אֲדֹנָי אִישׁ כִּדְרָכָיו אֶשְׁפּוֹט אֶתְכֶם בֵּית יִשְׂרָאֵל:

21 In the twelfth year of our exile, on the fifth day of the tenth month, a fugitive came to me from *Yerushalayim* and reported, "The city has fallen."

כא וַיְהִי בִּשְׁתֵּי עֶשְׂרֵה שָׁנָה בָּעֲשִׂרִי בַּחֲמִשָּׁה לַחֹדֶשׁ לְגָלוּתֵנוּ בָּא־אֵלַי הַפָּלִיט מִירוּשָׁלַ͏ִם לֵאמֹר הֻכְּתָה הָעִיר:

22 Now the hand of *Hashem* had come upon me the evening before the fugitive arrived, and He opened my mouth before he came to me in the morning; thus my mouth was opened and I was no longer speechless.

כב וְיַד־יְהֹוָה הָיְתָה אֵלַי בָּעֶרֶב לִפְנֵי בּוֹא הַפָּלִיט וַיִּפְתַּח אֶת־פִּי עַד־בּוֹא אֵלַי בַּבֹּקֶר וַיִּפָּתַח פִּי וְלֹא נֶאֱלַמְתִּי עוֹד:

23 The word of *Hashem* came to me:

כג וַיְהִי דְבַר־יְהֹוָה אֵלַי לֵאמֹר:

24 O mortal, those who live in these ruins in the land of *Yisrael* argue, "*Avraham* was but one man, yet he was granted possession of the land. We are many; surely, the land has been given as a possession to us."

כד בֶּן־אָדָם יֹשְׁבֵי הֶחֳרָבוֹת הָאֵלֶּה עַל־אַדְמַת יִשְׂרָאֵל אֹמְרִים לֵאמֹר אֶחָד הָיָה אַבְרָהָם וַיִּירַשׁ אֶת־הָאָרֶץ וַאֲנַחְנוּ רַבִּים לָנוּ נִתְּנָה הָאָרֶץ לְמוֹרָשָׁה:

25 Therefore say to them: Thus said *Hashem*: You eat with the blood, you raise your eyes to your fetishes, and you shed blood – yet you expect to possess the land!

כה לָכֵן אֱמֹר אֲלֵיהֶם כֹּה־אָמַר אֲדֹנָי יֱהֹוִה עַל־הַדָּם תֹּאכֵלוּ וְעֵינֵכֶם תִּשְׂאוּ אֶל־גִּלּוּלֵיכֶם וְדָם תִּשְׁפֹּכוּ וְהָאָרֶץ תִּירָשׁוּ:

26 You have relied on your sword, you have committed abominations, you have all defiled other men's wives – yet you expect to possess the land!

כו עֲמַדְתֶּם עַל־חַרְבְּכֶם עֲשִׂיתֶן תּוֹעֵבָה וְאִישׁ אֶת־אֵשֶׁת רֵעֵהוּ טִמֵּאתֶם וְהָאָרֶץ תִּירָשׁוּ:

27 Thus shall you speak to them: Thus said *Hashem*: As I live, those who are in the ruins shall fall by the sword, and those who are in the open I have allotted as food to the beasts, and those who are in the strongholds and caves shall die by pestilence.

כז כֹּה־תֹאמַר אֲלֵהֶם כֹּה־אָמַר אֲדֹנָי יֱהֹוִה חַי־אָנִי אִם־לֹא אֲשֶׁר בֶּחֳרָבוֹת בַּחֶרֶב יִפֹּלוּ וַאֲשֶׁר עַל־פְּנֵי הַשָּׂדֶה לַחַיָּה נְתַתִּיו לְאָכְלוֹ וַאֲשֶׁר בַּמְּצָדוֹת וּבַמְּעָרוֹת בַּדֶּבֶר יָמוּתוּ:

28 I will make the land a desolate waste, and her proud glory shall cease; and the mountains of *Yisrael* shall be desolate, with none passing through.

כח וְנָתַתִּי אֶת־הָאָרֶץ שְׁמָמָה וּמְשַׁמָּה וְנִשְׁבַּת גְּאוֹן עֻזָּהּ וְשָׁמְמוּ הָרֵי יִשְׂרָאֵל מֵאֵין עוֹבֵר:

²⁹ And they shall know that I am *Hashem*, when I make the land a desolate waste on account of all the abominations which they have committed.

כט וְיָדְעוּ כִּי־אֲנִי יְהֹוָה בְּתִתִּי אֶת־הָאָרֶץ שְׁמָמָה וּמְשַׁמָּה עַל כׇּל־תּוֹעֲבֹתָם אֲשֶׁר עָשׂוּ:

³⁰ Note well, O mortal: your fellow countrymen who converse about you by the walls and in the doorways of their houses and say to each other and propose to one another, "Come and hear what word has issued from *Hashem*."

ל וְאַתָּה בֶן־אָדָם בְּנֵי עַמְּךָ הַנִּדְבָּרִים בְּךָ אֵצֶל הַקִּירוֹת וּבְפִתְחֵי הַבָּתִּים וְדִבֶּר־חַד אֶת־אַחַד אִישׁ אֶת־אָחִיו לֵאמֹר בֹּאוּ־נָא וְשִׁמְעוּ מָה הַדָּבָר הַיּוֹצֵא מֵאֵת יְהֹוָה:

³¹ They will come to you in crowds and sit before you in throngs and will hear your words, but they will not obey them. For they produce nothing but lust with their mouths; and their hearts pursue nothing but gain.

לא וְיָבוֹאוּ אֵלֶיךָ כִּמְבוֹא־עָם וְיֵשְׁבוּ לְפָנֶיךָ עַמִּי וְשָׁמְעוּ אֶת־דְּבָרֶיךָ וְאוֹתָם לֹא יַעֲשׂוּ כִּי־עֲגָבִים בְּפִיהֶם הֵמָּה עֹשִׂים אַחֲרֵי בִצְעָם לִבָּם הֹלֵךְ:

³² To them you are just a singer of bawdy songs, who has a sweet voice and plays skillfully; they hear your words, but will not obey them.

לב וְהִנְּךָ לָהֶם כְּשִׁיר עֲגָבִים יְפֵה קוֹל וּמֵטִב נַגֵּן וְשָׁמְעוּ אֶת־דְּבָרֶיךָ וְעֹשִׂים אֵינָם אוֹתָם:

³³ But when it comes – and come it will – they shall know that a *Navi* has been among them.

לג וּבְבֹאָהּ הִנֵּה בָאָה וְיָדְעוּ כִּי נָבִיא הָיָה בְתוֹכָם:

34 ¹ The word of *Hashem* came to me:

לד א וַיְהִי דְבַר־יְהֹוָה אֵלַי לֵאמֹר:

² O mortal, prophesy against the shepherds of *Yisrael*. Prophesy, and say to them: To the shepherds: Thus said *Hashem*: Ah, you shepherds of *Yisrael*, who have been tending yourselves! Is it not the flock that the shepherds ought to tend?

ב בֶּן־אָדָם הִנָּבֵא עַל־רוֹעֵי יִשְׂרָאֵל הִנָּבֵא וְאָמַרְתָּ אֲלֵיהֶם לָרֹעִים כֹּה אָמַר אֲדֹנָי יְהֹוִה הוֹי רֹעֵי־יִשְׂרָאֵל אֲשֶׁר הָיוּ רֹעִים אוֹתָם הֲלוֹא הַצֹּאן יִרְעוּ הָרֹעִים:

³ You partake of the fat, you clothe yourselves with the wool, and you slaughter the fatlings; but you do not tend the flock

ג אֶת־הַחֵלֶב תֹּאכֵלוּ וְאֶת־הַצֶּמֶר תִּלְבָּשׁוּ הַבְּרִיאָה תִּזְבָּחוּ הַצֹּאן לֹא תִרְעוּ:

⁴ You have not sustained the weak, healed the sick, or bandaged the injured; you have not brought back the strayed, or looked for the lost; but you have driven them with harsh rigor,

ד אֶת־הַנַּחְלוֹת לֹא חִזַּקְתֶּם וְאֶת־הַחוֹלָה לֹא־רִפֵּאתֶם וְלַנִּשְׁבֶּרֶת לֹא חֲבַשְׁתֶּם וְאֶת־הַנִּדַּחַת לֹא הֲשֵׁבֹתֶם וְאֶת־הָאֹבֶדֶת לֹא בִקַּשְׁתֶּם וּבְחׇזְקָה רְדִיתֶם אֹתָם וּבְפָרֶךְ:

⁵ and they have been scattered for want of anyone to tend them; scattered, they have become prey for every wild beast.

ה וַתְּפוּצֶינָה מִבְּלִי רֹעֶה וַתִּהְיֶינָה לְאׇכְלָה לְכׇל־חַיַּת הַשָּׂדֶה וַתְּפוּצֶינָה:

⁶ My sheep stray through all the mountains and over every lofty hill; My flock is scattered all over the face of the earth, with none to take thought of them and none to seek them.

ו יִשְׁגּוּ צֹאנִי בְּכׇל־הֶהָרִים וְעַל כׇּל־גִּבְעָה רָמָה וְעַל כׇּל־פְּנֵי הָאָרֶץ נָפֹצוּ צֹאנִי וְאֵין דּוֹרֵשׁ וְאֵין מְבַקֵּשׁ:

⁷ Hear then, O shepherds, the word of *Hashem*!

ז לָכֵן רֹעִים שִׁמְעוּ אֶת־דְּבַר יְהֹוָה:

8 As I live – declares *Hashem*: Because My flock has been a spoil – My flock has been a prey for all the wild beasts, for want of anyone to tend them since My shepherds have not taken thought of My flock, for the shepherds tended themselves instead of tending the flock –

ח חַי־אָ֜נִי נְאֻ֣ם ׀ אֲדֹנָ֣י יֱהֹוִ֗ה אִם־לֹ֣א יַ֡עַן הֱיֽוֹת־צֹאנִ֣י ׀ לָבַ֡ז וַתִּהְיֶ֩ינָה֩ צֹאנִ֨י לְאׇכְלָ֜ה לְכׇל־חַיַּ֤ת הַשָּׂדֶה֙ מֵאֵ֣ין רֹעֶ֔ה וְלֹא־דָרְשׁ֥וּ רֹעַ֖י אֶת־צֹאנִ֑י וַיִּרְע֤וּ הָֽרֹעִים֙ אוֹתָ֔ם וְאֶת־צֹאנִ֖י לֹ֥א רָעֽוּ׃

9 hear indeed, O shepherds, the word of *Hashem*:

ט לָכֵ֣ן הָֽרֹעִ֔ים שִׁמְע֖וּ דְּבַר־יְהֹוָֽה׃

10 Thus said *Hashem*: I am going to deal with the shepherds! I will demand a reckoning of them for My flock, and I will dismiss them from tending the flock. The shepherds shall not tend themselves any more; for I will rescue My flock from their mouths, and it shall not be their prey.

י כֹּה־אָמַ֞ר אֲדֹנָ֣י יֱהֹוִ֗ה הִנְנִ֤י אֶֽל־הָֽרֹעִים֙ וְדָרַשְׁתִּ֤י אֶת־צֹאנִי֙ מִיָּדָ֔ם וְהִשְׁבַּתִּים֙ מֵרְע֣וֹת צֹ֔אן וְלֹא־יִרְע֥וּ ע֖וֹד הָֽרֹעִ֑ים אוֹתָ֔ם וְהִצַּלְתִּ֤י צֹאנִי֙ מִפִּיהֶ֔ם וְלֹֽא־תִהְיֶ֥יןָ לָהֶ֖ם לְאׇכְלָֽה׃

11 For thus said *Hashem*: Here am I! I am going to take thought for My flock and I will seek them out.

יא כִּ֛י כֹּ֥ה אָמַ֖ר אֲדֹנָ֣י יֱהֹוִ֑ה הִנְנִי־אָ֕נִי וְדָרַשְׁתִּ֥י אֶת־צֹאנִ֖י וּבִקַּרְתִּֽים׃

12 As a shepherd seeks out his flock when some [animals] in his flock have gotten separated, so I will seek out My flock, I will rescue them from all the places to which they were scattered on a day of cloud and gloom.

יב כְּבַקָּרַת֩ רֹעֶ֨ה עֶדְר֜וֹ בְּיֽוֹם־הֱיוֹת֤וֹ בְתֽוֹךְ־צֹאנוֹ֙ נִפְרָשׁ֔וֹת כֵּ֖ן אֲבַקֵּ֣ר אֶת־צֹאנִ֑י וְהִצַּלְתִּ֣י אֶתְהֶ֗ם מִכׇּל־הַמְּקוֹמֹת֙ אֲשֶׁ֣ר נָפֹ֣צוּ שָׁ֔ם בְּי֥וֹם עָנָ֖ן וַעֲרָפֶֽל׃

13 I will take them out from the peoples and gather them from the countries, and I will bring them to their own land, and will pasture them on the mountains of *Yisrael*, by the watercourses and in all the settled portions of the land.

יג וְהוֹצֵאתִ֣ים מִן־הָֽעַמִּ֗ים וְקִבַּצְתִּים֙ מִן־הָ֣אֲרָצ֔וֹת וַהֲבִיאֹתִ֖ים אֶל־אַדְמָתָ֑ם וּרְעִיתִ֞ים אֶל־הָרֵ֤י יִשְׂרָאֵל֙ בָּֽאֲפִיקִ֔ים וּבְכֹ֖ל מֽוֹשְׁבֵ֥י הָאָֽרֶץ׃

v'-ho-tzay-TEEM min ha-a-MEEM v'-ki-batz-TEEM min ha-a-ra-TZOT
va-ha-vee-o-TEEM el ad-ma-TAM ur-ee-TEEM el ha-RAY
yis-ra-AYL ba-a-fee-KEEM uv-KHOL mo-sh'-VAY ha-A-retz

14 I will feed them in good grazing land, and the lofty hills of *Yisrael* shall be their pasture. There, in the hills of *Yisrael*, they shall lie down in a good pasture and shall feed on rich grazing land.

יד בְּמִרְעֶה־טּ֣וֹב אֶרְעֶ֣ה אֹתָ֗ם וּבְהָרֵ֤י מְרֽוֹם־יִשְׂרָאֵל֙ יִהְיֶ֣ה נְוֵהֶ֔ם שָׁ֤ם תִּרְבַּ֙צְנָה֙ בְּנָ֣וֶה טּ֔וֹב וּמִרְעֶ֥ה שָׁמֵ֛ן תִּרְעֶ֖ינָה אֶל־הָרֵ֥י יִשְׂרָאֵֽל׃

15 I Myself will graze My flock, and I Myself will let them lie down – declares *Hashem*.

טו אֲנִ֨י אֶרְעֶ֤ה צֹאנִי֙ וַאֲנִ֣י אַרְבִּיצֵ֔ם נְאֻ֖ם אֲדֹנָ֥י יֱהֹוִֽה׃

34:13 I will take them out from the peoples and gather them The "ingathering of the exiles," known in Hebrew as *kibbutz galuyot* (קיבוץ גלויות), is promised in multiple places throughout the Bible. Although they are scattered throughout the four corners of the earth, *Yechezkel* declares that one day, God will gather the People of Israel and return them to their ancient soil, the Land of Israel. For centuries, Jews have been praying three times daily for the fulfillment of this prophecy in their central prayer, known as the *amidah*.

With the establishment of the State of Israel and the many waves of immigration that have taken place in recent history, we are fortunate to witness the beginning of the fulfillment of this tremendous miracle.

North American immigrants

16 I will look for the lost, and I will bring back the strayed; I will bandage the injured, and I will sustain the weak; and the fat and healthy ones I will destroy. I will tend them rightly.

טז אֶת־הָאֹבֶדֶת אֲבַקֵּשׁ וְאֶת־הַנִּדַּחַת אָשִׁיב וְלַנִּשְׁבֶּרֶת אֶחֱבֹשׁ וְאֶת־הַחוֹלָה אֲחַזֵּק וְאֶת־הַשְּׁמֵנָה וְאֶת־הַחֲזָקָה אַשְׁמִיד אֶרְעֶנָּה בְמִשְׁפָּט:

17 And as for you, My flock, thus said *Hashem*: I am going to judge between one animal and another. To the rams and the bucks:

יז וְאַתֵּנָה צֹאנִי כֹּה אָמַר אֲדֹנָי יֱהֹוִה הִנְנִי שֹׁפֵט בֵּין־שֶׂה לָשֶׂה לָאֵילִים וְלָעַתּוּדִים:

18 Is it not enough for you to graze on choice grazing ground, but you must also trample with your feet what is left from your grazing? And is it not enough for you to drink clear water, but you must also muddy with your feet what is left?

יח הַמְעַט מִכֶּם הַמִּרְעֶה הַטּוֹב תִּרְעוּ וְיֶתֶר מִרְעֵיכֶם תִּרְמְסוּ בְּרַגְלֵיכֶם וּמִשְׁקַע־מַיִם תִּשְׁתּוּ וְאֵת הַנּוֹתָרִים בְּרַגְלֵיכֶם תִּרְפֹּשׂוּן:

19 And must My flock graze on what your feet have trampled and drink what your feet have muddied?

יט וְצֹאנִי מִרְמַס רַגְלֵיכֶם תִּרְעֶינָה וּמִרְפַּשׂ רַגְלֵיכֶם תִּשְׁתֶּינָה:

20 Assuredly, thus said *Hashem* to them: Here am I, I am going to decide between the stout animals and the lean.

כ לָכֵן כֹּה אָמַר אֲדֹנָי יֱהֹוִה אֲלֵיהֶם הִנְנִי־אָנִי וְשָׁפַטְתִּי בֵּין־שֶׂה בִרְיָה וּבֵין שֶׂה רָזָה:

21 Because you pushed with flank and shoulder against the feeble ones and butted them with your horns until you scattered them abroad,

כא יַעַן בְּצַד וּבְכָתֵף תֶּהְדֹּפוּ וּבְקַרְנֵיכֶם תְּנַגְּחוּ כָּל־הַנַּחְלוֹת עַד אֲשֶׁר הֲפִיצוֹתֶם אוֹתָנָה אֶל־הַחוּצָה:

22 I will rescue My flock and they shall no longer be a spoil. I will decide between one animal and another.

כב וְהוֹשַׁעְתִּי לְצֹאנִי וְלֹא־תִהְיֶינָה עוֹד לָבַז וְשָׁפַטְתִּי בֵּין שֶׂה לָשֶׂה:

23 Then I will appoint a single shepherd over them to tend them – My servant *David*. He shall tend them, he shall be a shepherd to them.

כג וַהֲקִמֹתִי עֲלֵיהֶם רֹעֶה אֶחָד וְרָעָה אֶתְהֶן אֵת עַבְדִּי דָוִיד הוּא יִרְעֶה אֹתָם וְהוּא־יִהְיֶה לָהֶן לְרֹעֶה:

24 I *Hashem* will be their God, and My servant *David* shall be a ruler among them – I *Hashem* have spoken.

כד וַאֲנִי יֱהֹוָה אֶהְיֶה לָהֶם לֵאלֹהִים וְעַבְדִּי דָוִד נָשִׂיא בְתוֹכָם אֲנִי יֱהֹוָה דִּבַּרְתִּי:

25 And I will grant them a covenant of friendship. I will banish vicious beasts from their land, and they shall live secure in the wasteland, they shall even sleep in the woodland.

כה וְכָרַתִּי לָהֶם בְּרִית שָׁלוֹם וְהִשְׁבַּתִּי חַיָּה־רָעָה מִן־הָאָרֶץ וְיָשְׁבוּ בַמִּדְבָּר לָבֶטַח וְיָשְׁנוּ בַּיְּעָרִים:

26 I will make these and the environs of My hill a blessing: I will send down the rain in its season, rains that bring blessing.

כו וְנָתַתִּי אוֹתָם וּסְבִיבוֹת גִּבְעָתִי בְּרָכָה וְהוֹרַדְתִּי הַגֶּשֶׁם בְּעִתּוֹ גִּשְׁמֵי בְרָכָה יִהְיוּ:

27 The trees of the field shall yield their fruit and the land shall yield its produce. [My people] shall continue secure on its own soil. They shall know that I am *Hashem* when I break the bars of their yoke and rescue them from those who enslave them.

כז וְנָתַן עֵץ הַשָּׂדֶה אֶת־פִּרְיוֹ וְהָאָרֶץ תִּתֵּן יְבוּלָהּ וְהָיוּ עַל־אַדְמָתָם לָבֶטַח וְיָדְעוּ כִּי־אֲנִי יֱהֹוָה בְּשִׁבְרִי אֶת־מֹטוֹת עֻלָּם וְהִצַּלְתִּים מִיַּד הָעֹבְדִים בָּהֶם:

28 They shall no longer be a spoil for the nations, and the beasts of the earth shall not devour them; they shall dwell secure and untroubled.

כח וְלֹא־יִהְיוּ עוֹד בַּז לַגּוֹיִם וְחַיַּת הָאָרֶץ לֹא תֹאכְלֵם וְיָשְׁבוּ לָבֶטַח וְאֵין מַחֲרִיד:

29 I shall establish for them a planting of renown; they shall no more be carried off by famine, and they shall not have to bear again the taunts of the nations.

כט וַהֲקִמֹתִי לָהֶם מַטָּע לְשֵׁם וְלֹא־יִהְיוּ עוֹד אֲסֻפֵי רָעָב בָּאָרֶץ וְלֹא־יִשְׂאוּ עוֹד כְּלִמַּת הַגּוֹיִם:

30 They shall know that I *Hashem* their God am with them and they, the House of *Yisrael*, are My people – declares *Hashem*.

ל וְיָדְעוּ כִּי אֲנִי יְהֹוָה אֱלֹהֵיהֶם אִתָּם וְהֵמָּה עַמִּי בֵּית יִשְׂרָאֵל נְאֻם אֲדֹנָי יְהֹוִה:

31 For you, My flock, flock that I tend, are men; and I am your God – declares *Hashem*.

לא וְאַתֵּן צֹאנִי צֹאן מַרְעִיתִי אָדָם אַתֶּם אֲנִי אֱלֹהֵיכֶם נְאֻם אֲדֹנָי יְהֹוִה:

35

1 The word of *Hashem* came to me:

ה א וַיְהִי דְבַר־יְהֹוָה אֵלַי לֵאמֹר:

2 O mortal, set your face against Mount Seir and prophesy against it.

ב בֶּן־אָדָם שִׂים פָּנֶיךָ עַל־הַר שֵׂעִיר וְהִנָּבֵא עָלָיו:

3 Say to it: Thus said *Hashem*: I am going to deal with you, Mount Seir: I will stretch out My hand against you and make you an utter waste.

ג וְאָמַרְתָּ לּוֹ כֹּה אָמַר אֲדֹנָי יְהֹוִה הִנְנִי אֵלֶיךָ הַר־שֵׂעִיר וְנָטִיתִי יָדִי עָלֶיךָ וּנְתַתִּיךָ שְׁמָמָה וּמְשַׁמָּה:

4 I will turn your towns into ruins, and you shall be a desolation; then you shall know that I am *Hashem*.

ד עָרֶיךָ חָרְבָּה אָשִׂים וְאַתָּה שְׁמָמָה תִהְיֶה וְיָדַעְתָּ כִּי־אֲנִי יְהֹוָה:

5 Because you harbored an ancient hatred and handed the people of *Yisrael* over to the sword in their time of calamity, the time set for their punishment –

ה יַעַן הֱיוֹת לְךָ אֵיבַת עוֹלָם וַתַּגֵּר אֶת־בְּנֵי־יִשְׂרָאֵל עַל־יְדֵי־חָרֶב בְּעֵת אֵידָם בְּעֵת עֲוֹן קֵץ:

YA-an he-YOT l'-KHA ay-VAT o-LAM va-ta-GAYR et b'-nay yis-ra-AYL al y'-DAY KHA-rev b'-AYT ay-DAM b'-AYT a-VON KAYTZ

6 assuredly, as I live, declares *Hashem*, I will doom you with blood; blood shall pursue you; I swear that, for your bloodthirsty hatred, blood shall pursue you.

ו לָכֵן חַי־אָנִי נְאֻם אֲדֹנָי יְהֹוִה כִּי־לְדָם אֶעֶשְׂךָ וְדָם יִרְדְּפֶךָ אִם־לֹא דָם שָׂנֵאתָ וְדָם יִרְדְּפֶךָ:

7 I will make Mount Seir an utter waste, and I will keep all passersby away from it.

ז וְנָתַתִּי אֶת־הַר שֵׂעִיר לְשִׁמְמָה וּשְׁמָמָה וְהִכְרַתִּי מִמֶּנּוּ עֹבֵר וָשָׁב:

The Arava valley with the Edom Mountains in the background

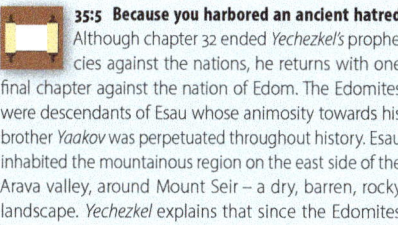

35:5 Because you harbored an ancient hatred
Although chapter 32 ended *Yechezkel's* prophecies against the nations, he returns with one final chapter against the nation of Edom. The Edomites were descendants of Esau whose animosity towards his brother *Yaakov* was perpetuated throughout history. Esau inhabited the mountainous region on the east side of the Arava valley, around Mount Seir – a dry, barren, rocky landscape. *Yechezkel* explains that since the Edomites constantly assisted Israel's enemies, God was personally against them (verse 3), and would ensure that their country would remain desolate (verse 4).

ח וּמִלֵּאתִי אֶת־הָרָיו חֲלָלָיו גִּבְעוֹתֶיךָ וְגֵאוֹתֶיךָ וְכָל־אֲפִיקֶיךָ חַלְלֵי־חֶרֶב יִפְּלוּ בָהֶם:

8 I will cover its mountains with the slain; men slain by the sword shall lie on your hills, in your valleys, and in all your watercourses.

ט שְׁמְמוֹת עוֹלָם אֶתֶּנְךָ וְעָרֶיךָ לֹא תֵישַׁבְנָה [תָשֹׁבְנָה] וִידַעְתֶּם כִּי־אֲנִי יְהוָה:

9 I will make you a desolation for all time; your towns shall never be inhabited. And you shall know that I am *Hashem*.

י יַעַן אֲמָרְךָ אֶת־שְׁנֵי הַגּוֹיִם וְאֶת־שְׁתֵּי הָאֲרָצוֹת לִי תִהְיֶינָה וִירַשְׁנוּהָ וַיהוָה שָׁם הָיָה:

10 Because you thought "The two nations and the two lands shall be mine and we shall possess them" – although *Hashem* was there –

יא לָכֵן חַי־אָנִי נְאֻם אֲדֹנָי יְהוִה וְעָשִׂיתִי כְּאַפְּךָ וּכְקִנְאָתְךָ אֲשֶׁר עָשִׂיתָה מִשִּׂנְאָתֶךָ בָּם וְנוֹדַעְתִּי בָם כַּאֲשֶׁר אֶשְׁפְּטֶךָ:

11 assuredly, as I live, declares *Hashem*, I will act with the same anger and passion that you acted with in your hatred of them. And I will make Myself known through them when I judge you.

יב וְיָדַעְתָּ כִּי־אֲנִי יְהוָה שָׁמַעְתִּי אֶת־כָּל־ נָאָצוֹתֶיךָ אֲשֶׁר אָמַרְתָּ עַל־הָרֵי יִשְׂרָאֵל לֵאמֹר שממה [שָׁמֵמוּ] לָנוּ נִתְּנוּ לְאָכְלָה:

12 You shall know that I *Hashem* have heard all the taunts you uttered against the hills of *Yisrael*: "They have been laid waste; they have been given to us as prey."

יג וַתַּגְדִּילוּ עָלַי בְּפִיכֶם וְהַעְתַּרְתֶּם עָלַי דִּבְרֵיכֶם אֲנִי שָׁמָעְתִּי:

13 And you spoke arrogantly against Me and multiplied your words against Me: I have heard it.

יד כֹּה אָמַר אֲדֹנָי יְהוִה כִּשְׂמֹחַ כָּל־הָאָרֶץ שְׁמָמָה אֶעֱשֶׂה־לָּךְ:

14 Thus said *Hashem*: When the whole earth rejoices, I will make you a desolation.

טו כְּשִׂמְחָתְךָ לְנַחְלַת בֵּית־יִשְׂרָאֵל עַל אֲשֶׁר־שָׁמֵמָה כֵּן אֶעֱשֶׂה־לָּךְ שְׁמָמָה תִהְיֶה הַר־שֵׂעִיר וְכָל־אֱדוֹם כֻּלָּהּ וְיָדְעוּ כִּי־אֲנִי יְהוָה:

15 As you rejoiced when the heritage of the House of *Yisrael* was laid waste, so will I treat you: the hill country of Seir and the whole of Edom, all of it, shall be laid waste. And they shall know that I am *Hashem*.

לו א וְאַתָּה בֶן־אָדָם הִנָּבֵא אֶל־הָרֵי יִשְׂרָאֵל וְאָמַרְתָּ הָרֵי יִשְׂרָאֵל שִׁמְעוּ דְּבַר־יְהוָה:

36 1 And you, O mortal, prophesy to the mountains of *Yisrael* and say: O mountains of *Yisrael*, hear the word of *Hashem*:

ב כֹּה אָמַר אֲדֹנָי יְהוִה יַעַן אָמַר הָאוֹיֵב עֲלֵיכֶם הֶאָח וּבָמוֹת עוֹלָם לְמוֹרָשָׁה הָיְתָה לָּנוּ:

2 Thus said *Hashem*: Because the enemy gloated over you, "Aha! Those ancient heights have become our possession!"

ג לָכֵן הִנָּבֵא וְאָמַרְתָּ כֹּה אָמַר אֲדֹנָי יְהוִה יַעַן בְּיַעַן שַׁמּוֹת וְשָׁאֹף אֶתְכֶם מִסָּבִיב לִהְיוֹתְכֶם מוֹרָשָׁה לִשְׁאֵרִית הַגּוֹיִם וַתֵּעֲלוּ עַל־שְׂפַת לָשׁוֹן וְדִבַּת־עָם:

3 therefore prophesy, and say: Thus said *Hashem*: Just because they eagerly lusted to see you become a possession of the other nations round about, so that you have become the butt of gossip in every language and of the jibes from every people –

ד לָכֵן הָרֵי יִשְׂרָאֵל שִׁמְעוּ דְּבַר־אֲדֹנָי יְהוִה כֹּה־אָמַר אֲדֹנָי יְהוִה לֶהָרִים וְלַגְּבָעוֹת לָאֲפִיקִים וְלַגֵּאָיוֹת וְלֶחֳרָבוֹת הַשֹּׁמְמוֹת וְלֶעָרִים הַנֶּעֱזָבוֹת אֲשֶׁר הָיוּ לְבַז וּלְלַעַג לִשְׁאֵרִית הַגּוֹיִם אֲשֶׁר מִסָּבִיב:

4 truly, you mountains of *Yisrael*, hear the word of *Hashem*: Thus said *Hashem* to the mountains and the hills, to the watercourses and the valleys, and to the desolate wastes and deserted cities which have become a prey and a laughingstock to the other nations round about:

5 Assuredly, thus said *Hashem*: I have indeed spoken in My blazing wrath against the other nations and against all of Edom which, with wholehearted glee and with contempt, have made My land a possession for themselves for pasture and for prey.

ה לָכֵן כֹּה־אָמַר אֲדֹנָי יֱהֹוִה אִם־לֹא בְּאֵשׁ קִנְאָתִי דִבַּרְתִּי עַל־שְׁאֵרִית הַגּוֹיִם וְעַל־אֱדוֹם כֻּלָּא אֲשֶׁר נָתְנוּ־אֶת־אַרְצִי לָהֶם לְמוֹרָשָׁה בְּשִׂמְחַת כָּל־לֵבָב בִּשְׁאָט נֶפֶשׁ לְמַעַן מִגְרָשָׁהּ לָבַז:

6 Yes, prophesy about the land of *Yisrael*, and say to the mountains and the hills, to the watercourses and to the valleys, Thus said *Hashem*: Behold, I declare in My blazing wrath: Because you have suffered the taunting of the nations,

ו לָכֵן הִנָּבֵא עַל־אַדְמַת יִשְׂרָאֵל וְאָמַרְתָּ לֶהָרִים וְלַגְּבָעוֹת לָאֲפִיקִים וְלַגֵּאָיוֹת כֹּה־אָמַר אֲדֹנָי יֱהֹוִה הִנְנִי בְקִנְאָתִי וּבַחֲמָתִי דִבַּרְתִּי יַעַן כְּלִמַּת גּוֹיִם נְשָׂאתֶם:

7 thus said *Hashem*: I hereby swear that the nations which surround you shall, in their turn, suffer disgrace.

ז לָכֵן כֹּה אָמַר אֲדֹנָי יֱהֹוִה אֲנִי נָשָׂאתִי אֶת־יָדִי אִם־לֹא הַגּוֹיִם אֲשֶׁר לָכֶם מִסָּבִיב הֵמָּה כְּלִמָּתָם יִשָּׂאוּ:

8 But you, O mountains of *Yisrael*, shall yield your produce and bear your fruit for My people *Yisrael*, for their return is near.

ח וְאַתֶּם הָרֵי יִשְׂרָאֵל עַנְפְּכֶם תִּתֵּנוּ וּפֶרְיְכֶם תִּשְׂאוּ לְעַמִּי יִשְׂרָאֵל כִּי קֵרְבוּ לָבוֹא:

v'-a-TEM ha-RAY yis-ra-AYL an-p'-KHEM ti-TAY-nu u-fer-y'-KHEM tis-U l'-a-MEE yis-ra-AYL kee kay-r'-VU la-VO

9 For I will care for you: I will turn to you, and you shall be tilled and sown.

ט כִּי הִנְנִי אֲלֵיכֶם וּפָנִיתִי אֲלֵיכֶם וְנֶעֱבַדְתֶּם וְנִזְרַעְתֶּם:

10 I will settle a large population on you, the whole House of *Yisrael*; the towns shall be resettled, and the ruined sites rebuilt.

י וְהִרְבֵּיתִי עֲלֵיכֶם אָדָם כָּל־בֵּית יִשְׂרָאֵל כֻּלֹּה וְנֹשְׁבוּ הֶעָרִים וְהֶחֳרָבוֹת תִּבָּנֶינָה:

11 I will multiply men and beasts upon you, and they shall increase and be fertile, and I will resettle you as you were formerly, and will make you more prosperous than you were at first. And you shall know that I am *Hashem*.

יא וְהִרְבֵּיתִי עֲלֵיכֶם אָדָם וּבְהֵמָה וְרָבוּ וּפָרוּ וְהוֹשַׁבְתִּי אֶתְכֶם כְּקַדְמוֹתֵיכֶם וְהֵטִבֹתִי מֵרִאשֹׁתֵיכֶם וִידַעְתֶּם כִּי־אֲנִי יְהֹוָה:

12 I will lead men – My people *Yisrael* – to you, and they shall possess you. You shall be their heritage, and you shall not again cause them to be bereaved.

יב וְהוֹלַכְתִּי עֲלֵיכֶם אָדָם אֶת־עַמִּי יִשְׂרָאֵל וִירֵשׁוּךָ וְהָיִיתָ לָהֶם לְנַחֲלָה וְלֹא־תוֹסִף עוֹד לְשַׁכְּלָם:

13 Thus said *Hashem*: Because they say to you, "You are [a land] that devours men, you have been a bereaver of your nations,"

יג כֹּה אָמַר אֲדֹנָי יֱהֹוִה יַעַן אֹמְרִים לָכֶם אֹכֶלֶת אָדָם אַתִּי [אָתְּ] וּמְשַׁכֶּלֶת גּוֹיֵךְ [גּוֹיַיִךְ] הָיִית:

36:8 But you, O mountains of *Yisrael*, shall yield your produce In this prophecy, *Hashem* promises that the land will again be inhabited by the house of Israel and that it will flourish, pledging that the mountains will grow trees and produce fruits for the sake of His returning nation. Since the Jewish people have returned to Israel, the land has indeed begun to flourish, and there are once again trees growing throughout the land. In fact, under the direction of the Jewish National Fund, over 250,000,000 trees have been planted in Israel since 1901.

While the world struggles with deforestation, Israel is the only country that ended the twentieth century with more trees than it had at its start. According to Rabbi Abba of the Talmud (*Sanhedrin* 98a), the flourishing of the Land of Israel described in this verse is a clear sign that the complete and final redemption is near.

Eshtaol Forest planted by the Jewish National Fund

¹⁴ assuredly, you shall devour men no more, you shall never again bereave your nations – declares *Hashem*.

לֶכֵן אָדָם לֹא־תֹאכְלִי עוֹד וְגוֹיַיִךְ [וְגוֹיַיִךְ] לֹא תְכַשְּׁלִי־[תְשַׁכְּלִי־] עוֹד נְאֻם אֲדֹנָי יֱהֹוִה: יד

¹⁵ No more will I allow the jibes of the nations to be heard against you, no longer shall you suffer the taunting of the peoples; and never again shall you cause your nations to stumble – declares *Hashem*.

וְלֹא־אַשְׁמִיעַ אֵלַיִךְ עוֹד כְּלִמַּת הַגּוֹיִם וְחֶרְפַּת עַמִּים לֹא תִשְׂאִי־עוֹד וְגוֹיַיִךְ [וְגוֹיַיִךְ] לֹא־תַכְשִׁלִי עוֹד נְאֻם אֲדֹנָי יֱהֹוִה: טו

¹⁶ The word of *Hashem* came to me:

וַיְהִי דְבַר־יְהֹוָה אֵלַי לֵאמֹר: טז

¹⁷ O mortal, when the House of *Yisrael* dwelt on their own soil, they defiled it with their ways and their deeds; their ways were in My sight like the uncleanness of a menstruous woman.

בֶּן־אָדָם בֵּית יִשְׂרָאֵל יֹשְׁבִים עַל־אַדְמָתָם וַיְטַמְּאוּ אוֹתָהּ בְּדַרְכָּם וּבַעֲלִילוֹתָם כְּטֻמְאַת הַנִּדָּה הָיְתָה דַרְכָּם לְפָנָי: יז

¹⁸ So I poured out My wrath on them for the blood which they shed upon their land, and for the fetishes with which they defiled it.

וָאֶשְׁפֹּךְ חֲמָתִי עֲלֵיהֶם עַל־הַדָּם אֲשֶׁר־שָׁפְכוּ עַל־הָאָרֶץ וּבְגִלּוּלֵיהֶם טִמְּאוּהָ: יח

¹⁹ I scattered them among the nations, and they were dispersed through the countries: I punished them in accordance with their ways and their deeds.

וָאָפִיץ אֹתָם בַּגּוֹיִם וַיִּזָּרוּ בָּאֲרָצוֹת כְּדַרְכָּם וְכַעֲלִילוֹתָם שְׁפַטְתִּים: יט

²⁰ But when they came to those nations, they caused My holy name to be profaned, in that it was said of them, "These are the people of *Hashem*, yet they had to leave His land."

וַיָּבוֹא אֶל־הַגּוֹיִם אֲשֶׁר־בָּאוּ שָׁם וַיְחַלְּלוּ אֶת־שֵׁם קָדְשִׁי בֶּאֱמֹר לָהֶם עַם־יְהֹוָה אֵלֶּה וּמֵאַרְצוֹ יָצָאוּ: כ

va-ya-VO el ha-go-YIM a-sher BA-u SHAM vai-kha-l'-LU et SHAYM kod-SHEE be-e-MOR la-HEM am a-do-NAI AY-leh u-may-ar-TZO ya-TZA-u

²¹ Therefore I am concerned for My holy name, which the House of *Yisrael* have caused to be profaned among the nations to which they have come.

וָאֶחְמֹל עַל־שֵׁם קָדְשִׁי אֲשֶׁר חִלְּלוּהוּ בֵּית יִשְׂרָאֵל בַּגּוֹיִם אֲשֶׁר־בָּאוּ שָׁמָּה: כא

²² Say to the House of *Yisrael*: Thus said *Hashem*: Not for your sake will I act, O House of *Yisrael*, but for My holy name, which you have caused to be profaned among the nations to which you have come.

לָכֵן אֱמֹר לְבֵית־יִשְׂרָאֵל כֹּה אָמַר אֲדֹנָי יֱהֹוִה לֹא לְמַעַנְכֶם אֲנִי עֹשֶׂה בֵּית יִשְׂרָאֵל כִּי אִם־לְשֵׁם־קָדְשִׁי אֲשֶׁר חִלַּלְתֶּם בַּגּוֹיִם אֲשֶׁר־בָּאתֶם שָׁם: כב

36:20 They caused My holy name to be profaned *Yechezkel* writes that the exile of the People of Israel among the nations caused a 'desecration of God's name,' in Hebrew, *chilul Hashem* (חילול השם). *Rashi* explains that in response to the exile, the nations of the world would say "these are the Lord's people and they left His land; apparently, He did not have the power to save His people and His land." Hence, the exile of the people from *Eretz Yisrael* causes the name of the Lord to be profaned. It therefore follows that the redemption of this people and their return to their homeland results in a *kiddush Hashem* (קידוש השם), 'sanctification of God's name.' As *Yechezkel* writes (verses 23–24), "And I will sanctify My great name, which has been profaned among the nations…I will take you from among the nations and gather you from all the countries, and I will bring you back to your own land."

Western Wall plaza crowded with Jews praying

23 I will sanctify My great name which has been profaned among the nations – among whom you have caused it to be profaned. And the nations shall know that I am *Hashem* – declares *Hashem* – when I manifest My holiness before their eyes through you.

כג וְקִדַּשְׁתִּי אֶת־שְׁמִי הַגָּדוֹל הַמְחֻלָּל בַּגּוֹיִם אֲשֶׁר חִלַּלְתֶּם בְּתוֹכָם וְיָדְעוּ הַגּוֹיִם כִּי־אֲנִי יְהוָה נְאֻם אֲדֹנָי יְהוִה בְּהִקָּדְשִׁי בָכֶם לְעֵינֵיהֶם:

v'-ki-dash-TEE et sh'-MEE ha-ga-DOL ham-khu-LAL ba-go-YIM a-SHER khi-lal-TEM b'-to-KHAM v'-ya-d'-U ha-go-YIM kee a-NEE a-do-NAI n'-UM a-do-NAI e-lo-HEEM b'-hi-ka-d'-SHEE va-KHEM l'-ay-nay-HEM

24 I will take you from among the nations and gather you from all the countries, and I will bring you back to your own land.

כד וְלָקַחְתִּי אֶתְכֶם מִן־הַגּוֹיִם וְקִבַּצְתִּי אֶתְכֶם מִכָּל־הָאֲרָצוֹת וְהֵבֵאתִי אֶתְכֶם אֶל־אַדְמַתְכֶם:

25 I will sprinkle clean water upon you, and you shall be clean: I will cleanse you from all your uncleanness and from all your fetishes.

כה וְזָרַקְתִּי עֲלֵיכֶם מַיִם טְהוֹרִים וּטְהַרְתֶּם מִכֹּל טֻמְאוֹתֵיכֶם וּמִכָּל־גִּלּוּלֵיכֶם אֲטַהֵר אֶתְכֶם:

26 And I will give you a new heart and put a new spirit into you: I will remove the heart of stone from your body and give you a heart of flesh;

כו וְנָתַתִּי לָכֶם לֵב חָדָשׁ וְרוּחַ חֲדָשָׁה אֶתֵּן בְּקִרְבְּכֶם וַהֲסִרֹתִי אֶת־לֵב הָאֶבֶן מִבְּשַׂרְכֶם וְנָתַתִּי לָכֶם לֵב בָּשָׂר:

27 and I will put My spirit into you. Thus I will cause you to follow My laws and faithfully to observe My rules.

כז וְאֶת־רוּחִי אֶתֵּן בְּקִרְבְּכֶם וְעָשִׂיתִי אֵת אֲשֶׁר־בְּחֻקַּי תֵּלֵכוּ וּמִשְׁפָּטַי תִּשְׁמְרוּ וַעֲשִׂיתֶם:

28 Then you shall dwell in the land which I gave to your fathers, and you shall be My people and I will be your God.

כח וִישַׁבְתֶּם בָּאָרֶץ אֲשֶׁר נָתַתִּי לַאֲבֹתֵיכֶם וִהְיִיתֶם לִי לְעָם וְאָנֹכִי אֶהְיֶה לָכֶם לֵאלֹהִים:

29 And when I have delivered you from all your uncleanness, I will summon the grain and make it abundant, and I will not bring famine upon you.

כט וְהוֹשַׁעְתִּי אֶתְכֶם מִכֹּל טֻמְאוֹתֵיכֶם וְקָרָאתִי אֶל־הַדָּגָן וְהִרְבֵּיתִי אֹתוֹ וְלֹא־אֶתֵּן עֲלֵיכֶם רָעָב:

30 I will make the fruit of your trees and the crops of your fields abundant, so that you shall never again be humiliated before the nations because of famine.

ל וְהִרְבֵּיתִי אֶת־פְּרִי הָעֵץ וּתְנוּבַת הַשָּׂדֶה לְמַעַן אֲשֶׁר לֹא תִקְחוּ עוֹד חֶרְפַּת רָעָב בַּגּוֹיִם:

31 Then you shall recall your evil ways and your base conduct, and you shall loathe yourselves for your iniquities and your abhorrent practices.

לא וּזְכַרְתֶּם אֶת־דַּרְכֵיכֶם הָרָעִים וּמַעַלְלֵיכֶם אֲשֶׁר לֹא־טוֹבִים וּנְקֹטֹתֶם בִּפְנֵיכֶם עַל עֲוֺנֹתֵיכֶם וְעַל תּוֹעֲבוֹתֵיכֶם:

32 Not for your sake will I act – declares *Hashem* – take good note! Be ashamed and humiliated because of your ways, O House of *Yisrael*!

לב לֹא לְמַעַנְכֶם אֲנִי־עֹשֶׂה נְאֻם אֲדֹנָי יְהוִה יִוָּדַע לָכֶם בּוֹשׁוּ וְהִכָּלְמוּ מִדַּרְכֵיכֶם בֵּית יִשְׂרָאֵל:

33 Thus said *Hashem*: When I have cleansed you of all your iniquities, I will people your settlements, and the ruined places shall be rebuilt;

לג כֹּה אָמַר אֲדֹנָי יְהוִה בְּיוֹם טַהֲרִי אֶתְכֶם מִכֹּל עֲוֺנוֹתֵיכֶם וְהוֹשַׁבְתִּי אֶת־הֶעָרִים וְנִבְנוּ הֶחֳרָבוֹת:

34 and the desolate land, after lying waste in the sight of every passerby, shall again be tilled.

לד וְהָאָרֶץ הַנְּשַׁמָּה תֵּעָבֵד תַּחַת אֲשֶׁר הָיְתָה שְׁמָמָה לְעֵינֵי כָּל־עוֹבֵר:

35 And men shall say, "That land, once desolate, has become like the garden of Eden and the cities, once ruined, desolate, and ravaged, are now populated and fortified."	לה וְאָמְרוּ הָאָרֶץ הַלֵּזוּ הַנְּשַׁמָּה הָיְתָה כְּגַן־עֵדֶן וְהֶעָרִים הֶחֲרֵבוֹת וְהַנְשַׁמּוֹת וְהַנֶּהֱרָסוֹת בְּצוּרוֹת יָשָׁבוּ:

36 And the nations that are left around you shall know that I *Hashem* have rebuilt the ravaged places and replanted the desolate land. I *Hashem* have spoken and will act.

לו וְיָדְעוּ הַגּוֹיִם אֲשֶׁר יִשָּׁאֲרוּ סְבִיבוֹתֵיכֶם כִּי אֲנִי יְהֹוָה בָּנִיתִי הַנֶּהֱרָסוֹת נָטַעְתִּי הַנְּשַׁמָּה אֲנִי יְהֹוָה דִּבַּרְתִּי וְעָשִׂיתִי:

37 Thus said *Hashem*: Moreover, in this I will respond to the House of *Yisrael* and act for their sake: I will multiply their people like sheep.

לז כֹּה אָמַר אֲדֹנָי יְהֹוִה עוֹד זֹאת אִדָּרֵשׁ לְבֵית־יִשְׂרָאֵל לַעֲשׂוֹת לָהֶם אַרְבֶּה אֹתָם כַּצֹּאן אָדָם:

38 As *Yerushalayim* is filled with sacrificial sheep during her festivals, so shall the ruined cities be filled with flocks of people. And they shall know that I am *Hashem*.

לח כְּצֹאן קָדָשִׁים כְּצֹאן יְרוּשָׁלַ͏ִם בְּמוֹעֲדֶיהָ כֵּן תִּהְיֶינָה הֶעָרִים הֶחֲרֵבוֹת מְלֵאוֹת צֹאן אָדָם וְיָדְעוּ כִּי־אֲנִי יְהֹוָה:

לז 1 The hand of *Hashem* came upon me. He took me out by the spirit of *Hashem* and set me down in the valley. It was full of bones.

א הָיְתָה עָלַי יַד־יְהֹוָה וַיּוֹצִאֵנִי בְרוּחַ יְהֹוָה וַיְנִיחֵנִי בְּתוֹךְ הַבִּקְעָה וְהִיא מְלֵאָה עֲצָמוֹת:

2 He led me all around them; there were very many of them spread over the valley, and they were very dry.

ב וְהֶעֱבִירַנִי עֲלֵיהֶם סָבִיב סָבִיב וְהִנֵּה רַבּוֹת מְאֹד עַל־פְּנֵי הַבִּקְעָה וְהִנֵּה יְבֵשׁוֹת מְאֹד:

3 He said to me, "O mortal, can these bones live again?" I replied, "O *Hashem*, only You know."

ג וַיֹּאמֶר אֵלַי בֶּן־אָדָם הֲתִחְיֶינָה הָעֲצָמוֹת הָאֵלֶּה וָאֹמַר אֲדֹנָי יְהֹוִה אַתָּה יָדָעְתָּ:

va-YO-mer ay-LAI ben a-DAM ha-tikh-YE-nah ha-a-tza-MOT ha-AY-leh va-o-MAR a-do-NAI e-lo-HEEM a-TAH ya-DA-ta

4 And He said to me, "Prophesy over these bones and say to them: O dry bones, hear the word of *Hashem*!

ד וַיֹּאמֶר אֵלַי הִנָּבֵא עַל־הָעֲצָמוֹת הָאֵלֶּה וְאָמַרְתָּ אֲלֵיהֶם הָעֲצָמוֹת הַיְבֵשׁוֹת שִׁמְעוּ דְּבַר־יְהֹוָה:

5 Thus said *Hashem* to these bones: I will cause breath to enter you and you shall live again.

ה כֹּה אָמַר אֲדֹנָי יְהֹוִה לָעֲצָמוֹת הָאֵלֶּה הִנֵּה אֲנִי מֵבִיא בָכֶם רוּחַ וִחְיִיתֶם:

37:3 'O mortal, can these bones live again?' This chapter contains *Yechezkel's* well-known vision of the valley in which dry bones come to life. There could be no greater metaphor for the restoration of the Jewish people to their land. *Yisrael* and *Yehuda* have been destroyed, the people scattered to the four corners of the earth. Just as no one could imagine that dead bones could live again, the exiles cannot imagine that they will survive as a nation, let alone ever return to their homeland. Yet, when God asks *Yechezkel* "can these bones live?" he doesn't express doubt or hopelessness. He answers that anything can happen if it is God's will. And so the dry bones arise from the dead. In a similarly miraculous fashion, in the years immediately following the Holocaust, the People of Israel came back to life in the Land of Israel. In fact, these verses are read on Israeli radio every year on Holocaust Remembrance Day.

Holocaust survivors arrive in Israel

Ezekiel

6 I will lay sinews upon you, and cover you with flesh, and form skin over you. And I will put breath into you, and you shall live again. And you shall know that I am *Hashem*!"

ו וְנָתַתִּי עֲלֵיכֶם גִּדִים וְהַעֲלֵתִי עֲלֵיכֶם בָּשָׂר וְקָרַמְתִּי עֲלֵיכֶם עוֹר וְנָתַתִּי בָכֶם רוּחַ וִחְיִיתֶם וִידַעְתֶּם כִּי־אֲנִי יְהוָה:

7 I prophesied as I had been commanded. And while I was prophesying, suddenly there was a sound of rattling, and the bones came together, bone to matching bone.

ז וְנִבֵּאתִי כַּאֲשֶׁר צֻוֵּיתִי וַיְהִי־קוֹל כְּהִנָּבְאִי וְהִנֵּה־רַעַשׁ וַתִּקְרְבוּ עֲצָמוֹת עֶצֶם אֶל־עַצְמוֹ:

8 I looked, and there were sinews on them, and flesh had grown, and skin had formed over them; but there was no breath in them.

ח וְרָאִיתִי וְהִנֵּה־עֲלֵיהֶם גִּדִים וּבָשָׂר עָלָה וַיִּקְרַם עֲלֵיהֶם עוֹר מִלְמָעְלָה וְרוּחַ אֵין בָּהֶם:

9 Then He said to me, "Prophesy to the breath, prophesy, O mortal! Say to the breath: Thus said *Hashem*: Come, O breath, from the four winds, and breathe into these slain, that they may live again."

ט וַיֹּאמֶר אֵלַי הִנָּבֵא אֶל־הָרוּחַ הִנָּבֵא בֶן־אָדָם וְאָמַרְתָּ אֶל־הָרוּחַ כֹּה־אָמַר אֲדֹנָי יְהוָה מֵאַרְבַּע רוּחוֹת בֹּאִי הָרוּחַ וּפְחִי בַּהֲרוּגִים הָאֵלֶּה וְיִחְיוּ:

10 I prophesied as He commanded me. The breath entered them, and they came to life and stood up on their feet, a vast multitude.

י וְהִנַּבֵּאתִי כַּאֲשֶׁר צִוָּנִי וַתָּבוֹא בָהֶם הָרוּחַ וַיִּחְיוּ וַיַּעַמְדוּ עַל־רַגְלֵיהֶם חַיִל גָּדוֹל מְאֹד־מְאֹד:

11 And He said to me, "O mortal, these bones are the whole House of *Yisrael*. They say, 'Our bones are dried up, our hope is gone; we are doomed.'

יא וַיֹּאמֶר אֵלַי בֶּן־אָדָם הָעֲצָמוֹת הָאֵלֶּה כָּל־בֵּית יִשְׂרָאֵל הֵמָּה הִנֵּה אֹמְרִים יָבְשׁוּ עַצְמוֹתֵינוּ וְאָבְדָה תִקְוָתֵנוּ נִגְזַרְנוּ לָנוּ:

12 Prophesy, therefore, and say to them: Thus said *Hashem*: I am going to open your graves and lift you out of the graves, O My people, and bring you to the land of *Yisrael*.

יב לָכֵן הִנָּבֵא וְאָמַרְתָּ אֲלֵיהֶם כֹּה־אָמַר אֲדֹנָי יְהוָה הִנֵּה אֲנִי פֹתֵחַ אֶת־קִבְרוֹתֵיכֶם וְהַעֲלֵיתִי אֶתְכֶם מִקִּבְרוֹתֵיכֶם עַמִּי וְהֵבֵאתִי אֶתְכֶם אֶל־אַדְמַת יִשְׂרָאֵל:

13 You shall know, O My people, that I am *Hashem*, when I have opened your graves and lifted you out of your graves.

יג וִידַעְתֶּם כִּי־אֲנִי יְהוָה בְּפִתְחִי אֶת־קִבְרוֹתֵיכֶם וּבְהַעֲלוֹתִי אֶתְכֶם מִקִּבְרוֹתֵיכֶם עַמִּי:

14 I will put My breath into you and you shall live again, and I will set you upon your own soil. Then you shall know that I *Hashem* have spoken and have acted" – declares *Hashem*.

יד וְנָתַתִּי רוּחִי בָכֶם וִחְיִיתֶם וְהִנַּחְתִּי אֶתְכֶם עַל־אַדְמַתְכֶם וִידַעְתֶּם כִּי־אֲנִי יְהוָה דִּבַּרְתִּי וְעָשִׂיתִי נְאֻם־יְהוָה:

15 The word of *Hashem* came to me:

טו וַיְהִי דְבַר־יְהוָה אֵלַי לֵאמֹר:

16 And you, O mortal, take a stick and write on it, "Of *Yehuda* and the Israelites associated with him"; and take another stick and write on it, "Of *Yosef* – the stick of *Efraim* – and all the House of *Yisrael* associated with him."

טז וְאַתָּה בֶן־אָדָם קַח־לְךָ עֵץ אֶחָד וּכְתֹב עָלָיו לִיהוּדָה וְלִבְנֵי יִשְׂרָאֵל חֲבֵרָו [חֲבֵרָיו] וּלְקַח עֵץ אֶחָד וּכְתוֹב עָלָיו לְיוֹסֵף עֵץ אֶפְרַיִם וְכָל־בֵּית יִשְׂרָאֵל חֲבֵרָו [חֲבֵרָיו]:

17 Bring them close to each other, so that they become one stick, joined together in your hand.

יז וְקָרַב אֹתָם אֶחָד אֶל־אֶחָד לְךָ לְעֵץ אֶחָד וְהָיוּ לַאֲחָדִים בְּיָדֶךָ:

18 And when any of your people ask you, "Won't you tell us what these actions of yours mean?"

יח וְכַאֲשֶׁר יֹאמְרוּ אֵלֶיךָ בְּנֵי עַמְּךָ לֵאמֹר הֲלוֹא־תַגִּיד לָנוּ מָה־אֵלֶּה לָּךְ:

19 answer them, "Thus said *Hashem*: I am going to take the stick of *Yosef* – which is in the hand of *Efraim* – and of the tribes of *Yisrael* associated with him, and I will place the stick of *Yehuda* upon it and make them into one stick; they shall be joined in My hand."

יט דַּבֵּר אֲלֵהֶם כֹּה־אָמַר אֲדֹנָי יֱהֹוִה הִנֵּה אֲנִי לֹקֵחַ אֶת־עֵץ יוֹסֵף אֲשֶׁר בְּיַד־אֶפְרַיִם וְשִׁבְטֵי יִשְׂרָאֵל חֲבֵרָו [חֲבֵרָיו] וְנָתַתִּי אוֹתָם עָלָיו אֶת־עֵץ יְהוּדָה וַעֲשִׂיתִם לְעֵץ אֶחָד וְהָיוּ אֶחָד בְּיָדִי:

*da-BAYR a-lay-HEM koh a-MAR a-do-NAI e-lo-HEEM hi-NAY a-NEE
lo-KAY-akh et AYTZ yo-SAYF a-SHER b'-YAD ef-RA-yim v'-shiv-TAY
yis-ra-AYL kha-vay-RAV v'-na-ta-TEE o-TAM a-LAV et AYTZ y'-hu-DAH
va-a-see-TEEM l'-AYTZ e-KHAD v'-ha-YU e-KHAD b'-ya-DEE*

20 You shall hold up before their eyes the sticks which you have inscribed,

כ וְהָיוּ הָעֵצִים אֲשֶׁר־תִּכְתֹּב עֲלֵיהֶם בְּיָדְךָ לְעֵינֵיהֶם:

21 and you shall declare to them: Thus said *Hashem*: I am going to take *B'nei Yisrael* from among the nations they have gone to, and gather them from every quarter, and bring them to their own land.

כא וְדַבֵּר אֲלֵיהֶם כֹּה־אָמַר אֲדֹנָי יֱהֹוִה הִנֵּה אֲנִי לֹקֵחַ אֶת־בְּנֵי יִשְׂרָאֵל מִבֵּין הַגּוֹיִם אֲשֶׁר הָלְכוּ־שָׁם וְקִבַּצְתִּי אֹתָם מִסָּבִיב וְהֵבֵאתִי אוֹתָם אֶל־אַדְמָתָם:

22 I will make them a single nation in the land, on the hills of *Yisrael*, and one king shall be king of them all. Never again shall they be two nations, and never again shall they be divided into two kingdoms.

כב וְעָשִׂיתִי אֹתָם לְגוֹי אֶחָד בָּאָרֶץ בְּהָרֵי יִשְׂרָאֵל וּמֶלֶךְ אֶחָד יִהְיֶה לְכֻלָּם לְמֶלֶךְ וְלֹא יִהְיֶה־[יִהְיוּ] עוֹד לִשְׁנֵי גוֹיִם וְלֹא יֵחָצוּ עוֹד לִשְׁתֵּי מַמְלָכוֹת עוֹד:

23 Nor shall they ever again defile themselves by their fetishes and their abhorrent things, and by their other transgressions. I will save them in all their settlements where they sinned, and I will cleanse them. Then they shall be My people, and I will be their God.

כג וְלֹא יִטַּמְּאוּ עוֹד בְּגִלּוּלֵיהֶם וּבְשִׁקּוּצֵיהֶם וּבְכֹל פִּשְׁעֵיהֶם וְהוֹשַׁעְתִּי אֹתָם מִכֹּל מוֹשְׁבֹתֵיהֶם אֲשֶׁר חָטְאוּ בָהֶם וְטִהַרְתִּי אוֹתָם וְהָיוּ־לִי לְעָם וַאֲנִי אֶהְיֶה לָהֶם לֵאלֹהִים:

24 My servant *David* shall be king over them; there shall be one shepherd for all of them. They shall follow My rules and faithfully obey My laws.

כד וְעַבְדִּי דָוִד מֶלֶךְ עֲלֵיהֶם וְרוֹעֶה אֶחָד יִהְיֶה לְכֻלָּם וּבְמִשְׁפָּטַי יֵלֵכוּ וְחֻקֹּתַי יִשְׁמְרוּ וְעָשׂוּ אוֹתָם:

25 Thus they shall remain in the land which I gave to My servant *Yaakov* and in which your fathers dwelt; they and their children and their children's children shall dwell there forever, with My servant *David* as their prince for all time.

כה וְיָשְׁבוּ עַל־הָאָרֶץ אֲשֶׁר נָתַתִּי לְעַבְדִּי לְיַעֲקֹב אֲשֶׁר יָשְׁבוּ־בָהּ אֲבוֹתֵיכֶם וְיָשְׁבוּ עָלֶיהָ הֵמָּה וּבְנֵיהֶם וּבְנֵי בְנֵיהֶם עַד־עוֹלָם וְדָוִד עַבְדִּי נָשִׂיא לָהֶם לְעוֹלָם:

37:19 They shall be joined in My hand *Yechezkel* again prophesies about the ingathering of the exiles. He stresses that this a promise for all of Israel; not only for the members of the kingdom of *Yehuda*, but also for the tribes from kingdom of *Yisrael* whose people have been considered lost since the Assyrian conquest of the northern kingdom. During the final redemption, all twelve tribes of Israel will return to the Promised Land, and they will re-unite to form one nation unified under one leader. Today, Jews are returning to *Eretz Yisrael* from all over the world, and are joining together to reestablish the Nation of Israel in the Land of Israel.

Members of the *Bnei Menashe* tribe arrive in Israel

²⁶ I will make a covenant of friendship with them – it shall be an everlasting covenant with them – I will establish them and multiply them, and I will place My Sanctuary among them forever.

כו וְכָרַתִּי לָהֶם בְּרִית שָׁלוֹם בְּרִית עוֹלָם יִהְיֶה אוֹתָם וּנְתַתִּים וְהִרְבֵּיתִי אוֹתָם וְנָתַתִּי אֶת־מִקְדָּשִׁי בְּתוֹכָם לְעוֹלָם:

²⁷ My Presence shall rest over them; I will be their God and they shall be My people.

כז וְהָיָה מִשְׁכָּנִי עֲלֵיהֶם וְהָיִיתִי לָהֶם לֵאלֹהִים וְהֵמָּה יִהְיוּ־לִי לְעָם:

²⁸ And when My Sanctuary abides among them forever, the nations shall know that I *Hashem* do sanctify *Yisrael*.

כח וְיָדְעוּ הַגּוֹיִם כִּי אֲנִי יְהוָה מְקַדֵּשׁ אֶת־יִשְׂרָאֵל בִּהְיוֹת מִקְדָּשִׁי בְּתוֹכָם לְעוֹלָם:

38 ¹ The word of *Hashem* came to me:

ח א וַיְהִי דְבַר־יְהוָה אֵלַי לֵאמֹר:

² O mortal, turn your face toward Gog of the land of Magog, the chief prince of Meshech and Tubal. Prophesy against him

ב בֶּן־אָדָם שִׂים פָּנֶיךָ אֶל־גּוֹג אֶרֶץ הַמָּגוֹג נְשִׂיא רֹאשׁ מֶשֶׁךְ וְתֻבָל וְהִנָּבֵא עָלָיו:

³ and say: Thus said *Hashem*: Lo, I am coming to deal with you, O Gog, chief prince of Meshech and Tubal!

ג וְאָמַרְתָּ כֹּה אָמַר אֲדֹנָי יְהוִה הִנְנִי אֵלֶיךָ גּוֹג נְשִׂיא רֹאשׁ מֶשֶׁךְ וְתֻבָל:

⁴ I will turn you around and put hooks in your jaws, and lead you out with all your army, horses, and horsemen, all of them clothed in splendor, a vast assembly, all of them with bucklers and shields, wielding swords.

ד וְשׁוֹבַבְתִּיךָ וְנָתַתִּי חַחִים בִּלְחָיֶיךָ וְהוֹצֵאתִי אוֹתְךָ וְאֶת־כָּל־חֵילֶךָ סוּסִים וּפָרָשִׁים לְבֻשֵׁי מִכְלוֹל כֻּלָּם קָהָל רָב צִנָּה וּמָגֵן תֹּפְשֵׂי חֲרָבוֹת כֻּלָּם:

⁵ Among them shall be Persia, Nubia, and Put, everyone with shield and helmet;

ה פָּרַס כּוּשׁ וּפוּט אִתָּם כֻּלָּם מָגֵן וְכוֹבָע:

⁶ Gomer and all its cohorts, Beth-togarmah [in] the remotest parts of the north and all its cohorts – the many peoples with you.

ו גֹּמֶר וְכָל־אֲגַפֶּיהָ בֵּית תּוֹגַרְמָה יַרְכְּתֵי צָפוֹן וְאֶת־כָּל־אֲגַפָּיו עַמִּים רַבִּים אִתָּךְ:

⁷ Be ready, prepare yourselves, you and all the battalions mustered about you, and hold yourself in reserve for them.

ז הִכֹּן וְהָכֵן לְךָ אַתָּה וְכָל־קְהָלֶךָ הַנִּקְהָלִים עָלֶיךָ וְהָיִיתָ לָהֶם לְמִשְׁמָר:

⁸ After a long time you shall be summoned; in the distant future you shall march against the land [of a people] restored from the sword, gathered from the midst of many peoples – against the mountains of *Yisrael*, which have long lain desolate – [a people] liberated from the nations, and now all dwelling secure.

ח מִיָּמִים רַבִּים תִּפָּקֵד בְּאַחֲרִית הַשָּׁנִים תָּבוֹא אֶל־אֶרֶץ מְשׁוֹבֶבֶת מֵחֶרֶב מְקֻבֶּצֶת מֵעַמִּים רַבִּים עַל הָרֵי יִשְׂרָאֵל אֲשֶׁר־הָיוּ לְחָרְבָּה תָּמִיד וְהִיא מֵעַמִּים הוּצָאָה וְיָשְׁבוּ לָבֶטַח כֻּלָּם:

⁹ You shall advance, coming like a storm; you shall be like a cloud covering the earth, you and all your cohorts, and the many peoples with you.

ט וְעָלִיתָ כַּשֹּׁאָה תָבוֹא כֶּעָנָן לְכַסּוֹת הָאָרֶץ תִּהְיֶה אַתָּה וְכָל־אֲגַפֶּיךָ וְעַמִּים רַבִּים אוֹתָךְ:

¹⁰ Thus said *Hashem*: On that day, a thought will occur to you, and you will conceive a wicked design.

י כֹּה אָמַר אֲדֹנָי יְהוִה וְהָיָה בַּיּוֹם הַהוּא יַעֲלוּ דְבָרִים עַל־לְבָבֶךָ וְחָשַׁבְתָּ מַחֲשֶׁבֶת רָעָה:

11 You will say, "I will invade a land of open towns, I will fall upon a tranquil people living secure, all of them living in unwalled towns and lacking bars and gates,

יא וְאָמַרְתָּ אֶעֱלֶה עַל־אֶרֶץ פְּרָזוֹת אָבוֹא הַשֹּׁקְטִים יֹשְׁבֵי לָבֶטַח כֻּלָּם יֹשְׁבִים בְּאֵין חוֹמָה וּבְרִיחַ וּדְלָתַיִם אֵין לָהֶם:

12 in order to take spoil and seize plunder" – to turn your hand against repopulated wastes, and against a people gathered from among nations, acquiring livestock and possessions, living at the center of the earth.

יב לִשְׁלֹל שָׁלָל וְלָבֹז בַּז לְהָשִׁיב יָדְךָ עַל־חֳרָבוֹת נוֹשָׁבֹת וְאֶל־עַם מְאֻסָּף מִגּוֹיִם עֹשֶׂה מִקְנֶה וְקִנְיָן יֹשְׁבֵי עַל־טַבּוּר הָאָרֶץ:

13 Sheba and Dedan, and the merchants and all the magnates of Tarshish will say to you, "Have you come to take spoil? Is it to seize plunder that you assembled your hordes – to carry off silver and gold, to make off with livestock and goods, to gather an immense booty?"

יג שְׁבָא וּדְדָן וְסֹחֲרֵי תַרְשִׁישׁ וְכָל־כְּפִרֶיהָ יֹאמְרוּ לְךָ הֲלִשְׁלֹל שָׁלָל אַתָּה בָא הֲלָבֹז בַּז הִקְהַלְתָּ קְהָלֶךָ לָשֵׂאת כֶּסֶף וְזָהָב לָקַחַת מִקְנֶה וְקִנְיָן לִשְׁלֹל שָׁלָל גָּדוֹל:

14 Therefore prophesy, O mortal, and say to Gog: Thus said *Hashem*: Surely, on that day, when My people *Yisrael* are living secure, you will take note,

יד לָכֵן הִנָּבֵא בֶן־אָדָם וְאָמַרְתָּ לְגוֹג כֹּה אָמַר אֲדֹנָי יֱהֹוִה הֲלוֹא בַּיּוֹם הַהוּא בְּשֶׁבֶת עַמִּי יִשְׂרָאֵל לָבֶטַח תֵּדָע:

la-KHAYN hi-na-VAY ven a-DAM v'-a-mar-TA l'-GOG
KOH a-MAR a-do-NAI e-lo-HEEM ha-LO ba-YOM ha-HU
b'-SHE-vet a-MEE yis-ra-AYL la-VE-takh tay-DA

15 and you will come from your home in the farthest north, you and many peoples with you – all of them mounted on horses, a vast horde, a mighty army –

טו וּבָאתָ מִמְּקוֹמְךָ מִיַּרְכְּתֵי צָפוֹן אַתָּה וְעַמִּים רַבִּים אִתָּךְ רֹכְבֵי סוּסִים כֻּלָּם קָהָל גָּדוֹל וְחַיִל רָב:

16 and you will advance upon My people *Yisrael*, like a cloud covering the earth. This shall happen on that distant day: I will bring you to My land, that the nations may know Me when, before their eyes, I manifest My holiness through you, O Gog!

טז וְעָלִיתָ עַל־עַמִּי יִשְׂרָאֵל כֶּעָנָן לְכַסּוֹת הָאָרֶץ בְּאַחֲרִית הַיָּמִים תִּהְיֶה וַהֲבִאוֹתִיךָ עַל־אַרְצִי לְמַעַן דַּעַת הַגּוֹיִם אֹתִי בְּהִקָּדְשִׁי בְךָ לְעֵינֵיהֶם גּוֹג:

17 Thus said *Hashem*: Why, you are the one I spoke of in ancient days through My servants, the *Neviim* of *Yisrael*, who prophesied for years in those days that I would bring you against them!

יז כֹּה־אָמַר אֲדֹנָי יֱהֹוִה הַאַתָּה־הוּא אֲשֶׁר־דִּבַּרְתִּי בְּיָמִים קַדְמוֹנִים בְּיַד עֲבָדַי נְבִיאֵי יִשְׂרָאֵל הַנִּבְּאִים בַּיָּמִים הָהֵם שָׁנִים לְהָבִיא אֹתְךָ עֲלֵיהֶם:

38:14 When My people *Yisrael* are living secure In *Yechezkel's* final apocalyptic vision, Gog and Magog make their evil preparations to invade Israel. They see the people dwelling in the land in security and prosperity, and feel that the time is ripe to attack. *Hashem* tells Gog and Magog that through their evil, they will be destroyed, and God's name will be sanctified throughout the world (verse 16). This verse gives us a hint into the mind of Israel's enemies. The sight of the People of Israel liv- ing in peace and quiet in *Eretz Yisrael* motivates them to attack. Although Israel poses no threat, her enemies are prepared to risk everything to see her destroyed. But as God makes clear, He will never allow that to happen.

Two brothers relaxing at the beach in Haifa

Ezekiel

יחזקאל

פרק לט

18 On that day, when Gog sets foot on the soil of *Yisrael* – declares *Hashem* – My raging anger shall flare up.

יח וְהָיָה בַּיּוֹם הַהוּא בְּיוֹם בּוֹא גוֹג עַל־אַדְמַת יִשְׂרָאֵל נְאֻם אֲדֹנָי יֱהֹוִה תַּעֲלֶה חֲמָתִי בְּאַפִּי:

19 For I have decreed in My indignation and in My blazing wrath: On that day, a terrible earthquake shall befall the land of *Yisrael*.

יט וּבְקִנְאָתִי בְאֵשׁ־עֶבְרָתִי דִּבַּרְתִּי אִם־לֹא בַּיּוֹם הַהוּא יִהְיֶה רַעַשׁ גָּדוֹל עַל אַדְמַת יִשְׂרָאֵל:

20 The fish of the sea, the birds of the sky, the beasts of the field, all creeping things that move on the ground, and every human being on earth shall quake before Me. Mountains shall be overthrown, cliffs shall topple, and every wall shall crumble to the ground.

כ וְרָעֲשׁוּ מִפָּנַי דְּגֵי הַיָּם וְעוֹף הַשָּׁמַיִם וְחַיַּת הַשָּׂדֶה וְכָל־הָרֶמֶשׂ הָרֹמֵשׂ עַל־הָאֲדָמָה וְכֹל הָאָדָם אֲשֶׁר עַל־פְּנֵי הָאֲדָמָה וְנֶהֶרְסוּ הֶהָרִים וְנָפְלוּ הַמַּדְרֵגוֹת וְכָל־חוֹמָה לָאָרֶץ תִּפּוֹל:

21 I will then summon the sword against him throughout My mountains – declares *Hashem* – and every man's sword shall be turned against his brother.

כא וְקָרָאתִי עָלָיו לְכָל־הָרַי חֶרֶב נְאֻם אֲדֹנָי יֱהֹוִה חֶרֶב אִישׁ בְּאָחִיו תִּהְיֶה:

22 I will punish him with pestilence and with bloodshed; and I will pour torrential rain, hailstones, and sulfurous fire upon him and his hordes and the many peoples with him.

כב וְנִשְׁפַּטְתִּי אִתּוֹ בְּדֶבֶר וּבְדָם וְגֶשֶׁם שׁוֹטֵף וְאַבְנֵי אֶלְגָּבִישׁ אֵשׁ וְגָפְרִית אַמְטִיר עָלָיו וְעַל־אֲגַפָּיו וְעַל־עַמִּים רַבִּים אֲשֶׁר אִתּוֹ:

23 Thus will I manifest My greatness and My holiness, and make Myself known in the sight of many nations. And they shall know that I am *Hashem*.

כג וְהִתְגַּדִּלְתִּי וְהִתְקַדִּשְׁתִּי וְנוֹדַעְתִּי לְעֵינֵי גּוֹיִם רַבִּים וְיָדְעוּ כִּי־אֲנִי יְהֹוָה:

39 **1** And you, O mortal, prophesy against Gog and say: Thus said *Hashem*: I am going to deal with you, O Gog, chief prince of Meshech and Tubal!

ט א וְאַתָּה בֶן־אָדָם הִנָּבֵא עַל־גּוֹג וְאָמַרְתָּ כֹּה אָמַר אֲדֹנָי יֱהֹוִה הִנְנִי אֵלֶיךָ גּוֹג נְשִׂיא רֹאשׁ מֶשֶׁךְ וְתֻבָל:

2 I will turn you around and drive you on, and I will take you from the far north and lead you toward the mountains of *Yisrael*.

ב וְשֹׁבַבְתִּיךָ וְשִׁשֵּׁאתִיךָ וְהַעֲלִיתִיךָ מִיַּרְכְּתֵי צָפוֹן וַהֲבִאוֹתִךָ עַל־הָרֵי יִשְׂרָאֵל:

3 I will strike your bow from your left hand and I will loosen the arrows from your right hand.

ג וְהִכֵּיתִי קַשְׁתְּךָ מִיַּד שְׂמֹאולֶךָ וְחִצֶּיךָ מִיַּד יְמִינְךָ אַפִּיל:

4 You shall fall on the mountains of *Yisrael*, you and all your battalions and the peoples who are with you; and I will give you as food to carrion birds of every sort and to the beasts of the field,

ד עַל־הָרֵי יִשְׂרָאֵל תִּפּוֹל אַתָּה וְכָל־אֲגַפֶּיךָ וְעַמִּים אֲשֶׁר אִתָּךְ לְעֵיט צִפּוֹר כָּל־כָּנָף וְחַיַּת הַשָּׂדֶה נְתַתִּיךָ לְאָכְלָה:

5 as you lie in the open field. For I have spoken – declares *Hashem*.

ה עַל־פְּנֵי הַשָּׂדֶה תִּפּוֹל כִּי אֲנִי דִבַּרְתִּי נְאֻם אֲדֹנָי יֱהֹוִה:

6 And I will send a fire against Magog and against those who dwell secure in the coastlands. And they shall know that I am *Hashem*.

ו וְשִׁלַּחְתִּי־אֵשׁ בְּמָגוֹג וּבְיֹשְׁבֵי הָאִיִּים לָבֶטַח וְיָדְעוּ כִּי־אֲנִי יְהֹוָה:

Ezekiel

7 I will make My holy name known among My
people *Yisrael*, and never again will I let My holy
name be profaned. And the nations shall know that
I *Hashem* am holy in *Yisrael*.

ז וְאֶת־שֵׁם קָדְשִׁי אוֹדִיעַ בְּתוֹךְ עַמִּי
יִשְׂרָאֵל וְלֹא־אַחֵל אֶת־שֵׁם־קָדְשִׁי
עוֹד וְיָדְעוּ הַגּוֹיִם כִּי־אֲנִי יְהֹוָה קָדוֹשׁ
בְּיִשְׂרָאֵל:

8 Ah! it has come, it has happened – declares
Hashem: this is that day that I decreed.

ח הִנֵּה בָאָה וְנִהְיָתָה נְאֻם אֲדֹנָי יְהֹוִה הוּא
הַיּוֹם אֲשֶׁר דִּבַּרְתִּי:

9 Then the inhabitants of the cities of *Yisrael* will
go out and make fires and feed them with the
weapons – shields and bucklers, bows and arrows,
clubs and spears; they shall use them as fuel for
seven years.

ט וְיָצְאוּ יֹשְׁבֵי עָרֵי יִשְׂרָאֵל וּבִעֲרוּ וְהִשִּׂיקוּ
בְּנֶשֶׁק וּמָגֵן וְצִנָּה בְּקֶשֶׁת וּבְחִצִּים
וּבְמַקֵּל יָד וּבְרֹמַח וּבִעֲרוּ בָהֶם אֵשׁ
שֶׁבַע שָׁנִים:

10 They will not gather firewood in the fields or cut
any in the forests, but will use the weapons as
fuel for their fires. They will despoil those who
despoiled them and plunder those who plundered
them – declares *Hashem*.

י וְלֹא־יִשְׂאוּ עֵצִים מִן־הַשָּׂדֶה וְלֹא יַחְטְבוּ
מִן־הַיְּעָרִים כִּי בַנֶּשֶׁק יְבַעֲרוּ־אֵשׁ וְשָׁלְלוּ
אֶת־שֹׁלְלֵיהֶם וּבָזְזוּ אֶת־בֹּזְזֵיהֶם נְאֻם
אֲדֹנָי יְהֹוִה:

11 On that day I will assign to Gog a burial site there
in *Yisrael* – the Valley of the Travelers, east of the
Sea. It shall block the path of travelers, for there
Gog and all his multitude will be buried. It shall be
called the Valley of Gog's Multitude.

יא וְהָיָה בַיּוֹם הַהוּא אֶתֵּן לְגוֹג מְקוֹם־שָׁם
קֶבֶר בְּיִשְׂרָאֵל גֵּי הָעֹבְרִים קִדְמַת הַיָּם
וְחֹסֶמֶת הִיא אֶת־הָעֹבְרִים וְקָבְרוּ שָׁם
אֶת־גּוֹג וְאֶת־כָּל־הֲמוֹנֹה וְקָרְאוּ גֵּיא
הֲמוֹן גּוֹג:

12 The House of *Yisrael* shall spend seven months
burying them, in order to cleanse the land;

יב וּקְבָרוּם בֵּית יִשְׂרָאֵל לְמַעַן טַהֵר אֶת־
הָאָרֶץ שִׁבְעָה חֳדָשִׁים:

13 all the people of the land shall bury them. The day
I manifest My glory shall bring renown to them –
declares *Hashem*.

יג וְקָבְרוּ כָּל־עַם הָאָרֶץ וְהָיָה לָהֶם לְשֵׁם
יוֹם הִכָּבְדִי נְאֻם אֲדֹנָי יְהֹוִה:

14 And they shall appoint men to serve permanently,
to traverse the land and bury any invaders who
remain above ground, in order to cleanse it. The
search shall go on for a period of seven months.

יד וְאַנְשֵׁי תָמִיד יַבְדִּילוּ עֹבְרִים בָּאָרֶץ
מְקַבְּרִים אֶת־הָעֹבְרִים אֶת־הַנּוֹתָרִים
עַל־פְּנֵי הָאָרֶץ לְטַהֲרָהּ מִקְצֵה שִׁבְעָה־
חֳדָשִׁים יַחְקֹרוּ:

15 As those who traverse the country make their
rounds, any one of them who sees a human bone
shall erect a marker beside it, until the buriers have
interred them in the Valley of Gog's Multitude.

טו וְעָבְרוּ הָעֹבְרִים בָּאָרֶץ וְרָאָה עֶצֶם
אָדָם וּבָנָה אֶצְלוֹ צִיּוּן עַד קָבְרוּ אֹתוֹ
הַמְקַבְּרִים אֶל־גֵּיא הֲמוֹן גּוֹג:

16 There shall also be a city named Multitude. And
thus the land shall be cleansed.

טז וְגַם שֶׁם־עִיר הֲמוֹנָה וְטִהֲרוּ הָאָרֶץ:

17 And you, O mortal, say to every winged bird and
to all the wild beasts: Thus said *Hashem*: Assemble,
come and gather from all around for the sacrificial
feast that I am preparing for you – a great sacrificial
feast – upon the mountains of *Yisrael*, and eat flesh
and drink blood.

יז וְאַתָּה בֶן־אָדָם כֹּה־אָמַר אֲדֹנָי יְהֹוִה
אֱמֹר לְצִפּוֹר כָּל־כָּנָף וּלְכֹל חַיַּת הַשָּׂדֶה
הִקָּבְצוּ וָבֹאוּ הֵאָסְפוּ מִסָּבִיב עַל־זִבְחִי
אֲשֶׁר אֲנִי זֹבֵחַ לָכֶם זֶבַח גָּדוֹל עַל הָרֵי
יִשְׂרָאֵל וַאֲכַלְתֶּם בָּשָׂר וּשְׁתִיתֶם דָּם:

¹⁸ You shall eat the flesh of warriors and drink the blood of the princes of the earth: rams, lambs, he-goats, and bulls – fatlings of Bashan all of them.

יח בְּשַׂר גִּבּוֹרִים תֹּאכֵלוּ וְדַם־נְשִׂיאֵי הָאָרֶץ תִּשְׁתּוּ אֵילִים כָּרִים וְעַתּוּדִים פָּרִים מְרִיאֵי בָשָׁן כֻּלָּם:

¹⁹ You shall eat fat to satiety and drink your fill of blood from the sacrificial feast that I have prepared for you.

יט וַאֲכַלְתֶּם־חֵלֶב לְשָׂבְעָה וּשְׁתִיתֶם דָּם לְשִׁכָּרוֹן מִזִּבְחִי אֲשֶׁר־זָבַחְתִּי לָכֶם:

²⁰ And you shall sate yourselves at My table with horses, charioteers, warriors, and all fighting men – declares *Hashem*.

כ וּשְׂבַעְתֶּם עַל־שֻׁלְחָנִי סוּס וָרֶכֶב גִּבּוֹר וְכָל־אִישׁ מִלְחָמָה נְאֻם אֲדֹנָי יְהֹוִה:

²¹ Thus will I manifest My glory among the nations, and all the nations shall see the judgment that I executed and the power that I wielded against them.

כא וְנָתַתִּי אֶת־כְּבוֹדִי בַּגּוֹיִם וְרָאוּ כָל־הַגּוֹיִם אֶת־מִשְׁפָּטִי אֲשֶׁר עָשִׂיתִי וְאֶת־יָדִי אֲשֶׁר־שַׂמְתִּי בָהֶם:

²² From that time on, the House of *Yisrael* shall know that I *Hashem* am their God.

כב וְיָדְעוּ בֵּית יִשְׂרָאֵל כִּי אֲנִי יְהֹוָה אֱלֹהֵיהֶם מִן־הַיּוֹם הַהוּא וָהָלְאָה:

²³ And the nations shall know that the House of *Yisrael* were exiled only for their iniquity, because they trespassed against Me, so that I hid My face from them and delivered them into the hands of their adversaries, and they all fell by the sword.

כג וְיָדְעוּ הַגּוֹיִם כִּי בַעֲוֺנָם גָּלוּ בֵית־יִשְׂרָאֵל עַל אֲשֶׁר מָעֲלוּ־בִי וָאַסְתִּר פָּנַי מֵהֶם וָאֶתְּנֵם בְּיַד צָרֵיהֶם וַיִּפְּלוּ בַחֶרֶב כֻּלָּם:

²⁴ When I hid My face from them, I dealt with them according to their uncleanness and their transgressions.

כד כְּטֻמְאָתָם וּכְפִשְׁעֵיהֶם עָשִׂיתִי אֹתָם וָאַסְתִּר פָּנַי מֵהֶם:

²⁵ Assuredly, thus said *Hashem*: I will now restore the fortunes of *Yaakov* and take the whole House of *Yisrael* back in love; and I will be zealous for My holy name.

כה לָכֵן כֹּה אָמַר אֲדֹנָי יְהֹוִה עַתָּה אָשִׁיב אֶת־שְׁבִית [שְׁבוּת] יַעֲקֹב וְרִחַמְתִּי כָּל־בֵּית יִשְׂרָאֵל וְקִנֵּאתִי לְשֵׁם קָדְשִׁי:

la-KHAYN KOH a-MAR a-do-NAI e-lo-HEEM a-TAH
a-SHEEV et sh'-VUT ya-a-KOV v'-ri-kham-TEE kol BAYT
yis-ra-AYL v'-ki-nay-TEE l'-SHAYM kod-SHEE

²⁶ They will bear their shame and all their trespasses that they committed against Me, when they dwell in their land secure and untroubled,

כו וְנָשׂוּ אֶת־כְּלִמָּתָם וְאֶת־כָּל־מַעֲלָם אֲשֶׁר מָעֲלוּ־בִי בְּשִׁבְתָּם עַל־אַדְמָתָם לָבֶטַח וְאֵין מַחֲרִיד:

²⁷ when I have brought them back from among the peoples and gathered them out of the lands of their enemies and have manifested My holiness through them in the sight of many nations.

כז בְּשׁוֹבְבִי אוֹתָם מִן־הָעַמִּים וְקִבַּצְתִּי אֹתָם מֵאַרְצוֹת אֹיְבֵיהֶם וְנִקְדַּשְׁתִּי בָם לְעֵינֵי הַגּוֹיִם רַבִּים:

רחמים

א **39:25 Take the whole House of *Yisrael* back in love** The root of the Hebrew word for 'compassion,' *rachamim* (רחמים), is from the same root as the word *rekhem* (רחם), which means 'womb.' The connection between these two ideas is that a mother has innate compassion for her children, the fruit of her womb, as it says in Isaiah (49:15), "Can a woman forget her baby, or disown the child of her womb?" *Yechezkel* teaches that when *Hashem* returns the captivity of *Yaakov*, He will shower them with mercy and compassion, comparable to the natural compassion a mother has for her child.

Mother and son at
the Dead Sea

28 They shall know that I *Hashem* am their God when, having exiled them among the nations, I gather them back into their land and leave none of them behind.

כח וְיָדְעוּ כִּי אֲנִי יְהֹוָה אֱלֹהֵיהֶם בְּהַגְלוֹתִי אֹתָם אֶל־הַגּוֹיִם וְכִנַּסְתִּים עַל־אַדְמָתָם וְלֹא־אוֹתִיר עוֹד מֵהֶם שָׁם:

29 I will never again hide My face from them, for I will pour out My spirit upon the House of *Yisrael* – declares *Hashem*.

כט וְלֹא־אַסְתִּיר עוֹד פָּנַי מֵהֶם אֲשֶׁר שָׁפַכְתִּי אֶת־רוּחִי עַל־בֵּית יִשְׂרָאֵל נְאֻם אֲדֹנָי יְהֹוִה:

0 1 In the twenty-fifth year of our exile, the fourteenth year after the city had fallen, at the beginning of the year, the tenth day of the month – on that very day – the hand of *Hashem* came upon me, and He brought me there.

מ א בְּעֶשְׂרִים וְחָמֵשׁ שָׁנָה לְגָלוּתֵנוּ בְּרֹאשׁ הַשָּׁנָה בֶּעָשׂוֹר לַחֹדֶשׁ בְּאַרְבַּע עֶשְׂרֵה שָׁנָה אַחַר אֲשֶׁר הֻכְּתָה הָעִיר בְּעֶצֶם הַיּוֹם הַזֶּה הָיְתָה עָלַי יַד־יְהֹוָה וַיָּבֵא אֹתִי שָׁמָּה:

2 He brought me, in visions of *Hashem*, to the Land of *Yisrael*, and He set me down on a very high mountain on which there seemed to be the outline of a city on the south.

ב בְּמַרְאוֹת אֱלֹהִים הֱבִיאַנִי אֶל־אֶרֶץ יִשְׂרָאֵל וַיְנִיחֵנִי אֶל־הַר גָּבֹהַּ מְאֹד וְעָלָיו כְּמִבְנֵה־עִיר מִנֶּגֶב:

*b'-mar-OT e-lo-HEEM he-vee-A-nee el E-retz yis-ra-AYL vai-nee-KHAY-nee
el HAR ga-VO-ha m'-OD v'-a-LAV k'-miv-nay EER mi-NE-gev*

3 He brought me over to it, and there, standing at the gate, was a man who shone like copper. In his hand were a cord of linen and a measuring rod.

ג וַיָּבִיא אוֹתִי שָׁמָּה וְהִנֵּה־אִישׁ מַרְאֵהוּ כְּמַרְאֵה נְחֹשֶׁת וּפְתִיל־פִּשְׁתִּים בְּיָדוֹ וּקְנֵה הַמִּדָּה וְהוּא עֹמֵד בַּשָּׁעַר:

4 The man spoke to me: "Mortal, look closely and listen attentively and note well everything I am going to show you – for you have been brought here in order to be shown – and report everything you see to the House of *Yisrael*."

ד וַיְדַבֵּר אֵלַי הָאִישׁ בֶּן־אָדָם רְאֵה בְעֵינֶיךָ וּבְאָזְנֶיךָ שְׁמַע וְשִׂים לִבְּךָ לְכֹל אֲשֶׁר־אֲנִי מַרְאֶה אוֹתָךְ כִּי לְמַעַן הַרְאוֹתְכָה הֻבָאתָה הֵנָּה הַגֵּד אֶת־כָּל־אֲשֶׁר־אַתָּה רֹאֶה לְבֵית יִשְׂרָאֵל:

5 Along the outside of the Temple [area] ran a wall on every side. The rod that the man held was six *amot* long, plus one *tefach* for each *amah*; and when he applied it to that structure, it measured one rod deep and one rod high.

ה וְהִנֵּה חוֹמָה מִחוּץ לַבַּיִת סָבִיב סָבִיב וּבְיַד הָאִישׁ קְנֵה הַמִּדָּה שֵׁשׁ־אַמּוֹת בָּאַמָּה וָטֹפַח וַיָּמָד אֶת־רֹחַב הַבִּנְיָן קָנֶה אֶחָד וְקוֹמָה קָנֶה אֶחָד:

Ezekiel

40:2 And He set me down on a very high mountain The final section of *Yechezkel's* prophecy describes the building of the third *Beit Hamikdash*, its operation, and the re-division of the Land of Israel among the people. These chapters contain the prophet's hopes for his people, and represent the closing of a circle that began in chapter 1. Decades earlier, *Yechezkel* envisioned the Divine Presence leaving *Eretz Yisrael* and the Temple prior to its destruction. Now, perched on the high mountain, the Temple Mount in *Yerushalayim*, *Yechezkel* can foresee the return of the People of Israel to the Land of Israel, and God's Presence returning to His city. According to the sages, this vision comes to *Yechezkel* at the beginning of the *yovel*, the Jubilee year. *Radak* emphasizes how appropriate the timing of this vision is, since during the *yovel*, all people are freed and returned to their ancestral homes.

The Temple Mount in *Yerushalayim*

⁶ He went up to the gate that faced eastward and mounted its steps. He measured the threshold of the gate; it was one rod deep – the one threshold was one rod deep.

ו וַיָּבוֹא אֶל־שַׁעַר אֲשֶׁר פָּנָיו דֶּרֶךְ הַקָּדִימָה וַיַּעַל בְּמַעֲלוֹתָו [בְּמַעֲלוֹתָיו] וַיָּמָד אֶת־סַף הַשַּׁעַר קָנֶה אֶחָד רֹחַב וְאֵת סַף אֶחָד קָנֶה אֶחָד רֹחַב:

⁷ Each recess was one rod wide and one rod deep, with [a partition of] 5 *amot* between recesses; and the threshold of the gate, at the inner vestibule of the gate, was one rod deep.

ז וְהַתָּא קָנֶה אֶחָד אֹרֶךְ וְקָנֶה אֶחָד רֹחַב וּבֵין הַתָּאִים חָמֵשׁ אַמּוֹת וְסַף הַשַּׁעַר מֵאֵצֶל אוּלָם הַשַּׁעַר מֵהַבַּיִת קָנֶה אֶחָד:

⁸ For when he measured it at the inner vestibule of the gate, it was one rod [deep].

ח וַיָּמָד אֶת־אֻלָם הַשַּׁעַר מֵהַבַּיִת קָנֶה אֶחָד:

⁹ Next he measured the vestibule of the gate, and it measured 8 *amot* and its supports 2 *amot*; the vestibule of the gate was at its inner end.

ט וַיָּמָד אֶת־אֻלָם הַשַּׁעַר שְׁמֹנֶה אַמּוֹת וְאֵילוֹ [וְאֵילָיו] שְׁתַּיִם אַמּוֹת וְאֻלָם הַשַּׁעַר מֵהַבָּיִת:

¹⁰ On either side of this eastern gate there were three recesses, all three of the same size; of identical sizes were also the supports on either side.

י וְתָאֵי הַשַּׁעַר דֶּרֶךְ הַקָּדִים שְׁלֹשָׁה מִפֹּה וּשְׁלֹשָׁה מִפֹּה מִדָּה אַחַת לִשְׁלָשְׁתָּם וּמִדָּה אַחַת לָאֵילִם מִפֹּה וּמִפֹּו:

¹¹ He measured the opening of the gate and found it 10 *amot* wide, while the gate itself measured 13 *amot* across.

יא וַיָּמָד אֶת־רֹחַב פֶּתַח־הַשַּׁעַר עֶשֶׂר אַמּוֹת אֹרֶךְ הַשַּׁעַר שְׁלוֹשׁ עֶשְׂרֵה אַמּוֹת:

¹² At the fronts of the recesses on either side were barriers of one *amah*; the recesses on either side were 6 *amot* [deep].

יב וּגְבוּל לִפְנֵי הַתָּאוֹת אַמָּה אֶחָת וְאַמָּה־אַחַת גְּבוּל מִפֹּה וְהַתָּא שֵׁשׁ־אַמּוֹת מִפֹּו וְשֵׁשׁ אַמּוֹת מִפֹּו:

¹³ Their openings faced each other directly across the gate passage, so that when he measured from rear of recess to rear of recess he obtained a width of 25 *amot*.

יג וַיָּמָד אֶת־הַשַּׁעַר מִגַּג הַתָּא לְגַגּוֹ רֹחַב עֶשְׂרִים וְחָמֵשׁ אַמּוֹת פֶּתַח נֶגֶד פָּתַח:

¹⁴ He made the vestibule – 60 *amot* – and the gate next to the support on every side of the court.

יד וַיַּעַשׂ אֶת־אֵילִים שִׁשִּׁים אַמָּה וְאֶל־אֵיל הֶחָצֵר הַשַּׁעַר סָבִיב סָבִיב:

¹⁵ And [the distance] from the front of the outer gate to the front of the inner vestibule of the gate was 50 *amot*.

טו וְעַל פְּנֵי הַשַּׁעַר הַיְאתוֹן [הָאִיתוֹן] עַל־לִפְנֵי אֻלָם הַשַּׁעַר הַפְּנִימִי חֲמִשִּׁים אַמָּה:

¹⁶ The recesses – and their supports – had windows with frames on the interior of the gate complex on both sides, and the interiors of the vestibules also had windows on both sides; and the supports were adorned with palms.

טז וְחַלֹּנוֹת אֲטֻמוֹת אֶל־הַתָּאִים וְאֶל אֵלֵיהֵמָה לִפְנִימָה לַשַּׁעַר סָבִיב סָבִיב וְכֵן לָאֵלַמּוֹת וְחַלּוֹנוֹת סָבִיב סָבִיב לִפְנִימָה וְאֶל־אַיִל תִּמֹרִים:

¹⁷ He took me into the outer court. There were chambers there, and there was a pavement laid out all around the court. There were 30 chambers on the pavement.

יז וַיְבִיאֵנִי אֶל־הֶחָצֵר הַחִיצוֹנָה וְהִנֵּה לְשָׁכוֹת וְרִצְפָה עָשׂוּי לֶחָצֵר סָבִיב סָבִיב שְׁלֹשִׁים לְשָׁכוֹת אֶל־הָרִצְפָה:

¹⁸ The pavements flanked the gates; the depth of the lower pavements paralleled that of the gates.

יח וְהָרִצְפָה אֶל־כֶּתֶף הַשְּׁעָרִים לְעֻמַּת אֹרֶךְ הַשְּׁעָרִים הָרִצְפָה הַתַּחְתּוֹנָה:

19 Then he measured the width of the lower court, from in front of the inner gate to in front of the outer gate – 100 *amot*. After the east [gate], the north [gate].

יט וַיָּמָד רֹחַב מִלִּפְנֵי הַשַּׁעַר הַתַּחְתּוֹנָה לִפְנֵי הֶחָצֵר הַפְּנִימִי מִחוּץ מֵאָה אַמָּה הַקָּדִים וְהַצָּפוֹן:

20 Next he measured the gate of the outer court that faced north: its length and its width,

כ וְהַשַּׁעַר אֲשֶׁר פָּנָיו דֶּרֶךְ הַצָּפוֹן לֶחָצֵר הַחִיצוֹנָה מָדַד אָרְכּוֹ וְרָחְבּוֹ:

21 its three recesses on either side and its supports, as also its vestibule. It measured, like the first gate, 50 *amot* in length and 25 *amot* in width.

כא ותאו [וְתָאָיו] שְׁלוֹשָׁה מִפּוֹ וּשְׁלֹשָׁה מִפּוֹ ואילו [וְאֵילָיו] ואלמו [וְאֵלַמָּיו] הָיָה כְּמִדַּת הַשַּׁעַר הָרִאשׁוֹן חֲמִשִּׁים אַמָּה אָרְכּוֹ וְרֹחַב חָמֵשׁ וְעֶשְׂרִים בָּאַמָּה:

22 Its windows and [those of] its vestibule, as also its palm trees, corresponded to those of the gate that faced east. [From the outside] one had to climb 7 steps to reach it, and its vestibule was ahead of them.

כב וחלונו [וְחַלּוֹנָיו] ואלמו [וְאֵלַמָּיו] ותמרו [וְתִמֹרָיו] כְּמִדַּת הַשַּׁעַר אֲשֶׁר פָּנָיו דֶּרֶךְ הַקָּדִים וּבְמַעֲלוֹת שֶׁבַע יַעֲלוּ־בוֹ ואילמו [וְאֵילַמָּיו] לִפְנֵיהֶם:

23 Like the east gate, the north gate faced a gate leading into the inner forecourt; and when he measured the distance from gate to gate, it was 100 *amot*.

כג וְשַׁעַר לֶחָצֵר הַפְּנִימִי נֶגֶד הַשַּׁעַר לַצָּפוֹן וְלַקָּדִים וַיָּמָד מִשַּׁעַר אֶל־שַׁעַר מֵאָה אַמָּה:

24 Then he took me to the south side. There was also a gate on the south side, and he got the same measurements as before for its supports and its vestibule.

כד וַיּוֹלִכֵנִי דֶּרֶךְ הַדָּרוֹם וְהִנֵּה־שַׁעַר דֶּרֶךְ הַדָּרוֹם וּמָדַד אילו [אֵילָיו] ואילמו [וְאֵילַמָּיו] כַּמִּדּוֹת הָאֵלֶּה:

25 Both it and its vestibule had windows like the aforementioned ones. It was 50 *amot* long and 25 *amot* wide.

כה וְחַלּוֹנִים לוֹ ולאילמו [וּלְאֵילַמָּיו] סָבִיב סָבִיב כְּהַחַלֹּנוֹת הָאֵלֶּה חֲמִשִּׁים אַמָּה אֹרֶךְ וְרֹחַב חָמֵשׁ וְעֶשְׂרִים אַמָּה:

26 Its staircase consisted of 7 steps; its vestibule was ahead of them, and its supports were decorated on both sides with palm trees.

כו וּמַעֲלוֹת שִׁבְעָה עלותו [עֹלוֹתָיו] ואלמו [וְאֵלַמָּיו] לִפְנֵיהֶם וְתִמֹרִים לוֹ אֶחָד מִפּוֹ וְאֶחָד מִפּוֹ אֶל־אילו [אֵילָיו]:

27 The inner court likewise had a gate facing south; and on the south side, too, he measured a distance of 100 *amot* from the [outer] gate to the [inner] gate.

כז וְשַׁעַר לֶחָצֵר הַפְּנִימִי דֶּרֶךְ הַדָּרוֹם וַיָּמָד מִשַּׁעַר אֶל־הַשַּׁעַר דֶּרֶךְ הַדָּרוֹם מֵאָה אַמּוֹת:

28 He now took me into the inner forecourt through its south gate. When he measured this south gate, it had the same measurements as the foregoing.

כח וַיְבִיאֵנִי אֶל־חָצֵר הַפְּנִימִי בְּשַׁעַר הַדָּרוֹם וַיָּמָד אֶת־הַשַּׁעַר הַדָּרוֹם כַּמִּדּוֹת הָאֵלֶּה:

29 Its recesses, its supports, and its vestibule had the same measurements. Both it and its vestibule had windows on both sides; it was 50 *amot* long and 25 *amot* wide –

כט ותאו [וְתָאָיו] ואילו [וְאֵילָיו] ואלמו [וְאֵלַמָּיו] כַּמִּדּוֹת הָאֵלֶּה וְחַלּוֹנוֹת לוֹ ולאלמו [וּלְאֵלַמָּיו] סָבִיב סָבִיב חֲמִשִּׁים אַמָּה אֹרֶךְ וְרֹחַב עֶשְׂרִים וְחָמֵשׁ אַמּוֹת:

30 vestibules on both sides, 25 *amot* long, 5 *amot* wide.

ל וְאֵלַמּוֹת סָבִיב סָבִיב אֹרֶךְ חָמֵשׁ וְעֶשְׂרִים אַמָּה וְרֹחַב חָמֵשׁ אַמּוֹת:

31 Its vestibule, however, gave on the outer court. Its supports were adorned on either side with palms, and its staircase consisted of 8 steps.

לא וְאֵלַמָּו אֶל־חָצֵר הַחִצוֹנָה וְתִמֹרִים אֶל־אֵילָו [אֵילָיו] וּמַעֲלוֹת שְׁמוֹנֶה מַעֲלוֹ [מַעֲלָיו]:

32 Then he took me to the eastern side of the inner forecourt; and when he measured the gate there, he got the same measurements:

לב וַיְבִיאֵנִי אֶל־הֶחָצֵר הַפְּנִימִי דֶּרֶךְ הַקָּדִים וַיָּמָד אֶת־הַשַּׁעַר כַּמִּדּוֹת הָאֵלֶּה:

33 its recesses, supports, and vestibule had the above measurements. Both it and its vestibule had windows on both sides; it was 50 *amot* long and 25 *amot* wide,

לג וְתָאָו [וְתָאָיו] וְאֵלָו [וְאֵלָיו] וְאֵלַמָּו [וְאֵלַמָּיו] כַּמִּדּוֹת הָאֵלֶּה וְחַלּוֹנוֹת לוֹ וּלְאֵלַמָּו [וּלְאֵלַמָּיו] סָבִיב סָבִיב אֹרֶךְ חֲמִשִּׁים אַמָּה וְרֹחַב חָמֵשׁ וְעֶשְׂרִים אַמָּה:

34 and its vestibule gave on the outer court. Its supports were decorated on both sides with palm trees, and its staircase consisted of 8 steps.

לד וְאֵלַמָּו [וְאֵלַמָּיו] לֶחָצֵר הַחִצוֹנָה וְתִמֹרִים אֶל־אֵלָו [אֵלָיו] מִפּוֹ וּמִפּוֹ וּשְׁמֹנֶה מַעֲלוֹת מַעֲלוֹ [מַעֲלָיו]:

35 Then he took me to the north gate, and found its measurements to be identical,

לה וַיְבִיאֵנִי אֶל־שַׁעַר הַצָּפוֹן וּמָדַד כַּמִּדּוֹת הָאֵלֶּה:

36 with the same recesses, supports, vestibule, windows on both sides, and a length of 50 *amot* and a width of 25 *amot*.

לו תָּאָו [תָּאָיו] אֵלָו [אֵלָיו] וְאֵלַמָּו [וְאֵלַמָּיו] וְחַלּוֹנוֹת לוֹ סָבִיב סָבִיב אֹרֶךְ חֲמִשִּׁים אַמָּה וְרֹחַב חָמֵשׁ וְעֶשְׂרִים אַמָּה:

37 Its supports gave on the outer court; its supports were decorated on both sides with palm trees; and its staircase consisted of eight steps.

לז וְאֵילָו [וְאֵילָיו] לֶחָצֵר הַחִצוֹנָה וְתִמֹרִים אֶל־אֵלָו [אֵילָיו] מִפּוֹ וּמִפּוֹ וּשְׁמֹנֶה מַעֲלוֹת מַעֲלוֹ [מַעֲלָיו]:

38 A chamber opened into the gate; there the burnt offering would be washed.

לח וְלִשְׁכָּה וּפִתְחָהּ בְּאֵילִים הַשְּׁעָרִים שָׁם יָדִיחוּ אֶת־הָעֹלָה:

39 And inside the vestibule of the gate, there were two tables on each side, at which the burnt offering, the sin offering, and the guilt offering were to be slaughtered;

לט וּבְאֻלָם הַשַּׁעַר שְׁנַיִם שֻׁלְחָנוֹת מִפּוֹ וּשְׁנַיִם שֻׁלְחָנוֹת מִפֹּה לִשְׁחוֹט אֲלֵיהֶם הָעוֹלָה וְהַחַטָּאת וְהָאָשָׁם:

40 while outside – as one goes up toward the opening of the north gate – there were two tables on one side, and there were two tables on the other side of the gate's vestibule.

מ וְאֶל־הַכָּתֵף מִחוּצָה לָעוֹלֶה לְפֶתַח הַשַּׁעַר הַצָּפוֹנָה שְׁנַיִם שֻׁלְחָנוֹת וְאֶל־הַכָּתֵף הָאַחֶרֶת אֲשֶׁר לְאֻלָם הַשַּׁעַר שְׁנַיִם שֻׁלְחָנוֹת:

41 Thus there were four tables on either flank of the gate – eight tables in all – at which [the sacrifices] were to be slaughtered.

מא אַרְבָּעָה שֻׁלְחָנוֹת מִפֹּה וְאַרְבָּעָה שֻׁלְחָנוֹת מִפֹּה לְכֶתֶף הַשָּׁעַר שְׁמוֹנֶה שֻׁלְחָנוֹת אֲלֵיהֶם יִשְׁחָטוּ:

42 As for the four tables for the burnt offering – they were of hewn stone, one and a half *amot* long, one and a half *amot* wide, and one *amah* high – on them were laid out the instruments with which burnt offerings and sacrifices were slaughtered.

מב וְאַרְבָּעָה שֻׁלְחָנוֹת לָעוֹלָה אַבְנֵי גָזִית אֹרֶךְ אַמָּה אַחַת וָחֵצִי וְרֹחַב אַמָּה אַחַת וָחֵצִי וְגֹבַהּ אַמָּה אֶחָת אֲלֵיהֶם וְיַנִּיחוּ אֶת־הַכֵּלִים אֲשֶׁר יִשְׁחֲטוּ אֶת־הָעוֹלָה בָּם וְהַזָּבַח:

43 Shelves, one *tefach* wide, were attached all around the inside; and the sacrificial flesh was [laid] on the tables.

מג וְהַשְׁפַתַּיִם טֹפַח אֶחָד מוּכָנִים בַּבַּיִת סָבִיב סָבִיב וְאֶל־הַשֻּׁלְחָנוֹת בְּשַׂר הַקָּרְבָּן:

44 There were chambers for singers in the inner forecourt: [one] beside the north gate facing south, and one beside the east gate facing north.

מד וּמִחוּצָה לַשַּׁעַר הַפְּנִימִי לִשְׁכוֹת שָׁרִים בֶּחָצֵר הַפְּנִימִי אֲשֶׁר אֶל־כֶּתֶף שַׁעַר הַצָּפוֹן וּפְנֵיהֶם דֶּרֶךְ הַדָּרוֹם אֶחָד אֶל־כֶּתֶף שַׁעַר הַקָּדִים פְּנֵי דֶּרֶךְ הַצָּפֹן:

45 [The man] explained to me: "The chamber that faces south is for the *Kohanim* who perform the duties of the Temple;

מה וַיְדַבֵּר אֵלָי זֶה הַלִּשְׁכָּה אֲשֶׁר פָּנֶיהָ דֶּרֶךְ הַדָּרוֹם לַכֹּהֲנִים שֹׁמְרֵי מִשְׁמֶרֶת הַבָּיִת:

46 and the chamber that faces north is for the *Kohanim* who perform the duties of the *Mizbayach* – they are the descendants of *Tzadok*, who alone of the descendants of *Levi* may approach *Hashem* to minister to Him."

מו וְהַלִּשְׁכָּה אֲשֶׁר פָּנֶיהָ דֶּרֶךְ הַצָּפוֹן לַכֹּהֲנִים שֹׁמְרֵי מִשְׁמֶרֶת הַמִּזְבֵּחַ הֵמָּה בְנֵי־צָדוֹק הַקְּרֵבִים מִבְּנֵי־לֵוִי אֶל־יְהוָה לְשָׁרְתוֹ:

47 He then measured the forecourt: 100 *amot* long and 100 *amot* broad – foursquare. In front of the Temple stood the *Mizbayach*.

מז וַיָּמָד אֶת־הֶחָצֵר אֹרֶךְ מֵאָה אַמָּה וְרֹחַב מֵאָה אַמָּה מְרֻבָּעַת וְהַמִּזְבֵּחַ לִפְנֵי הַבָּיִת:

48 He took me into the portico of the Temple and measured it. The jambs of the portico were 5 *amot* deep on either side. The width of the gate-opening was [14 *amot*, and the flanking wall of the gate was] 3 *amot* on either side.

מח וַיְבִאֵנִי אֶל־אֻלָם הַבַּיִת וַיָּמָד אֵל אֻלָם חָמֵשׁ אַמּוֹת מִפֹּה וְחָמֵשׁ אַמּוֹת מִפֹּה וְרֹחַב הַשַּׁעַר שָׁלֹשׁ אַמּוֹת מִפּוֹ וְשָׁלֹשׁ אַמּוֹת מִפּוֹ:

49 The portico was 20 *amot* wide and 11 *amot* deep, and it was by steps that it was reached. There were columns by the jambs on either side.

מט אֹרֶךְ הָאֻלָם עֶשְׂרִים אַמָּה וְרֹחַב עַשְׁתֵּי עֶשְׂרֵה אַמָּה וּבַמַּעֲלוֹת אֲשֶׁר יַעֲלוּ אֵלָיו וְעַמֻּדִים אֶל־הָאֵילִים אֶחָד מִפֹּה וְאֶחָד מִפֹּה:

41 1 He then led me into the great hall. He measured the jambs, 6 *amot* on either side; such was the depth of each jamb.

מא א וַיְבִיאֵנִי אֶל־הַהֵיכָל וַיָּמָד אֶת־הָאֵילִים שֵׁשׁ־אַמּוֹת רֹחַב־מִפּוֹ וְשֵׁשׁ־אַמּוֹת־רֹחַב מִפּוֹ רֹחַב הָאֹהֶל:

2 The entrance was 10 *amot* wide, and the flanking walls of the entrance were each 5 *amot* wide. Next he measured the depth [of the hall], 40 *amot*, and the width, 20 *amot*.

ב וְרֹחַב הַפֶּתַח עֶשֶׂר אַמּוֹת וְכִתְפוֹת הַפֶּתַח חָמֵשׁ אַמּוֹת מִפּוֹ וְחָמֵשׁ אַמּוֹת מִפּוֹ וַיָּמָד אָרְכּוֹ אַרְבָּעִים אַמָּה וְרֹחַב עֶשְׂרִים אַמָּה:

3 And then he entered the inner room. He measured each jamb of the entrance, 2 *amot* [deep]; the entrance itself, 6 *amot* across; and the width of [the flanking wall on either side of] the entrance, 7 *amot*.

ג וּבָא לִפְנִימָה וַיָּמָד אֵיל־הַפֶּתַח שְׁתַּיִם אַמּוֹת וְהַפֶּתַח שֵׁשׁ אַמּוֹת וְרֹחַב הַפֶּתַח שֶׁבַע אַמּוֹת:

4 Then he measured the depth, 20 *amot*; and the width at the inner end of the great hall was also 20 *amot*. And he said to me, "This is the Holy of Holies."

ד וַיָּמָד אֶת־אָרְכּוֹ עֶשְׂרִים אַמָּה וְרֹחַב עֶשְׂרִים אַמָּה אֶל־פְּנֵי הַהֵיכָל וַיֹּאמֶר אֵלָי זֶה קֹדֶשׁ הַקֳּדָשִׁים:

5 Then he measured the wall of the Temple. [It was] 6 *amot* [thick] on every side of the Temple, and the side-chamber measured 4 *amot* [across].

ה וַיָּמָד קִיר־הַבַּיִת שֵׁשׁ אַמּוֹת וְרֹחַב הַצֵּלָע אַרְבַּע אַמּוֹת סָבִיב סָבִיב לַבַּיִת סָבִיב:

6 The side chambers were arranged one above the other, in 33 sections. All around, there were projections in the Temple wall to serve the side chambers as supports, so that [their] supports should not be the Temple wall itself.

ו וְהַצְּלָעוֹת צֵלָע אֶל־צֵלָע שָׁלוֹשׁ וּשְׁלֹשִׁים פְּעָמִים וּבָאוֹת בַּקִּיר אֲשֶׁר־לַבַּיִת לַצְּלָעוֹת סָבִיב סָבִיב לִהְיוֹת אֲחוּזִים וְלֹא־יִהְיוּ אֲחוּזִים בְּקִיר הַבָּיִת:

7 The winding passage of the side chambers widened from story to story; and since the structure was furnished all over with winding passages from story to story, the structure itself became wider from story to story. It was by this means that one ascended from the bottom story to the top one by way of the middle one.

ז וְרָחֲבָה וְנָסְבָה לְמַעְלָה לְמַעְלָה לַצְּלָעוֹת כִּי מוּסַב־הַבַּיִת לְמַעְלָה לְמַעְלָה סָבִיב סָבִיב לַבַּיִת עַל־כֵּן רֹחַב־לַבַּיִת לְמָעְלָה וְכֵן הַתַּחְתּוֹנָה יַעֲלֶה עַל־הָעֶלְיוֹנָה לַתִּיכוֹנָה:

8 I observed that the Temple was surrounded by a raised pavement – the foundations of the side chambers; its elevation was a rod's length, or 6 *amot*.

ח וְרָאִיתִי לַבַּיִת גֹּבַהּ סָבִיב סָבִיב מיסדות [מוּסְדוֹת] הַצְּלָעוֹת מְלוֹ הַקָּנֶה שֵׁשׁ אַמּוֹת אַצִּילָה:

9 The outer wall of the side chamber was 5 *amot* thick, and that which served as a walk between the Temple's side chambers

ט רֹחַב הַקִּיר אֲשֶׁר־לַצֵּלָע אֶל־הַחוּץ חָמֵשׁ אַמּוֹת וַאֲשֶׁר מֻנָּח בֵּית צְלָעוֹת אֲשֶׁר לַבָּיִת:

10 and the chamber complexes was 20 *amot* wide all around the Temple.

י וּבֵין הַלְּשָׁכוֹת רֹחַב עֶשְׂרִים אַמָּה סָבִיב לַבַּיִת סָבִיב סָבִיב:

11 Of entrances to the side chambers giving on the walk, there was one entrance on the north side and one entrance on the south side; and the space of the walk was 5 *amot* thick all around.

יא וּפֶתַח הַצֵּלָע לַמֻּנָּח פֶּתַח אֶחָד דֶּרֶךְ הַצָּפוֹן וּפֶתַח אֶחָד לַדָּרוֹם וְרֹחַב מְקוֹם הַמֻּנָּח חָמֵשׁ אַמּוֹת סָבִיב סָבִיב:

12 And the structure that fronted on the vacant space at the [Temple's] western end was 70 *amot* deep; the walls of the structure were 5 *amot* thick on every side; and it was 90 *amot* wide.

יב וְהַבִּנְיָן אֲשֶׁר אֶל־פְּנֵי הַגִּזְרָה פְּאַת דֶּרֶךְ־הַיָּם רֹחַב שִׁבְעִים אַמָּה וְקִיר הַבִּנְיָן חָמֵשׁ־אַמּוֹת רֹחַב סָבִיב סָבִיב וְאָרְכּוֹ תִּשְׁעִים אַמָּה:

13 He measured the [total] depth of the Temple, 100 *amot*; and the depth of the vacant space and of the structure, with its walls, also came to 100 *amot*.

יג וּמָדַד אֶת־הַבַּיִת אֹרֶךְ מֵאָה אַמָּה וְהַגִּזְרָה וְהַבִּנְיָה וְקִירוֹתֶיהָ אֹרֶךְ מֵאָה אַמָּה:

14 The front side of the Temple, like the vacant space on the east, was 100 *amot* wide.

יד וְרֹחַב פְּנֵי הַבַּיִת וְהַגִּזְרָה לַקָּדִים מֵאָה אַמָּה:

15 He also measured the width of the structure facing the vacant space in the rear, inclusive of its ledges, 100 *amot*. Both the great hall inside and the portico next to the court –

טו וּמָדַד אֹרֶךְ־הַבִּנְיָן אֶל־פְּנֵי הַגִּזְרָה אֲשֶׁר עַל־אַחֲרֶיהָ ואתוקיהא [וְאַתִּיקֶיהָא] מִפּוֹ וּמִפּוֹ מֵאָה אַמָּה וְהַהֵיכָל הַפְּנִימִי וְאֻלַמֵּי הֶחָצֵר:

16 the thresholds – and the windows with frames and the ledges at the threshold, all over the three parts of each, were completely overlaid with wood. There was wainscoting from the floor to the windows, including the window [frame]s

טז הַסִּפִּים וְהַחַלּוֹנִים הָאֲטֻמוֹת וְהָאַתִּיקִים סָבִיב לִשְׁלָשְׁתָּם נֶגֶד הַסַּף שְׂחִיף עֵץ סָבִיב ׀ סָבִיב וְהָאָרֶץ עַד־הַחַלּוֹנוֹת וְהַחַלֹּנוֹת מְכֻסּוֹת:

17 and extending above the openings, both in the inner Temple and outside. And all over the wall, both in the inner one and in the outer, ran a pattern.

יז עַל־מֵעַל הַפֶּתַח וְעַד־הַבַּיִת הַפְּנִימִי וְלַחוּץ וְאֶל־כָּל־הַקִּיר סָבִיב ׀ סָבִיב בַּפְּנִימִי וּבַחִיצוֹן מִדּוֹת:

18 It consisted of cherubs and palm trees, with a palm tree between every two cherubs. Each cherub had two faces:

יח וְעָשׂוּי כְּרוּבִים וְתִמֹרִים וְתִמֹרָה בֵּין־ כְּרוּב לִכְרוּב וּשְׁנַיִם פָּנִים לַכְּרוּב:

*v'-a-SUY k'-ru-VEEM v'-ti-mo-REEM v'-ti-mo-RAH bayn
k'-RUV likh-RUV ush-NA-yim pa-NEEM la-k'-RUV*

19 a human face turned toward the palm tree on one side and a lion's face turned toward the palm tree on the other side. This was repeated all over the Temple;

יט וּפְנֵי אָדָם אֶל־הַתִּמֹרָה מִפּוֹ וּפְנֵי־כְפִיר אֶל־הַתִּמֹרָה מִפּוֹ עָשׂוּי אֶל־כָּל־הַבַּיִת סָבִיב ׀ סָבִיב:

20 the cherubs and the palm trees were carved on the wall from the floor to above the openings. As regards the great hall,

כ מֵהָאָרֶץ עַד־מֵעַל הַפֶּתַח הַכְּרוּבִים וְהַתִּמֹרִים עֲשׂוּיִם וְקִיר הַהֵיכָל:

21 the great hall had four doorposts; and before the Shrine was something resembling

כא הַהֵיכָל מְזוּזַת רְבֻעָה וּפְנֵי הַקֹּדֶשׁ הַמַּרְאֶה כַּמַּרְאֶה:

22 a wooden *Mizbayach* 3 *amot* high and 2 *amot* long and having inner corners; and its length and its walls were of wood. And he said to me, "This is the table that stands before *Hashem.*"

כב הַמִּזְבֵּחַ עֵץ שָׁלוֹשׁ אַמּוֹת גָּבֹהַּ וְאָרְכּוֹ שְׁתַּיִם־אַמּוֹת וּמִקְצֹעוֹתָיו לוֹ וְאָרְכּוֹ וְקִירֹתָיו עֵץ וַיְדַבֵּר אֵלַי זֶה הַשֻּׁלְחָן אֲשֶׁר לִפְנֵי יְהֹוָה:

23 The great hall had a double door, and the Shrine likewise had

כג וּשְׁתַּיִם דְּלָתוֹת לַהֵיכָל וְלַקֹּדֶשׁ:

24 a double door, and each door had two swinging leaves: two for the one door and two such leaves for the other.

כד וּשְׁתַּיִם דְּלָתוֹת לַדְּלָתוֹת שְׁתַּיִם מוּסַבּוֹת דְּלָתוֹת שְׁתַּיִם לְדֶלֶת אֶחָת וּשְׁתֵּי דְלָתוֹת לָאַחֶרֶת:

41:18 It consisted of cherubs and palm trees On the walls of the inner and outer chambers of the *Beit Hamikdash* in *Yechezkel's* vision are cherubs and palm trees. These two items also appear in *Shlomo's* Temple (II Kings 6:29–36). The significance of the cherubs as dividers between mankind and God has been discussed in chapter 10. The palm tree symbolizes both righteousness (Psalms 92:13) and longevity. In fact, in 2005, a date palm was successfully grown from a two-thousand-year-old seed found on Masada, becoming the oldest seed ever to be brought back to life. The tree, nicknamed "Methuselah" after the longest-living figure in the Bible (Genesis 5:27), is now over two meters tall and has sprouted flowers. Ancient Judean dates were known to have healing properties and Israeli researchers are hoping that Methuselah will also have medicinal qualities that will benefit future generations.

Methuselah date palm tree

25 Cherubs and palm trees were carved on these – on the doors of the hall – just as they were carved on the walls; and there was a lattice of wood outside in front of the portico.

26 And there were windows with frames and palm trees on the flanking walls of the portico on either side [of the entrance] and [on] the Temple's side chambers and [on] the lattices.

42 1 He took me out, by way of the northern gate, into the outer court, and he led me [westward] up to a complex of chambers that ran parallel to the northern ends of the vacant space and the structure.

2 The width of its fa³ade – its north side, the one from which it was entered – was 100 *amot*, and its depth was 50 *amot*.

3 At right angles to the 20 *amot* of the inner court and to the pavement of the outer court, the complex rose ledge by ledge in three tiers.

4 There was an areaway, 10 *amot* wide and a road of one *amah*, running along the inner-court side of the chamber complex, but its entrances were on its north side.

5 Here its upper chambers were cut back, because ledges took away from them as construction proceeded backward from the bottom ones and then from the middle ones.

6 For they were arranged in three tiers, and they had no columns like those of the chambers in the courts. That is why the rise proceeded by stages: from the ground, from the bottom ones, and from the middle ones.

7 In the outer court, a wall 50 *amot* long ran parallel to the chamber complex up to the chambers in the outer court;

8 for the chambers in the outer court were themselves 50 *amot* deep, thus completing 100 *amot* alongside the edifice.

9 Thus, at the foot of that complex of chambers ran a passage – of a width set by the wall in the outer court – which one entered from the east in order to gain access to them from the outer court.*

10 There was another chamber complex to the east of the vacant space and the structure,

כה וַעֲשׂוּיָה אֲלֵיהֶן אֶל־דַּלְתוֹת הַהֵיכָל כְּרוּבִים וְתִמֹרִים כַּאֲשֶׁר עֲשׂוּיִם לַקִּירוֹת וְעָב עֵץ אֶל־פְּנֵי הָאוּלָם מֵהַחוּץ:

כו וְחַלּוֹנִים אֲטֻמוֹת וְתִמֹרִים מִפּוֹ וּמִפּוֹ אֶל־כִּתְפוֹת הָאוּלָם וְצַלְעוֹת הַבַּיִת וְהָעֻבִּים:

ב א וַיּוֹצִאֵנִי אֶל־הֶחָצֵר הַחִיצוֹנָה הַדֶּרֶךְ דֶּרֶךְ הַצָּפוֹן וַיְבִאֵנִי אֶל־הַלִּשְׁכָּה אֲשֶׁר נֶגֶד הַגִּזְרָה וַאֲשֶׁר־נֶגֶד הַבִּנְיָן אֶל־הַצָּפוֹן:

ב אֶל־פְּנֵי־אֹרֶךְ אַמּוֹת הַמֵּאָה פֶּתַח הַצָּפוֹן וְהָרֹחַב חֲמִשִּׁים אַמּוֹת:

ג נֶגֶד הָעֶשְׂרִים אֲשֶׁר לֶחָצֵר הַפְּנִימִי וְנֶגֶד רִצְפָה אֲשֶׁר לֶחָצֵר הַחִיצוֹנָה אַתִּיק אֶל־פְּנֵי־אַתִּיק בַּשְּׁלִשִׁים:

ד וְלִפְנֵי הַלְּשָׁכוֹת מַהֲלַךְ עֶשֶׂר אַמּוֹת רֹחַב אֶל־הַפְּנִימִית דֶּרֶךְ אַמָּה אֶחָת וּפִתְחֵיהֶם לַצָּפוֹן:

ה וְהַלְּשָׁכוֹת הָעֶלְיוֹנֹת קְצֻרוֹת כִּי־יוֹכְלוּ אַתִּיקִים מֵהֵנָה מֵהַתַּחְתֹּנוֹת וּמֵהַתִּכֹנוֹת בִּנְיָן:

ו כִּי מְשֻׁלָּשׁוֹת הֵנָּה וְאֵין לָהֶן עַמּוּדִים כְּעַמּוּדֵי הַחֲצֵרוֹת עַל־כֵּן נֶאֱצַל מֵהַתַּחְתּוֹנוֹת וּמֵהַתִּיכֹנוֹת מֵהָאָרֶץ:

ז וְגָדֵר אֲשֶׁר־לַחוּץ לְעֻמַּת הַלְּשָׁכוֹת דֶּרֶךְ הֶחָצֵר הַחִצוֹנָה אֶל־פְּנֵי הַלְּשָׁכוֹת אָרְכּוֹ חֲמִשִּׁים אַמָּה:

ח כִּי־אֹרֶךְ הַלְּשָׁכוֹת אֲשֶׁר לֶחָצֵר הַחִצוֹנָה חֲמִשִּׁים אַמָּה וְהִנֵּה עַל־פְּנֵי הַהֵיכָל מֵאָה אַמָּה:

ט וּמִתַּחְתָּה לשכות [וּמִתַּחַת] [הַלְּשָׁכוֹת] הָאֵלֶּה המבוא [הַמֵּבִיא] מֵהַקָּדִים בְּבֹאוֹ לָהֵנָּה מֵהֶחָצֵר הַחִצֹנָה:

י בְּרֹחַב גֶּדֶר הֶחָצֵר דֶּרֶךְ הַקָּדִים אֶל־פְּנֵי הַגִּזְרָה וְאֶל־פְּנֵי הַבִּנְיָן לְשָׁכוֹת:

---

* "of a width set by the wall in the outer court" moved up from verse 10 for clarity

11 likewise with a passage in front – just like the complex on the north side, with which this one agreed in width and depth and in the exact layout of its exits and entrances.

12 Accordingly, the entrances to the chamber complex on the south side were approached from the east by the entrance at the head of the corresponding passage along the matching wall.

13 And he said to me, "The northern chambers and the southern chambers by the vacant space are the consecrated chambers in which the *Kohanim* who have access to *Hashem* shall eat the most holy offerings. There they shall deposit the most holy offerings – the meal offerings, the sin offerings, and the guilt offerings, for the place is consecrated.

14 When the *Kohanim* enter, they shall not proceed from the consecrated place to the outer court without first leaving here the vestments in which they minister; for the [vestments] are consecrated. Before proceeding to the area open to the people, they shall put on other garments."

15 When he had finished the measurements of the inner Temple [area], he led me out by way of the gate which faces east, and he measured off the entire area.

16 He measured the east side with the measuring rod, 500 [*amot*] – in rods, by the measuring rod. He turned

17 [and] measured the north side: 500 [*amot*] – in rods, by the measuring rod. He turned

18 [and] measured the south side: 500 [*amot*] – in rods, by the measuring rod.

19 Then he turned to the west side [and] measured it: 500 *amot* – in rods, by the measuring rod.

20 Thus he measured it on the four sides; it had a wall completely surrounding it, 500 [*amot*] long on each side, to separate the consecrated from the unconsecrated.

יא וְדֶרֶךְ לִפְנֵיהֶם כְּמַרְאֵה הַלְּשָׁכוֹת אֲשֶׁר דֶּרֶךְ הַצָּפוֹן כְּאָרְכָּן כֵּן רָחְבָּן וְכֹל מוֹצָאֵיהֶן וּכְמִשְׁפְּטֵיהֶן וּכְפִתְחֵיהֶן:

יב וּכְפִתְחֵי הַלְּשָׁכוֹת אֲשֶׁר דֶּרֶךְ הַדָּרוֹם פֶּתַח בְּרֹאשׁ דָּרֶךְ דֶּרֶךְ בִּפְנֵי הַגְּדֶרֶת הַגִּנָה דֶּרֶךְ הַקָּדִים בְּבוֹאָן:

יג וַיֹּאמֶר אֵלַי לִשְׁכוֹת הַצָּפוֹן לִשְׁכוֹת הַדָּרוֹם אֲשֶׁר אֶל־פְּנֵי הַגִּזְרָה הֵנָּה לִשְׁכוֹת הַקֹּדֶשׁ אֲשֶׁר יֹאכְלוּ־שָׁם הַכֹּהֲנִים אֲשֶׁר־קְרוֹבִים לַיהוָֹה קָדְשֵׁי הַקֳּדָשִׁים שָׁם יַנִּיחוּ קָדְשֵׁי הַקֳּדָשִׁים וְהַמִּנְחָה וְהַחַטָּאת וְהָאָשָׁם כִּי הַמָּקוֹם קָדֹשׁ:

יד בְּבֹאָם הַכֹּהֲנִים וְלֹא־יֵצְאוּ מֵהַקֹּדֶשׁ אֶל־הֶחָצֵר הַחִיצוֹנָה וְשָׁם יַנִּיחוּ בִגְדֵיהֶם אֲשֶׁר־יְשָׁרְתוּ בָהֶן כִּי־קֹדֶשׁ הֵנָּה יִלְבְּשׁוּ [וְלָבְשׁוּ] בְּגָדִים אֲחֵרִים וְקָרְבוּ אֶל־אֲשֶׁר לָעָם:

טו וְכִלָּה אֶת־מִדּוֹת הַבַּיִת הַפְּנִימִי וְהוֹצִיאַנִי דֶּרֶךְ הַשַּׁעַר אֲשֶׁר פָּנָיו דֶּרֶךְ הַקָּדִים וּמְדָדוֹ סָבִיב סָבִיב:

טז מָדַד רוּחַ הַקָּדִים בִּקְנֵה הַמִּדָּה חֲמֵשׁ־אֵמוֹת [מֵאוֹת] קָנִים בִּקְנֵה הַמִּדָּה סָבִיב:

יז מָדַד רוּחַ הַצָּפוֹן חֲמֵשׁ־מֵאוֹת קָנִים בִּקְנֵה הַמִּדָּה סָבִיב:

יח אֵת רוּחַ הַדָּרוֹם מָדָד חֲמֵשׁ־מֵאוֹת קָנִים בִּקְנֵה הַמִּדָּה:

יט סָבַב אֶל־רוּחַ הַיָּם מָדַד חֲמֵשׁ־מֵאוֹת קָנִים בִּקְנֵה הַמִּדָּה:

כ לְאַרְבַּע רוּחוֹת מְדָדוֹ חוֹמָה לוֹ סָבִיב סָבִיב אֹרֶךְ חֲמֵשׁ מֵאוֹת וְרֹחַב חֲמֵשׁ מֵאוֹת לְהַבְדִּיל בֵּין הַקֹּדֶשׁ לְחֹל:

Surrounding walls of the Temple Mount in *Yerushalayim*

42:20 To separate the consecrated from the unconsecrated *Yechezkel's* vision of the rebuilt *Beit Hamikdash* concludes with a description of its surrounding walls. These walls form a perfect square, five-hundred cubits on each side, and serve to distin-

l'-ar-BA ru-KHOT m'-da-DO KHO-mah LO sa-VEEV sa-VEEV
O-rekh kha-MAYSH may-OT v'-RO-khav kha-MAYSH
may-OT l'-hav-DEEL BAYN ha-KO-desh l'-KHOL

43 ¹ Then he led me to a gate, the gate that faced east.

א וַיּוֹלִכֵנִי אֶל־הַשָּׁעַר שַׁעַר אֲשֶׁר פֹּנֶה דֶּרֶךְ הַקָּדִים:

² And there, coming from the east with a roar like the roar of mighty waters, was the Presence of the God of *Yisrael*, and the earth was lit up by His Presence.

ב וְהִנֵּה כְּבוֹד אֱלֹהֵי יִשְׂרָאֵל בָּא מִדֶּרֶךְ הַקָּדִים וְקוֹלוֹ כְּקוֹל מַיִם רַבִּים וְהָאָרֶץ הֵאִירָה מִכְּבֹדוֹ:

³ The vision was like the vision I had seen when I came to destroy the city, the very same vision that I had seen by the Chebar Canal. Forthwith, I fell on my face.

ג וּכְמַרְאֵה הַמַּרְאֶה אֲשֶׁר רָאִיתִי כַּמַּרְאֶה אֲשֶׁר־רָאִיתִי בְּבֹאִי לְשַׁחֵת אֶת־הָעִיר וּמַרְאוֹת כַּמַּרְאֶה אֲשֶׁר רָאִיתִי אֶל־נְהַר־כְּבָר וָאֶפֹּל אֶל־פָּנָי:

⁴ The Presence of *Hashem* entered the Temple by the gate that faced eastward.

ד וּכְבוֹד יְהֹוָה בָּא אֶל־הַבָּיִת דֶּרֶךְ שַׁעַר אֲשֶׁר פָּנָיו דֶּרֶךְ הַקָּדִים:

⁵ A spirit carried me into the inner court, and lo, the Presence of *Hashem* filled the Temple;

ה וַתִּשָּׂאֵנִי רוּחַ וַתְּבִיאֵנִי אֶל־הֶחָצֵר הַפְּנִימִי וְהִנֵּה מָלֵא כְבוֹד־יְהֹוָה הַבָּיִת:

⁶ and I heard speech addressed to me from the Temple, though [the] man was standing beside me.

ו וָאֶשְׁמַע מִדַּבֵּר אֵלַי מֵהַבָּיִת וְאִישׁ הָיָה עֹמֵד אֶצְלִי:

⁷ It said to me: O mortal, this is the place of My throne and the place for the soles of My feet, where I will dwell in the midst of the people *Yisrael* forever. The House of *Yisrael* and their kings must not again defile My holy name by their apostasy and by the corpses of their kings at their death.

ז וַיֹּאמֶר אֵלַי בֶּן־אָדָם אֶת־מְקוֹם כִּסְאִי וְאֶת־מְקוֹם כַּפּוֹת רַגְלַי אֲשֶׁר אֶשְׁכָּן־שָׁם בְּתוֹךְ בְּנֵי־יִשְׂרָאֵל לְעוֹלָם וְלֹא יְטַמְּאוּ עוֹד בֵּית־יִשְׂרָאֵל שֵׁם קָדְשִׁי הֵמָּה וּמַלְכֵיהֶם בִּזְנוּתָם וּבְפִגְרֵי מַלְכֵיהֶם בָּמוֹתָם:

⁸ When they placed their threshold next to My threshold and their doorposts next to My doorposts with only a wall between Me and them, they would defile My holy name by the abominations that they committed, and I consumed them in My anger.

ח בְּתִתָּם סִפָּם אֶת־סִפִּי וּמְזוּזָתָם אֵצֶל מְזוּזָתִי וְהַקִּיר בֵּינִי וּבֵינֵיהֶם וְטִמְּאוּ אֶת־שֵׁם קָדְשִׁי בְּתוֹעֲבוֹתָם אֲשֶׁר עָשׂוּ וָאֲכַל אֹתָם בְּאַפִּי:

⁹ Therefore, let them put their apostasy and the corpses of their kings far from Me, and I will dwell among them forever.

ט עַתָּה יְרַחֲקוּ אֶת־זְנוּתָם וּפִגְרֵי מַלְכֵיהֶם מִמֶּנִּי וְשָׁכַנְתִּי בְתוֹכָם לְעוֹלָם:

¹⁰ [Now] you, O mortal, describe the Temple to the House of *Yisrael*, and let them measure its design. But let them be ashamed of their iniquities:

י אַתָּה בֶן־אָדָם הַגֵּד אֶת־בֵּית־יִשְׂרָאֵל אֶת־הַבַּיִת וְיִכָּלְמוּ מֵעֲוֹנוֹתֵיהֶם וּמָדְדוּ אֶת־תָּכְנִית:

guish between the holiness of *Har Habayit,* the Temple Mount, and the rest of *Yerushalayim,* where sacrifices could not be offered. The *Mishna* (*Keilim* 1:6–9) teaches that the Land of Israel possesses ten ascending levels of holiness, starting from the outskirts of the country and culminating with the Holy of Holies, the resting place of God's Divine Presence.

11 When they are ashamed of all they have done, make known to them the plan of the Temple and its layout, its exits and entrances – its entire plan, and all the laws and instructions pertaining to its entire plan. Write it down before their eyes, that they may faithfully follow its entire plan and all its laws.

יא וְאִם־נִכְלְמוּ מִכֹּל אֲשֶׁר־עָשׂוּ צוּרַת הַבַּיִת וּתְכוּנָתוֹ וּמוֹצָאָיו וּמוֹבָאָיו וְכָל־צוּרֹתָו וְאֵת כָּל־חֻקֹּתָיו וְכָל־צוּרֹתָי [צוּרֹתָיו] וְכָל־תּוֹרֹתָו [תּוֹרֹתָיו] הוֹדַע אוֹתָם וּכְתֹב לְעֵינֵיהֶם וְיִשְׁמְרוּ אֶת־כָּל־ צוּרָתוֹ וְאֶת־כָּל־חֻקֹּתָיו וְעָשׂוּ אוֹתָם:

v'-im nikh-l'-MU mi-KOL a-sher a-SU tzu-RAT ha-BA-yit ut-khu-na-TO u-mo-tza-AV u-mo-va-AV v'-khol tzu-ro-TAV v'-AYT kol khu-ko-TAV v'-khol tzu-ro-TAV v'-khol to-ro-TAV ho-DA o-TAM ukh-TOV l'-ay-nay-HEM v'-yish-m'-RU et kol tzu-ra-TO v'-et kol khu-ko-TAV v'-a-SU o-TAM

12 Such are the instructions for the Temple on top of the mountain: the entire area of its enclosure shall be most holy. Thus far the instructions for the Temple.

יב זֹאת תּוֹרַת הַבָּיִת עַל־רֹאשׁ הָהָר כָּל־ גְּבֻלוֹ סָבִיב סָבִיב קֹדֶשׁ קׇדָשִׁים הִנֵּה־ זֹאת תּוֹרַת הַבָּיִת:

13 And these are the dimensions of the *Mizbayach*, in *amot* where each is an *amah* and a *tefach*. The trench shall be an *amah* deep and an *amah* wide, with a rim one *zeret* high around its edge. And the height shall be as follows:

יג וְאֵלֶּה מִדּוֹת הַמִּזְבֵּחַ בָּאַמּוֹת אַמָּה אַמָּה וָטֹפַח וְחֵיק הָאַמָּה וְאַמָּה־רֹחַב וּגְבוּלָהּ אֶל־שְׂפָתָהּ סָבִיב זֶרֶת הָאֶחָד וְזֶה גַּב הַמִּזְבֵּחַ:

14 From the trench in the ground to the lower ledge, which shall be an *amah* wide: 2 *amot*; from the lower ledge to the upper ledge, which shall likewise be an *amah* wide: 4 *amot*;

יד וּמֵחֵיק הָאָרֶץ עַד־הָעֲזָרָה הַתַּחְתּוֹנָה שְׁתַּיִם אַמּוֹת וְרֹחַב אַמָּה אֶחָת וּמֵהָעֲזָרָה הַקְּטַנָּה עַד־הָעֲזָרָה הַגְּדוֹלָה אַרְבַּע אַמּוֹת וְרֹחַב הָאַמָּה:

15 and the height of the *Mizbayach* hearth shall be 4 *amot*, with 4 horns projecting upward from the hearth: 4 *amot*.

טו וְהָהַרְאֵל אַרְבַּע אַמּוֹת וּמֵהָאֲרִאֵיל וּלְמַעְלָה הַקְּרָנוֹת אַרְבַּע:

16 Now the hearth shall be 12 *amot* long and 12 broad, square, with 4 equal sides.

טז וְהָאֲרִאֵיל [וְהָאֲרִאֵל] שְׁתֵּים עֶשְׂרֵה אֹרֶךְ בִּשְׁתֵּים עֶשְׂרֵה רֹחַב רָבוּעַ אֶל אַרְבַּעַת רְבָעָיו:

17 Hence, the [upper] base shall be 14 *amot* broad, with 4 equal sides. The surrounding rim shall be half an *amah* [high], and the surrounding trench shall measure one *amah*. And the ramp shall face east.

יז וְהָעֲזָרָה אַרְבַּע עֶשְׂרֵה אֹרֶךְ בְּאַרְבַּע עֶשְׂרֵה רֹחַב אֶל אַרְבַּעַת רְבָעֶיהָ וְהַגְּבוּל סָבִיב אוֹתָהּ חֲצִי הָאַמָּה וְהַחֵיק־לָהּ אַמָּה סָבִיב וּמַעֲלֹתֵהוּ פְּנוֹת קָדִים:

Replica of the Temple *menorah*

43:11 Make known to them the plan of the Temple and its layout The Sages describe a conversation that took place between *Hashem* and *Yechezkel* after the prophet had been exiled to Babylonia. The Lord tells *Yechezkel* to teach the design of the third *Beit Hamikdash* to the Children of Israel. *Yechezkel* answers, "Let it wait until we return to the Land of Israel … we cannot build it here in Babylonia." *Hashem* turns to the prophet and responds, "No, teach it to the people now, because when the people study the design of your *Beit Hamikdash*, I will consider it as if they have already begun to build it." Today, scholars in Jerusalem are studying the design of the third Temple, and are already building vessels to use in it, including the solid gold *menorah* prominently displayed at the top of the stairs leading down to the *Kotel*.

18 Then he said to me: O mortal, thus said *Hashem*: These are the directions for the *Mizbayach* on the day it is erected, so that burnt offerings may be offered up on it and blood dashed against it.

וַיֹּאמֶר אֵלַי בֶּן־אָדָם כֹּה אָמַר אֲדֹנָי יְהוִה אֵלֶּה חֻקּוֹת הַמִּזְבֵּחַ בְּיוֹם הֵעָשׂוֹתוֹ לְהַעֲלוֹת עָלָיו עוֹלָה וְלִזְרֹק עָלָיו דָּם:

19 You shall give to the levitical *Kohanim* who are of the stock of *Tzadok*, and so eligible to minister to Me – declares *Hashem* – a young bull of the herd for a sin offering.

וְנָתַתָּה אֶל־הַכֹּהֲנִים הַלְוִיִּם אֲשֶׁר הֵם מִזֶּרַע צָדוֹק הַקְּרֹבִים אֵלַי נְאֻם אֲדֹנָי יְהוִה לְשָׁרְתֵנִי פַּר בֶּן־בָּקָר לְחַטָּאת:

20 You shall take some of its blood and apply it to the four horns [of the *Mizbayach*], to the four corners of the base, and to the surrounding rim; thus you shall purge it and perform purification upon it.

וְלָקַחְתָּ מִדָּמוֹ וְנָתַתָּה עַל־אַרְבַּע קַרְנֹתָיו וְאֶל־אַרְבַּע פִּנּוֹת הָעֲזָרָה וְאֶל־הַגְּבוּל סָבִיב וְחִטֵּאתָ אוֹתוֹ וְכִפַּרְתָּהוּ:

21 Then you shall take the bull of sin offering and burn it in the designated area of the Temple, outside the Sanctuary.

וְלָקַחְתָּ אֵת הַפָּר הַחַטָּאת וּשְׂרָפוֹ בְּמִפְקַד הַבָּיִת מִחוּץ לַמִּקְדָּשׁ:

22 On the following day, you shall offer a goat without blemish as a sin offering; and the *Mizbayach* shall be purged [with it] just as it was purged with the bull.

וּבַיּוֹם הַשֵּׁנִי תַּקְרִיב שְׂעִיר־עִזִּים תָּמִים לְחַטָּאת וְחִטְּאוּ אֶת־הַמִּזְבֵּחַ כַּאֲשֶׁר חִטְּאוּ בַּפָּר:

23 When you have completed the ritual of purging, you shall offer a bull of the herd without blemish and a ram of the flock without blemish.

בְּכַלּוֹתְךָ מֵחַטֵּא תַּקְרִיב פַּר בֶּן־בָּקָר תָּמִים וְאַיִל מִן־הַצֹּאן תָּמִים:

24 Offer them to *Hashem*; let the *Kohanim* throw salt on them and offer them up as a burnt offering to *Hashem*.

וְהִקְרַבְתָּם לִפְנֵי יְהוָה וְהִשְׁלִיכוּ הַכֹּהֲנִים עֲלֵיהֶם מֶלַח וְהֶעֱלוּ אוֹתָם עֹלָה לַיהוָה:

25 Every day, for seven days, you shall present a goat of sin offering, as well as a bull of the herd and a ram of the flock; you shall present unblemished ones.

שִׁבְעַת יָמִים תַּעֲשֶׂה שְׂעִיר־חַטָּאת לַיּוֹם וּפַר בֶּן־בָּקָר וְאַיִל מִן־הַצֹּאן תְּמִימִים יַעֲשׂוּ:

26 Seven days they shall purge the *Mizbayach* and cleanse it; thus shall it be consecrated.

שִׁבְעַת יָמִים יְכַפְּרוּ אֶת־הַמִּזְבֵּחַ וְטִהֲרוּ אֹתוֹ וּמִלְאוּ יָדוֹ [יָדָיו:]

27 And when these days are over, then from the eighth day onward the *Kohanim* shall offer your burnt offerings and your offerings of well-being on the *Mizbayach*; and I wil extend My favor to you – declares *Hashem*.

וִיכַלּוּ אֶת־הַיָּמִים וְהָיָה בַיּוֹם הַשְּׁמִינִי וָהָלְאָה יַעֲשׂוּ הַכֹּהֲנִים עַל־הַמִּזְבֵּחַ אֶת־עוֹלוֹתֵיכֶם וְאֶת־שַׁלְמֵיכֶם וְרָצִאתִי אֶתְכֶם נְאֻם אֲדֹנָי יְהוִה:

44 1 Then he led me back to the outer gate of the Sanctuary that faced eastward; it was shut.

וַיָּשֶׁב אֹתִי דֶּרֶךְ שַׁעַר הַמִּקְדָּשׁ הַחִיצוֹן הַפֹּנֶה קָדִים וְהוּא סָגוּר:

2 And *Hashem* said to me: This gate is to be kept shut and is not to be opened! No one shall enter by it because *Hashem*, the God of *Yisrael*, has entered by it; therefore it shall remain shut.

וַיֹּאמֶר אֵלַי יְהוָה הַשַּׁעַר הַזֶּה סָגוּר יִהְיֶה לֹא יִפָּתֵחַ וְאִישׁ לֹא־יָבֹא בוֹ כִּי יְהוָה אֱלֹהֵי־יִשְׂרָאֵל בָּא בוֹ וְהָיָה סָגוּר:

3 Only the prince may sit in it and eat bread before *Hashem*, since he is a prince; he shall enter by way of the vestibule of the gate, and shall depart by the same way.

ג אֶת־הַנָּשִׂיא נָשִׂיא הוּא יֵשֶׁב־בּוֹ לֶאֱכָל־לֶחֶם לִפְנֵי יְהֹוָה מִדֶּרֶךְ אֻלָם הַשַּׁעַר יָבוֹא וּמִדַּרְכּוֹ יֵצֵא:

4 Then he led me, by way of the north gate, to the front of the Temple. I looked, and lo! the Presence of *Hashem* filled the Temple of *Hashem*; and I fell upon my face.

ד וַיְבִיאֵנִי דֶּרֶךְ־שַׁעַר הַצָּפוֹן אֶל־פְּנֵי הַבַּיִת וָאֵרֶא וְהִנֵּה מָלֵא כְבוֹד־יְהֹוָה אֶת־בֵּית יְהֹוָה וָאֶפֹּל אֶל־פָּנָי:

5 Then *Hashem* said to me: O mortal, mark well, look closely and listen carefully to everything that I tell you regarding all the laws of the Temple of *Hashem* and all the instructions regarding it. Note well who may enter the Temple and all who must be excluded from the Sanctuary.

ה וַיֹּאמֶר אֵלַי יְהֹוָה בֶּן־אָדָם שִׂים לִבְּךָ וּרְאֵה בְעֵינֶיךָ וּבְאָזְנֶיךָ שְׁמָע אֵת כָּל־אֲשֶׁר אֲנִי מְדַבֵּר אֹתָךְ לְכָל־חֻקּוֹת בֵּית־יְהֹוָה וּלְכָל־תּורתו [תּוֹרֹתָיו] וְשַׂמְתָּ לִבְּךָ לִמְבוֹא הַבַּיִת בְּכֹל מוֹצָאֵי הַמִּקְדָּשׁ:

6 And say to the rebellious House of *Yisrael*: Thus said *Hashem*: Too long, O House of *Yisrael*, have you committed all your abominations,

ו וְאָמַרְתָּ אֶל־מֶרִי אֶל־בֵּית יִשְׂרָאֵל כֹּה אָמַר אֲדֹנָי יְהֹוָה רַב־לָכֶם מִכָּל־תּוֹעֲבוֹתֵיכֶם בֵּית יִשְׂרָאֵל:

7 admitting aliens, uncircumcised of spirit and uncircumcised of flesh, to be in My Sanctuary and profane My very Temple, when you offer up My food – the fat and the blood. You have broken My covenant with all your abominations.

ז בַּהֲבִיאֲכֶם בְּנֵי־נֵכָר עַרְלֵי־לֵב וְעַרְלֵי בָשָׂר לִהְיוֹת בְּמִקְדָּשִׁי לְחַלְּלוֹ אֶת־בֵּיתִי בְּהַקְרִיבְכֶם אֶת־לַחְמִי חֵלֶב וָדָם וַיָּפֵרוּ אֶת־בְּרִיתִי אֶל כָּל־תּוֹעֲבוֹתֵיכֶם:

8 You have not discharged the duties concerning My sacred offerings, but have appointed them to discharge the duties of My Sanctuary for you.

ח וְלֹא שְׁמַרְתֶּם מִשְׁמֶרֶת קָדָשָׁי וַתְּשִׂימוּן לְשֹׁמְרֵי מִשְׁמַרְתִּי בְּמִקְדָּשִׁי לָכֶם:

9 Thus said *Hashem*: Let no alien, uncircumcised in spirit and flesh, enter My Sanctuary – no alien whatsoever among the people of *Yisrael*.

ט כֹּה־אָמַר אֲדֹנָי יְהֹוִה כָּל־בֶּן־נֵכָר עֶרֶל לֵב וְעֶרֶל בָּשָׂר לֹא יָבוֹא אֶל־מִקְדָּשִׁי לְכָל־בֶּן־נֵכָר אֲשֶׁר בְּתוֹךְ בְּנֵי יִשְׂרָאֵל:

10 But the *Leviim* who forsook Me when *Yisrael* went astray – straying from Me to follow their fetishes – shall suffer their punishment:

י כִּי אִם־הַלְוִיִּם אֲשֶׁר רָחֲקוּ מֵעָלַי בִּתְעוֹת יִשְׂרָאֵל אֲשֶׁר תָּעוּ מֵעָלַי אַחֲרֵי גִּלּוּלֵיהֶם וְנָשְׂאוּ עֲוֹנָם:

11 They shall be servitors in My Sanctuary, appointed over the Temple gates, and performing the chores of My Temple; they shall slaughter the burnt offerings and the sacrifices for the people. They shall attend on them and serve them.

יא וְהָיוּ בְמִקְדָּשִׁי מְשָׁרְתִים פְּקֻדּוֹת אֶל־שַׁעֲרֵי הַבַּיִת וּמְשָׁרְתִים אֶת־הַבָּיִת הֵמָּה יִשְׁחֲטוּ אֶת־הָעֹלָה וְאֶת־הַזֶּבַח לָעָם וְהֵמָּה יַעַמְדוּ לִפְנֵיהֶם לְשָׁרְתָם:

12 Because they served the House of *Yisrael* in the presence of their fetishes and made them stumble into guilt, therefore – declares *Hashem* – I have sworn concerning them that they shall suffer their punishment:

יב יַעַן אֲשֶׁר יְשָׁרְתוּ אוֹתָם לִפְנֵי גִלּוּלֵיהֶם וְהָיוּ לְבֵית־יִשְׂרָאֵל לְמִכְשׁוֹל עָוֹן עַל־כֵּן נָשָׂאתִי יָדִי עֲלֵיהֶם נְאֻם אֲדֹנָי יְהֹוִה וְנָשְׂאוּ עֲוֹנָם:

13 They shall not approach Me to serve Me as *Kohanim*, to come near any of My sacred offerings, the most holy things. They shall bear their shame for the abominations that they committed.

יג וְלֹא־יִגְּשׁוּ אֵלַי לְכַהֵן לִי וְלָגֶשֶׁת עַל־כָּל־קָדָשַׁי אֶל־קָדְשֵׁי הַקֳּדָשִׁים וְנָשְׂאוּ כְּלִמָּתָם וְתוֹעֲבוֹתָם אֲשֶׁר עָשׂוּ:

14 I will make them watchmen of the Temple, to perform all its chores, everything that needs to be done in it.

יד וְנָתַתִּי אוֹתָם שֹׁמְרֵי מִשְׁמֶרֶת הַבָּיִת לְכֹל עֲבֹדָתוֹ וּלְכֹל אֲשֶׁר יֵעָשֶׂה בּוֹ:

15 But the levitical *Kohanim* descended from *Tzadok*, who maintained the service of My Sanctuary when the people of *Yisrael* went astray from Me – they shall approach Me to minister to Me; they shall stand before Me to offer Me fat and blood – declares *Hashem*.

טו וְהַכֹּהֲנִים הַלְוִיִּם בְּנֵי צָדוֹק אֲשֶׁר שָׁמְרוּ אֶת־מִשְׁמֶרֶת מִקְדָּשִׁי בִּתְעוֹת בְּנֵי־יִשְׂרָאֵל מֵעָלַי הֵמָּה יִקְרְבוּ אֵלַי לְשָׁרְתֵנִי וְעָמְדוּ לְפָנַי לְהַקְרִיב לִי חֵלֶב וָדָם נְאֻם אֲדֹנָי יְהֹוִה:

v'-ha-ko-ha-NEEM hal-vi-YIM b'-NAY tza-DOK a-SHER sha-m'-RU et mish-ME-ret mik-da-SHEE bit-OT b'-nay yis-ra-AYL may-a-LAI HAY-mah yik-r'-VU ay-LAI l'-sha-r'-TAY-nee v'-a-m'-DU l'-fa-NAI l'-hak-REEV LEE KHAY-lev va-DAM n'-UM a-do-NAI e-lo-HEEM

16 They alone may enter My Sanctuary and they alone shall approach My table to minister to Me; and they shall keep My charge.

טז הֵמָּה יָבֹאוּ אֶל־מִקְדָּשִׁי וְהֵמָּה יִקְרְבוּ אֶל־שֻׁלְחָנִי לְשָׁרְתֵנִי וְשָׁמְרוּ אֶת־מִשְׁמַרְתִּי:

17 And when they enter the gates of the inner court, they shall wear linen vestments: they shall have nothing woolen upon them when they minister inside the gates of the inner court.

יז וְהָיָה בְּבוֹאָם אֶל־שַׁעֲרֵי הֶחָצֵר הַפְּנִימִית בִּגְדֵי פִשְׁתִּים יִלְבָּשׁוּ וְלֹא־יַעֲלֶה עֲלֵיהֶם צֶמֶר בְּשָׁרְתָם בְּשַׁעֲרֵי הֶחָצֵר הַפְּנִימִית וָבָיְתָה:

18 They shall have linen turbans on their heads and linen breeches on their loins; they shall not gird themselves with anything that causes sweat.

יח פַּאֲרֵי פִשְׁתִּים יִהְיוּ עַל־רֹאשָׁם וּמִכְנְסֵי פִשְׁתִּים יִהְיוּ עַל־מָתְנֵיהֶם לֹא יַחְגְּרוּ בַּיָּזַע:

19 When they go out to the outer court – the outer court where the people are – they shall remove the vestments in which they minister and shall deposit them in the sacred chambers; they shall put on other garments, lest they make the people consecrated by [contact with] their vestments.

יט וּבְצֵאתָם אֶל־הֶחָצֵר הַחִיצוֹנָה אֶל־הֶחָצֵר הַחִיצוֹנָה אֶל־הָעָם יִפְשְׁטוּ אֶת־בִּגְדֵיהֶם אֲשֶׁר־הֵמָּה מְשָׁרְתִם בָּם וְהִנִּיחוּ אוֹתָם בְּלִשְׁכֹת הַקֹּדֶשׁ וְלָבְשׁוּ בְּגָדִים אֲחֵרִים וְלֹא־יְקַדְּשׁוּ אֶת־הָעָם בְּבִגְדֵיהֶם:

20 They shall neither shave their heads nor let their hair go untrimmed; they shall keep their hair trimmed.

כ וְרֹאשָׁם לֹא יְגַלֵּחוּ וּפֶרַע לֹא יְשַׁלֵּחוּ כָּסוֹם יִכְסְמוּ אֶת־רָאשֵׁיהֶם:

Minister of Justice Ayelet Shaked, President Reuven Rivlin, and President of the Supreme Court Miriam Naor, at an induction ceremony of new judges (2015).

44:15 Descended from *Tzadok*
For their loyalty to *Hashem*, *Yechezkel* nominates the members of the house of *Tzadok* to serve as teachers (verse 23) and judges (verse 24), and to serve in the *Beit Hamikdash*. Given their enhanced positions of power, it is not surprising that the house of *Tzadok* will face the burden of greater restrictions, as described in the rest of the chapter. Those who lead God's people in *Eretz Yisrael* must be prepared to make sacrifices others won't make, in order to maintain their character and purity.

Ezekiel

²¹ No *Kohen* shall drink wine when he enters into the inner court.

כא וְיַיִן לֹא־יִשְׁתּוּ כָּל־כֹּהֵן בְּבוֹאָם אֶל־הֶחָצֵר הַפְּנִימִית:

²² They shall not marry widows or divorced women; they may marry only virgins of the stock of the House of *Yisrael*, or widows who are widows of *Kohanim*.

כב וְאַלְמָנָה וּגְרוּשָׁה לֹא־יִקְחוּ לָהֶם לְנָשִׁים כִּי אִם־בְּתוּלֹת מִזֶּרַע בֵּית יִשְׂרָאֵל וְהָאַלְמָנָה אֲשֶׁר תִּהְיֶה אַלְמָנָה מִכֹּהֵן יִקָּחוּ:

²³ They shall declare to My people what is sacred and what is profane, and inform them what is clean and what is unclean.

כג וְאֶת־עַמִּי יוֹרוּ בֵּין קֹדֶשׁ לְחֹל וּבֵין־טָמֵא לְטָהוֹר יוֹדִעֻם:

²⁴ In lawsuits, too, it is they who shall act as judges; they shall decide them in accordance with My rules. They shall preserve My teachings and My laws regarding all My fixed occasions; and they shall maintain the sanctity of My *Shabbatot*.

כד וְעַל־רִיב הֵמָּה יַעַמְדוּ לשפט [לְמִשְׁפָּט] בְּמִשְׁפָּטַי ושפטהו [יִשְׁפְּטוּהוּ] וְאֶת־תּוֹרֹתַי וְאֶת־חֻקֹּתַי בְּכָל־מוֹעֲדַי יִשְׁמֹרוּ וְאֶת־שַׁבְּתוֹתַי יְקַדֵּשׁוּ:

²⁵ [A *Kohen*] shall not defile himself by entering [a house] where there is a dead person. He shall defile himself only for father or mother, son or daughter, brother or unmarried sister.

כה וְאֶל־מֵת אָדָם לֹא יָבוֹא לְטָמְאָה כִּי אִם־לְאָב וּלְאֵם וּלְבֵן וּלְבַת לְאָח וּלְאָחוֹת אֲשֶׁר־לֹא־הָיְתָה לְאִישׁ יִטַּמָּאוּ:

²⁶ After he has become clean, seven days shall be counted off for him;

כו וְאַחֲרֵי טָהֳרָתוֹ שִׁבְעַת יָמִים יִסְפְּרוּ־לוֹ:

²⁷ and on the day that he reenters the inner court of the Sanctuary to minister in the Sanctuary, he shall present his sin offering – declares *Hashem*.

כז וּבְיוֹם בֹּאוֹ אֶל־הַקֹּדֶשׁ אֶל־הֶחָצֵר הַפְּנִימִית לְשָׁרֵת בַּקֹּדֶשׁ יַקְרִיב חַטָּאתוֹ נְאֻם אֲדֹנָי יֱהֹוִה:

²⁸ This shall be their portion, for I am their portion; and no holding shall be given them in *Yisrael*, for I am their holding.

כח וְהָיְתָה לָהֶם לְנַחֲלָה אֲנִי נַחֲלָתָם וַאֲחֻזָּה לֹא־תִתְּנוּ לָהֶם בְּיִשְׂרָאֵל אֲנִי אֲחֻזָּתָם:

²⁹ The meal offerings, sin offerings, and guilt offerings shall be consumed by them. Everything proscribed in *Yisrael* shall be theirs.

כט הַמִּנְחָה וְהַחַטָּאת וְהָאָשָׁם הֵמָּה יֹאכְלוּם וְכָל־חֵרֶם בְּיִשְׂרָאֵל לָהֶם יִהְיֶה:

³⁰ All the choice first fruits of every kind, and all the gifts of every kind – of all your contributions – shall go to the *Kohanim*. You shall further give the first of the yield of your baking to the *Kohen*, that a blessing may rest upon your home.

ל וְרֵאשִׁית כָּל־בִּכּוּרֵי כֹל וְכָל־תְּרוּמַת כֹּל מִכֹּל תְּרוּמוֹתֵיכֶם לַכֹּהֲנִים יִהְיֶה וְרֵאשִׁית עֲרִסוֹתֵיכֶם תִּתְּנוּ לַכֹּהֵן לְהָנִיחַ בְּרָכָה אֶל־בֵּיתֶךָ:

³¹ *Kohanim* shall not eat anything, whether bird or animal, that died or was torn by beasts.

לא כָּל־נְבֵלָה וּטְרֵפָה מִן־הָעוֹף וּמִן־הַבְּהֵמָה לֹא יֹאכְלוּ הַכֹּהֲנִים:

45 ¹ When you allot the land as an inheritance, you shall set aside from the land, as a gift sacred to *Hashem*, an area 25,000 [*amot*] long and 10,000 wide: this shall be holy through its entire extent.

מה א וּבְהַפִּילְכֶם אֶת־הָאָרֶץ בְּנַחֲלָה תָּרִימוּ תְרוּמָה לַיהֹוָה קֹדֶשׁ מִן־הָאָרֶץ אֹרֶךְ חֲמִשָּׁה וְעֶשְׂרִים אֶלֶף אֹרֶךְ וְרֹחַב עֲשָׂרָה אָלֶף קֹדֶשׁ־הוּא בְכָל־גְּבוּלָהּ סָבִיב:

ב יִהְיֶה מִזֶּה אֶל־הַקֹּדֶשׁ חֲמֵשׁ מֵאוֹת בַּחֲמֵשׁ מֵאוֹת מְרֻבָּע סָבִיב וַחֲמִשִּׁים אַמָּה מִגְרָשׁ לוֹ סָבִיב:

ג וּמִן־הַמִּדָּה הַזֹּאת תָּמוֹד אֹרֶךְ חמש [חֲמִשָּׁה] וְעֶשְׂרִים אֶלֶף וְרֹחַב עֲשֶׂרֶת אֲלָפִים וּבוֹ־יִהְיֶה הַמִּקְדָּשׁ קֹדֶשׁ קָדָשִׁים:

ד קֹדֶשׁ מִן־הָאָרֶץ הוּא לַכֹּהֲנִים מְשָׁרְתֵי הַמִּקְדָּשׁ יִהְיֶה הַקְּרֵבִים לְשָׁרֵת אֶת־יְהוָה וְהָיָה לָהֶם מָקוֹם לְבָתִּים וּמִקְדָּשׁ לַמִּקְדָּשׁ:

ה וַחֲמִשָּׁה וְעֶשְׂרִים אֶלֶף אֹרֶךְ וַעֲשֶׂרֶת אֲלָפִים רֹחַב יהיה [וְהָיָה] לַלְוִיִּם מְשָׁרְתֵי הַבַּיִת לָהֶם לַאֲחֻזָּה עֶשְׂרִים לְשָׁכֹת:

ו וַאֲחֻזַּת הָעִיר תִּתְּנוּ חֲמֵשֶׁת אֲלָפִים רֹחַב וְאֹרֶךְ חֲמִשָּׁה וְעֶשְׂרִים אֶלֶף לְעֻמַּת תְּרוּמַת הַקֹּדֶשׁ לְכָל־בֵּית יִשְׂרָאֵל יִהְיֶה:

ז וְלַנָּשִׂיא מִזֶּה וּמִזֶּה לִתְרוּמַת הַקֹּדֶשׁ וְלַאֲחֻזַּת הָעִיר אֶל־פְּנֵי תְרוּמַת־הַקֹּדֶשׁ וְאֶל־פְּנֵי אֲחֻזַּת הָעִיר מִפְּאַת־יָם יָמָּה וּמִפְּאַת־קֵדְמָה קָדִימָה וְאֹרֶךְ לְעֻמּוֹת אַחַד הַחֲלָקִים מִגְּבוּל יָם אֶל־גְּבוּל קָדִימָה:

ח לָאָרֶץ יִהְיֶה־לּוֹ לַאֲחֻזָּה בְּיִשְׂרָאֵל וְלֹא־יוֹנוּ עוֹד נְשִׂיאַי אֶת־עַמִּי וְהָאָרֶץ יִתְּנוּ לְבֵית־יִשְׂרָאֵל לְשִׁבְטֵיהֶם:

ט כֹּה־אָמַר אֲדֹנָי יְהוִה רַב־לָכֶם נְשִׂיאֵי יִשְׂרָאֵל חָמָס וָשֹׁד הָסִירוּ וּמִשְׁפָּט וּצְדָקָה עֲשׂוּ הָרִימוּ גְרֻשֹׁתֵיכֶם מֵעַל עַמִּי נְאֻם אֲדֹנָי יְהוִה:

² Of this, a square measuring a full 500 by 500 shall be reserved for the Sanctuary, and 50 *amot* for an open space all around it.

³ Of the aforesaid area, you shall measure off, as most holy and destined to include the Sanctuary, [a space] 25,000 long by 10,000 wide;

⁴ it is a sacred portion of the land; it shall provide space for houses for the *Kohanim*, the ministrants of the Sanctuary who are qualified to minister to *Hashem*, as well as holy ground for the Sanctuary.

⁵ Another [space], 25,000 long by 10,000 wide, shall be the property of the *Leviim*, the servants of the Temple – twenty chambers.

⁶ Alongside the sacred reserve, you shall set aside [a space] 25,000 long by 5,000 wide, as the property of the city; it shall belong to the whole House of *Yisrael*.

⁷ And to the prince shall belong, on both sides of the sacred reserve and the property of the city and alongside the sacred reserve and the property of the city, on the west extending westward and on the east extending eastward, a portion corresponding to one of the [tribal] portions that extend from the western border to the eastern border

⁸ of the land. That shall be his property in *Yisrael*; and My princes shall no more defraud My people, but shall leave the rest of the land to the several tribes of the House of *Yisrael*.

⁹ Thus said *Hashem*: Enough, princes of *Yisrael*! Make an end of lawlessness and rapine, and do what is right and just! Put a stop to your evictions of My people – declares *Hashem*.

> koh a-MAR a-do-NAI e-lo-HEEM rav la-KHEM n'-see-AY yis-ra-AYL
> kha-MAS va-SHOD ha-SEE-ru u-mish-PAT utz-da-KAH a-SU ha-REE-mu
> g'-ru-sho-tay-KHEM may-AL a-MEE n'-UM a-do-NAI e-lo-HEEM

Weighing diamonds at the new diamond exchange building in Ramat Gan (1969)

45:9 Do what is right and just In the middle of discussing the division of the land between the priests, princes, and the people, *Yechezkel* suddenly stops to warn the leaders against false weights and measures. The previous *Beit Hamikdash* fell because of dishonesty and injustice (see Amos 8). *Yechezkel* understands that the strongest foundation for rebuilding the *Beit*

10 Have honest balances, an honest *efah*, and an honest *bat*.

י מֹאזְנֵי־צֶדֶק וְאֵיפַת־צֶדֶק וּבַת־צֶדֶק יְהִי לָכֶם:

11 The *efah* and the *bat* shall comprise the same volume, the *bat* a tenth of a *chomer* and the *efah* a tenth of a *chomer*; their capacity shall be gauged by the *chomer*.

יא הָאֵיפָה וְהַבַּת תֹּכֶן אֶחָד יִהְיֶה לָשֵׂאת מַעְשַׂר הַחֹמֶר הַבַּת וַעֲשִׂירִת הַחֹמֶר הָאֵיפָה אֶל־הַחֹמֶר יִהְיֶה מַתְכֻּנְתּוֹ:

12 And the *shekel* shall weigh 20 *geira*. 20 *shekalim*, 25 *shekalim* [and] 10 plus 5 *shekalim* shall count with you as a *maneh*.

יב וְהַשֶּׁקֶל עֶשְׂרִים גֵּרָה עֶשְׂרִים שְׁקָלִים חֲמִשָּׁה וְעֶשְׂרִים שְׁקָלִים עֲשָׂרָה וַחֲמִשָּׁה שֶׁקֶל הַמָּנֶה יִהְיֶה לָכֶם:

13 This is the contribution you shall make: One-sixth of an *efah* from every *chomer* of wheat and one-sixth of an *efah* from every *chomer* of barley,

יג זֹאת הַתְּרוּמָה אֲשֶׁר תָּרִימוּ שִׁשִּׁית הָאֵיפָה מֵחֹמֶר הַחִטִּים וְשִׁשִּׁיתֶם הָאֵיפָה מֵחֹמֶר הַשְּׂעֹרִים:

14 while the due from the oil – the oil being measured by the *bat* – shall be one-tenth of a *bat* from every *kor.* – As 10 *batim* make a *chomer*, so 10 *batim* make a *chomer*. –

יד וְחֹק הַשֶּׁמֶן הַבַּת הַשֶּׁמֶן מַעְשַׂר הַבַּת מִן־הַכֹּר עֲשֶׂרֶת הַבַּתִּים חֹמֶר כִּי־עֲשֶׂרֶת הַבַּתִּים חֹמֶר:

15 And [the due] from the flock shall be one animal from every 200. [All these shall be contributed] from *Yisrael*'s products for meal offerings, burnt offerings, and offerings of well-being, to make expiation for them – declares *Hashem*.

טו וְשֶׂה־אַחַת מִן־הַצֹּאן מִן־הַמָּאתַיִם מִמַּשְׁקֵה יִשְׂרָאֵל לְמִנְחָה וּלְעוֹלָה וְלִשְׁלָמִים לְכַפֵּר עֲלֵיהֶם נְאֻם אֲדֹנָי יְהוִֹה:

16 In this contribution, the entire population must join with the prince in *Yisrael*.

טז כֹּל הָעָם הָאָרֶץ יִהְיוּ אֶל־הַתְּרוּמָה הַזֹּאת לַנָּשִׂיא בְּיִשְׂרָאֵל:

17 But the burnt offerings, the meal offerings, and the libations on festivals, new moons, *Shabbatot* – all fixed occasions – of the House of *Yisrael* shall be the obligation of the prince; he shall provide the sin offerings, the meal offerings, the burnt offerings, and the offerings of well-being, to make expiation for the House of *Yisrael*.

יז וְעַל־הַנָּשִׂיא יִהְיֶה הָעוֹלוֹת וְהַמִּנְחָה וְהַנֵּסֶךְ בַּחַגִּים וּבֶחֳדָשִׁים וּבַשַּׁבָּתוֹת בְּכָל־מוֹעֲדֵי בֵּית יִשְׂרָאֵל הוּא־יַעֲשֶׂה אֶת־הַחַטָּאת וְאֶת־הַמִּנְחָה וְאֶת־הָעוֹלָה וְאֶת־הַשְּׁלָמִים לְכַפֵּר בְּעַד בֵּית־יִשְׂרָאֵל:

18 Thus said *Hashem*: On the first day of the first month, you shall take a bull of the herd without blemish, and you shall cleanse the Sanctuary.

יח כֹּה־אָמַר אֲדֹנָי יְהוִֹה בָּרִאשׁוֹן בְּאֶחָד לַחֹדֶשׁ תִּקַּח פַּר־בֶּן־בָּקָר תָּמִים וְחִטֵּאתָ אֶת־הַמִּקְדָּשׁ:

19 The *Kohen* shall take some of the blood of the sin offering and apply it to the doorposts of the Temple, to the four corners of the ledge of the *Mizbayach*, and to the doorposts of the gate of the inner court.

יט וְלָקַח הַכֹּהֵן מִדַּם הַחַטָּאת וְנָתַן אֶל־מְזוּזַת הַבַּיִת וְאֶל־אַרְבַּע פִּנּוֹת הָעֲזָרָה לַמִּזְבֵּחַ וְעַל־מְזוּזַת שַׁעַר הֶחָצֵר הַפְּנִימִית:

Hamikdash, and residing in *Eretz Yisrael*, is a sense of justice. The same rules of honesty and integrity that apply in the marketplace (see Leviticus 19) apply in the *Beit Hamikdash*, and throughout the Land of Israel. *Yechezkel* therefore interrupts his division of the land to emphasize the importance of honest dealings in settling Israel. Just as dishonesty and injustice led to the destruction of the *Beit Hamikdash* and exile from the land, it is through honesty and justice that the people will merit resettling and dwelling in *Eretz Yisrael*.

20 You shall do the same on the seventh day of the month to purge the Temple from uncleanness caused by unwitting or ignorant persons.

כ וְכֵן תַּעֲשֶׂה בְּשִׁבְעָה בַחֹדֶשׁ מֵאִישׁ שֹׁגֶה וּמִפֶּתִי וְכִפַּרְתֶּם אֶת־הַבָּיִת:

21 On the fourteenth day of the first month you shall have the *Pesach* sacrifice; and during a festival of seven days unleavened bread shall be eaten.

כא בָּרִאשׁוֹן בְּאַרְבָּעָה עָשָׂר יוֹם לַחֹדֶשׁ יִהְיֶה לָכֶם הַפָּסַח חָג שְׁבֻעוֹת יָמִים מַצּוֹת יֵאָכֵל:

22 On that day, the prince shall provide a bull of sin offering on behalf of himself and of the entire population;

כב וְעָשָׂה הַנָּשִׂיא בַּיּוֹם הַהוּא בַּעֲדוֹ וּבְעַד כָּל־עַם הָאָרֶץ פַּר חַטָּאת:

23 and during the seven days of the festival, he shall provide daily – for seven days – seven bulls and seven rams, without blemish, for a burnt offering to *Hashem*, and one goat daily for a sin offering.

כג וְשִׁבְעַת יְמֵי־הֶחָג יַעֲשֶׂה עוֹלָה לַיהֹוָה שִׁבְעַת פָּרִים וְשִׁבְעַת אֵילִים תְּמִימִם לַיּוֹם שִׁבְעַת הַיָּמִים וְחַטָּאת שְׂעִיר עִזִּים לַיּוֹם:

24 He shall provide a meal offering of an *efah* for each bull and an *efah* for each ram, with a *hin* of oil to every *efah*.

כד וּמִנְחָה אֵיפָה לַפָּר וְאֵיפָה לָאַיִל יַעֲשֶׂה וְשֶׁמֶן הִין לָאֵיפָה:

25 So, too, during the festival of the seventh month, for seven days from the fifteenth day on, he shall provide the same sin offerings, burnt offerings, meal offerings, and oil.

כה בַּשְּׁבִיעִי בַּחֲמִשָּׁה עָשָׂר יוֹם לַחֹדֶשׁ בֶּחָג יַעֲשֶׂה כָאֵלֶּה שִׁבְעַת הַיָּמִים כַּחַטָּאת כָּעֹלָה וְכַמִּנְחָה וְכַשָּׁמֶן:

46 1 Thus said *Hashem*: The gate of the inner court which faces east shall be closed on the six working days; it shall be opened on the *Shabbat* day and it shall be opened on the day of the new moon.

מו א כֹּה־אָמַר אֲדֹנָי יֱהֹוִה שַׁעַר הֶחָצֵר הַפְּנִימִית הַפֹּנֶה קָדִים יִהְיֶה סָגוּר שֵׁשֶׁת יְמֵי הַמַּעֲשֶׂה וּבְיוֹם הַשַּׁבָּת יִפָּתֵחַ וּבְיוֹם הַחֹדֶשׁ יִפָּתֵחַ:

2 The prince shall enter by way of the vestibule outside the gate, and shall attend at the gatepost while the *Kohanim* sacrifice his burnt offering and his offering of well-being; he shall then bow low at the threshold of the gate and depart. The gate, however, shall not be closed until evening.

ב וּבָא הַנָּשִׂיא דֶּרֶךְ אוּלָם הַשַּׁעַר מִחוּץ וְעָמַד עַל־מְזוּזַת הַשַּׁעַר וְעָשׂוּ הַכֹּהֲנִים אֶת־עוֹלָתוֹ וְאֶת־שְׁלָמָיו וְהִשְׁתַּחֲוָה עַל־מִפְתַּן הַשַּׁעַר וְיָצָא וְהַשַּׁעַר לֹא־יִסָּגֵר עַד־הָעָרֶב:

3 The common people shall worship before *Hashem* on *Shabbatot* and new moons at the entrance of the same gate.

ג וְהִשְׁתַּחֲווּ עַם־הָאָרֶץ פֶּתַח הַשַּׁעַר הַהוּא בַּשַּׁבָּתוֹת וּבֶחֳדָשִׁים לִפְנֵי יְהֹוָה:

4 The burnt offering which the prince presents to *Hashem* on the *Shabbat* day shall consist of six lambs without blemish and one ram without blemish –

ד וְהָעֹלָה אֲשֶׁר־יַקְרִב הַנָּשִׂיא לַיהֹוָה בְּיוֹם הַשַּׁבָּת שִׁשָּׁה כְבָשִׂים תְּמִימִם וְאַיִל תָּמִים:

5 with a meal offering of an *efah* for the ram, a meal offering of as much as he wishes for the lambs, and a *hin* of oil with every *efah*.

ה וּמִנְחָה אֵיפָה לָאַיִל וְלַכְּבָשִׂים מִנְחָה מַתַּת יָדוֹ וְשֶׁמֶן הִין לָאֵיפָה:

6 And on the day of the new moon, it shall consist of a bull of the herd without blemish, and six lambs and a ram – they shall be without blemish.

ו וּבְיוֹם הַחֹדֶשׁ פַּר בֶּן־בָּקָר תְּמִימִם וְשֵׁשֶׁת כְּבָשִׂם וְאַיִל תְּמִימִם יִהְיוּ:

7 And he shall provide a meal offering of an *efah* for the bull, an *efah* for the ram, and as much as he can afford for the lambs, with a *hin* of oil to every *efah*.

ז וְאֵיפָה לַפָּר וְאֵיפָה לָאַיִל יַעֲשֶׂה מִנְחָה וְלַכְּבָשִׂים כַּאֲשֶׁר תַּשִּׂיג יָדוֹ וְשֶׁמֶן הִין לָאֵיפָה:

8 When the prince enters, he shall come in by way of the vestibule of the gate, and he shall go out the same way.

ח וּבְבוֹא הַנָּשִׂיא דֶּרֶךְ אוּלָם הַשַּׁעַר יָבוֹא וּבְדַרְכּוֹ יֵצֵא:

9 But on the fixed occasions, when the common people come before *Hashem*, whoever enters by the north gate to bow low shall leave by the south gate; and whoever enters by the south gate shall leave by the north gate. They shall not go back through the gate by which they came in, but shall go out by the opposite one.

ט וּבְבוֹא עַם־הָאָרֶץ לִפְנֵי יְהֹוָה בַּמּוֹעֲדִים הַבָּא דֶרֶךְ־שַׁעַר צָפוֹן לְהִשְׁתַּחֲוֹת יֵצֵא דֶּרֶךְ־שַׁעַר נֶגֶב וְהַבָּא דֶּרֶךְ־שַׁעַר נֶגֶב יֵצֵא דֶּרֶךְ־שַׁעַר צָפוֹנָה לֹא יָשׁוּב דֶּרֶךְ הַשַּׁעַר אֲשֶׁר־בָּא בוֹ כִּי נִכְחוֹ יצאו [יֵצֵא]:

u-v'-VO am ha-A-retz lif-NAY a-do-NAI ba-mo-a-DEEM ha-BA DE-rekh SHA-ar tza-FON l'-hish-ta-kha-VOT yay-TZAY de-rekh SHA-ar NE-gev v'-ha-BA de-rekh SHA-ar NE-gev yay-TZAY de-rekh SHA-ar tza-FO-nah LO ya-SHUV DE-rekh ha-SHA-ar a-sher BA VO KEE nikh-KHO yay-TZAY

10 And as for the prince, he shall enter with them when they enter and leave when they leave.

י וְהַנָּשִׂיא בְּתוֹכָם בְּבוֹאָם יָבוֹא וּבְצֵאתָם יֵצֵאוּ:

11 On festivals and fixed occasions, the meal offering shall be an *efah* for each bull, an *efah* for each ram, and as much as he wishes for the lambs, with a *hin* of oil for every *efah*.

יא וּבַחַגִּים וּבַמּוֹעֲדִים תִּהְיֶה הַמִּנְחָה אֵיפָה לַפָּר וְאֵיפָה לָאַיִל וְלַכְּבָשִׂים מַתַּת יָדוֹ וְשֶׁמֶן הִין לָאֵיפָה:

12 The gate that faces east shall also be opened for the prince whenever he offers a freewill offering – be it burnt offering or offering of well-being – freely offered to *Hashem*, so that he may offer his burnt offering or his offering of well-being just as he does on the *Shabbat* day. Then he shall leave, and the gate shall be closed after he leaves.

יב וְכִי־יַעֲשֶׂה הַנָּשִׂיא נְדָבָה עוֹלָה אוֹ־שְׁלָמִים נְדָבָה לַיהֹוָה וּפָתַח לוֹ אֶת הַשַּׁעַר הַפֹּנֶה קָדִים וְעָשָׂה אֶת־עֹלָתוֹ וְאֶת־שְׁלָמָיו כַּאֲשֶׁר יַעֲשֶׂה בְּיוֹם הַשַּׁבָּת וְיָצָא וְסָגַר אֶת־הַשַּׁעַר אַחֲרֵי צֵאתוֹ:

13 Each day you shall offer a lamb of the first year without blemish, as a daily burnt offering to *Hashem*; you shall offer one every morning.

יג וְכֶבֶשׂ בֶּן־שְׁנָתוֹ תָּמִים תַּעֲשֶׂה עוֹלָה לַיּוֹם לַיהֹוָה בַּבֹּקֶר בַּבֹּקֶר תַּעֲשֶׂה אֹתוֹ:

Ancient pilgrim stairs leading up to the southern wall of the Temple Mount

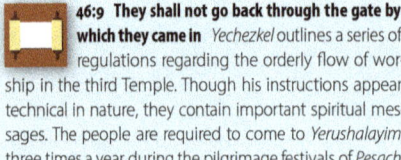

46:9 They shall not go back through the gate by which they came in *Yechezkel* outlines a series of regulations regarding the orderly flow of worship in the third Temple. Though his instructions appear technical in nature, they contain important spiritual messages. The people are required to come to *Yerushalayim* three times a year during the pilgrimage festivals of *Pesach*, *Shavuot*, and *Sukkot*. All pilgrims were expected to leave the *Beit Hamikdash* courtyard from the gate on the opposite side from where they had entered. One suggestion to explain this procedure is that it incorporates a sense of variety, so that worshippers at the Holy Temple will feel enhanced excitement as they enter, and even as they exit, the complex.

14 And every morning regularly you shall offer a meal offering with it: a sixth of an *efah*, with a third of a *hin* of oil to moisten the choice flour, as a meal offering to *Hashem* – a law for all time.

יד וּמִנְחָה תַעֲשֶׂה עָלָיו בַּבֹּקֶר בַּבֹּקֶר שִׁשִּׁית הָאֵיפָה וְשֶׁמֶן שְׁלִישִׁית הַהִין לָרֹס אֶת־הַסֹּלֶת מִנְחָה לַיהוָה חֻקּוֹת עוֹלָם תָּמִיד:

15 The lamb, the meal offering, and oil shall be presented every morning as a regular burnt offering.

טו ועשו [יַעֲשׂוּ] אֶת־הַכֶּבֶשׂ וְאֶת־הַמִּנְחָה וְאֶת־הַשֶּׁמֶן בַּבֹּקֶר בַּבֹּקֶר עוֹלַת תָּמִיד:

16 Thus said *Hashem*: If the prince makes a gift to any of his sons, it shall become the latter's inheritance; it shall pass on to his sons; it is their holding by inheritance.

טז כֹּה־אָמַר אֲדֹנָי יְהוִֹה כִּי־יִתֵּן הַנָּשִׂיא מַתָּנָה לְאִישׁ מִבָּנָיו נַחֲלָתוֹ הִיא לְבָנָיו תִּהְיֶה אֲחֻזָּתָם הִיא בְּנַחֲלָה:

17 But if he makes a gift from his inheritance to any of his subjects, it shall only belong to the latter until the year of release. Then it shall revert to the prince; his inheritance must by all means pass on to his sons.

יז וְכִי־יִתֵּן מַתָּנָה מִנַּחֲלָתוֹ לְאַחַד מֵעֲבָדָיו וְהָיְתָה לּוֹ עַד־שְׁנַת הַדְּרוֹר וְשָׁבַת לַנָּשִׂיא אַךְ נַחֲלָתוֹ בָּנָיו לָהֶם תִּהְיֶה:

18 But the prince shall not take property away from any of the people and rob them of their holdings. Only out of his own holdings shall he endow his sons, in order that My people may not be dispossessed of their holdings.

יח וְלֹא־יִקַּח הַנָּשִׂיא מִנַּחֲלַת הָעָם לְהוֹנֹתָם מֵאֲחֻזָּתָם מֵאֲחֻזָּתוֹ יַנְחִל אֶת־בָּנָיו לְמַעַן אֲשֶׁר לֹא־יָפֻצוּ עַמִּי אִישׁ מֵאֲחֻזָּתוֹ:

19 Then he led me into the passage at the side of the gate to the sacred chambers of the *Kohanim*, which face north, and there, at the rear of it, in the west, I saw a space.

יט וַיְבִיאֵנִי בַמָּבוֹא אֲשֶׁר עַל־כֶּתֶף הַשַּׁעַר אֶל־הַלִּשְׁכוֹת הַקֹּדֶשׁ אֶל־הַכֹּהֲנִים הַפֹּנוֹת צָפוֹנָה וְהִנֵּה־שָׁם מָקוֹם בירכתם [בַּיַּרְכָתַיִם] יָמָּה:

20 He said to me, "This is the place where the *Kohanim* shall boil the guilt offerings and the sin offerings, and where they shall bake the meal offerings, so as not to take them into the outer court and make the people consecrated."

כ וַיֹּאמֶר אֵלַי זֶה הַמָּקוֹם אֲשֶׁר יְבַשְּׁלוּ־שָׁם הַכֹּהֲנִים אֶת־הָאָשָׁם וְאֶת־הַחַטָּאת אֲשֶׁר יֹאפוּ אֶת־הַמִּנְחָה לְבִלְתִּי הוֹצִיא אֶל־הֶחָצֵר הַחִיצוֹנָה לְקַדֵּשׁ אֶת־הָעָם:

21 Then he led me into the outer court and led me past the four corners of the court; and in each corner of the court there was an enclosure.

כא וַיּוֹצִיאֵנִי אֶל־הֶחָצֵר הַחִיצֹנָה וַיַּעֲבִירֵנִי אֶל־אַרְבַּעַת מִקְצוֹעֵי הֶחָצֵר וְהִנֵּה חָצֵר בְּמִקְצֹעַ הֶחָצֵר חָצֵר בְּמִקְצֹעַ הֶחָצֵר:

22 These unroofed enclosures, [each] 40 [*amot*] long and 30 wide, were in the four corners of the court; the four corner enclosures had the same measurements.

כב בְּאַרְבַּעַת מִקְצֹעוֹת הֶחָצֵר חֲצֵרוֹת קְטֻרוֹת אַרְבָּעִים אֹרֶךְ וּשְׁלֹשִׁים רֹחַב מִדָּה אַחַת לְאַרְבַּעְתָּם מְהֻקְצָעוֹת:

23 [On the inside,] running round the four of them, there was a row of masonry, equipped with hearths under the rows all around.

כג וְטוּר סָבִיב בָּהֶם סָבִיב לְאַרְבַּעְתָּם וּמְבַשְּׁלוֹת עָשׂוּי מִתַּחַת הַטִּירוֹת סָבִיב:

24 He said to me, "These are the kitchens where the Temple servitors shall boil the sacrifices of the people."

כד וַיֹּאמֶר אֵלַי אֵלֶּה בֵּית הַמְבַשְּׁלִים אֲשֶׁר יְבַשְּׁלוּ־שָׁם מְשָׁרְתֵי הַבַּיִת אֶת־זֶבַח הָעָם:

47 1 He led me back to the entrance of the Temple, and I found that water was issuing from below the platform of the Temple – eastward, since the Temple faced east – but the water was running out at the south of the *Mizbayach,* under the south wall of the Temple.

א וַיְשִׁבֵנִי אֶל־פֶּתַח הַבַּיִת וְהִנֵּה־מַיִם יֹצְאִים מִתַּחַת מִפְתַּן הַבַּיִת קָדִימָה כִּי־פְנֵי הַבַּיִת קָדִים וְהַמַּיִם יֹרְדִים מִתַּחַת מִכֶּתֶף הַבַּיִת הַיְמָנִית מִנֶּגֶב לַמִּזְבֵּחַ:

2 Then he led me out by way of the northern gate and led me around to the outside of the outer gate that faces in the direction of the east; and I found that water was gushing from [under] the south wall.

ב וַיּוֹצִאֵנִי דֶּרֶךְ־שַׁעַר צָפוֹנָה וַיְסִבֵּנִי דֶּרֶךְ חוּץ אֶל־שַׁעַר הַחוּץ דֶּרֶךְ הַפּוֹנֶה קָדִים וְהִנֵּה־מַיִם מְפַכִּים מִן־הַכָּתֵף הַיְמָנִית:

3 As the man went on eastward with a measuring line in his hand, he measured off a thousand *amot* and led me across the water; the water was ankle deep.

ג בְּצֵאת־הָאִישׁ קָדִים וְקָו בְּיָדוֹ וַיָּמָד אֶלֶף בָּאַמָּה וַיַּעֲבִרֵנִי בַמַּיִם מֵי אָפְסָיִם:

4 Then he measured off another thousand and led me across the water; the water was knee deep. He measured off a further thousand and led me across the water; the water was up to the waist.

ד וַיָּמָד אֶלֶף וַיַּעֲבִרֵנִי בַמַּיִם מַיִם בִּרְכָּיִם וַיָּמָד אֶלֶף וַיַּעֲבִרֵנִי מֵי מָתְנָיִם:

5 When he measured yet another thousand, it was a stream I could not cross; for the water had swollen into a stream that could not be crossed except by swimming.

ה וַיָּמָד אֶלֶף נַחַל אֲשֶׁר לֹא־אוּכַל לַעֲבֹר כִּי־גָאוּ הַמַּיִם מֵי שָׂחוּ נַחַל אֲשֶׁר לֹא־יֵעָבֵר:

6 "Do you see, O mortal?" he said to me; and he led me back to the bank of the stream.

ו וַיֹּאמֶר אֵלַי הֲרָאִיתָ בֶן־אָדָם וַיּוֹלִכֵנִי וַיְשִׁבֵנִי שְׂפַת הַנָּחַל:

7 As I came back, I saw trees in great profusion on both banks of the stream.

ז בְּשׁוּבֵנִי וְהִנֵּה אֶל־שְׂפַת הַנַּחַל עֵץ רַב מְאֹד מִזֶּה וּמִזֶּה:

8 "This water," he told me, "runs out to the eastern region, and flows into the Arabah; and when it comes into the sea, into the sea of foul waters, the water will become wholesome.

ח וַיֹּאמֶר אֵלַי הַמַּיִם הָאֵלֶּה יוֹצְאִים אֶל־הַגְּלִילָה הַקַּדְמוֹנָה וְיָרְדוּ עַל־הָעֲרָבָה וּבָאוּ הַיָּמָּה אֶל־הַיָּמָּה הַמּוּצָאִים וְנִרְפְּאוּ [וְנִרְפּוּ] הַמָּיִם:

9 Every living creature that swarms will be able to live wherever this stream goes; the fish will be very abundant once these waters have reached there. It will be wholesome, and everything will live wherever this stream goes.

ט וְהָיָה כָל־נֶפֶשׁ חַיָּה אֲשֶׁר־יִשְׁרֹץ אֶל כָּל־אֲשֶׁר יָבוֹא שָׁם נַחֲלַיִם יִחְיֶה וְהָיָה הַדָּגָה רַבָּה מְאֹד כִּי בָאוּ שָׁמָּה הַמַּיִם הָאֵלֶּה וְיֵרָפְאוּ וָחָי כֹּל אֲשֶׁר־יָבוֹא שָׁמָּה הַנָּחַל:

10 Fishermen shall stand beside it all the way from *Ein Gedi* to En-eglaim; it shall be a place for drying nets; and the fish will be of various kinds [and] most plentiful, like the fish of the Great Sea.

י וְהָיָה יעמדו [עָמְדוּ] עָלָיו דַּוָּגִים מֵעֵין גֶּדִי וְעַד־עֵין עֶגְלַיִם מִשְׁטוֹחַ לַחֲרָמִים יִהְיוּ לְמִינָה תִּהְיֶה דְגָתָם כִּדְגַת הַיָּם הַגָּדוֹל רַבָּה מְאֹד:

11 But its swamps and marshes shall not become wholesome; they will serve to [supply] salt.

יא בצאתו [בִּצֹּאתָיו] וּגְבָאָיו וְלֹא יֵרָפְאוּ לְמֶלַח נִתָּנוּ:

12 All kinds of trees for food will grow up on both banks of the stream. Their leaves will not wither nor their fruit fail; they will yield new fruit every month, because the water for them flows from the Temple. Their fruit will serve for food and their leaves for healing."

יב וְעַל־הַנַּחַל יַעֲלֶה עַל־שְׂפָתוֹ מִזֶּה וּמִזֶּה כָּל־עֵץ־מַאֲכָל לֹא־יִבּוֹל עָלֵהוּ וְלֹא־יִתֹּם פִּרְיוֹ לֶחֳדָשָׁיו יְבַכֵּר כִּי מֵימָיו מִן־הַמִּקְדָּשׁ הֵמָּה יוֹצְאִים וְהָיוּ [וְהָיָה] פִּרְיוֹ לְמַאֲכָל וְעָלֵהוּ לִתְרוּפָה:

13 Thus said *Hashem*: These shall be the boundaries of the land that you shall allot to the twelve tribes of *Yisrael*. *Yosef* shall receive two portions,

יג כֹּה אָמַר אֲדֹנָי יֱהֹוִה גֵּה גְבוּל אֲשֶׁר תִּתְנַחֲלוּ אֶת־הָאָרֶץ לִשְׁנֵי עָשָׂר שִׁבְטֵי יִשְׂרָאֵל יוֹסֵף חֲבָלִים:

14 and you shall share the rest equally. As I swore to give it to your fathers, so shall this land fall to you as your heritage.

יד וּנְחַלְתֶּם אוֹתָהּ אִישׁ כְּאָחִיו אֲשֶׁר נָשָׂאתִי אֶת־יָדִי לְתִתָּהּ לַאֲבֹתֵיכֶם וְנָפְלָה הָאָרֶץ הַזֹּאת לָכֶם בְּנַחֲלָה:

un-khal-TEM o-TAH EESH k'-a-KHEEV a-SHER na-SA-tee et ya-DEE l'-ti-TAH la-a-vo-tay-KHEM v'-NA-f'-LAH ha-A-retz ha-ZOT la-KHEM b'-na-kha-LAH

15 These are the boundaries of the land: As the northern limit: From the Great Sea by way of Hethlon, Lebo-hamath,* Zedad,

טו וְזֶה גְּבוּל הָאָרֶץ לִפְאַת צָפוֹנָה מִן־הַיָּם הַגָּדוֹל הַדֶּרֶךְ חֶתְלֹן לְבוֹא צְדָדָה:

16 Berathah, Sibraim – which lies between the border of Damascus and the border of Hamath – [down to] Hazer-hatticon, which is on the border of Hauran.

טז חֲמָת בֵּרוֹתָה סִבְרַיִם אֲשֶׁר בֵּין־גְּבוּל דַּמֶּשֶׂק וּבֵין גְּבוּל חֲמָת חָצֵר הַתִּיכוֹן אֲשֶׁר אֶל־גְּבוּל חַוְרָן:

17 Thus the boundary shall run from the Sea to Hazar-enon, to the north of the territory of Damascus, with the territory of Hamath to the north of it. That shall be the northern limit.

יז וְהָיָה גְבוּל מִן־הַיָּם חֲצַר עֵינוֹן גְּבוּל דַּמֶּשֶׂק וְצָפוֹן צָפוֹנָה וּגְבוּל חֲמָת וְאֵת פְּאַת צָפוֹן:

18 As the eastern limit: A line between Hauran and Damascus, and between *Gilad* and the land of *Yisrael*: with the *Yarden* as a boundary, you shall measure down to the Eastern Sea. That shall be the eastern limit.

יח וּפְאַת קָדִים מִבֵּין חַוְרָן וּמִבֵּין־דַּמֶּשֶׂק וּמִבֵּין הַגִּלְעָד וּמִבֵּין אֶרֶץ יִשְׂרָאֵל הַיַּרְדֵּן מִגְּבוּל עַל־הַיָּם הַקַּדְמוֹנִי תָּמֹדּוּ וְאֵת פְּאַת קָדִימָה:

19 The southern limit shall run: A line from Tamar to the waters of Meriboth-kadesh, along the Wadi [of Egypt and] the Great Sea. That is the southern limit.

יט וּפְאַת נֶגֶב תֵּימָנָה מִתָּמָר עַד־מֵי מְרִיבוֹת קָדֵשׁ נַחֲלָה אֶל־הַיָּם הַגָּדוֹל וְאֵת פְּאַת־תֵּימָנָה נֶגְבָּה:

20 And as the western limit: The Great Sea shall be the boundary up to a point opposite Lebo-hamath. That shall be the western limit.

כ וּפְאַת־יָם הַיָּם הַגָּדוֹל מִגְּבוּל עַד־נֹכַח לְבוֹא חֲמָת זֹאת פְּאַת־יָם:

---

* "hamath" brought up from verse 16 for clarity

נַחֲלָה
נַחַל

47:14 So shall this land fall to you as your heritage In biblical Hebrew, the word for 'inheritance' is *nachalah* (נחלה). The root of this word, *nakhal* (נחל), also means 'a flowing stream', as in *Devarim* (8:7), "a land with streams and springs and fountains." These two ideas are connected: Just like a stream of water flows downward, so too, the inheritance of a precious legacy passes from one generation to the next. Such is the connection between the Children of Israel and the Land of Israel. Their inheritance was given to *Avraham* to be passed down to *Yitzchak* and to all subsequent generations.

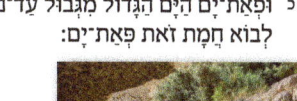

Nachal Arugot, the Arugot stream, in Ein Gedi

21 This land you shall divide for yourselves among the tribes of *Yisrael*.

וְחִלַּקְתֶּם אֶת־הָאָרֶץ הַזֹּאת לָכֶם לְשִׁבְטֵי יִשְׂרָאֵל: כא

22 You shall allot it as a heritage for yourselves and for the strangers who reside among you, who have begotten children among you. You shall treat them as Israelite citizens; they shall receive allotments along with you among the tribes of *Yisrael*.

וְהָיָה תַּפִּלוּ אוֹתָהּ בְּנַחֲלָה לָכֶם וּלְהַגֵּרִים הַגָּרִים בְּתוֹכְכֶם אֲשֶׁר־הוֹלִדוּ בָנִים בְּתוֹכְכֶם וְהָיוּ לָכֶם כְּאֶזְרָח בִּבְנֵי יִשְׂרָאֵל אִתְּכֶם יִפְּלוּ בְנַחֲלָה בְּתוֹךְ שִׁבְטֵי יִשְׂרָאֵל: כב

23 You shall give the stranger an allotment within the tribe where he resides – declares *Hashem*.

וְהָיָה בַשֵּׁבֶט אֲשֶׁר־גָּר הַגֵּר אִתּוֹ שָׁם תִּתְּנוּ נַחֲלָתוֹ נְאֻם אֲדֹנָי יֱהֹוִה: כג

48 1 These are the names of the tribes: At the northern end, along the Hethlon road, [from] Lebo-hamath to Hazar-enan – which is the border of Damascus, with Hamath to the north – from the eastern border to the Sea: *Dan* – one [tribe].

וְאֵלֶּה שְׁמוֹת הַשְּׁבָטִים מִקְצֵה צָפוֹנָה אֶל־יַד דֶּרֶךְ־חֶתְלֹן לְבוֹא־חֲמָת חֲצַר עֵינָן גְּבוּל דַּמֶּשֶׂק צָפוֹנָה אֶל־יַד חֲמָת וְהָיוּ־לוֹ פְאַת־קָדִים הַיָּם דָּן אֶחָד: **מח** א

v'-AY-leh sh'-MOT ha-sh'-va-TEEM mik-TZAY tza-FO-nah el YAD de-rekh khet-LON l'-vo kha-MAT kha-TZAR ay-NAN g'-VUL da-ME-sek tza-FO-nah el YAD kha-MAT v'-ha-yu LO f'-at ka-DEEM ha-YAM DAN e-KHAD

2 Adjoining the territory of *Dan*, from the eastern border to the western border: *Asher* – one.

וְעַל גְּבוּל דָּן מִפְּאַת קָדִים עַד־פְּאַת־יָמָה אָשֵׁר אֶחָד: ב

3 Adjoining the territory of *Asher*, from the eastern border to the western border: *Naftali* – one.

וְעַל גְּבוּל אָשֵׁר מִפְּאַת קָדִימָה וְעַד־פְּאַת־יָמָה נַפְתָּלִי אֶחָד: ג

4 Adjoining the territory of *Naftali*, from the eastern border to the western border: *Menashe* – one.

וְעַל גְּבוּל נַפְתָּלִי מִפְּאַת קָדְמָה עַד־פְּאַת־יָמָה מְנַשֶּׁה אֶחָד: ד

5 Adjoining the territory of *Menashe*, from the eastern border to the western border: *Efraim* – one.

וְעַל גְּבוּל מְנַשֶּׁה מִפְּאַת קָדְמָה עַד־פְּאַת־יָמָה אֶפְרַיִם אֶחָד: ה

6 Adjoining the territory of *Efraim*, from the eastern border to the western border: *Reuven* – one.

וְעַל גְּבוּל אֶפְרַיִם מִפְּאַת קָדִים וְעַד־פְּאַת־יָמָה רְאוּבֵן אֶחָד: ו

7 Adjoining the territory of *Reuven*, from the eastern border to the western border: *Yehuda* – one.

וְעַל גְּבוּל רְאוּבֵן מִפְּאַת קָדִים עַד־פְּאַת־יָמָה יְהוּדָה אֶחָד: ז

8 Adjoining the territory of *Yehuda*, from the eastern border to the western border, shall be the reserve that you set aside: 25,000 [*amot*] in breadth and in length equal to one of the portions from the eastern border to the western border; the Sanctuary shall be in the middle of it.

וְעַל גְּבוּל יְהוּדָה מִפְּאַת קָדִים עַד־פְּאַת־יָמָה תִּהְיֶה הַתְּרוּמָה אֲשֶׁר־תָּרִימוּ חֲמִשָּׁה וְעֶשְׂרִים אֶלֶף רֹחַב וְאֹרֶךְ כְּאַחַד הַחֲלָקִים מִפְּאַת קָדִימָה עַד־פְּאַת־יָמָה וְהָיָה הַמִּקְדָּשׁ בְּתוֹכוֹ: ח

48:1 From the eastern border to the Sea The final chapter of *Yechezkel* begins with the inheritance of the land and apportionment among the twelve tribes. By returning to the tribal arrangement, *Yechezkel* promises a return to traditional family groupings. This final lesson of *Yechezkel* teaches that the viability of Israel's existence in their ancestral land is intimately connected to the strength of the families who dwell within it. When feelings of love permeate and strengthen the families of Israel in *Eretz Yisrael*, then the God of Israel blesses His people and dwells among them in eternal harmony.

A family playing in the snow on Mount Hermon

Ezekiel

9 The reserve that you set aside for *Hashem* shall be 25,000 long and 10,000 wide.

ט הַתְּרוּמָה אֲשֶׁר תָּרִימוּ לַיהוָֹה אֹרֶךְ חֲמִשָּׁה וְעֶשְׂרִים אֶלֶף וְרֹחַב עֲשֶׂרֶת אֲלָפִים:

10 It shall be apportioned to the following: The sacred reserve for the *Kohanim* shall measure 25,000 [*amot*] on the north, 10,000 on the west, 10,000 on the east, and 25,000 on the south, with *Hashem's* Sanctuary in the middle of it.

י וּלְאֵלֶּה תִּהְיֶה תְרוּמַת־הַקֹּדֶשׁ לַכֹּהֲנִים צָפוֹנָה חֲמִשָּׁה וְעֶשְׂרִים אֶלֶף וְיָמָּה רֹחַב עֲשֶׂרֶת אֲלָפִים וְקָדִימָה רֹחַב עֲשֶׂרֶת אֲלָפִים וְנֶגְבָּה אֹרֶךְ חֲמִשָּׁה וְעֶשְׂרִים אָלֶף וְהָיָה מִקְדַּשׁ־יְהוָֹה בְּתוֹכוֹ:

11 This consecrated area shall be for the *Kohanim* of the line of *Tzadok*, who kept My charge and did not go astray, as the *Leviim* did when the people of *Yisrael* went astray.

יא לַכֹּהֲנִים הַמְקֻדָּשׁ מִבְּנֵי צָדוֹק אֲשֶׁר שָׁמְרוּ מִשְׁמַרְתִּי אֲשֶׁר לֹא־תָעוּ בִּתְעוֹת בְּנֵי יִשְׂרָאֵל כַּאֲשֶׁר תָּעוּ הַלְוִיִּם:

12 It shall be a special reserve for them out of the [total] reserve from the land, most holy, adjoining the territory of the *Leviim*.

יב וְהָיְתָה לָהֶם תְּרוּמִיָּה מִתְּרוּמַת הָאָרֶץ קֹדֶשׁ קָדָשִׁים אֶל־גְּבוּל הַלְוִיִּם:

13 Alongside the territory of the *Kohanim*, the *Leviim* shall have [an area] 25,000 long by 10,000 wide; the total length shall be 25,000 and the breadth 10,000.

יג וְהַלְוִיִּם לְעֻמַּת גְּבוּל הַכֹּהֲנִים חֲמִשָּׁה וְעֶשְׂרִים אֶלֶף אֹרֶךְ וְרֹחַב עֲשֶׂרֶת אֲלָפִים כָּל־אֹרֶךְ חֲמִשָּׁה וְעֶשְׂרִים אֶלֶף וְרֹחַב עֲשֶׂרֶת אֲלָפִים:

14 None of it – the choicest of the land – may be sold, exchanged, or transferred; it is sacred to *Hashem*.

יד וְלֹא־יִמְכְּרוּ מִמֶּנּוּ וְלֹא יָמֵר וְלֹא יַעֲבוֹר [יַעֲבִיר] רֵאשִׁית הָאָרֶץ כִּי־קֹדֶשׁ לַיהוָֹה:

15 The remaining 5,000 in breadth by 25,000 shall be for common use – serving the city for dwellings and pasture. The city itself shall be in the middle of it;

טו וַחֲמֵשֶׁת אֲלָפִים הַנּוֹתָר בָּרֹחַב עַל־פְּנֵי חֲמִשָּׁה וְעֶשְׂרִים אֶלֶף חֹל־הוּא לָעִיר לְמוֹשָׁב וּלְמִגְרָשׁ וְהָיְתָה הָעִיר בְּתוֹכֹה [בְּתוֹכוֹ]:

16 and these shall be its measurements: On the north side 4,500 *amot*, on the south side 4,500, on the east side 4,500, and on the west side 4,500.

טז וְאֵלֶּה מִדּוֹתֶיהָ פְּאַת צָפוֹן חֲמֵשׁ מֵאוֹת וְאַרְבַּעַת אֲלָפִים וּפְאַת־נֶגֶב חֲמֵשׁ מֵאוֹת וְאַרְבַּעַת אֲלָפִים וּמִפְּאַת קָדִים חֲמֵשׁ מֵאוֹת וְאַרְבַּעַת אֲלָפִים וּפְאַת־יָמָּה חֲמֵשׁ מֵאוֹת וְאַרְבַּעַת אֲלָפִים:

17 The pasture shall extend 250 *amot* to the north of the city, 250 to the south, 250 to the east, and 250 to the west.

יז וְהָיָה מִגְרָשׁ לָעִיר צָפוֹנָה חֲמִשִּׁים וּמָאתַיִם וְנֶגְבָּה חֲמִשִּׁים וּמָאתָיִם וְקָדִימָה חֲמִשִּׁים וּמָאתַיִם וְיָמָּה חֲמִשִּׁים וּמָאתָיִם:

18 As for the remaining 10,000 to the east and 10,000 to the west, adjoining the long side of the sacred reserve, the produce of these areas adjoining the sacred reserve shall serve as food for the workers in the city;

יח וְהַנּוֹתָר בָּאֹרֶךְ לְעֻמַּת תְּרוּמַת הַקֹּדֶשׁ עֲשֶׂרֶת אֲלָפִים קָדִימָה וַעֲשֶׂרֶת אֲלָפִים יָמָּה וְהָיָה לְעֻמַּת תְּרוּמַת הַקֹּדֶשׁ וְהָיְתָה תְבוּאָתֹה [תְבוּאָתוֹ] לְלֶחֶם לְעֹבְדֵי הָעִיר:

19 the workers in the city from all the tribes of *Yisrael* shall cultivate it.

יט וְהָעֹבֵד הָעִיר יַעַבְדוּהוּ מִכֹּל שִׁבְטֵי יִשְׂרָאֵל:

Ezekiel

20 The entire reserve, 25,000 square, you shall set aside as the sacred reserve plus the city property.

כ כָּל־הַתְּרוּמָה חֲמִשָּׁה וְעֶשְׂרִים אֶלֶף בַּחֲמִשָּׁה וְעֶשְׂרִים אֶלֶף רְבִיעִית תָּרִימוּ אֶת־תְּרוּמַת הַקֹּדֶשׁ אֶל־אֲחֻזַּת הָעִיר:

21 What remains on either side of the sacred reserve and the city property shall belong to the prince. The prince shall own [the land] from the border of the 25,000 of the reserve up to the eastern boundary, and from the border of the 25,000 on the west up to the western boundary, corresponding to the [tribal] portions. The sacred reserve, with the Temple Sanctuary in the middle of it

כא וְהַנּוֹתָר לַנָּשִׂיא מִזֶּה וּמִזֶּה לִתְרוּמַת־ הַקֹּדֶשׁ וְלַאֲחֻזַּת הָעִיר אֶל־פְּנֵי חֲמִשָּׁה וְעֶשְׂרִים אֶלֶף תְּרוּמָה עַד־גְּבוּל קָדִימָה וְיָמָּה עַל־פְּנֵי חֲמִשָּׁה וְעֶשְׂרִים אֶלֶף עַל־ גְּבוּל יָמָּה לְעֻמַּת חֲלָקִים לַנָּשִׂיא וְהָיְתָה תְּרוּמַת הַקֹּדֶשׁ וּמִקְדַּשׁ הַבַּיִת בְּתוֹכה [בְּתוֹכוֹ:]

22 and the property of the *Leviim* and the city property as well, shall be in the middle of the [area belonging] to the prince; [the rest of the land] between the territory of *Yehuda* and the territory of *Binyamin* shall belong to the prince.

כב וּמֵאֲחֻזַּת הַלְוִיִּם וּמֵאֲחֻזַּת הָעִיר בְּתוֹךְ אֲשֶׁר לַנָּשִׂיא יִהְיֶה בֵּין גְּבוּל יְהוּדָה וּבֵין גְּבוּל בִּנְיָמִן לַנָּשִׂיא יִהְיֶה:

23 As for the remaining tribes: From the eastern border to the western border: *Binyamin* – one.

כג וְיֶתֶר הַשְּׁבָטִים מִפְּאַת קָדִימָה עַד־ פְּאַת־יָמָּה בִּנְיָמִן אֶחָד:

24 Adjoining the territory of *Binyamin*, from the eastern border to the western border: *Shimon* – one.

כד וְעַל גְּבוּל בִּנְיָמִן מִפְּאַת קָדִימָה עַד־ פְּאַת־יָמָּה שִׁמְעוֹן אֶחָד:

25 Adjoining the territory of *Shimon*, from the eastern border to the western border: *Yissachar* – one.

כה וְעַל גְּבוּל שִׁמְעוֹן מִפְּאַת קָדִימָה עַד־ פְּאַת־יָמָּה יִשָּׂשכָר אֶחָד:

26 Adjoining the territory of *Yissachar*, from the eastern border to the western border: *Zevulun* – one.

כו וְעַל גְּבוּל יִשָּׂשכָר מִפְּאַת קָדִימָה עַד־ פְּאַת־יָמָּה זְבוּלֻן אֶחָד:

27 Adjoining the territory of *Zevulun*, from the eastern border to the western border: *Gad* – one.

כז וְעַל גְּבוּל זְבוּלֻן מִפְּאַת קָדְמָה עַד־ פְּאַת־יָמָּה גָּד אֶחָד:

28 The other border of *Gad* shall be the southern boundary. This boundary shall run from *Tamar* to the waters of Meribath-kadesh, to the Wadi [of Egypt], and to the Great Sea.

כח וְעַל גְּבוּל גָּד אֶל־פְּאַת נֶגֶב תֵּימָנָה וְהָיָה גְבוּל מִתָּמָר מֵי מְרִיבַת קָדֵשׁ נַחֲלָה עַל־הַיָּם הַגָּדוֹל:

29 That is the land which you shall allot as a heritage to the tribes of *Yisrael*, and those are their portions – declares *Hashem*.

כט זֹאת הָאָרֶץ אֲשֶׁר־תַּפִּילוּ מִנַּחֲלָה לְשִׁבְטֵי יִשְׂרָאֵל וְאֵלֶּה מַחְלְקוֹתָם נְאֻם אֲדֹנָי יֱהוִֹה:

30 And these are the exits from the city: On its northern side, measuring 4,500 *amot*,

ל וְאֵלֶּה תּוֹצְאֹת הָעִיר מִפְּאַת צָפוֹן חֲמֵשׁ מֵאוֹת וְאַרְבַּעַת אֲלָפִים מִדָּה:

31 the gates of the city shall be – three gates on the north – named for the tribes of *Yisrael*: the *Reuven* Gate: one; the *Yehuda* Gate: one; the *Levi* Gate: one.

לא וְשַׁעֲרֵי הָעִיר עַל־שְׁמוֹת שִׁבְטֵי יִשְׂרָאֵל שְׁעָרִים שְׁלוֹשָׁה צָפוֹנָה שַׁעַר רְאוּבֵן אֶחָד שַׁעַר יְהוּדָה אֶחָד שַׁעַר לֵוִי אֶחָד:

32 On the eastern side, [measuring] 4,500 *amot* – there shall be three gates: the *Yosef* Gate: one; the *Binyamin* Gate: one; and the *Dan* Gate: one.

לב וְאֶל־פְּאַת קָדִימָה חֲמֵשׁ מֵאוֹת וְאַרְבַּעַת אֲלָפִים וּשְׁעָרִים שְׁלֹשָׁה וְשַׁעַר יוֹסֵף אֶחָד שַׁעַר בִּנְיָמִן אֶחָד שַׁעַר דָּן אֶחָד׃

33 On the southern side, measuring 4,500 *amot*, there shall be three gates: the *Shimon* Gate: one; the *Yissachar* Gate: one; and the *Zevulun* Gate: one.

לג וּפְאַת־נֶגְבָּה חֲמֵשׁ מֵאוֹת וְאַרְבַּעַת אֲלָפִים מִדָּה וּשְׁעָרִים שְׁלֹשָׁה שַׁעַר שִׁמְעוֹן אֶחָד שַׁעַר יִשָּׂשכָר אֶחָד שַׁעַר זְבוּלֻן אֶחָד׃

34 And on the western side, [measuring] 4,500 *amot* – there shall be three gates: the *Gad* Gate: one; the *Asher* Gate: one; the *Naftali* Gate: one.

לד פְּאַת־יָמָּה חֲמֵשׁ מֵאוֹת וְאַרְבַּעַת אֲלָפִים שַׁעֲרֵיהֶם שְׁלֹשָׁה שַׁעַר גָּד אֶחָד שַׁעַר אָשֵׁר אֶחָד שַׁעַר נַפְתָּלִי אֶחָד׃

35 Its circumference [shall be] 18,000 [*amot*]; and the name of the city from that day on shall be "*Hashem* Is There."

לה סָבִיב שְׁמֹנָה עָשָׂר אָלֶף וְשֵׁם־הָעִיר מִיּוֹם יְהֹוָה שָׁמָּה׃

List of Transliterated Words in *The Israel Bible*

The following is a list of nouns which have been transliterated into Hebrew in the English translation and commentary of *The Israel Bible*:

Hebrew Name	English Name	Pronunciation	Hebrew
Achan	Achan	a-KHAN	עָכָן
Achav	Ahab	akh-AV	אַחְאָב
Achaz	Ahaz	a-KHAZ	אָחָז
Achazyahu	Ahaziah	a-khaz-YA-hu	אֲחַזְיָהוּ
Achiezer	Ahiezer	a-khee-E-zer	אֲחִיעֶזֶר
Achihud	Ahihud	a-khee-HUD	אֲחִיהוּד
Achikam	Ahikam	a-khee-KAM	אֲחִיקָם
Achilud	Ahilud	a-khee-LUD	אֲחִילוּד
Achimelech	Ahimelech	a-khee-ME-lekh	אֲחִימֶלֶךְ
Achira	Ahira	a-khee-RA	אֲחִירַע
Achisamach	Ahisamach	a-khee-sa-MAKH	אֲחִיסָמָךְ
Achitofel	Ahithophel	a-khee-TO-fel	אֲחִיתֹפֶל
Achituv	Ahitub	a-khee-TUV	אֲחִיטוּב
Achiya	Ahijah	a-khi-YAH	אֲחִיָּה
Adam	Adam	a-DAM	אָדָם
Adar	Adar	a-DAR	אֲדָר
Adoniyahu	Adonijah	a-do-ni-YA-hu	אֲדֹנִיָּהוּ
Adulam	Adullam	a-du-LAM	עֲדֻלָּם
Agur	Agur	a-GUR	אָגוּר
Aharon	Aaron	a-ha-RON	אַהֲרֹן
Amasa	Amasa	a-ma-SA	עֲמָשָׂא
Amatzya	Amaziah	a-matz-YAH	אֲמַצְיָה
Amen	Amen	a-MAYN	אָמֵן
Amiel	Ammiel	a-mee-AYL	עַמִּיאֵל
Aminadav	Amminadab	a-mee-na-DAV	עַמִּינָדָב
Amitai	Amittai	a-mi-TAI	אֲמִתַּי
Amnon	Amnon	am-NON	אַמְנֹן

Hebrew Name	English Name	Pronunciation	Hebrew
Amon	Amon	a-MON	אָמוֹן
Amos	Amos	a-MOS	עָמוֹס
Amotz	Amoz	a-MOTZ	אָמוֹץ
Amram	Amram	am-RAM	עַמְרָם
Anatot	Anathoth	a-na-TOT	עֲנָתוֹת
Aron	Ark	a-RON	אָרוֹן
Aron HaBrit	Ark of the Covenant	a-RON ha-b'-REET	אָרוֹן הַבְּרִית
Arpachshad	Arpachshad	ar-pakh-SHAD	אַרְפַּכְשַׁד
Asa	Asa	a-SA	אָסָא
Asael	Asahel	a-sah-AYL	עֲשָׂהאֵל
Asaf	Asaph	a-SAF	אָסָף
Ashdod	Ashdod	ash-DOD	אַשְׁדּוֹד
Asher	Asher	a-SHAYR	אָשֵׁר
Ashkelon	Ashkelon	ash-k'-LON	אַשְׁקְלוֹן
Atalya	Athaliah	a-tal-YAH	עֲתַלְיָה
Avdon	Abdon	av-DON	עַבְדּוֹן
Avichayil	Abihail	a-vee-KHA-yil	אֲבִיחַיִל
Avidan	Abidan	a-vee-DAN	אֲבִידָן
Avigail	Abigail	a-vee-GA-yil	אֲבִיגַיִל
Avihu	Abihu	a-vee-HU	אֲבִיהוּא
Avimelech	Abimelech	a-vee-ME-lekh	אֲבִימֶלֶךְ
Avinadav	Abinadab	a-vee-na-DAV	אֲבִינָדָב
Aviram	Abiram	a-vee-RAM	אֲבִירָם
Avishai	Abishai	a-vee-SHAI	אֲבִישַׁי
Aviya	Abijah	a-vi-YAH	אֲבִיָּה
Aviyam	Abijam	a-vi-YAM	אֲבִיָם
Avner	Abner	av-NAYR	אַבְנֵר
Avraham	Abraham	av-ra-HAM	אַבְרָהָם
Avram	Abram	av-RAM	אַבְרָם
Avshalom	Absalom	av-sha-LOM	אַבְשָׁלוֹם
Azarya	Azariah	a-zar-YAH	עֲזַרְיָה
Azeika	Azekah	a-zay-KAH	עֲזֵקָה
Azza	Gaza	a-ZAH	עַזָּה

Hebrew Name	English Name	Pronunciation	Hebrew
B'nei Yisrael	The Children of Israel	b'-NAY yis-ra-AYL	בְּנֵי יִשְׂרָאֵל
Barak	Barak	ba-rakh-AYL	בָּרָק
Baruch	Baruch	ba-RUKH	בָּרוּךְ
Barzilai	Barzillai	bar-zi-LAI	בַּרְזִלַּי
Basha	Baasa	ba-SHA	בַּעְשָׁא
Batsheva	Bath-sheba	bat-SHE-va	בַּת־שֶׁבַע
Be'er Sheva	Beer-sheba	b'-AYR SHE-va	בְּאֵר שֶׁבַע
Be'eri	Beeri	b'-ay-REE	בְּאֵרִי
Beit Aven	Beth-aven	bayt A-ven	בֵּית אָוֶן
Beit El	Beth-el	bayt el	בֵּית אֵל
Beit Hamikdash	Temple	bayt ha-mik-DASH	בֵּית הַמִּקְדָּשׁ
Beit Lechem	Beth-lehem	bayt LE-khem	בֵּית לֶחֶם
Beit Shean	Beth-shean	bayt sh'-AN	בֵּית שְׁאָן
Beit Shemesh	Beth-shemesh	bayt SHE-mesh	בֵּית שֶׁמֶשׁ
Berechya	Berechiah	be-rekh-YAH	בֶּרֶכְיָה
Betzalel	Bezalel	b'-tzal-AYL	בְּצַלְאֵל
Bilha	Bilhah	bil-HAH	בִּלְהָה
Binyamin	Benjamin	bin-ya-MIN	בִּנְיָמִין
Boaz	Boaz	BO-az	בֹּעַז
Buki	Bukki	bu-KEE	בֻּקִּי
Buzi	Buzi	bu-ZEE	בּוּזִי
Carmel	Carmel	kar-MEL	כַּרְמֶל
Chachalya	Hacaliah	kha-khal-YAH	חֲכַלְיָה
Chagai	Haggai	kha-GAI	חַגַּי
Chana	Hannah	kha-NAH	חַנָּה
Chanamel	Hanamel	kha-nam-AYL	חֲנַמְאֵל
Chanani	Hanani	kha-NA-nee	חֲנָנִי
Chananya	Hananiah	kha-nan-YAH	חֲנַנְיָה
Chaniel	Hanniel	kha-nee-AYL	חַנִּיאֵל
Chanoch	Enoch	kha-NOKH	חֲנוֹךְ
Chava	Eve	kha-VAH	חַוָּה
Chavakuk	Habakkuk	kha-va-KUK	חֲבַקּוּק
Chermon	Hermon	kher-MON	חֶרְמוֹן

Hebrew Name	English Name	Pronunciation	Hebrew
Chetzron	Hezron	khetz-RON	חֶצְרוֹן
Chever	Heber	KHE-ver	חֶבֶר
Chevron	Hebron	khev-RON	חֶבְרוֹן
Chilkiyahu	Hilkiah	khil-ki-YA-hu	חִלְקִיָּהוּ
Chizkiyahu	Hezekiah	khiz-ki-YA-hu	חִזְקִיָּהוּ
Chofni	Hophni	khof-NEE	חָפְנִי
Chogla	Hoglah	khog-LAH	חָגְלָה
Chulda	Hulda	khul-DAH	חֻלְדָּה
Chur	Hur	Khur	חוּר
Dan	Dan	Dan	דָּן
Daniel	Daniel	da-ni-YAYL	דָּנִיֵּאל
Datan	Dathan	da-TAN	דָּתָן
David	David	da-VID	דָּוִד
Devora	Deborah	d'-vo-RAH	דְּבוֹרָה
Dina	Dinah	DEE-nah	דִּינָה
Doeg Ha'adomi	Doeg the Edomite	do-AYG ha-a-do-MEE	דּוֹאֵג הָאֲדֹמִי
Efraim	Ephraim	ef-RA-yim	אֶפְרַיִם
Efrat	Ephrat	ef-RAT	אֶפְרָתָה
Efrat	Ephrathah	ef-RA-tah	אֶפְרָתָה
Ehud	Ehud	ay-HUD	אֵהוּד
Eila	Elah	AY-lah	אֵלָה
Eilon	Elon	ay-LON	אֵילוֹן
Ein Gedi	En-gedi	ayn GE-dee	עֵין גֶּדִי
Elazar	Eleazar	el-a-ZAR	אֶלְעָזָר
Elchanan	Elhanan	el-kha-NAN	אֶלְחָנָן
Eli	Eli	ay-LEE	עֵלִי
Eliav	Eliab	e-lee-AV	אֱלִיאָב
Elidad	Elidad	e-lee-DAD	אֱלִידָד
Eliezer	Eliezer	e-lee-E-zer	אֱלִיעֶזֶר
Elimelech	Elimelech	e-lee-ME-lekh	אֱלִימֶלֶךְ
Elisha	Elisha	e-lee-SHA	אֱלִישָׁע
Elishama	Elishama	e-lee-sha-MA	אֱלִישָׁמָע
Elisheva	Elisheba	e-lee-SHE-va	אֱלִישֶׁבַע

Hebrew Name	English Name	Pronunciation	Hebrew
Elitzafan	Eli-zaphan	e-lee-tza-FAN	אֱלִיצָפָן
Elitzur	Elizur	e-lee-TZUR	אֱלִיצוּר
Eliyahu	Elijah	ay-li-YA-hu	אֵלִיָּהוּ
Elkana	Elkanah	el-ka-NAH	אֶלְקָנָה
Elyasaf	Eliasaph	el-ya-SAF	אֶלְיָסָף
Elyashiv	Eliashib	el-ya-SHEEV	אֶלְיָשִׁיב
Enosh	Enosh	e-NOSH	אֱנוֹשׁ
Er	Er	ayr	עֵר
Eshtaol	Eshtaol	esh-ta-OL	אֶשְׁתָּאֹל
Esther	Esther	es-TAYR	אֶסְתֵּר
Eved Melech	Ebed-melech	E-ved ME-lekh	עֶבֶד־מֶלֶךְ
Even Ha-Ezer	Eben-Ezer	E-ven ha-E-zer	אֶבֶן הָעֶזֶר
Ever	Eber	AY-ver	עֵבֶר
Evyatar	Abiathar	ev-ya-TAR	אֶבְיָתָר
Ezra	Ezra	ez-RA	עֶזְרָא
Gad	Gad	gad	גָּד
Gadi	Gaddi	ga-DEE	גַּדִּי
Gadiel	Gaddiel	ga-dee-AYL	גַּדִּיאֵל
Gamliel	Gamaliel	gam-lee-AYL	גַּמְלִיאֵל
Gedalia	Gedaliah	g'-dal-YA (hu)	גְּדַלְיָהוּ
Gedera	Gederah	g'-day-RAH	גְּדֵרָה
Gershom	Gershom	gay-r'-SHOM	גֵּרְשׁוֹם
Gershon	Gershon	gay-r'-SHON	גֵּרְשׁוֹן
Geshem	Geshem	GE-shem	גֶּשֶׁם
Geuel	Geuel	g'-u-AYL	גְּאוּאֵל
Gidon	Gideon	gid-ON	גִּדְעוֹן
Gilad	Gilead	gil-AD	גִּלְעָד
Gilgal	Gilgal	gil-GAL	גִּלְגָּל
Giva	Gibeah	giv-AH	גִּבְעָה
Givon	Gibeon	giv-ON	גִּבְעוֹן
Hadassa	Hadassah	ha-da-SAH	הֲדַסָּה
Har Eival	Mount Ebal	ay-VAL	הַר עֵיבָל
Har Gerizim	Mount Gerizim	g'-ri-ZEEM	הַר גְּרִזִים

125

Hebrew Name	English Name	Pronunciation	Hebrew
Har HaBayit	Temple Mount	har ha-BA-yit	הַר הַבַּיִת
Har HaZeitim	the Mount of Olives	har ha-zay-TEEM	הַר הַזֵּיתִים
Hashem	Lord/God		
Hayman	Heman	hay-MAN	הֵימָן
Hoshea	Hosea	ho-SHAY-a	הוֹשֵׁעַ
Ido	Iddo	i-DO	עִדּוֹ
Imanu-El	Immanuel	i-MA-nu ayl	עִמָּנוּ אֵל
Ish-boshet	Ish-bosheth	eesh BO-shet	אִישׁ־בֹּשֶׁת
Itamar	Ithamar	ee-ta-MAR	אִיתָמָר
Itiel	Ithiel	ee-tee-AYL	אִיתִיאֵל
Ivtzan	Ibzan	iv-TZAN	אִבְצָן
Iyov	Job	i-YOV	אִיּוֹב
Kadmiel	Kadmiel	kad-mee-AYL	קַדְמִיאֵל
Kalev	Caleb	ka-LAYV	כָּלֵב
Keesh	Kish	keesh	קִישׁ
Kehat	Kohath	k'-HAT	קְהָת
Keinan	Kenan	kay-NAN	קֵינָן
Kemuel	Kemuel	k'-mu-AYL	קְמוּאֵל
Keruvim	Cherubim	k'-ru-VEEM	כְּרוּבִים
Kilyon	Chilion	kil-YON	כִּלְיוֹן
Kiryat Arba	Kiriath-arba	keer-YAT AR-bah	קִרְיַת אַרְבַּע
Kiryat Sefer	Kiriath-sepher	keer-YAT SAY-fer	קִרְיַת־סֵפֶר
Kiryat Ye'arim	Kiriath-jearim	keer-YAT y'-a-REEM	קִרְיַת יְעָרִים
Kislev	Chislev	kis-LAYV	כִּסְלֵו
Kohanim	Priests	ko-ha-NEEM	כֹּהֲנִים
Kohelet	Koheleth	ko-HE-let	קֹהֶלֶת
Kohen	Priest	ko-HAYN	כֹּהֵן
Kohen Gadol	High Priest	ko-HAYN ga-DOL	כֹּהֵן גָּדוֹל
Korach	Korah	KO-rakh	קֹרַח
Kushi	Cushi	ku-SHEE	כּוּשִׁי
Lachish	Lachish	la-KHEESH	לָכִישׁ
Leah	Leah	lay-AH	לֵאָה
Lemech	Lamech	LE-mekh	לֶמֶךְ

Hebrew Name	English Name	Pronunciation	Hebrew
Lemuel	Lemuel	l'-mu-AYL	לְמוֹאֵל
Levi	Levi	lay-VEE	לֵוִי
Leviim	Levites	l'-vee-IM	לְוִיִּם
Machla	Mahlah	makh-LAH	מַחְלָה
Machlon	Mahlon	makh-LON	מַחְלוֹן
Machseya	Mahseiah	makh-say-YAH	מַחְסֵיָה
Malachi	Malachi	mal-a-KHEE	מַלְאָכִי
Manoach	Manoah	ma-NO-akh	מָנוֹחַ
Mashiach	Messiah	ma-SHEE-akh	מָשִׁיחַ
Mefiboshet	Mephibosheth	m'-fee-VO-shet	מְפִיבֹשֶׁת
Mehalalel	Mahalalel	ma-ha-lal-AYL	מַהֲלַלְאֵל
Menachem	Menahem	m'-na-KHAYM	מְנַחֵם
Menashe	Menasseh	m'-na-SHEH	מְנַשֶּׁה
Menorah	Candlestick	m'-no-RAH	מְנֹרָה
Merari	Merari	m'-ra-REE	מְרָרִי
Metushelach	Methusaleh	m'-tu-SHE-lakh	מְתוּשָׁלַח
Micha	Micah	mee-KHAH	מִיכָה
Michael	Michael	mee-kha-AYL	מִיכָאֵל
Michaihu	Micaiah	mee-KHAI-hu	מִיכָיְהוּ
Michal	Michal	mee-KHAL	מִיכַל
Milka	Milcah	mil-KAH	מִלְכָּה
Miriam	Miriam	mir-YAM	מִרְיָם
Mishael	Mishael	mee-sha-AYL	מִישָׁאֵל
Mishkan	Tabernacle	mish-KAN	מִשְׁכַּן
Mitzpa	Mizpah	mitz-PAH	מִצְפָּה
Mizbayach	Altar	miz-BAY-akh	מִזְבֵּחַ
Mordechai	Mordecai	mor-d'-KHAI	מָרְדְּכַי
Moriah	Moriah	mo-ri-YAH	מוֹרִיָּה
Moshe	Moses	mo-SHEH	מֹשֶׁה
Nachbi	Nahbi	nakh-BEE	נַחְבִּי
Nachor	Nahor	na-KHOR	נָחוֹר
Nachshon	Nahshon	nakh-SHON	נַחְשׁוֹן
Nachum	Nahum	na-KHUM	נַחוּם

Hebrew Name	English Name	Pronunciation	Hebrew
Nadav	Nadab	na-DAV	נָדָב
Naftali	Naphtali	naf-ta-LEE	נַפְתָּלִי
Naomi	Naomi	na-o-MEE	נָעֳמִי
Natan	Nathan	na-TAN	נָתָן
Naval	Nabal	na-VAL	נָבָל
Navi	Prophet	na-VEE	נָבִיא
Navot	Naboth	na-VAL	נָבָל
Nechemya	Nehemiah	n'-khem-YAH	נְחֶמְיָה
Negev	Negeb	NE-gev	נֶגֶב
Nerya	Neriah	nay-ri-YAH	נֵרִיָּה
Netanel	Nethanel	n'-tan-AYL	נְתַנְאֵל
Neviah	Prophetess	n'-vee-AH	נְבִיאָה
Neviim	Prophets	n'-vee-EEM	נְבִיאִים
Nisan	Nisan	nee-SAN	נִיסָן
Noa	Noah	no-AH	נֹעָה
Noach	Noah	NO-akh	נֹחַ
Nov	Nob	nov	נֹב
Nun	Nun	nun	נוּן
Oded	Oded	o-DAYD	עוֹדֵד
Ohola	Oholah	a-ho-LAH	אָהֳלָה
Oholiav	Oholiab	o-ha-lee-AV	אָהֳלִיאָב
Oholiva	Oholibah	a-ho-lee-VAH	אָהֳלִיבָה
Omri	Omri	om-REE	עָמְרִי
Onan	Onan	o-NAN	אוֹנָן
Otniel	Othniel	ot-nee-AYL	עָתְנִיאֵל
Ovadya	Obadiah	o-vad-YAH	עֹבַדְיָה
Oved	Obed	o-VAYD	עוֹבֵד
Oved Edom	Obed Edom	o-VAYD e-DOM	עוֹבֵד אֱדוֹם
Pagiel	Pagiel	pag-ee-AYL	פַּגְעִיאֵל
Palti	Palti	pal-TEE	פַּלְטִי
Paltiel	Paltiel	pal-tee-AYL	פַּלְטִיאֵל
Pekach	Pekah	PE-kakh	פֶּקַח
Pedael	Pedahel	p'-da-AYL	פְּדָהְאֵל

Hebrew Name	English Name	Pronunciation	Hebrew
Pekachya	Pekahiah	p'-kakh-YAH	פְּקַחְיָה
Peleg	Peleg	PE-leg	פֶּלֶג
Penina	Peninnah	p'-ni-NAH	פְּנִנָּה
Peretz	Perez	PE-retz	פֶּרֶץ
Petuel	Pethuel	p'-tu-AYL	פְּתוּאֵל
Pinchas	Phinehas	peen-KHAS	פִּינְחָס
Rachel	Rachel	ra-KHAYL	רָחֵל
Ram	Ram	ram	רָם
Rama	Ramah	ra-MAH	רָמָה
Re'u	Reu	r'-U	רְעוּ
Rechovam	Rehoboam	r'-khav-AM	רְחַבְעָם
Reuven	Reuben	r'-u-VAYN	רְאוּבֵן
Rivka	Rebecca	riv-KAH	רִבְקָה
Rut	Ruth	rut	רוּת
Salma	Salmon/Salmah	sal-MAH	שַׂלְמָה
Salmon	Salmon	sal-MON	שַׂלְמוֹן
Sara	Sarah	sa-RAH	שָׂרָה
Sarai	Sarai	sa-RAI	שָׂרַי
Selah	Selah	SE-lah	סֶלָה
Seraya	Seraiah	s'-ra-YAH	שְׂרָיָה
Serug	Serug	s'-RUG	שְׂרוּג
Setur	Sethur	s'-TUR	סְתוּר
Shaarayim	Shaaraim	sha-a-RA-yim	שַׁעֲרַיִם
Shabbat	Sabbath	sha-BAT	שַׁבַּת
Shabbatot	Sabbaths	sha-ba-TOT	שַׁבָּתוֹת
Shafan	Shaphan	sha-FAN	שָׁפָן
Shafat	Shaphat	sha-FAT	שָׁפָט
Shalem	Salem	sha-LAYM	שָׁלֵם
Shalum	Shallum	sha-LUM	שַׁלּוּם
Shamgar	Shamgar	sham-GAR	שַׁמְגַּר
Shamua	Shammua	sha-MU-a	שַׁמּוּעַ
Shaul	Saul	sha-UL	שָׁאוּל
Shealtiel	Shealtiel	sh'-al-tee-AYL	שְׁאַלְתִּיאֵל

Hebrew Name	English Name	Pronunciation	Hebrew
Shear Yashuv	Shear-Jashub	sh'-AR ya-SHUV	שְׁאָר יָשׁוּב
Shechanya	Shecaniah	sh'-khan-YAH	שְׁכַנְיָה
Shechem	Shechem	sh'-KHEM	שְׁכֶם
Sheila	Shelah	shay-LAH	שֵׁלָה
Shelach	Shelah	SHE-lakh	שֶׁלַח
Shelumiel	Shelumiel	sh'-lu-mee-AYL	שְׁלֻמִיאֵל
Shem	Shem	Shaym	שֵׁם
Shemaya	Shemaiah	sh'-ma-YAH	שְׁמַעְיָה
Sheshbatzar	Sheshbazzar	shaysh-ba-TZAR	שֵׁשְׁבַּצַּר
Shet	Seth	Shayt	שֵׁת
Shevat	Shebat	sh'-VAT	שְׁבָט
Shilo	Shiloh	shi-LOH	שִׁלֹה
Shim'i	Shimei	shim-EE	שִׁמְעִי
Shimon	Simeon	shim-ON	שִׁמְעוֹן
Shimshon	Samson	shim-SHON	שִׁמְשׁוֹן
Shlomo	Solomon	sh'-lo-MOH	שְׁלֹמֹה
Shmuel	Samuel	sh'-mu-AYL	שְׁמוּאֵל
Shofar	Horn	sho-FAR	שׁוֹפָר
Shofarot	Horns	sho-fa-ROT	שׁוֹפָרוֹת
Shomron	Samaria	sho-m'-RON	שֹׁמְרוֹן
Sivan	Sivan	see-VAN	סִיוָן
Tamar	Tamar	ta-MAR	תָּמָר
Tanakh	Hebrew Bible	ta-NAKH	תָּנָ"ךְ
Tapuach	Tappuah	ta-PU-akh	תַּפּוּחַ
Tavor	Tabor	ta-VOR	תָּבוֹר
Tekoa	Tekoa	t'-KO-a	תְּקוֹעָה
Terach	Terah	TE-rakh	תֶּרַח
Teveria	Tiberias	t'-ver-YAH	טְבֶרְיָה
Tevet	Tebeth	tay-VAYT	טֵבֵת
Tirtza	Tirzah	tir-TZAH	תִּרְצָה
Tola	Tola	to-LA	תּוֹלָע
Tzadok	Zadok	tza-DOK	צָדוֹק
Tzefanya	Zephaniah	tz'-fan-YAH	צְפַנְיָה

Hebrew Name	English Name	Pronunciation	Hebrew
Tzelofchad	Zelophehad	tz'-lo-f-KHAD	צְלָפְחָד
Tzeruya	Zeruiah	tz'-ru-YAH	צְרוּיָה
Tzfat	Safed	tz'-FAT	צְפַת
Tzidkiyahu	Zedekiah	tzid-ki-YA-hu	צִדְקִיָּהוּ
Tziklag	Ziklag	tzi-k'-LAG	צִקְלַג
Tzion	Zion	tzi-YON	צִיּוֹן
Tzipora	Zipporah	tzi-po-RAH	צִפֹּרָה
Tzora	Zorah	tzor-AH	צָרְעָה
Tzuriel	Zuriel	tzu-ree-AYL	צוּרִיאֵל
Ukal	Ucal	u-KAL	אֻכָל
Uri	Uri	u-REE	אוּרִי
Uriya	Uriah	u-ri-YAH	אוּרִיָּה
Utz	Uz	Utz	עוּץ
Uzziyahu	Uzziah	u-zi-YA-hu	עֻזִּיָּהוּ
Yaakov	Jacob	ya-a-KOV	יַעֲקֹב
Yachaziel	Jahaziel	ya-kha-zee-AYL	יַחֲזִיאֵל
Yael	Jael	ya-AYL	יָעֵל
Yaffo	Joppa/Jaffa	ya-FO	יָפוֹ
Yair	Jair	ya-EER	יָאִיר
Yakeh	Jakeh	ya-KEH	יָקֶה
Yarden	Jordan	yar-DAYN	יַרְדֵּן
Yarmut	Jarmuth	yar-MUT	יַרְמוּת
Yechezkel	Ezekiel	y'-khez-KAYL	יְחֶזְקֵאל
Yechiel	Jehiel	y'-khee-AYL	יְחִיאֵל
Yechonya	Jeconiah	y'-khon-YAH	יְכָנְיָה
Yedutun	Jeduthun	y'-du-TUN	יְדוּתוּן
Yehoachaz	Jehoahaz	y'-ho-a-KHAZ	יְהוֹאָחָז
Yehoash	Jehoash	y'-ho-ASH	יְהוֹאָשׁ
Yehochanan	Jehohanan	y'-ho-kha-NAN	יְהוֹחָנָן
Yehonatan	Jonathan	y'-ho-na-TAN	יְהוֹנָתָן
Yehoram	Jehoram	y'-ho-RAM	יְהוֹרָם
Yehoshafat	Jehoshaphat	y'-ho-sha-FAT	יְהוֹשָׁפָט
Yehoshavat	Jehoshabeath	y'-ho-shav-AT	יְהוֹשַׁבְעַת

Hebrew Name	English Name	Pronunciation	Hebrew
Yehosheva	Jehosheba	y-ho-SHE-va	יְהוֹשֶׁבַע
Yehoshua	Joshua	y'-ho-SHU-a	יְהוֹשֻׁעַ
Yehotzadak	Jehozadak	y'-ho-tza-DAK	יְהוֹצָדָק
Yehoyachin	Jehoiachin	y'-ho-ya-KHEEN	יְהוֹיָכִין
Yehoyada	Jehoiada	y'-ho-ya-DA	יְהוֹיָדָע
Yehoyakim	Jehoiakim	y'-ho-ya-KEEM	יְהוֹיָקִים
Yehu	Jehu	yay-HU	יֵהוּא
Yehuda	Judah	y'-hu-DAH	יהוּדָה
Yehudi	Jew	y'-hu-DEE	יהוּדִי
Yehudim	Jews	y'-hu-DEEM	יהוּדִים
Yered	Jared	YE-red	יֶרֶד
Yericho	Jericho	y'-ree-KHO	יְרִיחוֹ
Yerovam	Jeroboam	ya-rov-AM	יָרָבְעָם
Yerubaal	Jerubbaal	y'-ru-BA-al	יְרֻבַּעַל
Yerushalayim	Jerusalem	y'-ru-sha-LA-yim	יְרוּשָׁלַיִם
Yeshayahu	Isaiah	y'-sha-YA-hu	יְשַׁעְיָהוּ
Yeshua	Jeshua	yay-SHU-a	יֵשׁוּעַ
Yiftach	Jephthah	yif-TAKH	יִפְתָּח
Yigal	Igal	yig-AL	יִגְאָל
Yirmiyahu	Jeremiah	yir-m'-YA-hu	יִרְמְיָהוּ
Yishai	Jesse	yi-SHAI	יִשַׁי
Yisrael	Israel	yis-ra-AYL	יִשְׂרָאֵל
Yissachar	Issachar	yi-sa-KHAR	יִשָּׂשכָר
Yitzchak	Issac	yitz-KHAK	יִצְחָק
Yizrael	Jezreel	yiz-r'-EL	יִזְרְעָאל
Yoash	Joash	yo-ASH	יוֹאָשׁ
Yoav	Joab	yo-AV	יוֹאָב
Yochanan	Johanan	yo-kha-NAN	יוֹחָנָן
Yocheved	Jochebed	yo-KHE-ved	יוֹכֶבֶד
Yoel	Joel	yo-AYL	יוֹאֵל
Yona	Jonah	yo-NAH	יוֹנָה
Yonadav	Jonadab	yo-na-DAV	יוֹנָדָב
Yonatan	Jonathan	yo-na-TAN	יוֹנָתָן

Hebrew Name	English Name	Pronunciation	Hebrew
Yoram	Joram	yo-RAM	יוֹרָם
Yosef	Joseph	yo-SAYF	יוֹסֵף
Yoshiyahu	Josiah	yo-shi-YA-hu	יאשִׁיָהוּ
Yotam	Jotham	yo-TAM	יוֹתָם
Yotzadak	Jozadak	yo-tza-DAK	יוֹצָדָק
Yozavad	Jozabad	yo-za-VAD	יוֹזָבָד
Zanoach	Zanoah	za-NO-akh	זָנוֹחַ
Zecharya	Zechariah	z'-khar-YAH	זְכַרְיָה
Zerach	Zerah	ZE-rakh	זֶרַח
Zerubavel	Zerubbabel	z'-ru-ba-VEL	זְרֻבָּבֶל
Zevulun	Zebulun	z'-vu-LUN	זְבוּלֻן
Zilpa	Zilpah	zil-PAH	זִלְפָּה
Zimri	Zimri	zim-REE	זִמְרִי

Jewish Holidays

Chanukah	Hanukkah	kha-nu-KAH	חֲנוּכָּה
Pesach	Passover	PE-sakh	פֶּסַח
Purim	Purim	pu-REEM	פּוּרִים
Rosh Hashana	Jewish New Year	rosh ha-sha-NAH	רֹאשׁ הַשָּׁנָה
Shavuot	Feast of Weeks	sha-vu-OT	שָׁבוּעוֹת
Shemini Atzeret	Eight Day of Assembly	sh'-mee-NEE a-TZE-ret	שְׁמִינִי עֲצֶרֶת
Sukkot	Feast of Tabernacles	su-KOT	סֻכּוֹת
Yom Kippur	Day of Atonement	yom kee-PUR	יוֹם כִּיפּוּר

Biblical Measurements

Amah	Cubit	a-MAH	אַמָּה
Amot	Cubits	a-MOT	אַמּוֹת
Bat	Bath	bat	בַּת
Batim	Baths	ba-TEEM	בָּתִים
Beka	half-shekel	BE-ka	בֶּקַע
Chomarim	Homers	kho-ma-REEM	חֳמָרִים
Chomer	Homer	KHO-mer	חֹמֶר
Efah	Ephah	ay-FAH	אֵיפָה
Geira	Gerah	gay-RAH	גֵּרָה

Hebrew Name	English Name	Pronunciation	Hebrew
Gomed	Gomed	GO- med	גֹּמֶד
Hin	Hin	heen	הִין
Kav	kab	kav	קַב
Kesita	kesitah	k'-see-TAH	קְשִׂיטָה
Kikar	talent	ki-KAR	כִּכָּר
Kikarim	talents	ki-ka-RIM	כִּכָּרִים
Kor	kor	kor	כֹּר
Letek	lethech	LE-tek	לֶתֶךְ
Log	Log	log	לֹג
Maneh	Mina	ma-NEH	מָנֶה
Manim	Minas	ma-NEEM	מָנִים
Omer	Omer	O-mer	עֹמֶר
Pim	Pim	peem	פִּים
Se'ah	Seah	say-AH	סְאָה
Se'eem	Seahs	s'-EEM	סְאִים
Shekalim	Shekels	sh'-ka-LEEM	שְׁקָלִים
Shekel	Shekel	SHE-kel	שֶׁקֶל
Tefach	Handbreadth	TE-fakh	טֶפַח
Zeret	Span	ZE-ret	זֶרֶת

Photo Credits

1:3 John Theodor/Shutterstock.com, 2:3 Courtesy Israel365, 3:15 StockStudio/ Shutterstock.com 4:9 Barbarajo/Shutterstock.com, 5:5 public domain, 6:2 Twinkle Studio/Shutterstock.com, 7:13 Ilia Falco/Shutterstock.com, 8:12 Dubova/Shutterstock.com, 9:4 Oren Ravid/Shutterstock.com, 10:1 alefbet/ Shutterstock.com, 11:25 By Eic413 (talk) – Own work (Original text: I created this work entirely by myself.), Public Domain, https://commons.wikimedia .org/w/index.php?curid=22600955, 12:10 John Theodor/Shutterstock.com, 13:4 Felagund, Wikimedia Commons, 14:14 Altosvic/Shutterstock.com, 15:6 Avi Ohayon, Government Press Office (Israel), 16:60 John Theodor/Shutterstock. com, 17:23 EMILY19/Shutterstock.com, 18:2 ChameleonsEye/Shutterstock. com, 19:7 Evgeny Meerson/Shutterstock.com, 20:6 Sergei25/Shutterstock. com, 21:2 Andrew Shiva, Wikimedia Commons, 22:24 courtesy of Israel365, 23:4 TI/Shutterstock.com, 24:1 John Theodor/Shutterstock.com, 25:17 Oren Ravid/Shutterstock.com, 26:2 Anton_Ivanov/Shutterstock.com, 27:3 vblinov/ Shutterstock.com, 28:25 Chaim, Wikimedia Commons, 29:3 Yokypics/ Shutterstock.com, 30:22 KrispelSlavin/Shutterstock.com, 31:3 AlinaAme/ Shutterstock.com, 32:2 Avi Ohayon, Government Press Office (Israel), 33:3 Mark Neyman, Government Press Office (Israel), 34:13 Mark Neyman, Government Press Office (Israel), 35:5 Ilan Ejzykowicz/Shutterstock.com, 36:8 Wikimedia Commons, 36:20 Yuri Yavnik/Shutterstock.com, 37:3 By Unknown author – To the Promised Land by Uri Dan (Doubleday, 1987) ISBN 0385245971 p. 58, Public Domain, https://commons.wikimedia.org/w/index .php?curid=5669592, 37:19 Moshe Milner, Government Press Office (Israel), 38:14 Evgeny Pylayev/Shutterstock.com, 39:25 Slepitssskaya/Shutterstock.com, 40:2 Leonid Andronov/Shutterstock.com, 41:18 Avishai Teicher, Wikimedia Commons, 42:20 Kobby Dagan/Shutterstock.com, 43:11 Amos Ben Gershom, Government Press Office (Israel), 44:15 Mark Neyman, Government Press Office (Israel), 45:9 Fritz Cohen, Government Press Office (Israel), 46:9 Sarit Richerson/Shutterstock.com, 47:14 Yair Aronshtam/Shutterstock.com, 48:1 len4ik/Shutterstock.com

Map of Modern-Day Israel and its Neighbors

The following is a map of modern-day Israel and the surrounding countries

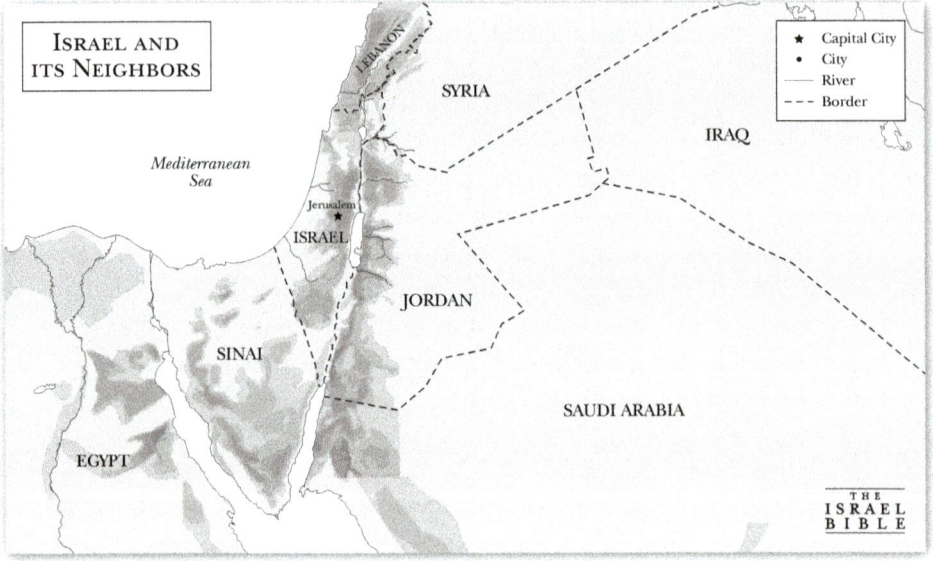

NOTES

NOTES

NOTES

NOTES

NOTES

For more inspiring commentary,
interactive maps, educational videos,
vivid photographs and more,
please visit our website

www.TheIsraelBible.com

THE
ISRAEL
BIBLE